INTRODUCTION TO THE HISTORY OF THE MUSLIM EAST

Published under the Auspices of the

NEAR EASTERN CENTER

UNIVERSITY OF CALIFORNIA

LOS ANGELES

JEAN SAUVAGET'S

INTRODUCTION TO THE HISTORY OF THE MUSLIM EAST

A Bibliographical Guide

BASED ON THE SECOND EDITION AS RECAST BY

CLAUDE CAHEN

UNIVERSITY OF CALIFORNIA PRESS

BERKELEY AND LOS ANGELES · 1965

UNIVERSITY OF CALIFORNIA PRESS
BERKELEY AND LOS ANGELES
CALIFORNIA

CAMBRIDGE UNIVERSITY PRESS
LONDON, ENGLAND

LIBRARY OF CONGRESS CATALOG NUMBER: 64-25271

Foreword

Perhaps the most striking evidence of the effect of Sauvaget's *Introduction à l'histoire musulmane* on the scholarly world and beyond is that the urge to add to its wealth has been so widely felt. Professor Cahen's *refonte* was a major step toward working into the *Introduction* the advances made by Islamic history in the past twenty years. The Near Eastern Center, University of California, Los Angeles, desiring to increase the effectiveness of the work, arranged for its translation into English and decided to use this translation to amplify some of the bibliographical statements, to include additional materials, in part chosen for their special usefulness for the English-speaking student and scholar, and to correct such errors as would almost inevitably slip into a book of this kind.

Our thanks and appreciation go to Mme. Paira-Pemberton, who prepared the translation, and to the scholars, among them notably Professor Cahen himself, who have given freely of their time to make the English edition authoritative: Professors Franz Rosenthal (Yale), Nikki Keddie, Moshe Perlmann, and Andreas Tietze (UCLA). Mr. D. P. Little and Mr. R. W. J. Austin, and above all, Mr. B. May, Research Assistants at the Near Eastern Center, devoted many months to checking and adding to the data and, on occasion, modifying the statements (but not the perspective) of the French original. Mrs. Teresa Joseph did infinitely more than an editor may be expected to do. In making reference to my own participation, I merely wish to assume my fair share in the responsibility for remaining imperfections.

G. E. von Grunebaum
Director

Near Eastern Center
University of California, Los Angeles
February 11, 1964.

Preface to the English Edition

In adding a few words at the beginning of this English edition of the *Introduction* with whose preparation I have been associated only at a distance, I am discharging a duty both imperative and pleasant.

My French recasting of the *Introduction* was on the whole awarded a favorable reception with regard to substance. But numerous errors in the data were noted as well as certain inadequacies in the presentation of which I had to take cognizance. The English edition, which had been decided upon even before the appearance of the French version, provided a welcome opportunity to make the necessary corrections. It also permitted taking advantage of information provided by book reviewers to whom I am grateful. Since, obviously, the preparation took some time, it was possible to include works appearing after 1961, date of the French publication. Finally, it was agreed upon that certain references, better suited to the needs of the English-speaking student and which did not appear in the French edition, would be added. The book that the reader now has before him is much more than a translation; it is a new and corrected edition which should therefore be consulted by the French-speaking student as well whenever possible. Having said this, I will have fulfilled only the least of my obligations if I did not add an expression of my profound gratitude to all my colleagues, led by Professor G. E. von Grunebaum, who have devoted so much of their time to the realization of the present work. It is a pleasure to me that they have judged my work worthy of their efforts, but it is also an embarrassment that it required so much effort. And if in spite of all this, there still remain some errors—inevitable in this genre of publication—it goes without saying that I alone am to be held responsible.

To one criticism, a word of explanation. It has been the cause of some surprise that a chapter on the Muslim West has been included in an

Introduction to the History of the Muslim East. Is it necessary to reiterate that the title does not express a confrontation of East and West within Islam, but of the Muslim world as a whole, including its western part, with other parts of the East and the non-Muslim West? It is merely that within this world of Islam we have placed our emphasis on the East.

Claude Cahen

October, 1964

Preface to the Second French Edition

In 1943, when the *Introduction à l'histoire de l'Orient musulman* was published, it was the answer to an urgent and obvious need. The lack of such a work for students had been brought home to Jean Sauvaget first at the École des Hautes Études, later at the Collège de France, when he had added teaching to his scholarly activity. Any work that is largely bibliographical, however, needs periodic revision, and the *Introduction* is no exception; by 1946, Sauvaget himself had already included addenda; and, in our field of study, the ever-increasing rate of progress makes increasingly frequent revision indispensable. Sauvaget also made no secret of the fact that he had written his book in haste in order to provide students quickly with a reference work and that he might later modify certain opinions or even revise at least partially the whole conception of the book in the light of his increased experience in research and teaching. Once the first edition had been exhausted, he would undoubtedly have availed himself of the opportunity to revise his work completely. His tragic fate left the realization of this revision to others.* A feeling of duty toward the memory of a departed friend and master, combined with an awareness of the needs of our discipline, has moved me to accept the responsibility of this revision. As the work progressed, I became more and more aware of the technical and scientific difficulties involved, and, with regard to Sauvaget, of the awkward one-sidedness of this kind of collaboration. Briefly, then, I must explain how I went about my task.

It would, of course, have been possible merely to have made the bibliographical additions and cuts necessitated by the passage of time. Had I done so, I would have respected Sauvaget's text but not his intentions—

* An excellent biographical note (by L. Robert), a bibliography, and selected articles by Sauvaget will be found in the *Mémorial Jean Sauvaget*, edited by D. Sourdel and Mme. J. Sourdel-Thomine, two volumes (Damascus, 1954 and 1961); Vol. II contains an index to his work.

nor the needs of the reader. Or, I could have substituted a completely new work for the old; this would have been easier in some respects—Sauvaget would certainly not have thought that respect for the dead ought to restrict the freedom of the living, but it would have meant disregarding the parts of the original that are still fundamentally valid, either because it would be impossible in some cases to improve the terminology or tone adopted by Sauvaget or because, in a more general way, the overall conception and intention of the work could still provide the inspiration and framework even of such chapters as had to be completely rewritten. For this reason, I decided upon a composite method. I have felt justified in following my views although they are not always the same as Sauvaget's and are sometimes irreconcilable with them or at least with those he expressed in 1943. On the other hand, I have made no attempt to suppress certain particularly felicitous passages, especially in the first part of the book, even though retaining them occasionally upset the balance of the work as a whole. It follows that we are perhaps not entirely justified in keeping Sauvaget's name on the title page; but there is little—or less—justification for omitting it: the present work is not by Sauvaget, but it would never have existed without him; without him it would not have been planned as it is. And though he would perhaps have been shocked by certain passages, it is none the less true that I have been constantly aware of his presence as I wrote. I can do no more than assume the responsibility for what I have written in the eyes of his friends and colleagues, his former students, and his children, in the hope that I have not fallen too far short of my model or what the *Introduction* would have been, had Sauvaget lived to revise it himself.

The 1943 *Introduction* reflects in some respects Sauvaget's oral teaching. This explains the vigorously personal style of the work and its somewhat erratic method; it also accounts for certain gaps. In the present work we have attempted to conform to a somewhat stricter plan, both in the descriptive sections and in the classification adopted for the bibliographical lists. In doing so, we have obviously detracted from the evocative quality of the book for those who attended Sauvaget's lectures. But since, in my opinion, the more personal passages strike fewer chords for the new generation of readers who have not known Sauvaget in person, it seemed more important to try to compensate for the loss of what only he could have done better. The general outline is untouched: the general remarks on documentation, contained in the first part, are followed by a study of the main works of reference and all the questions which could not be classified chronologically; finally, in the third part, we have dealt with the bibliography of works which could be classified more exactly according to period or region. Admittedly, it is sometimes difficult to draw the lines of demarcation; and we have included frequent cross references from one chapter to

another, even at the expense of appearing tedious, rather than run the risk of leaving serious gaps. The economic, social, and cultural questions discussed in part two cannot be studied thoroughly unless the bibliography is expanded to include the more specialized studies now indicated in the various historical chapters. Books by Near Eastern authors may be envisaged in one place as sources, in another as cultural documents. In the historical chapters, or their subsections, care has been taken to describe first the sources, then the modern works, more systematically than was done by Sauvaget.

Without aiming at being exhaustive, we have attempted to extend the range of subjects and, here and there, to enter into more detail than did Sauvaget, in accordance with the development of modern interests. At the same time, we have tried to stress the gaps in our knowledge, indicating the lines along which research should be encouraged. The work has thus become a little bulkier—though we wanted to avoid making it much longer—than the original *Introduction*: it is a work which should be accessible, both scientifically and financially, primarily to the undergraduate, even though it may be of incidental use to teachers and more advanced research workers. I have thus had to eliminate a certain amount of "marginal" information and adopt a more condensed style of writing, which would be tiring if one were to read the book from end to end but will perhaps be acceptable in the bibliographical sections which are intended primarily for reference. I must apologize for two omissions as compared with the original *Introduction*: I did not think it necessary in practice to give the names of collections to which works belong when the latter are catalogued in all libraries individually; and frequently the place of publication has been omitted, though not of course the date, which situates the work in the history of scholarship.* Nor have I felt it necessary to keep the library numbers of works which are almost all to be found in the libraries normally frequented by students in Paris; otherwise it would have been necessary to extend investigation to other libraries, without thereby profiting the non-Parisian or even the non-French student, to whom the work also appeals as its success proves.

It goes without saying that our bibliographies are not complete. And naturally, since a choice has been made, the ideas guiding the choice and the manner in which it was made are open to discussion. It must also be admitted, as may well be imagined, that I do not pretend to know all there is to be known in such a wide field and that I must inevitably be guilty of mistakes and omissions. I shall be grateful if my colleagues will kindly point these out to me in view of possible further editions. Otherwise, I have tried

* It should perhaps be noted that, for the English translation, a not inconsiderable number of references have been added. (G.E.v.G.)

to steer a middle course between two extremes: on the one hand, to save the undergraduate's time by providing the necessary elementary and practical information and, on the other hand, to suggest ideas for further study for the young research worker by giving, if not a bibliography of the subject, at least the fundamental references on which to base his investigations. For this reason, I wished neither to confine myself to the essential general works nor drown the reader in a sea of references. Above all, I have tried to demonstrate the diversity of the questions to be asked and have sometimes cited works which, though slight in themselves, for want of others, seemed likely to contribute to this aim. I could not cite all the works of scholars active in the field; but I have tried not to omit any name of importance, not in order to compose a roll of honor nor for fear of discontenting anyone, but simply because the mere fact of citing various writers is a means of indicating various points of view.* And not being able to cite everything, I have tried above all to cite the recent works that replace or refer to previous publications and are not yet in other bibliographies. I may be reproached for citing books and articles in languages with which some of my readers may not be familiar. I felt it was necessary to draw attention to the fact that Oriental studies are becoming increasingly international and that there are questions that cannot easily be studied without a knowledge of certain languages. I also wanted the Western student to realize the part that Eastern scholars are beginning to play in our studies, at the same time pointing out to the Eastern student the works by his compatriots that rank as scholarly productions of value in the eyes of specialists.

Sauvaget and I have been paid the honor of a request, received before the French edition went to press, for an English translation. Although the bibliography is of course basically the same for students everywhere, it may be worthwhile replacing certain popular works or translations—of use to students in one country—by equivalent works in the language of another; similarly, certain subsidiary problems may be topical in one place for special reasons which do not pertain elsewhere. While not forgetting that the present work is intended primarily for the French reader, I have tried to give it an international flavor with a view to a wider audience, and particular attention has been paid to works in English. But, with my consent, the English edition will undergo certain modifications so that it will not be an exact translation.

Without the generous collaboration of several colleagues, this book would

* Obviously, my opinion of the value of a scholar's work is not in proportion to the number of times he is cited. There are important scholars whose work is contained in but a few works or deals with subjects unrelated to our work as historians, or else is now somewhat antiquated, so that the space they occupy in the index is less than that of others whose work is more diffuse, nearer our interests, or more recent.

not have been possible. Chief among them, in alphabetical order, are Mlle. M.-Th. d'Alverny (for the final chapter); Messrs. J. Aubin (post-Mongol Iran); R. Mantran (Ottoman Empire); M. Rodinson (pre-Islamic Arabia and sociology-ethnography); D. Schlumberger, Mme. J. Sourdel-Thomine, and M. D. Sourdel (archaeology). My thanks go out to these and to many others; naturally they are in no way responsible for the errors which may have found their way even into the pages for which they have given their help.

Finally I am most grateful to the publisher, Adrien-Maisonneuve; faithful to the memory of Sauvaget, instead of allowing the old *Introduction* to go out of print or to reissue it unchanged, he appreciated the necessity of a complete revision and honored me by entrusting it to me.

Cl. C.

February, 1961

Contents

FOREWORD v
PREFACE TO THE ENGLISH EDITION vii
PREFACE TO THE SECOND FRENCH EDITION ix
ABBREVIATIONS xix
INTRODUCTION: THE SCOPE OF THE WORK 3

Part I. The Sources of Muslim History

1. LANGUAGE AND SCRIPTS 11
2. ARCHIVES 16
3. NARRATIVE SOURCES 22
The Arabic Oral Tradition and Historical Romances—The Ḥadīth—Annals and Chronicles—Persian and Turkish Historiography—Historiography in Other Languages
4. TRAVEL BOOKS AND GEOGRAPHICAL WORKS 37
Travel Books—Geographies
5. LEGAL AND ADMINISTRATIVE SOURCES 40
6. OTHER LITERARY SOURCES 46
7. LITERARY SOURCES: BIO-BIBLIOGRAPHICAL WORKS 49
8. ARCHAEOLOGICAL SOURCES 52
Epigraphy—Numismatics—Archaeology
9. CONTEMPORARY GEOGRAPHICAL AND ETHNOLOGICAL MATERIAL . 61

Part II. Tools of Research and General Works

10. GENERAL INFORMATION 65
Histories and Reference Works—Periodicals
11. SPECIAL DISCIPLINES 76
Geography, Historical Topography, and Ethnology—Chronology

12. DYNASTIC SERIES AND TRIBAL GENEALOGIES 82
Personal Names—Metrology—Quotations

13. THE MAIN OUTLINES OF MUSLIM HISTORY 85
Introduction—Economic and Social Life—Law—Family Life; Slavery; Religion; Races—Technology and Warfare—Land Tenure, Iqṭā', and Waqf or Ḥubus—Urban Dwellers—Trade—Political and Administrative Institutions—Cultural Life—Religion—Philosophy and Science—Literature—History of Art

Part III. Historical Bibliography

14. THE NEAR EAST AND ARABIA ON THE EVE OF THE ADVENT OF ISLAM 107
The Near East (excluding Arabia)—Pre-Islamic Arabia

15. MUḤAMMAD 115
The Man—The Koran

16. THE RĀSHIDŪN (RIGHTLY-GUIDED) AND UMAYYAD CALIPHS AND THE ARAB CONQUESTS 121
Sources—The Arab Conquest—The Rāshidūn and Umayyad Periods—Literature and Art

17. THE 'ABBĀSID CALIPHATE AND THE SUCCESSOR STATES (TO THE MIDDLE OF THE ELEVENTH CENTURY) 130
Sources—General and Political History—Economic and Social Institutions—National Movements and Successor States—Religious Life—Cultural Life, Literature, and Art

18. THE ISMĀ'ĪLĪS AND FĀṬIMIDS 146
Sources—General History: Ismā'īlism; the Fāṭimid State; Sects; the Yemen

19. SELJUKS AND THEIR DESCENDANTS (ELEVENTH TO THIRTEENTH CENTURY). ISLAM AND THE CRUSADES 151
The Advent of the Turks—Tools of Research in Old Turkish History—General Sources and Sources on Seljuk History—The Seljuks of the East, Modern Works—The Caliphate after the Reign of the Seljuks—Turkish Asia Minor—The Crusades—Zengids and Ayyūbids: Sources—Modern Works

20. THE MUSLIM WORLD UNDER THE MONGOLS AND THE TIMURIDS . 168
Sources—General History—Asia Minor—The Golden Horde

21. THE MAMLŪKS AND THE ARAB EAST (TWELFTH TO FOURTEENTH CENTURY) 176
Sources—History—Arabia

22. IRAN AND THE NON-OTTOMAN MUSLIM EAST (FROM THE ADVENT OF THE ṢAFAVIDS TO THE BEGINNING OF THE NINETEENTH CENTURY) 184
Sources—History of Iran—Central Asia and the Russian Steppes—Muslim India—Expansion around the Indian Ocean

23. THE OTTOMAN EMPIRE 191
Period of its Origin—Sources of Ottoman History: Archives, Literary, and Foreign—General Works and Political History—Institutions—Foreign Policy—Economic and Social Life—Provinces—Religious Life, Literature, and Art

24. THE MUSLIM WEST 216
Sources—North Africa, Sicily and Spain (to the Eleventh Century)—Almoravid and Almohad Periods and the Kingdom of Granada—North Africa (from the Thirteenth to the Nineteenth Century)

25. THE INFLUENCE OF MUSLIM CULTURE IN EUROPE 228

INDEX OF NAMES 233

Abbreviations

AEDB	[Univ. de Lyon] *Annales de l'École du Droit de Beyrouth*
AESC	*Annales. Économies, societés, civilisations*
AGG	*Abhandlungen der Gesellschaft der Wissenschaften zu Göttingen*
AI	*Ars Islamica*
AIEO	*Annales de l'Institut des Études Orientales*
AJSL	*American Journal for Semitic Languages and Literatures*
AKM	*Abhandlungen für die Kunde des Morgenlandes*
ALFAV	*Accademia Nazionale dei Lincei. Fondazione Alessandro Volta. Atti dei Convegni*
AO	*Acta Orientalia*
AOASH	*Acta Orientalia Academiae Scientiarum Hungaricae*
ArO	*Archiv orientální*
AÜDTCFD	*Ankara Üniversitesi Dil ve Tarih-Coğrafya Fakültesi Dergisi*
AÜDTCFYay	*Ankara Üniversitesi Dil ve Tarih-Coğrafya Fakültesi Yayınları*
BEA	*Bulletin des études arabes*
Belleten	*Türk Tarih Kurumu Belleten*
BEOD	*Bulletin d'études orientales de l'Institut Français de Damas*
BGA	*Bibliotheca geographorum Arabicorum*
BIFAO	*Bulletin de l'Institut Français d'Archéologie Orientale*
BSOAS	*Bulletin of the School of Oriental and African Studies*
CIA	*Corpus Inscriptionum Arabicarum*
CT	*Cahiers de Tunisie*
CSCO	*Corpus Scriptorum Christianorum Orientalium*
EI	*Encyclopaedia of Islam*
EI²	*Encyclopaedia of Islam*. Second edition

EV	*Epigrafika Vostoka*
GAL	C. Brockelmann. *Geschichte der arabischen Litteratur*
GMS	Gibb Memorial Series
HO	B. Spuler. *Handbuch der Orientalistik*
IBLA	*Institut des Belles Lettres Arabes*
IC	*Islamic Culture*
IFM	[*Istanbul Üniversitesi*] *Iktisat Fakültesi Mecmuası* (Also: *Revue de la Faculté des Sciences Économiques d'Istanbul*)
IQ	*Islamic Quarterly*
IS	*Islamic Studies*
JA	*Journal asiatique*
JAOS	*Journal of the American Oriental Society*
JBBRAS	*Journal of the Bombay Branch of the Royal Asiatic Society*
JESHO	*Journal of the Economic and Social History of the Orient*
JRAS	*Journal of the Royal Asiatic Society*
JWH	*Journal of World History*
KSIV	*Kratkie Soobshcheniia Instituta Vostokovedeniia*
MFO	*Mélanges de la faculté orientale de l'Université St. Joseph de Beyrouth* (continued as *Mélanges de l'Université Saint-Joseph*, since 1956)
MIDEO	*Mélanges de l'Institut Dominicain d'Études Orientales du Caire*
MIE	*Mémoires de l'Institut d'Égypte*
MIF	*Mémoires de l'Institut de France*
MIFAO	*Mémoires de l'Institut Français d'Archéologie Orientale*
MK	*60 doğum yılı münasebetiyle Fuad Köprülü armağanı* (*Mélanges Fuad Köprülü*)
MSOA	*Mitteilungen des Seminars für Orientalische Sprachen*
MW	*Muslim World*
PO	*Patrologia Orientalis*
Prilozi	*Prilozi za orijentalni filologiju i istoriju jugoslovenskih naroda pod turskom vladavinom*
RA	*Revue Africaine*
REI	*Revue des études islamiques*
REJ	*Revue des études juives*
RH	*Revue historique*
RHC	*Recueil des historiens des croisades*
——— Arm	———. *Documents arméniens*
——— Hoc	———. *Historiens occidentaux*
——— Hor	———. *Historiens orientaux*
RIMA	*Revue de l'Institut des Manuscrits Arabes*

RL	*Rendiconti dell Accademia Nazionale dei Lincei, Classe di Scienze morali, storiche e filologiche*
RMM	*Revue du monde musulman*
RO	*Rocznik orientalistyczny*
ROC	*Revue de l'orient chrêtien*
RSO	*Rivista degli studi orientali*
RT	*Revue tunisienne*
SBAW	*Sitzungsberichte der Akademie der Wissenschaften zu Wien*
SBBA	*Sitzungsberichte der Bayrischen Akademie der Wissenschaften*
SPBA	*Sitzungsberichte der Preussischen Akademie der Wissenschaften zu Berlin*
SI	*Studia Islamica*
Storey	C. Storey. *Persian Literature, a Bio-Bibliographical Survey*
SV	*Sovetskoe Vostokovedenie*
TD	*[Edebiyat Fakültesi] Tarih Dergisi*
TOEM	*Tarih-i Osmani Encümeni Mecmuası*
TTKYay	*Türk Tarih Kurumu Yayınları*
UZIV	*Uchenye Zapiski Instituta Vostokovedeniia*
WI	*Die Welt des Islams*
WO	*Die Welt des Orients*
WZKM	*Wiener Zeitschrift für die Kunde des Morgenlandes*
ZA	*Zeitschrift für Assyriologie*
ZDMG	*Zeitschrift der Deutschen Morgenländischen Gesellschaft*

Introduction

The transliteration of words follows the accepted English system. Spelling in titles of non-English books where other systems were used has not been altered. For Turkish titles, the current official orthography was used. Books that are considered of special importance are printed in small caps. On the question of variant spellings of names, see the introductory note to the index.

The Scope of the Work

The field of research into which this book proposes to initiate the beginner is not indicated with sufficient clarity by the words *Muslim East* that occur in the title of the work. At the outset a more precise definition must be given.

The geographical extent of Islam is immense, covering at the present time a large part of Asia and Africa, while in the past it even included a considerable portion of Europe (Spain, Sicily, the Balkans, Southern Russia); far from representing a civilization of the past, it is today manifestly capable of attracting new adherents. It would hardly be feasible in a work of this kind to trace at the same time and in the same way the history of so many different countries. Little would be gained by such an ambitious program.

The Islamic world is by no means homogeneous. On the one hand there are the regions that were early converted to Islam and that have been the principal centers of Muslim civilization, as well as certain regions converted later but in which Muslims soon predominated numerically and culturally. On the other hand there are the countries recently or only partially converted wherein Islam has not succeeded in becoming the main factor in historical development. It would not be logical to treat them all in the same way. Java, with its thirty million faithful—some ten times the number in Iraq at the height of its splendor, when Baghdad was the political and intellectual center of the world—came into contact with Islam only in the fourteenth century, has not been socially molded by it, and has only just begun to exercise a certain influence in the Islamic Community; obviously it should not be treated in the same way as medieval Iraq. We shall not deal with the countries which form "outer Islam"—the Sudan and East Africa, India proper and the Indian Archipelago, or China—but merely refer to the expansion of Islam in due time and place. But we shall study the

Ottoman Empire (but not the history of the Balkan peoples as such, as they were mainly Christian), for the Ottoman Empire was felt to be basically Muslim; it dominated and influenced a large part of the Muslim world, and its capital, Istanbul, became the greatest center of Muslim culture. Our distinction, then, is based on history, not on geography.

Moreover, among the essentially Muslim countries that will form the object of our study, roughly two groups may be distinguished: the West (North Africa, Spain in the Middle Ages, and, for a time, Sicily) and the East (Arabia, Syria-Palestine and Mesopotamia, Egypt, Iran and neighboring countries, and, from the eleventh century on, Turkey). The second group will claim most of our attention.

In the first place, Islam originated in the East, and its center of gravity has always been there; to understand Islam, a close study of the eastern part of the Muslim world is indispensable. The West, except perhaps for Spain during a short period, does not have the same importance: less rich and less original, it has always been dependent on the East, which constituted its most fertile source of inspiration. This is our fundamental reason for stressing the Muslim East.

It so happens that there is also an incidental reason. Linked with French ways of life for a century, North Africa has inspired many important works by French scholars. To them must be added works by their Italian and Spanish colleagues who were intrigued by the Islamic past of their own countries or, like the French, interested in the culture of those Muslim areas that came within the spheres of influence of their respective countries. Obviously, the history of the West has not been exhausted (what history ever is?), but the study of it is at least less retarded than that of the history of the East, even though it is the East which should have come first. Most of the Eastern countries—excluding Egypt to some extent—have only recently been opened up to research, and as yet too few specialists are devoted to their study. We do not mean to underestimate the importance of the West, but it must be emphasized that to restrict oneself to the West and to look at Islam from there is to run the risk of distorting historical perspective and remaining blind to some of the most important factors in Muslim history.

Nevertheless, we shall not neglect the West, which for a time was politically a part of the Islamic Community and has never ceased to share its religion and culture. The history of the Fāṭimids, who left the East to cast in their lot with that of North Africa, only to meet with their real destiny in Egypt, is adequate proof—if proof be necessary—that we cannot afford to ignore the history of the West. Moreover, the Muslim West—and especially Spain, by dint of its proximity to Western Europe and the circumstances of the Christian reconquest of Spain at the moment when Latin Christianity was awakening to civilization—rather than the East, was responsible for the transmission of the cultural treasures of Islam and in this respect has played a vital part in the history of civilization as a whole. For this reason, a special chapter is devoted to this question (chap. 25).

It will not be difficult to delimit the extent of our study in time, for Islam did not experience the general upheaval in its social life and spiritual values that marks the beginning of the modern era in Europe. Not until the nineteenth century can the first symptoms of a similar evolution, owing to European pressure, be observed. Admittedly, European intervention and the regeneration which it brought about in the very nature of our sources of information initiated, at the very moment when the Ottoman Empire was forming, a certain change which might be said to alter the situation sufficiently to justify a division similar to that which it is customary to make in the history of the West. Seen from within Islam itself, as is more logical, such a division is more or less meaningless. Islam is just emerging from the Middle Ages, and the only logical demarcation that might be set between the Middle Ages and modern times was the moment when it was diverted from its independent path by pressure from Europe. This data varies with the different countries but nowhere antedates the nineteenth century. Therefore the study of Islamic history, perhaps more than any other segment of historical study, proves to be of practical value: it serves as an immediate introduction to the understanding of the Islamic world of our time.

Obviously, here as elsewhere, the study of history must be conducted with the methods and intellectual qualities that it both demands and develops: that is, it requires a feeling for exactitude and accuracy and, above all, critical judgment. The historian who refuses to accept what has not been correctly established or to confuse certainty with supposition must of necessity possess two characteristics: intellectual probity, implying a critical attitude toward his own work, and a love of truth. He must be aware of the possibilities of evolution and of the interrelationship of the various elements of a history. He should be able to fit each part into the whole and see the differences and resemblances between related societies: the historian of Islam can no more afford to neglect the history of the peripheral non-Muslim countries than the historian of the latter may neglect the Muslim world. Comparisons of this kind will help the historian of Islam to become aware of the different types of problems confronting Muslim history, of the inadequacy of the studies which have so far been devoted to certain questions (e.g., economic and social history), and, in a general way—despite the individual merit of a great many works and scholars—of the relative backwardness of the studies concerning the Islamic world. The linguistic problem and the academic habit of dividing studies into watertight compartments have given rise to a cleavage between Orientalists and historians—as though there were two kinds of humanity and not a common history—and are partly responsible for this backwardness. This cleavage has been further aggravated by the fact that Western Oriental studies have naturally given precedence to the questions which seemed more important from the Western point of view, while the curiosity of the East about its own past seemed to be dormant so long.

The broadening of the Western mind on the one hand, and the growing activity of the native scholars of Islamic lands on the other, should help correct a situation that is detrimental to the study of man in general and that cannot be explained as due exclusively to the difficulties involved in the study of the sources. Historians and Orientalists must learn to collaborate. The former must realize that Islam is a part of their history, and those who wish to devote themselves to the study of Islam should take the trouble to acquire a sufficient knowledge of Arabic and, eventually, of the other languages used in the country they wish to study. And the Arabists should realize in their turn that they cannot become impromptu historians and that the young students who wish to study the history and civilization of the peoples whose tongue they already know or are learning must first undergo a thorough historical apprenticeship.

On the history of Islamology (apart from the problem of cultural relations in the Middle Ages, for which see below, chap. 25), the student may consult J. W. Fück, *Die arabischen Studien in Europa bis in den Anfang des 20. Jahrhunderts* (Leipzig, 1955), which emphasizes German works without ignoring contributions from other nations, and V. Barthold, *La découverte de l'Asie* (Moscow, 1925), French translation by B. Nikitine (Paris, 1947), which goes beyond the scope of Islamology. On the question of Islamology in the various countries, we can only refer to certain detailed studies of limited scope, which are generally insufficient. See also *Historians of the Middle East*, edited by Bernard Lewis and P. Holt (London, 1962), part two, pp. 271–387. On Russian Islamology, the student may usefully consult N. Elisséeff, "L'Islamologie en U.R.S.S. d'après un ouvrage récent," *Mélanges Louis Massignon*, II (Damascus, 1957), 23–76, and the analysis by Ann K. S. Lambton in *Islam and Russia* (London, 1956) of N. Smirnov's *Ocherki istorii izucheniia islama* (*Panorama of the History of Islamology in the USSR*) (Moscow, 1954), while the career of an excellent Arabist is evoked in I. I. Krachkovskii [Kratchkovsky], *Nad arabskimi rukopisiami* (3d ed., Moscow, 1948), English translation by T. Minorsky, *Among Arabic*

Manuscripts (Leiden, 1953), French translation by M. Canard, *Avec les manuscrits arabes* (Algiers, 1954)—an extremely captivating narrative.

On French Islamology, see C. Déhérain, *Sylvestre de Sacy, ses contemporains et ses disciples*, Bibliothèque archéologique et historique, XXVII (Paris, 1938), and J. Alazard and E. Albertini, *Histoire et historiens de l'Algérie*, Vol. IV of *Collection du centenaire de l'Algérie* (1931).

For Oriental studies in England, see A. J. Arberry, *Oriental Essays* (1960), and Bernard Lewis, *British Contributions to Arabic Studies* (London, 1941). Read E. G. Browne's *A Year amongst the Persians* (London, 1893) for the experiences of an eminent British Orientalist. The participants of the Colloque sur la Sociologie Musulmane, the *Actes* of which are cited on pp. 96 and 128, occupied themselves, among other subjects, with certain methods of Islamology. (See especially G. E. von Grunebaum, cited p. 96.)

Some stimulating suggestions will be found in the collective brochure *Orientalism and History* by D. Sinor, published on the occasion of the International Congress of Orientalists held at Cambridge, England, in 1954.

PART I

The Sources of Muslim History

1

Language and Scripts

The research worker interested in the history of Islam is confronted with a considerable number of possible sources; but unfortunately they are not all of equal value, nor are they evenly distributed in time and space. Archives, on which historians of medieval European societies and economic systems rely almost exclusively, have been preserved in insufficient numbers. On the other hand, literary works, especially in the early Middle Ages, are much more numerous than their European counterparts and are often far more interesting; but the various countries and periods are not equally well represented. Archaeological evidence, on the average, is definitely less well preserved than in Europe in the corresponding period—not so well even as monuments of ancient times. In addition, in all these fields, research is far from having put at our disposal, conveniently, or in any manner whatsoever all the materials to which we should have access. In the present state of scholarship and particularly with reference to Muslim history the study of the sources and the careful publication of the more important are especially urgent tasks.

Obviously, the history of a society cannot be studied without a knowledge of at least its main language. Some texts, of course, have been translated; many others have not. In any case, the best of translations—and very many are second-rate—can never adequately replace the original. Certain technical problems call among other things, for a precise knowledge of terminology and for the ability to choose the exact meaning of a word among several possibilities. Many problems have remained unsolved through the fault of Orientalists who have unwittingly passed over a new formula, a precise technical nuance in the meaning of a word, a revealing etymology. One cannot learn all there is to be known; and we do not claim that a perfect acquaintance with all the aspects of a language, such as the linguist or the student of literature should possess, is indispensable for the historian.

But he must at least be fully cognizant of the absolute necessity of being able to understand the precise technical meaning of words—a meaning that is often variable. Many translations by eminent linguists are inadequate for the historian, for a general literary knowledge of the language is not sufficient to determine the meaning of terms used in special technical contexts.

We do not intend to give here a complete list of the grammars and textbooks which, ever since the classic work by Sylvestre de Sacy, *Grammaire arabe*, which first appeared in 1810 and has been reprinted many times, have enabled students of all nationalities to acquire an elementary knowledge of Arabic or to improve their command of the language. For the French student unable to attend a course in Arabic we would simply draw attention to the *Méthode d'arabe littéral* by G. Lecomte and A. Ghedira (1956), useful for beginners; the *Grammaire de l'arabe classique* by R. Blachère and M. Gaudefroy-Demombynes (3d ed., 1952), a more detailed scientific description; and lastly *L'arabe classique* by H. Fleisch (1956). The German student has had at his disposal for many years the excellent successive editions of the *Arabische Grammatik* by A. Socin and C. Brockelmann, English translation by R. Kennedy, *Arabic Grammar* (1895). The most important grammar in English is W. Wright's *A Grammar of the Arabic Language* in its third edition revised by W. Robertson Smith and M. J. de Goeje (1896–1898), an essential work for all Arabists of any nationality. In Russian there is G. Sharbatov's *The Structure of Arabic* (1961); N. Iushmanov's *The Structure of the Arabic Language* (1938), English translation by M. Perlmann (1961), and Iushmanov's *Grammatika Literaturnogo Arabskogo . . .* (1928, 2d ed., 1963); D. Cowan, *An Introduction to Modern Literary Arabic* (Cambridge, 1958); J. Kapliwatzky, *Arabic Language and Grammar*, four volumes (Jerusalem, Mass., 1940–1953). The standard work defining the place of Arabic in the general context of Semitic languages is still C. Brockelmann, *Grundriss der vergleichenden Grammatik der semitischen Sprachen* (New York, 1908–1913; reprinted Hildesheim, 1961); useful too is his *Semitische Sprachwissenschaft* (1906) with its French translation by M. Cohen and W. Marçais, *Précis de linguistique sémitique* (1910). The best recent statement on the question is that by H. Fleisch, *Introduction à l'étude des langues sémitiques* (1947).

Knowledge of spoken or modern written Arabic, naturally useful for the direct contact it makes possible, may also be of more immediate interest from the historical point of view, in that dialects occasionally retain words and meanings not admitted into their works by the classical lexicographers. In this respect J. Cowan, *A Dictionary of Modern Arabic* (1961), a translation of H. Wehr's *Arabisches Wörterbuch* (1952), as well as V. Monteil's *L'arabe moderne* (1960) can be helpful.

For the historian, the most valuable works are those which concern the historical evolution of Arabic. J. W. Fück's contribution in this field is of the highest importance: "Arabiya," *Abhandlungen der Sächsischen Akademie der Wissenschaften Leipzig. Philos.-hist. Kl.*, XLV/1 (1950), French translation by C. Denizeau, *'Arabīya; recherches sur l'histoire de la langue et du style arabe* (1955) (up to approximately the twelfth century). Of great significance, too, is the article " 'Arabiyya" in *EI*². Among the more specialized studies, those by C. Rabin should be mentioned; an introduction to these will be found in his article, "The Beginnings of Classical Arabic," *SI*, IV (1955), 19–38. See also *HO* (cited p. 67 f.), I, III/3.

For French-speaking students, the chief Arabic-French dictionary is by A. de Biberstein-Kazimirski, four volumes (1846; new ed., 2 vols., Paris, 1960). The small *Vocabulaire arabe-français* by J. Belot (17th ed., Beirut, 1955), much easier to handle, is substantially the same. The English edition of the Beirut dictionary goes under the name of J. Hava's *Arabic-English Dictionary*, many editions of which have been published. The sources on which E. W. Lane's *An Arabic-English Lexicon*, eight volumes (1863–1893), is based are more complete, and the references are given for each meaning; although richly documented in parts 1–5, it is less substantial in parts 6–8, which were completed by S. Lane-Poole after the author's death. Until quite recently, however, all general dictionaries were based exclusively on the work of Arab lexicographers who indisputably merit our admiration but who, we must not forget, are essentially concerned with purely literary old Arabic. The work will have to be done all over again from the very beginning, card-indexing as large a range of texts as possible. This tremendous task, which had been recognized as necessary and in fact begun by Th. Nöldeke and A. Fischer, is being taken up again at the present time; and two fascicles devoted to the letter *k* have already been published by A. Spitaler, J. Kraemer, and H. Gätje, *Wörterbuch der klassischen arabischen Sprache* (1957, 1960). Furthermore, the Cairo Arabic Academy has begun the publication of a dictionary, *al-Mu'jam al-kabīr*, I (1956) from *hamza* to *kha*, by Murād Kāmil and I. al-Ibyārī.

For the moment and for a long time to come, the historian's best dictionary remains R. Dozy, SUPPLÉMENT AUX DICTIONNAIRES ARABES (1881–1927) which draws on the author's own wide reading to complete the definitions found in the classical dictionaries and adds formations and meanings derived from scientific, administrative, and other texts. His work is valid mainly for Spanish Arabic, Dozy's own special field of research; for the East he has used in the main the more fragmentary notes by E. Quatremère and M. J. de Goeje. E. Fagnan has also published *Additions aux dictionnaires arabes* (1923) but these are less important.

For dialectal Arabic, one should consult A. Barthélémy, *Dictionnaire arabe-français. Dialectes de Syrie*, five parts (1935–1954) supplemented by C. Denizeau, *Dictionnaire des parlers arabes de Syrie, Liban, et Palestine* (1960). A dictionary of Northwest African Arabic, W. Marçais' life work, has been published under the title *Textes arabes de Takruna*, eight volumes (1925–1961).

It is interesting to consult the voluminous dictionary of Arabic technical terms composed in the eleventh/seventeenth century by Ibn Sīda, *Kitāb al-mukhaṣṣaṣ*, seventeen volumes (Būlāq, A.H. 1316–1321).

For the Persian language, see: Ann K. S. Lambton, *Persian Grammar* (1953); J. T. Platts and G. S. A. Ranking, *A Persian Grammar* (Oxford, 1911); D. C. Phillott, *Higher Persian Grammar* (Calcutta, 1919); G. Lazard, *Grammaire du Persan contemporain* (1957); C. Salemann, and V. Shukovski, *Persische Grammatik*, Porta Linguarum Orientalium, XII (Leipzig, 1947); H. Jensen, *Neupersische Grammatik mit Berücksichtigung der historischen Entwicklung*, Indogermanische Bibliothek, Abt. I, Reihe I, Bd. 22 (Heidelberg, 1931); J. Desmaisons, four volumes (1908–1914), the best Persian-French dictionary; and F. Steingass (1892) and S. Haïm (Ḥayyim), two volumes (1934), the best Persian-English dictionaries; B. Miller, *Persidsko-russkii Slovar'* (Moscow, 1953), a good Persian-Russian dictionary.

For Turkish, we have the excellent *Grammaire de la langue turque* by J. Deny (Paris, 1921); for the beginner, it is preferable to keep to the simpler manuals such as the *Lehrbuch der türkischen Sprache* by H. Jansky, translated into French under the title *Élements de langue turque* (1949). Also consult H. J. Kissling, *Osmanisch-türkische Grammatik*, Porta linguarum Orientalium, Ser. II, Vol. III (Wiesbaden, 1960), and L. Peters, *Grammatik der türkischen Sprache*, Berlin (1947). J. Redhouse, *A Turkish and English Lexicon* (2d ed., (Constantinople, 1921), devotes considerable space to administrative vocabulary. Two good and more recent dictionaries are H. C. Hony and F. İz, *A Turkish-English Dictionary* (Oxford, 1957), and F. Heuser and İ. Ṣevket, *Türkisch-deutsches Wörterbuch* (3d ed., Wiesbaden, 1953; 5th ed., 1962). For Old Turkish, we should consult the dictionaries mentioned on p. 154 as well as the modern dictionaries. It is also useful to compare words used in Osmanlı Turkish with those in other Turkish dialects, as may have retained forms and meanings lacking in the former.

It is not sufficient to understand the language only in printed texts, for many of the sources are still unpublished. A work on paleography would be useful even though the calligraphy of Arabic literary manuscripts—in contrast to that of documents and frequently that of Persian and Turkish manuscripts—presents little basic difficulty. Unfortunately, in spite of its title, B. Moritz's *Arabic Palaeography* (Cairo, 1905), is merely a collection —albeit a useful one—of specimens of different hands, as are the more recent *Specimens of Arabic and Persian Palaeography by* A. J. Arberry (1939); the *Album de Paléographie arabe* (1958) by G. Vajda; and by Ṣ. al-Munajjid, *al-Kitāb al-'arabi al-makhṭūṭ ilā l'-qarn al-'āshir al-hijrī* (*The Arab Manuscript Up to the Tenth Century A.H.*) (Cairo, 1960). Among the contributions to the history of Arabic scripts later than B. Moritz's article of 1908 in *EI*, *s.v.* "Arabia," section d, must be mentioned especially A. Grohmann, *Einführung*, cited p. 17, and N. Abbott, *The Rise of the North-Arabic Script and its Ḳur'ānic Development*, University of Chicago Oriental Publications, L (1939). A work on Arabic paleography till the year A.H. 1000 has been announced by Grohmann as *HO* (cited p. 67 f.). Erg. Bd. II. One should also consult the articles "Khaṭṭ" and "Epigraphy" in *EI*² by J. Sourdel-Thomine. For the essential numerical notations, see A. Pihan, *Exposé des numerations usités chez les peuples orientaux* (1860); and, as a small specimen of the overdue modern study of this important subject, R. Irani, "Arabic Numeral Forms," *Centaurus*, IV (1955), 1–12. For Turkish paleography, see below, p. 193 ff.

The editing and translating of texts require technical precautions similar to those developed in Western historiography, added to which are the problems of transcribing and transliterating for which Orientalists have not been able to find a solution agreeable to all. We can only refer here to the general advice given on the subject by R. Blachère and J. Sauvaget, *Règles pour éditions et traductions de textes arabes* (1945) and Ṣ. Munajjid, "Règles pour l'édition des textes arabes," *RIMA*, I, in Arabic; French translation in *MIDEO*, III (1956), 359–374. On rules for setting Arabic in type, see H. Ritter, "Über einige Regeln, die beim Drucken mit arabischen Typen zu beachten sind," *ZDMG*, 100 (1950).

For the locating of manuscripts, see chapter 7.

2

Archives

History is based on documents—that is, on the "traces left by the thoughts and acts of men of old [C. Seignobos]."

For the historian of the European Middle Ages, such documents consist above all of what are called archives—authentic records established to deal with definite needs of daily life (administrative and juridical records, accounts, and private correspondence), forming in almost all cases a direct and impartial source of information that is naturally taken by the student as the basis for his research. Unfortunately, as far as Islamic history is concerned—especially in the earlier centuries, with the exception of Egypt—we are faced with an almost complete lack of documents of this kind. For the later centuries, the situation is somewhat better but in no way comparable with that of the historian of the West, although it must be admitted that the documents which do exist have not been sufficiently edited or exploited. For the present state of work in hand, see H. R. Roemer, "Über Urkunden zur Geschichte Ägyptens und Persiens in islamischer Zeit," *ZDMG*, CVII (1957), 519–538.

For the centuries preceding the Seljuks and the Crusades, the documents which have come down to us directly are almost exclusively concerned with Egypt immediately after the Arab conquest. Up to the tenth century, they are in the main written on papyrus; afterward they are on paper, sometimes on parchment, or other materials. Most have been found at Aphrodito (Kōm Eshqauh) and at Edfu: they are for the most part administrative, financial, and juridical documents or private letters and seem to date mainly from the eighth to the eleventh centuries. A few similar documents have been found outside Egypt, for example, in Palestine.

Pioneer works were J. von Karabaček's discussion of the papyri in the *Papyrus Erzherzog Rainer, Führer durch die Ausstellung* (Vienna, 1894), and, above all, C. H. Becker's demonstration of the historical significance of Arabic papyri in part one of his *Papyrus Schott-Reinhardt*, Vol. III of *Veröffentlichungen aus der Heidelberger Papyrussammlung* (Heidelberg, 1906).

The most important publications at the present time are by A. Grohmann, especially *Arabic Papyri in the Egyptian Library*, six volumes of which have been published (1934–1963). Each document is described, transcribed, annotated, and accompanied with a photographic facsimile. Grohmann gives a list of all publications prior to 1954 in his *Einführung*, cited p. 17.

Among recent works must be noted A. Dietrich, *Arabische Briefe aus der Papyrussammlung der Hamburger . . . Bibliothek* (1955) and the rather different type of work by N. Abbott, cited p. 29. N. Abbott's *The Ḳurrah Papyri from Aphrodito in the Oriental Institute* [of Chicago], Studies in Ancient Oriental Civilization, XV (1938), gives a clear view of the nature and value of an important group of papyri.

In the first century of Islam and sometimes even later, the Egyptian and Palestinian papyri were written in Greek (occasionally, in Egypt, in Coptic). Sometimes they are bilingual. Here the basic study is H. I. Bell's "The Aphrodito Papyri," *Journal of Hellenic Studies*, XXVIII (1908), 97–147, with the translations and commentary in *Islam*, II (1911), 269–283 and 372–384; III (1912), 132–140 and 369–373; IV (1913), 87–96; and XVII (1928), 4–8.

There are two important recent publications: the first dealing with Egypt, by R. Remondon, *Papyrus grecs d'Apollônos Ano* (Cairo, 1953); the second with Palestine, *Non-literary Papyri*, Vol. III of *Excavations at Nessana*, edited by C. J. Kraemer (Princeton, 1958).

In analogy to Greek papyrology, the discipline concerned with the study of these documents has been called Arabic papyrology. This name is unfortunate, implying as it does that the only existing such documents are on papyrus, whereas even in Egypt paper was used from the eleventh century on; and there is no difference in content between the documents on paper and those written on papyrus. In reality, papyrology, when it is concerned with mere deciphering, is a branch of paleography; when interpretation is involved, it is exclusively a branch of history. With these reservations and in the absence of a genuine methodical treatise on papyrology, much vital information will be found in A. Grohmann, *Einführung und Chrestomathie zur arabischen Papyruskunde*, I (Prague, 1954), replacing his older "Aperçu de papyrologie arabe," *Études de papyrologie* I (1932), 23–95. There is also a short introduction by A. Grohmann in English, *From the World of Arabic Papyri* (Cairo, 1952). See also his forthcoming contribution to *HO*.

From the period of the Crusades and of the Turkish domination, documents resulting from the diplomatic relations between Christian and Muslim states and, in exceptional cases, the correspondence of merchants have been preserved in medieval European archives (Venice, Genoa, Pisa, the Vatican, Paris, and Barcelona). Reports by diplomatic agents and deeds executed by notary in Latin or in the vernaculars of the West are often concerned with relations with the Muslim world though only indirectly. The Arabic documents themselves come from all the states touching on the Mediterranean and only occasionally from other regions (Mongol period, thirteenth and fourteenth centuries). See particularly M. Amari, *I diplomi arabi del R. Archivio Fiorentino* (Florence, 1863); G. Thomas and R. Predelli, *Diplomatarium Veneto-Levantinum* (Venice, 1880–1899); G. Thomas and G. Tafel, *Urkunden zur ältern Handels- und Staatsgeschichte der Republik Venedig* (Vienna, 1856); and M. A. Alarcón y Santón and R. García de Linares, *Los documentos árabes diplomáticos del Archivo de la Corona de Aragón* (Madrid and Granada, 1940).

A certain number of documents in Arabic have been preserved in Sicily and Southern Italy, recalling Arabic rule in these regions but usually dating actually from the time of Norman rule. See S. Cusa, *I diplomi greci ed arabi di Sicilia* (1868). See also p. 222.

Lastly, side by side with the Arabic documents, an extensive collection called the Geniza documents has been found at Cairo. These originated in Jewish circles in Egypt and other countries (from the Maghrib and Spain to India) having relations with Egypt (dating especially from the eleventh and twelfth centuries) and are generally drawn up in Hebrew or in Arabic with Hebrew characters. See P. Kahle, *The Cairo Geniza* (2d ed., 1959) and S. D. Goitein, "The Cairo Geniza as a Source for the History of Muslim Civilization," *SI*, III (1955), and "L'État actuel de la recherche sur les documents de la Geniza," *REJ*, CXVIII (1959–1960), 9–27.

A few isolated documents or collections—usually *waqf* deeds—have been discovered by chance. In Turkey, the secularization of former religious collections has brought to light deeds of this kind or legal documents dating back to the beginning of the thirteenth century. Recently, an inventory of the Mount Sinai monastery collection was made. The unusual isolation of the monastery accounts for the preservation of these documents, some of which date from the twelfth century. See the catalogue by A. S. Atiya, *The Arabic Manuscripts of Mount Sinai* (Baltimore, 1955), J. Ernst, *Die mamlukischen Sultansurkunden des Sinai-Klosters* (1960), and S. M. Stern, cited p. 21.

In addition to preserved documents, we take into account—though not without critical examination—those copied in chronicles and other literary works. Above all should be noticed the model collections of *inshā'* (the composition of documents), some of which are preserved from as early as the tenth century, and also the treatises written for use by government officials, the most impressive example being the work of al-Qalqashandī in Egypt in the fifteenth century (see below, p. 179).

It may even be useful to consult the formularies for legal deeds (*shurūṭ*). And the *fatwās* (juridical responses) might also be mentioned in this connection (see below, p. 44).

Finally, for the modern period (except for the quite recent past with which we are not concerned here), we have in process of classification the Ottoman archives, comparable to the richest collections of European archives but scarcely exploited till now. Minor collections dating from the Ottoman period are to be found in the countries which formed part of the Ottoman Empire (Egypt, Tunisia, and so forth). Similar collections have recently been discovered in Morocco, while other finds still remain possible elsewhere (in Iran, for example). See below p. 193 ff.

Though these documents taken altogether represent a considerable collection—even without reference to the modern period or the Ottoman archives—they do not measure up to the European archives either in quantity or quality. They are too unevenly distributed in time and space, and they lack variety; they are composed almost exclusively of governmental and administrative documents, and almost totally lack those private deeds which provide the historian of the West with such a store of information on economic and social questions. What we have, in fact, is a sample: whereas only a large number of documents makes it possible to generalize by assuring the student that the information found in isolated documents is not exceptional.

This relative lack of documents is not exclusively the result of circumstances beyond the control of Orientalists. Attracted by the literary works, they have sometimes been so completely reconciled to using these that they all have practically forgotten the existence—on their very doorstep, as it were—of a collection of documents as rich as that in Vienna. Nevertheless, it is true that the Muslim world has not preserved its archives for us as has Christian Europe. This situation is all the more paradoxical since the Muslims of the Middle Ages had reached a higher standard of culture than the Europeans of the same period, that writing was widespread among them, and that their administrative services were no less subject to red tape than ours. There must be a reason for this paradox.

The explanation is to be found in the nature of the political institutions of Islam and in certain characteristics of its history.

The great majority of our archives derive from legally constituted social bodies (churches, feudal households, towns, trades, and so forth) which carefully preserved in their "treasury of deeds" all facts that favored them. In the absence of any true law—so characteristic of our Middle Ages where custom, strengthened day by day on the basis of individual precedents, was paramount—all documents giving evidence of a precedent had to be preserved. The situation is quite different in Islam, with its horror of exemptive privileges. Islamic Law recognizes only the Community of Believers, which is one and indivisible, admitting no constituted bodies, so that there can be none but state archives.

On the other hand, the will of the sovereign could not by itself create law in this civilization. Caliphs and sultans, faced with an established jurisprudence, were merely instruments of a written law divinely revealed—the Koran and the Custom of the Prophet, the latter of which was soon codified, filling the gaps left by the Koran. Individual documents can therefore back up a particular title; but they do not really constitute law, so that there is no encouragement either for the formation of private archives or the preservation of individual documents in public archives.

Moreover, in our civilization, many documents were juridical in origin. Islamic civilization also had judges who were responsible for the administration of justice, the drawing up of contract deeds, and the management of the *waqf*s; but the prevailing rules of procedure made the number of documents to be recorded very small: the use of witnesses rather than written evidence was responsible for the fact that only the judgment was recorded; the contracts were not given to the parties but kept by the judge, whose archives were in fact state archives subject to the same vicissitudes as the royal chancelleries. And finally, though the Oriental tradition which holds that "the way to hell is paved with judges" is no doubt an exaggeration, it is nevertheless certain that the management of the *waqf*s gave rise to innumerable malversations; when the resources of a *waqf* were exhausted, the deeds which instituted it were destroyed, thereby removing all trace of the spoliation.

One must not exaggerate; the archives of the judges and of the administrative services responsible for the *waqf*s still contain a mass of authentic and important documents. But the older ones, having become useless, have often disappeared; and the more recent, or those which might still be supposed to be of practical value, are for that very reason not easily accessible to the disinterested scholar (as was formerly the case in Christian countries, and occasionally still is to this day).

However that may be, the task of seeking out and publishing rapidly those archives which have survived is an urgent and immediate one. A sound inventory of those which are already known would in itself be extremely useful; it would be necessary to collect quotations from literary works and anthologies of *inshā'* and submit them to critical examination by comparing them with authentic documents of the same type; above all the archives of the judges and those relating to the *waqf*s should be investigated as far as possible, and the ancient documents still preserved by many families collected. A task of this kind cannot easily be undertaken by Europeans for obvious reasons, both psychological and political, but could either devolve on young Muslims or be done in collaboration with them. Most commendably a few scholars have already begun to realize the importance of this work and should, naturally, be encouraged. It will not be long before the Muslim states—following the example of Turkey and of a few pioneers—will understand the value of their archives for the elaboration of their national history and will take measures to render them accessible.

One can easily understand why no general or comprehensive treatise on Arab archival material exists as yet. See, however, the *Einführung* by A. Grohmann, cited p. 17, and the new article "Diplomacy" in *EI*² (Arab section, by W. Björkman, uneven). For the Persian and Turkish see H. Busse, cited p. 185 and L. Fekete, cited p. 195. A good example for diplomatic study on Arabic documents is S. M. Stern, *Fatimid Decrees* (London, 1964). Further material will be found in C. Cahen, "Pour une diplomatique Arabo-Musulmane," *JA*, 1963.

3

Narrative Sources

Even though the historian of Islam is at a definite disadvantage with respect to archives, he at least has access to a large quantity of literary resources, larger perhaps than any other civilization has produced until modern times. These are not exclusively works of a historic nature; indeed, some would seem a priori to have nothing in common with history and yet are indispensable to the historian. Of these the first, naturally, is the Koran, on which see below, p. 117 ff.

Historiography proper was to be influenced in its development by Iranian-Sassanian, and to a lesser extent, Byzantine or Syriac models; but in its earliest manifestations it depends basically on Arab traditions and on the Islamic modes of elaboration, about which a word must be said.

Some valuable information about Muslim historiography in general may be found in the two articles "Ta'rīkh" in *EI*, IV and *Supplement*; in *Historians of the Middle East*, edited by Bernard Lewis and P. Holt, Vol. IV (London, 1962) of *Historical Writings of the Peoples of Asia*; and in F. Rosenthal, *A History of Muslim Historiography* (Leiden, 1952), conceived from the point of view of Muslim culture rather than its documentary value for the modern historian.

THE ARABIC ORAL TRADITION AND HISTORICAL ROMANCES

Arab historiography is primarily a development of oral tradition, not only as a natural consequence of illiteracy, but above all for reasons directly related to a particular social context and mental outlook.

Before Islam, one of the Arab's chief driving forces was a concern for his reputation, for his "honor" (*'irḍ*), based on nobility of race and the nobility acquired through cultivation of the traditional virtues. Every individual kept in mind not only his family tree but also the exploits of his ancestors, especially feats of arms performed in the course of tribal quarrels. But, in the pre-Islamic social structure, the individual counts for little except as a member of a group—clan or tribe—with its own *'irḍ* and a fame that is also based mainly on its feats of arms. Thus the oral tradition fostered by the *'irḍ* conserves a kind of historical documentation expressed in the old poetry and particularly in the "boasting contests" (*mufākhara*), between representatives of two rival tribes (just as "titles of glory" and "titles of infamy" were later to be used as arguments in the controversies between Arabs and non-Arabs). Such traditions do not find their expression so much in the poetry itself as in the prose setting accompanying it. It is practically certain that nomadic Arabs, then as now, introduced a poem (*qaṣīda*) with a narrative explaining in familiar language the deeds that inspired the poet. The later anthologies of poetry we possess follow the same pattern. Thus the historical content will be found in the prefatory narrative, and mere allusion to fact will be found in the poetry itself.

There is every reason to believe that the oldest form of "history" known to the Arabs originated in this genre: an unconscious history whose only aim was to divert and edify, stories, rather than history, that nevertheless presuppose an awareness of the past that other civilizations (India, for example) have scarcely known. Mu'āwiya was a passionate admirer of these narratives; it is in this form that the stories of the "Historical Days," which constitute the essence of the oral historical traditions of pre-Islamic times, have been collected.

For the "Historical Days," see W. Caskel, "Aijām al-'arab," *Islamica*, III (1930 Supplement), 1–99.

For the modern historian, the aim of these narratives obviously restricts their usefulness; they remain schematic, are concerned only with episodes and anecdotes, lack depth and amplitude, present facts unrelated to each other, and lack that historical perspective which would give them significance. They remain "index cards," so to speak.

As time passed, other imperfections were added to these. Memory, even an Arab's, had its limits. Old memories blurred, and more recent ones supervened. Often only contradictions make us aware of the fact that the original data have undergone change. Moreover, when the facts became very remote in time, the transmitter (*rāwī*) was not too concerned with the truth of his tale; what mattered was that he should be seen to his own best advantage and be able to hold his audience. The meaning of the legend thus became distorted. Nor was this the only distortion. Eventually in the first centuries of Islam, the oral narratives were written down in order to protect them from the tricks of memory; they, of course reached us in this form. But this drafting was done by "scholars" eager to find philological material in the old tales or arguments for use in the politico-religious disputes in which they were involved, thus giving rise, consciously or unconsciously, to a new factor of distortion.

See R. Blachère, *Histoire de la littérature arabe*, cited p. 102, especially pages 83 ff., and by the same author, "Regards sur la littérature narrative arabe au 1er siècle de l'hégire," *Semitica*, VI (1956), and G. Widengren, "Oral Tradition and Written Literature . . . ," *AO*, XXIII (1959).

During the Islamic period, there arose on the basis of these oral traditions, and in their own right, vast historical romances, rather like the French *chansons de geste*, except that they are written not in verse but in a simple prose style with the occasional insertion of poetry. This was to be the form of the *Thousand and One Nights*, which incorporated certain stories of this type. Only in Persia, with Firdausī (see p. 144), was the historical legend to take the form of poetry of high literary merit, although prose romances in Persian were not unknown (Abū Muslim). The later Turkish narratives sometimes adopted the Iranian genre, sometimes the Arab (Sayyid Baṭṭāl Ghāzī).

Legends based on historical fact grew up first around the military campaigns (*maghāzī*) of the Prophet, but later other subjects presented themselves and became sources of inspiration, such as the Byzantine wars and the Hilālian migration into the Maghrib. In spite of this, the stories woven around the symbolic figure of the pre-Islamic Bedouin, 'Antar, have remained popular.

See R. Paret, *Die legendäre Maghāzī-Literatur* (Tübingen, 1930); M. Hartmann, "Die Beni-Hilâl Geschichten," *Zeitschrift für afrikanische, ozeanische und ostasiatische Sprachen*, IV (1899), 289 ff.; B. Heller, *Der arabische 'Antarroman* (Hanover, 1925), with summary by the same author in *EI*². For the narrative literature in a more general way, see the recent restatement of the problems concerning the *Thousand and One Nights* in *EI*², *s.v.* "Alf laila wa laila," and below, p. 46 ff.

The epic romances inspired by the Byzantine wars in their Arabic form and in their later Turkish form, hold a unique interest for the historian because of the milieu in which they arose, the facts they relate, and because of the existence on the Byzantine side of an epic poem inspired by the same events, that of Digenis Acritas. We owe a comparative study of the two cycles mainly to H. Grégoire and his circle (e.g., Grégoire and R. Goossens, "Byzantinisches Epos und arabischer Ritterroman," *ZDMG*, LXXXVII [1934], 213–232) and to M. Canard (e.g., "Delhemma," *Byzantion*, XIII [1937], 183–188). See also the article "Dhū 'l-Himma" in *EI*², and "Les principaux personnages du roman de chevalerie arabe *Dhāt al-himma wa-l-Baṭṭāl*," *Arabica*, VIII (1961), 158–173.

For a somewhat similar romance from the time of the Mamlūks, see below, p. 183.

The historian cannot afford to ignore these stories which reveal to him, in the unfolding of the events they report, an ideal that reflects feelings deeply rooted among the people in the Arabic-speaking countries and elsewhere in the Muslim area.

See, for instance, R. Paret, *Die Geschichte des Islams im Spiegel der arabischen Volksliteratur* (Tübingen, 1927).

THE ḤADĪTH

The narratives which we have just discussed are not the only ones to be handed down by oral tradition and later committed to writing. There are others, conventionally called *ḥadīth* in the singular and collectively, the grouping and transmission of which are bound up with the development of primitive Islam. Although used in this connection in a very unhistorical way, they are nevertheless not without points of contact with history.

For the *ḥadīth* from the point of view of the formation of Islam, see p. 41 ff., the works of I. Goldziher, J. Schacht, and others.

In Europe, history soon became a more or less independent genre; the medieval clerks, continuing in their fashion the tradition of the ancients, set down for the use of future generations the events they had themselves witnessed or found related in earlier works. But among the Arabs, history was to be very slow in gaining its independence as a result of the more rapid formation of a more influential "science"—the *ḥadīth.*

A *ḥadīth* is a narrative—almost always short—containing or thought to contain a statement or an action of the Prophet. The science of the *ḥadīth* was developed in order to compensate for the deficiencies of the Koran as a source of concrete legal prescriptions. It was thought that complementary information might be found, when the Koran was not very precise, in the "imitation of Muḥammad," whose life, it was believed, must of necessity illustrate the Law that it was his mission to teach. The example of the Prophet created a precedent that was irrefutable and binding. In the absence of a *ḥadīth* of the Prophet, one could refer to the actions of his "companions."

The content of the *ḥadīth* thus touches upon the life of Muḥammad, his followers, and his immediate successors: it is, in fact, exactly what the historian of this period seeks. This is especially true since Muslim law impinges upon all aspects of life, public and private, in the community, so that the *ḥadīth* sometimes deals with questions that would not fall within the scope of jurisprudence in our sense of the word, questions such as genealogy or matters of policy.

At first the methods of the *ḥadīth* and of historiography were identical: each had recourse to the oral tradition, it being the only source of information available to the collectors of *ḥadīth* as well as to the first Muslim historians. Better still, their informants were the same people: Wahb b. Munabbih and 'Abbās are authorities that may be cited for a prophetic tradition or for a historical narrative. Indeed, for a long time the historians of Islam were simultaneously traditionalists (i.e., *ḥadīth* scholars) and historians; and some, among the earliest, obviously made no clear distinction between their work as traditionalists and their work as historians, regarding the two as linked. In theory there is a wide difference between the two points of view. In one the aim is to establish precedents having practical value for the life of the community in the time of the author; in the other the goal is merely to recount the past and save it from oblivion. In reality, however, it has been possible to show that many a historian, under the pretext of relating the past, was seeking to establish historical precedents, and exactly the same traditions nourish a collection of *ḥadīth* such as that of Yaḥyā b. Ādam on taxes and a history of the Arab conquests such as that of al-Balādhurī (see below, p. 122).

We owe an interesting analysis of the case of Ibn 'Abd al-Ḥakam to R. Brunschvig, "Ibn 'Abdalḥakam et la conquête de l'Afrique du Nord par les Arabes," *AIEO*, VI (1942–1947), 108–155.

The collusion between the genres is particularly flagrant in the case of the *sīra*, the "historical" biography of the Prophet (see below, p. 115 ff.).

Thus the earliest histories follow exactly the same pattern as the collection of *ḥadīth;* each narrative is preceded by its "chain of transmitters" (*isnād*), a list of the people who have handed down the tradition by word of mouth. Then follow other recensions in the same form containing variant readings and different, sometimes contradictory, versions of the same event. In particular, all the traditions that have been collected in al-Ṭabarī's voluminous history (see below, p. 121)—the work of a historian who was also a traditionist and a commentator on the Koran—are presented in this form. This gives an unexpected pungency to the narrative; since it reproduces an oral tradition, it retains the easy turn of phrase and spontaneity of conversation. Remarks are reported—or are claimed to be reported—in direct speech, in the speaker's own words, using the vigorous, imaginative, and highly-colored language of the first centuries of Islam. Rich in evocative detail, told sometimes with verve, many of these narratives combine the warmth of life with the charm of fairy tales. Some, in fact, are models of style. But from the historian's point of view, the habit of naming the sources, of handing everything over wholesale to the reader, leaving him free to make his choice, makes it possible to some extent to submit the different testimonies to critical study and go back to the original texts. With a little practice, one can recognize when one version is derived from another, in spite of the insertion of a detail, contamination by another narrative, or the distortion of an expression that has been misunderstood; it must not be forgotten that we are dealing here with oral traditions which would belong to the domain of folklore, rather than history, were it not for the fact that many alterations have been made for historical reasons, on which they help to throw light.

Books composed in this way are themselves not without their grave defects. The most obvious is the discontinuity of the narrative, which results in the juxtaposition of short anecdotes with no link between them other than the central character or event and with no attempt at chronological order. The claims of transmitters, repetitions, variants, parenthetical remarks by the author, gaps (which are frequent because of the lack of logical order), break up the narrative and make it impossible to take one's bearings so long as this incoherent collection of "index cards" has not been classified —a most disappointing impression. Yet it is with these grains of sand that the history of the first centuries of Islam must be written.

Like the histories, the collections of *ḥadīth* are full of traditions made up in part or entirely to justify a doctrinal or political position; for a long time the history of the Umayyads was seen in a completely false light because of "traditions" spread abroad for the purposes of 'Abbāsid propaganda. The *ḥadīth*, then, is just as useful for the time in which it was circulated as for the time to which it was supposed to refer. It is true that Muslim scholars were themselves aware of these frauds and tried to set up a method for detecting them. Such a healthy attempt at criticism should not be disparaged for being external—mere biographical *isnād* criticism. It explains, though, why so much importance came to be attached to the study of biographies, usually classified by generations (*ṭabaqāt*), in order to ensure that a connection between two links in a chain of transmission was in fact chronologically possible. Unfortunately, modern research has shown that "false" *aḥādīth* are far from lacking an *isnād*. In fact, the later *ḥadīth*, or those at least which received attention latest, were endowed by their transmitters with *isnād*s that were formally beyond all reproach and included the most trustworthy persons. One must not, of course, exaggerate; and there is no reason to deny that the collections of *ḥadīth* and the histories may transmit authentic evidence. But the work of sorting them into sound and unsound, though indispensable, is particularly unrewarding. Only a systematic comparison can show whether a particular version of an incident merely appears at a given time or in a given milieu or whether it derives from an older version. There is very little to go on apart from elusive details or proper names which may not be identifiable in view of the number of names used for one and the same person. Obviously there is still much to be done before a complete critical edition of the traditions is made available.

The most famous and easily accessible of the traditional collections of *ḥadīth* is the *Ṣaḥīḥ* by al-Bukhārī, edited by L. Krehl and T. Juynboll, four volumes (Leiden, 1862–1908) of which there is a French translation by O. Houdas (and W. Marçais for Vol. I), *Les traditions islamiques*, four volumes (1903–1914); an index was prepared by O. Rescher, *Sachindex zu Bokhari nach der Ausgabe Krehl-Juynboll und der Übersetzung Houdas-Marçais* (Stuttgart, 1923). Only Vol. V, parts 1–4, of a complete edition and English translation planned by M. Asad was published (Lahore, 1938). *Al-Madhkal ilā ma'rifat al-iklīl* by Muḥammad b. al-Bayyi' al-Ḥākim al-Nīsābūrī was edited and translated by J. Robson under the title *An Introduction to the Science of Tradition* (London, 1953).

A concordance of *ḥadīth* was begun by A. J. Wensinck, CONCORDANCE ET INDICES DE LA TRADITION MUSULMANE. The first fascicle was published in Leiden in 1933, and thirty fascicles (to *gh-m-r*) have appeared up to 1963; after the death of Wensinck and his successor, J. Mensing, the editorship was assumed by W. de Haas, J. Van Loon, M. F. Abdelbaky ('Abd al-Bāqī), J. T. P. Bruyn, and H. C. Ruyter. This monumental concordance lists the context and references of all the important words contained in the classical "six books" of *ḥadīth*. There are indexes to proper names, geographical names, and Koranic quotations.

A. J. Wensinck is also the author of a less detailed *Handbook of Early Muhammadan Tradition, Alphabetically Arranged* (Leiden, 1927), often adequate for those who want information about a given topic.

The critical study of the *ḥadīth* as practiced by the Muslims draws on the rudimentary forms of history (biography, genealogy, chronology). It is cultivated less for its own sake than as an auxiliary discipline of the legal sciences. In this way it aims indirectly at least, at a truly scientific exactness.

Muslim historiography has always remained marked by its origins. Even after its emancipation, it shows a strong leaning toward biographical studies of all kinds (see below, p. 33 ff.)—a direct result of the intellectual formation of Muslim historians. In fact, some books which are called "history books" are mere collections of biographies of traditionalists chosen exclusively for the traditions they have transmitted.

The beginnings of Muslim historiography are not well known, however, for very little has come down to us directly. A number of quotations have been preserved by later writers, and these should be collected and examined. Some fragments have also been preserved directly on papyrus and may be of great interest. See N. Abbott, *Studies in Arabic Literary Papyri*, University of Chicago Oriental Publications, LXXV (1959).

ANNALS AND CHRONICLES

From the ninth century on, historical works of a new type begin to appear, presenting events in the form of a continuous narrative. At first they merely list events (*akhbār*) but later on aim more and more at a chronological classification (this is the exact meaning of the word *ta'rīkh*, which came to be used to designate history) generally by division into years (in the same way as our European "annals"). The historiography of Sassanian Iran, so far as it existed, has for all practical purposes been preserved only in Arabic or neo-Persian Muslim translations or adaptations, so that it is difficult to say exactly how far it may have influenced this new development. But that such influence did exist seems almost certain if it is remembered that practically all the history written in Arabic in the ninth and tenth centuries was the work of Iranians writing for the aristocracy of government secretaries. It shows more distinctly in the sustained narratives about dynasties (with their tendency toward the moralizing or picturesque anecdote) than in the striving for chronological order. The precedent for such order, if there is need to invoke one, would appear to be in Greek Christian historiography and its Syrian adaptations, even though their influence in general on Muslim culture seems less clear-cut than that of other branches of the ancient Mediterranean heritage.

However that may be this new type was finally that most favored by historians of the Islamic East, and it remains the genre to the present day. There are hundreds of such chronologies of varying lengths, from the simple booklet on a limited subject to the monumental encyclopedia relating in detail the history of Islam in general, even that of all mankind (so far as it was known), and, finally, in connection with it, that of the whole physical world.

Compared with early historiography, these chronicles represent a more important innovation than one of mere form because they use new sources of information. It is true that the oral tradition never disappears and authors continue directly to record events they have themselves witnessed. But in the Muslim states of this period with their administrative services and records, with their chancelleries exchanging regular correspondence with others, keeping journals, and receiving detailed communiqués from the director of the postal service, it became more and more possible to draw on written documents, thus avoiding the uncertainty of oral transmission. The filing and preservation of the "archives" was probably uneven, with public and private sectors mixed; and access to them must have been very uncertain, depending in practice on the authors' luck, curiosity, astuteness, or their connections in society; but that such sources of information were considered important is quite clear from the chronicles, the quotations they contain, and the authors' statements on the question. Occasionally some of these investigators made use of archaeological monuments, ancient coins, epigraphy, and so forth—working, in fact, as historians in the modern sense of the word.

Access to these new sources of information resulted not only in the transmission of texts, if the author was a faithful copyist or excerptor; it also meant diversification in the content of the texts. The historian's audience, moreover, was not the same as in the early ages. Here again there was no complete break with the past; but the historians were now linked with the secretaries of the administration—the cultured elite of the age, who set the fashion in cultural matters—and with princes, who liked to hear their exploits celebrated and be told of the example of their predecessors. This does not mean, of course, that the modern historian, born of a more advanced civilization, will find all he needs to satisfy his curiosity in the works of his Muslim predecessors; it does, however, represent an enriching of the historical material at his disposal. Both in quantity and quality Islamic historiography is far superior to its Western medieval counterpart, although really great works are rare on both sides. Even when the intellectual life of the Muslim world began to flag for lack of fresh stimuli and original works became rarer, the writing of history continued active in all regions until the fifteenth century and here and there even later, for it still held the attention of the great, while the unfolding of new events kept it furnished with new material, if not with a new conception.

A fundamental distinction between types of historiographical works, which is generally observed by historians of the West but which has not always been respected in Oriental studies, must be made by the historian in his treatment of Muslim material. Naturally it was expedient for those who made the first attempt at writing Muslim history to work on the sources which they came upon by chance and to limit themselves to a certain extent to adapting these in a Western language. But such "emergency" methods are no longer adequate if the history of Islam is to be raised to the level of that of other societies. The early Muslim historiographical works we have at our disposal may be reduced to the following two types:

1. Sources in the strict sense of the word: the writer is describing events he has himself witnessed or is, at any rate, the first to describe—in short, reports based on firsthand information.

2. Compilations of various complexity, not reporting events at first hand but relying on earlier authors. These are by far the more numerous, and

generally each of them is represented in libraries by a far greater number of manuscripts than are the original sources, for in a society where there is a wide audience capable of taking an interest in history, works of a general nature are usually more successful than those of a specialized nature. For the same reason, they were the first works to be known and translated in Europe (al-Makīn, Christian, in 1625; Abū al-Fidā', Muslim, in 1722). They furnished the main chronological outlines which later research filled in from other sources. Some of them are voluminous, and the author's talented style has often supplied an additional, well-deserved reason for their success.

Today they cannot, of course, be assigned the same documentary value, though some of them retain their value for us as literary works. This does not mean that they should be automatically depreciated or neglected. Copying a predecessor in literature is plagiarism, though the Middle Ages did not have the same conception of literary copyright in this respect as we do; in historical works, which are not based on the imagination but on documentation, it is not possible, even today, to be anything other than dependent to a very large extent on the authors who were the first to supply the documentation. The medieval Muslim historian's methods are not basically different in this respect from those of his modern counterpart; one must merely distinguish between those who are content to collect and classify quotations and those with a more personal style who try to reassess the facts and produce a synthesis of the whole. In spite of their obvious intellectual superiority, the latter are the least useful and most dangerous for the modern historian if he has to use them.

Regardless of their intrinsic value, these compilations should be evaluated according to whether the information they contain has come down to us directly from the original sources or whether the original sources are lost and their content is not known to us except by the later compilations. and only to the extent that they are recorded in them. Many original sources have unfortunately disappeared, precisely because they did not have as wide an audience as the compilations; they can be reconstituted to some extent only with the help of later historical works: where they have been quoted *in extenso*, an inestimable service has been rendered to posterity. This means that the compilations cannot all be used in the same way, or any one of them in the same way throughout. Usually a work that is essentially a compilation will end with a number of pages that relate facts contemporaneous with the author himself, thus becoming original evidence. Up to this point, it will be necessary to distinguish between what we know from the original sources and the parts for which the sources no longer exist. To do this, every compilation will have to be studied paragraph by paragraph, sometimes detail by detail, in order to discover, by a comparison of the texts, the sources from which they are derived.

The methods of source criticism that have proved their worth for a century in the study of the history of the Christian lands must therefore be introduced or applied generally in the study of Muslim history. Classifying the works and discovering their filiations is a tedious but indispensable task if the true value of the versions of the events under consideration given in such texts is to be correctly appreciated. This is not always easy, for too many essential works are still in manuscript form, precisely because the editors of the chronicles have not observed the fundamental rules of criticism just formulated. Publication thus remains the principal task of the present day; at the same time, however, it is necessary to observe not only the rules for establishing a sound text but also to consider carefully the choice of the text to be published, which choice, in the age of the camera, cannot be dependent on a library's holdings. It would also be useful if editors of texts would supply footnotes giving observations concerning their author's sources that might be suggested by comparison with other known works on the subject. That and not philological annotation should be the task of the editor of a historical text, which for the historian is not primarily a literary text.

The original evidence itself must be studied critically. As a rule, the direct sources give concrete, vivid, and substantial evidence about the facts of which only the bare skeleton remains in the compilations. Chronicles such as those by al-Ṣūlī and al-Qalānisī (see below, pp. 132 and 163) rightly deserve for their humanistic value to rank among the masterpieces of Arabic literature. Nevertheless, the documentation in a given work—in Muslim chronicles as in European—is uneven, according to whether the author was an eyewitness of the events or was merely reporting hearsay, whether they took place in his own town or in a strange, distant region, and, finally, whether he was reporting honestly or for political or religious reasons was distorting or suppressing the facts: the greater part, for instance, of the historical works we possess is Sunnite and plays down the role of Muslims of other allegiances. Every author in fact can be trusted only within certain limits and for a certain period in a given area. The first thing to be done is to fix his "zone of credibility."

Far too often we must regret the fact that the chronicles say almost nothing about the institutions and economic and social life of the mass of the people. They take it for granted that these facts are known and refer to them only in allusions which remain dead letters for us. As we shall see, other works compensate to some extent for these defects. On the whole, the chronicles are especially useful for the history of politics and events. Some however, such as Miskawaih's chronicle (see below, p. 131), have a wider scope; and too often perhaps, knowing that the booty will not be rich, historians have tended to abandon the search for what can be found because it is fragmentary—but the pieces can be assembled. One should not put into a text more than it actually says; there is nevertheless an art of making explicit what was hitherto latent in it.

The historical works—or what are classified as such by Muslim bibliographers according to the usage of the word *ta'rīkh*—can be divided roughly into the following groups:

1. Chronicles, some universal, others dealing with a period or, intentionally or not, restricting themselves to one region; some aim to be exhaustive; others try to sum up the essential points which their readers should know. The ages of great states were naturally more favorable for chronicles covering a large geographical area; periods of political division favored the regional chronicle. While the deeds of princes play a large part in all, some, in autocratic periods, are formal dynastic histories or even histories of a single sovereign. The most limited but often the most vivid form of chronicle in periods of political fragmentation is the history of a town whose characteristic atmosphere it illustrates in its own way. Closely bound up with Arab or 'Alid preoccupations are the genealogical treatises and, occasionally, histories of great families and autobiographies. The histories of viziers and judges, intermediate between this and the following group, are particularly valuable.

The main chronicles will be found in the chapters in Part III dealing with the periods and lands with which they are concerned.

2. Biographical dictionaries, sometimes universal, but more often in categories of scholars or literary men. For instance, with reference to a particular law school, there is an alphabetical list of the legal scholars belonging to that school. There are also dictionary-anthologies of poets; after the rise of Ṣūfism, edifying lives (*manāqib*) of saintly persons were written. There are no biographies of merchants or of people who were neither public figures nor scholars. There is the biographical dictionary conceived on a regional basis, usually a large city, and a listing of all the learned men who ever stayed there. The eleventh-century *Ta'rīkh Baghdād* by al-Khaṭīb al-Baghdādī, fourteen volumes (Cairo, 1349/1931), and the twelfth-century *Ta'rīkh Madīnat Dimashq* (Damascus) by Ibn 'Asākir of which an edition by Ṣ. Munajjid is in course of publication (Damascus, 1951—) are especially famous. The as yet unpublished *Bughya* by Kamāl al-Dīn b. al-'Adīm, dealing with Aleppo, is more valuable for our purposes; it has the pleasant diversity of a chronicle and relies on the same sources a

chronicle would. For extracts see A. C. Barbier de Meynard, "Extraits du dictionnaire biographique de Kemāl ed-Dīn," *RHCHor*, III (Paris, 1884), 691–732. On the whole, these works resemble the early historiography rather than the more advanced chronicles in documentary methods.

From the sixth/twelfth century on, the habit of combining the chronicle type of narrative and the biographical articles of the dictionaries in the same work becomes more and more current, the articles now being arranged in chronological order.

The fullest of the biographical dictionaries is the monumental and invaluable *Wāfī bi-al-wafāyāt* by al-Ṣafadī (d. Damascus, 1363). It uses material which has much in common with the chronologically arranged obituary lists of the somewhat earlier *Ta'rīkh al-islām* by his compatriot, al-Dhahabī. An edition is now being published by H. Ritter and S. Dedering, four volumes of which have appeared in *Bibliotheca Islamica*, 6/a-d (1931–1959); in the meantime consult the "Indice alfabetico di tutte le biografie contenute nel *Wafi*, ... " by G. Gabrieli, *RL*, XXII-XXV (1913–1916). The introduction, listing the sources, has been translated into French by E. Amar, *JA* (1911–1912).

The best-known biographical dictionary is the *Wafayāt al-a'yān* by the Damascene, Ibn Khallikān (thirteenth century), which is selective and well written; equally divided between scholars and politicians, it became so to speak, the historical dictionary of the man of culture. There is a good translation in English by Wm. MacGuckin de Slane, *Ibn Khallikan's Biographical Dictionary*, four volumes (1843–1871, reprinted, 1961); based on F. Wüstenfeld's edition, four volumes (1835–1843), instead of which the Cairo edition (1881) may be used, this version was responsible for the recognition of the value of the work in Europe.

The *Ta'rīkh al-ḥukamā'* by Ibn al-Qifṭī, edited by J. Lippert (1903), and the *Kitāb . . . al-aṭibbā'* by Ibn abī Uṣaibi'a, edited by A. Müller, two volumes (1884), are most valuable for the biographies of scholars; on literary men see Yāqūt's *Irshād al-arīb*, edited by D. S. Margoliouth, seven volumes *GMS*, *VI* (1907–1927). All three belong to the seventh/thirteenth century.

3. Works of an archaeological, geographical, or administrative nature also exist and, as we shall see later, devote considerable space to history.

4. Arab historiography is not identical with Muslim historiography. There exists on the one hand—and we shall return to it later—a non-Arab Muslim historiography; and, on the other, an Arab non-Muslim historiography, which is, in fact, exclusively Christian and especially Coptic and Melkite (i.e., Christians of Greek rite but Arabic speaking), while the Nestorians and Monophysites used either Arabic or Syriac. Generally speaking, we may combine this literature with the non-Arab Christian historiography (within the Muslim world) to be considered later.

Inexperienced students and readers who have no knowledge of Arabic may learn a little about the different types of Arab histories from the *Morceaux choisis des historiens arabes* by J. Sauvaget (1946).

PERSIAN AND TURKISH HISTORIOGRAPHY

Neo-Persian historiography—i.e., in the Persian language but written in Arabic script by Muslim writers and with a vocabulary strongly influenced by Arabic—appears in the tenth century (not much later than the appearance of neo-Persian poetry) in the form of translations and adaptations of earlier Arabic chronicles (al-Ṭabarī). In the eleventh century, it acquires an original and independent style, concurrently with the Arab chronicles, while, from the thirteenth century on, it covers the whole field of Iranian culture to the exclusion of Arabic works. For this reason the history of Iran from the eleventh century on cannot be studied without a knowledge of Persian; and it would be fallacious to think that such knowledge was not required even for the earlier periods. Many Arabic works and documents of the earlier times have, in fact, reached us only in the form of translations or by incorporation in larger Persian works.

The genres and methods of neo-Persian historiography are not basically different from the Arab. Generally they show less insistence on exact chronological order and classification by years, a more marked preference for the continuous narrative, a tendency—in an age of autocratic dynasties—to regard the history of Islam as a series of dynasties, and a predilection for edifying anecdotes. This goes hand in hand with a certain lack of interest in the history of the Arabic-speaking countries, that is to say, a pronounced and exclusive leaning toward Iranian national history. In the field of biographical literature, there are fewer dictionaries of all other kinds, but more lives and dictionaries of saints, as we might expect in view of the part played by Iran in the development of Ṣūfism.

Turkish historical literature is not of great interest to us until the Ottoman Empire reaches its height, and even then it only gradually eliminated competition from Arabic and, above all, Persian works. Until the thirteenth century, all historical documentation concerning the Turks is Persian and remains so, with few exceptions, until the fifteenth century. The genres and methods developed afterward are practically the same as in Persia. But even for the remoter periods a knowledge of Turkish is useful because of the number of Turkish terms found in non-Turkish literature as well as for the ability to read modern Turkish historians on their national past.

HISTORIOGRAPHY IN OTHER LANGUAGES

This is not the place to discuss the literature of non-Muslim communities written in their own languages. But, even without taking into account peripheral Greek, Latin, Georgian, and other sources, attention must be drawn to the existence of Christian historiographical sources originating in Muslim territory, written in the Armenian and especially Syriac languages (in Mesopotamia and the northern regions until at least the thirteenth century). The latter are primarily denominational, but they frequently bring us into contact with popular milieux ignored by Muslim writers. As a rule, historiography in one language is completely independent of others; the Armenians, however, are frequently acquainted with Greek and Syriac authors, and Syriac writers have some knowledge of Arabic and even Persian writers (after the end of the period of translation from Greek, which provided a knowledge of pre-Islamic history). In the critical analysis of the sources, as necessary here as elsewhere, this possibility should be borne in mind. The opposite—that is, acquaintance on the part of Arab or Persian Muslims with peripheral sources—seems as a rule to be excluded except in the case of writers interested in pre-Islamic history (Iranian and Biblical, rarely Greco-Roman) and one or two writers of the period of inter-denominational universalism under the Mongol domination.

Medieval Jewish historiography in Muslim countries is practically non-existent.

4

Travel Books and Geographical Works

It is convenient to classify under the heading "geographical works" an important category of writing that is extremely useful to us. But it must be understood that the notion of geography as we know it emerged very slowly in Islam, and the works we group under this heading belong to genres whose limits go beyond those of geography.

TRAVEL BOOKS

Travel books are one of the sources of geographical works, and some that have come down to us can be used as direct sources. As we might expect, the Muslim travelers who wrote about their wanderings are mainly those who visited countries outside the Muslim world—India, China, or Russia—countries that are a source of wonder for themselves and their readers. But for us, they can be used only as documentation for the study of Muslim relations with the outside world. Journeys in Muslim countries hardly acquire a place in literature until the Turkish conquest and the Crusades. When they do, the travelers in question are almost exclusively Western Muslims drawn to the East by the Pilgrimage or by study—or, after a while, even by curiosity, for the ever-increasing gap between East and West in the Muslim world leads to inevitable surprises for the Western Muslim, especially in Turkish lands, which enhanced the incentive to travel. On the other hand, we have nothing written by Oriental travelers in the West of Islam; however, a few Persians and Turks have left accounts of their travels in the Levant.

If the first Muslim travelers to write about their journeys were those who went outside the Muslim world, we may safely expect in return some profitable descriptions by foreigners of their visits to Muslim countries: a few isolated Chinese and Jews, and later, especially from the time of the Crusades, Europeans of many walks of life. Before there had been only pilgrims interested in little beyond their itinerary, but now, besides the pilgrims, were missionaries, merchants, diplomatic agents, and so on. Their accounts are often extremely interesting, but they constitute a body of writing foreign to the Muslim world, and we cannot dwell on them here. It must be emphasized, however, that the historian must not neglect them. From the sixteenth century on, hundreds of such reports exist (see chap. 22 for the Ottomans and chap. 21 for other Muslim states of the modern period).

GEOGRAPHIES

Until the age of discovery, the geographical sciences were almost entirely a monopoly of Islamic culture; in spite of all that has been lost, Muslim geographers and particularly those of the great age (fourth/tenth century) are still of considerable interest for us.

On Muslim geography see: the article "Djughrāfiyā" by J. H. Kramers in *EI*, *Supplement*, or, by the same author, the partly identical article in *Analecta orientalia*, I (Leiden, 1954), published posthumously; the old *Introduction générale à la géographie des Orientaux* by M. Reinaud—the preface to his translation (1848) of Abū al-Fidā''s work on geography, which can still be usefully consulted; or, in Russian, the comprehensive study by I. I. Krachkovskii, to be found in his *Izbrannie Sochineniia* (*Selected Works*), six volumes (Moscow and Leningrad 1955–1960), IV, of which there is a partial French translation by M. Canard in *AIEO*, XVIII-XIX (1960–1961). A simpler but accurate introduction will be found in the *Extraits des principaux géographes arabes* by R. Blachère (2d ed., Paris, 1958), in collaboration with H. Darmaun.

A category of works devoted to mathematical geography in connection with cosmography and astronomy aims at charting localities and is of interest to the historian (excluding the historian of science) only so far as it may help to identify certain old place names.

Richer in information are the works arising out of administrative needs and based on official documents combined with the author's personal experience. Their object is to give names and precise information on administrative districts, production for fiscal purposes, road stages for the postal services, and sea routes. This category borders imprecisely on other types of work, such as the *adab* literature (see below, p. 46 ff.) which aims to instruct as well. Far from limiting themselves, the authors of these works were not only cosmographers, geographers, and naturalists but also "annalists, economists, moral and religious historians, sometimes even jurists, theologians, or philosophers [Blachère]." Their wide range of interests is a godsend for the historian, who reaps a rich harvest of facts from their usually detailed and accurate works—facts not to be found elsewhere and compensating in part for what one might otherwise expect to find in public records, were these not all too rare. Works of this kind are particularly numerous in the third/ninth and fourth/tenth centuries (see below, p. 134 and p. 179).

Certain dictionaries of geographical names were specially composed as aids for the historian—in particular for the historian of the origins of Islam or for the philologist commenting on ancient texts. In short, history is mingled here with geography. The monumental *Mu'jam al-buldān* by Yāqūt (d. 1229) belongs to this category. It was edited by F. Wüstenfeld, six volumes (1866–1873), and O. Rescher prepared for it *Sachindex zu Wüstenfeld's Ausgabe von Jâqûts "mu'ǧam el-buldân" nebst einem Verzeichnis der darin angeführten Werke* (Stuttgart, 1928). A new edition of the *Mu'jam* has appeared (Beirut, 1957). The introduction has been translated and commented upon by Wadie Jwaideh (Wadī' Juwaida), *The Introductory Chapters of Yāqūt's Mu'jam al-buldān* (1959).

After the breakup of the empire of the caliphs, a new genre—local topography—emerges. The author envisages the world no longer as a whole but merely as a political area in which he lives. The result was a number of detailed monographs that are often sources of the highest importance. They sometimes preface histories of a region or a town and are inspired by the same local patriotism. In any case, history mingled with topographical description in them throws light on the present—and explains archaeological monuments, for example.

This preoccupation with history is not without danger. It is excellent when the authors quote their sources or are careful at least to specify to which period their information relates. But often the later geographers, like their colleagues in other disciplines, are content to reproduce their predecessors' information without making any distinction between different chronological strata. Thus, if we are not careful, we may be tempted to relate to the time of the writer such descriptions as had been valid several centuries earlier. Here too, then, preliminary textual criticism is indispensable.

5

Legal and Administrative Sources

In theory, the comparative lack of archives should give added importance to legal works. But their special nature confronts the historian wishing to make use of them with a delicate preliminary problem.

That the limits of the Islamic legal system are not the same as ours is not of practical importance; the Islamic system makes no distinction between the spiritual and the temporal, so there is continual overlapping of questions which for us would come under ecclesiastical jurisdiction and questions of purely social legislation; in the *fiqh* works, public or private law stands side by side with ritual matters, and the existence of any distinction between them is not realized. For us it is much more important that since, in theory, their fountainhead of law is revelation supplemented by the "custom" of the Prophet (the *sunna*) then the Koran together with the *ḥadīth* will constitute the only collection of laws of universal and indisputable value. Muslim jurists were passionately attached to the idea of constructing a Muslim system of law, elaborated, that is, within a conceptual framework deduced from these texts. They were not responsible for the fact that the texts did not provide exact answers to all the problems of real life in their time; and they could not entirely ignore the existence in actual fact of practices which derived from pre-Islamic times or which had developed later—practices which it was not in their power to suppress and which in many cases could be brought more or less into line with Islam. To draw up Muslim law, they had to find ways of deriving from the sacred texts consequences which are not explicitly contained in them. It is not surprising that the jurists hesitated for a long time over the choice of such methods and were unable to reach complete agreement: there are four schools recognized as orthodox at the present time, to say nothing of the others. For the historian, however, the differences between them are minimal, for they are not so much concerned with practical problems, which are, naturally, common to them all, nor with the concrete solutions proposed by them, as with the theoretical foundations of the law.

The study of the methods which made its development possible and the conditions under which it came into being originated in the long and masterly article, which still deserves study, by I. Goldziher, "Über die Entwicklung des Ḥadīth," in his *Muhammedanische Studien*, II (1890; reprinted 1961), French translation by L. Bercher, *Études sur la tradition islamique* (1952); the essential information can be found in A. Guillaume, *The Traditions of Islam* (1924), less detailed but more accessible; a new and decisive advance has been made however with the publication of J. Schacht's *The Origins of Muhammadan Jurisprudence* (1950). This, however, is a difficult work; and the student will find the essentials in the *Esquisse d'une histoire du droit musulman* (1953) by the same author (up to modern times included). See also the new work by N. J. Coulson cited on p. 88. Nevertheless, although we now know how the jurists went about their work, much study is still required to define the credibility of their individual prescripts.

The most difficult question is whether the legal situation presented by an author does in fact correspond to normal practice at the time or whether it possesses a merely intellectual interest. Undoubtedly, many cases set forth by jurists were purely hypothetical—invented cases or reflections of an ideal without any historical application. The *fiqh* treatises should therefore be regarded with great suspicion before being used as material for the study of social conditions. One need not generalize, however, as long as Muslim legal literature is approached with the following in mind.

In the first place, all Muslim jurists undoubtedly accept the necessity of relating their work to the custom of the Prophet and the Koran. But in practice this can lead to two diametrically opposed results; one either remains faithful to the custom at the risk of coming into conflict with actual practice, or one ratifies the current usage while trying to find justification for it in the sacred texts, forcing them, if necessary, or inventing *ḥadīth*. The two methods have in common the fact that the presentation and theoretical justification of their prescripts are determined by the traditional framework of Islamic conceptions established by the early generations of Muslims. But it does not necessarily follow from the theoretical nature of the presentation that the concrete prescripts are unreal.

One must distinguish to a large extent, between different fields, periods, and regions. A *ḥadīth* usually expresses the preoccupations of the milieu in which it began to circulate rather than those of the person on whose authority it is reported. As for the general legal rules, the gap between the legal works and actual practice appears to be greater in the field of public than in that of civil law. With certain reservations, it is greater in the later works, which copy their predecessors, than in the earlier ones, which, being charged with the elaboration of a body of law in a period not far removed from the origins of Islam, were obliged, after a fashion, to meet the demands of the judges and to take into account simultaneously the demands of their law and the environmental actualities of custom. Finally, the gap is widest in the societies which continued to be governed basically by customary law —recognized by the jurists—such as the Berbers of the Maghrib. There are, moreover, works devoted to this customary law. One should also notice that in the later works and compilations the author juxtaposes as equally valid rules with which he is acquainted either through juridical sources or through the observation of practices that derive from various moments in history and that may even be in conflict; in the jurist's static and normative work, the historian must in fact be careful to distinguish between successive chronological strata.

Methodologically, it is prudent to consider that one cannot, in any given case affirm the reality or unreality of a rule found in a *fiqh* treatise. One must consider concrete situations—even each individual case—trying as far as possible to verify the date obtained through other sources of information. This is a difficult and exacting yet indispensable task—but is the only way of knowing where, when, and especially for what a given law is valid. At any rate, the legal literature cannot be rejected outright as useless; it is one of the means by which social reality finds expression.

On Muslim law viewed from this angle, see: J. Schacht, "Zur soziologischen Betrachtung des islamischen Rechts," *Islam*, XXII (1935); the article cited below by R. Brunschvig; N. J. Coulson, "Doctrine and Practice in Islamic Law," *BSOAS*, XVIII (1956); and J. Berque, "Problèmes initiaux de la sociologie juridique en Afrique du Nord," *SI*, I (1953).

The ordinary law treatises are individual works, not in any way official codes; but in practice they may have guided magistrates and officials. Besides ritual law, they cover the whole field of what we call civil and commercial law, as well as the rudiments of fiscal and penal law, public order, and international relations according to a plan that soon became fixed. They are not concerned, however, with the mechanism and concrete workings of the administrative services that had in fact evolved without much reference to Islam.

The four legal "schools" regarded as orthodox gradually developed in the course of the second Muslim century. The inspirer of the Ḥanafite school, Abū Ḥanīfa, left no work of his own; and the essential treatises, or those used most frequently, are those by his successors Abū Yūsuf (see below, p. 134), al-Shaibānī, *al-Jāmi' al-ṣaghīr*, and later al-Qudūrī, *al-*

Mukhtaṣar, al-Marghīnānī, *al-Hidāya*, al-Kāshānī, *Badā'i' al-ṣanā'i'*, al-Ḥalabī, *Multaqā al-abḥur*, and others; al-Sarakhsī, *al-Mabsūṭ*, is also useful because of the volume of material collected. For the Mālikites, the voluminous collection by Mālik, *al-Muwaṭṭa'*, has survived in various recensions; the basic work for North Africa is the *Mudawwana* of Saḥnūn; the most famous of the "handbooks" are the *Risāla* by al-Qairawānī (fourth/tenth century), the *Tuḥfat al-ḥukkām* by Ibn 'Āṣim, edited and translated by L. Bercher (1958) and the *Mukhtaṣar* by Khalīl b. Isḥāq, of which there now exists, in addition to the old French translation by M. Perron, *Précis ...* (1848–1854), a new translation by G.-H. Bousquet, *Khalîl Ben Ish'âq, Abrégé de la Loi Musulmane selon le Rite l'Imâm Mâlek*, four volumes (Algiers, 1956–1962), of which Vol. I appeared as Vol. XVII of Publications de l'Institut d'Études Orientales de la Faculté des Lettres d'Alger, and Vols. II–IV as Volumes XXIX, XXXIX, and XL of the Bibliothèque de la Faculté de Droit de l'Université d'Alger. An Italian translation by I. Guidi and D. Santillana appeared in 1919. For the Shāfi'ites, the basic work is the *Kitāb al-umm* by al-Shāfi'ī, of which the most popular adaptations are the *Tanbīh* by al-Shīrāzī (fifth/eleventh century), edited by T. Juynboll (1879), and the *Minhāj al-ṭālibīn* by al-Nawawī (seventh/thirteenth century) of which there is a French translation by L. Van den Berg (Batavia, 1882–1884). An English translation of al-Shāfi'ī's *Risāla* has been published by M. Khadduri (1961). Lastly, for the Ḥanbalites, the famous *Musnad* by Ibn Ḥanbal is a *ḥadīth* work, but the juridical opinions it contains have also been of importance. The most outstanding figure of this school is Ibn Taimiyya (eighth/fourteenth century), who has been studied by H. Laoust (see below, p. 181); the same author has translated into French the *Précis* by Ibn Qudāma (seventh/thirteenth century), published in 1956.

Outside the orthodox schools, the most important work for the historian is the *Corpus Juris*, which goes under the authorship of the Zaidite imam, Zaid b. 'Alī, edited by G. Griffini (1919); if its authenticity were established, this would be the oldest known treatise, but it was undoubtedly put into its present form at a later date.

There are naturally many smaller works devoted to particular legal questions all of which cannot be enumerated here. We cite as examples, besides Abū Yūsuf (below, p. 134), those by Hilāl b. Yaḥyā and al-Khaṣṣāf, which perfected the doctrine of the *waqf* in the 'Abbāsid period. (All the legal sources listed above have been published in the Near Eastern countries.)

Naturally the study of even the most theoretical works cannot be neglected for they reveal certain tendencies and claims which are real enough, however theoretical the works may be. In the case of the positive prescripts of a more realistic nature, it is particularly interesting to discover the divergencies, however limited, among the different schools, as R. Brunschvig's article, "Considerations sociologiques sur le droit musulman ancien," *SI*, III (1955) proves; besides the theoretical controversies, others arise out of the practice of superimposing upon the Islamic norm customs that are often pre-Islamic and cannot be assimilated or that result from conflict among different milieux or different moments in early Islamic society. Equally instructive is the study of works denouncing "innovations" (*bid'a*), almost always revivals of old customs, against which the conscience of the devout revolted, or, vice versa, the study of the "dodges" (*ḥiyal*) devised by some of the most highly respected jurists in order to evade the letter of the law in favor of an existing practice. See J. Schacht, "Die arabische Ḥijal-Literatur," *Islam*, XV (1926), 211–323.

The most useful type of legal work for the historian is that which is presented not in the form of a systematic treatise but as a collection of legal responses (*fatwā*) actually given by legal experts on certain difficult cases. Sometimes these collections differ from the dogmatic treatises only in their method of presentation, the questions being imaginary; but more often they deal with real problems and events and can be used for information about the changing aspects of Muslim life. The collections of judicial cases (*nawāzil*) in North Africa belong to the same kind of work. On the formularies, see above, p. 19.

Lastly, on the periphery of works that can justifiably be classified as legal, there is another type of book, written as a rule by high-ranking officials to meet the particular needs of the various government services. These works either describe the way in which the government functions or formulate the principles of such matters as financial management. In spite of tendencies to schematize and to indulge in artificial classifications, these works usually contain truthful accounts of a situation and merit our attention. A particular category of works connected with the needs of a public office are the *ḥisba* treatises for the *muḥtasib;* if the date and place of composition can be determined—which is not always easy—they furnish technical information of great interest on economic matters. See below, p. 165.

One book, which is practically unique in the Muslim world, forms a kind of synthesis of these two groups: *al-Aḥkām al-sulṭāniyya* (*Statutes of Rulership*) by al-Māwardī (eleventh century), an outstanding treatise of public law, combining an almost utopian program of reform of the caliphate with reflections on the actual practice of successive Muslim governments.

Legal works by members of the non-Muslim religions rarely deal with public law but may give information on various aspects of the social life of their community and of the period in general. Examples may be found in the works on Syro-Roman law, of Christian origin, edited by E. Bruns and E. Sachau, *Jus Syro-romanus*, three volumes (1880), written as we now know under the 'Abbāsids; the *Fiqh an-naṣrānīya* by Ibn al-Ṭayyib, edited by O. Spies and W. Hoenerbach, two volumes (1955–1957), or the *Responsa* (i.e., *fatwās*) by the Jewish scholar, Maimonides, edited by J. Blau (1957 ff.).

6

Other Literary Sources

Though the sources already discussed are the most important for the historian, he should not neglect other literary genres, because often he may find in them a particular aspect of some information that will compensate for the usual deficiencies in its documentation.

Under the title *adab* may be classed the whole category of works that aim to teach a "gentleman" the code of correct behavior, the notion of duty, and current morality in relation to his position in society as well as a little knowledge of everything he should know and the customs he should respect in order to hold his own in society and conversation. Side by side with works addressed to all cultured people are works concerned more especially with a particular social group or, more specifically with princes. On the latter, see G. Richter, *Studien zur Geschichte der älteren arabischen Fürstenspiegel* (Leipzig, 1932).

Such works are interesting for both form and content. They are not presented in the guise of moralizing and boring homilies logically arranged but are anthologies of unrelated anecdotes, whose significance automatically becomes apparent without the help of a commentary. The anecdotes are usually given an *isnād*, for they are not drawn from the imagination but from an oral tradition relating to true historical figures whose renown gives added weight to the story. The *adab* anthologies, then, are not fundamentally different from the old history books, and occasionally the same anecdote appears in both. The *adab* authors often quote documents and works which have not otherwise come down to us. Above all, since they seek to regulate man's behavior in society, they present a variety of aspects of social life; on these grounds, they must of necessity be included among the historian's sources of information. And sometimes, as in the case of the history of the Umayyads, the part they play in compensating for the inadequacy or the partiality of the chronicles is greater than usual.

Other works similar to these and difficult to differentiate from them consist simply of anthologies of anecdotes, intended to amuse and to enliven conversation without any higher moral or educational pretensions. Often they are stories about poets, gathered in the process of making an anthology of their verse. The *Kitab al-Aghānī* (*Book of Songs*), discussed on p. 123, is the masterpiece of this genre and a mine of information for the historian.

But all these works have one defect in common: history is merely a pretext for them, so there is no rigor whatsoever in their choice of documentation, and often themes of current folklore are ascribed to people with whose characters they seem compatible and are presented as historically authentic anecdotes: in this way, the caliph, 'Umar, or the governor of Iraq, al-Ḥajjāj, have become semilegendary figures, and their personalities have been overaccentuated by tradition. Here too a strict critical attitude is necessary which must take into account the inadvertent use of anachronisms and, above all, make systematic comparisons with other sources. In addition, these works become uninteresting from the eleventh century on; in general, they merely reproduce in a modified order stories mentioned by their predecessors (one should make sure that they do indeed occur in older collections) or tend toward mere pursuit of the piquant, which is of no use to the historian.

Many of the biographical dictionaries and lives of saints mentioned above resemble in form and type of documentation the *adab* works rather than the strictly historical works they claim to be.

Poetry too develops into a repetition of clichés and so gradually loses the interest it may have held for the historian. It cannot, however, be entirely neglected; nor, above all, can the commentaries which continue to be written. In the absence of normal historiographical sources, their meager allusions may for certain moments or certain regions still possess a practical value.

Scientific works should not be forgotten; not only because they are necessary (inevitably) for the historian of science, nor because they may contain incidental allusions or anecdotes whose interest lies beyond the scope of their actual subject, but because they are frequently written to meet the needs of a profession about which they furnish concrete details: for instance, mathematical treatises for merchants, tax agents, or surveyors; works on agriculture or jewelry; pharmacopoeias; even books on astrology predicting prices or events, sometimes after the fact, and so on. This category is too often neglected.

Naturally works of a "philosophical" nature form the raw material of cultural history; some, indeed, impinge on other aspects of history as in the case of the heresiographies which touch on the history of politico-religious movements; see below, pp. 136, 147 and 223.

Generally speaking, one should guard against relying too exclusively on texts of one type, even those that are most closely related to the question under consideration. One should vary them as much as possible, so as to compare the various points of view, compensate for the inadequacy of one kind of text by using material of a different genre, check statements, and complete the data.

7

Literary Sources: Bio-bibliographical Works

Various works list the literary sources that the student will have to use and include notes on the authors concerned.

For the Arabic sources, the indispensable work of reference is C. Brockelmann, GESCHICHTE DER ARABISCHEN LITTERATUR (*GAL*), two volumes, which one should consult in the second edition (Leiden, 1945–1949), and three supplementary volumes (Leiden, 1937–1942). The distribution of the subject matter is somewhat complicated. In the first place, three supplementary volumes were added to the original *GAL* of 1898–1902; subsequently, as these were also incomplete, a second edition of the original volumes was published, adding whatever was lacking in the supplements: this means that the two series of volumes must always be consulted concomitantly and only the old 1898–1902 volumes are no longer necessary. The page numbers of the first edition are printed in the margins of the supplementary volumes and of the second edition, thus facilitating reference, and the supplementary volumes (except for the third, which deals with contemporary literature) are divided in the same way as the original volumes in both editions. The index, which, in the 1902 edition, followed the Arabic alphabetical order, is now to be found in volume three of the supplements, in the order of the Latin alphabet, with references to the page numbers of either the supplements or the early volumes. There is an index of names of authors and an index of titles but unfortunately no index of subjects. The literary production in Arabic is divided chronologically into the main periods and, within each division, classified according to literary genres. The notes on each author give (*a*) all the necessary biographical information and (*b*) a complete list of works, with mention of all the known manuscripts and editions as well as the abridged versions, commentaries, or critical studies that may exist.

Errors and omissions are inevitable in a work of this scope, and, while it provides an invaluable and indispensable basis for research, it should always be verified in the course of more detailed study. The method of classification is a little artificial in that authors who wrote on different subjects are listed only in the section to which they have been assigned so that works dealing with a particular subject may appear in different sections. Anonyma are rarely listed. Finally, the investigation of manuscripts, especially in the East, has advanced at such a rate in recent times, and so many catalogues have been published that the *GAL*, even with its supplements, is no longer up to date. Periodical proposals for bringing it up to date have so far come to nothing.

For the Arabic-speaking Christian authors we have a somewhat more detailed work by G. Graf, *Geschichte der christlichen-arabischen Literatur*, five volumes (Rome, 1944–1953). Since many authors wrote in Syriac, and because Syriac literature is also of interest for the history of the Near East, it will sometimes be useful to consult A. Baumstark, *Geschichte der syrischen Literatur* (Bonn, 1922), similar to the two preceding works in its general plan. Similarly, one should consult M. Steinschneider, *Arabische Literatur der Juden* (Frankfurt, 1902), and A. S. Halkin's survey in *The Jews, their History, Culture and Religion*, edited by Louis Finkelstein (Philadelphia, 1949), pp. 784–816.

Most of C. Brockelmann's information is drawn from Ṣafadī, Yāqūt, and others, cited on p. 34 f. But it is still necessary to use, after verification, the monumental catalogue entitled *Kashf ẓal-unūn* in which the seventeenth-century Ottoman polygraph, Ḥājjī Khalīfa (Kātib Chelebi), listed all available Arabic books, especially those in Istanbul; in Europe, the convenient edition by G. Flügel, seven volumes (1835–1858), is used. Reference should be made to the edition in two volumes (Istanbul, 1941–1943), as well as to the supplement *Keşf-el-zunun Zeyli*, two volumes (Istanbul, 1945–1947) and the *Asmā' al-Mu'allifīn*, two volumes (1951–1955), by Bagdatlı Ismail Paşa. Sakhāwī, in the fifteenth century, made a less ambitious list of all the historical works known to him; and this will be found in F. Rosenthal, *History . . . Historiography*, cited p. 22.

Lists of the Shī'ite authors will be found in al-Tūnkī *Mu'jam al-muṣannifīn*, four volumes (Beirut, 1344/1925), and Āghā Buzurg al-Ṭihrānī, *al-Dharī'a ilā taṣānīf al-Shī'a*, two volumes (Teheran, 1955–1956).

Serious research, as everyone knows, cannot be conducted without consulting library catalogues, and the task is facilitated by G. Vajda, *Répertoire des catalogues et inventaires de manuscrits arabes* (1949). Certain catalogues contain substantial information on the works and authors they describe; W. Ahlwardt's catalogue for Berlin (ten volumes) takes first rank in this respect.

A guide to Persian literature, similar to that of C. Brockelmann's *GAL* but more reliable, is in course of publication: C. Storey, *Persian Literature, a Bio-Bibliographical Survey*, of which Vol. I/1, section 1, *Qur'ānic Literature* (1927), and section 2, *History and Biography* (1935–1955), and Vol. II/1, *Mathematics, Weights and Measures, Astronomy, Geography* (1958) have so far been published.

The only equivalent catalogue for Turkish is devoted to historiography: F. Babinger, *Die Geschichtsschreiber der Osmanen und ihre Werke* (Leipzig, 1927). For other kinds of works, consult the somewhat antiquated work by Bursalı Mehmet Tahir, *Osmanlı muellifleri*, three volumes (Istanbul, A.H. 1333), in Turkish.

Byzantine sources are listed in K. Krumbacher, *Geschichte der byzantinischen Literatur . . .* (527–1453), *Handbuch der klassischen Altertumswissenschaft*, IX. Bd., 1. Abt. (Munich, 1891), second edition in collaboration with A. Ehrhard and H. Gelzer (Munich, 1897; reprinted, 1958), supplemented with the first volume of G. Moravcsik, *Byzantino-Turcica*, cited p. 153, which is virtually a complete survey of Byzantine historical literature. There are only general histories of Armenian literature, no list of manuscripts and editions aiming to be exhaustive. On Syriac, see p. 50. The Georgian sources will be found in the compilation edited and translated by M. Brosset under the title *Histoire de la Géorgie*, five volumes (1849–1858).

8

Archaeological Sources

EPIGRAPHY

Although Islamic archives are rare, this handicap is offset to some extent not only by the comparative profusion of literary works but also by the abundance of inscriptions. These are authentic, firsthand documents contemporaneous with the events; few civilizations can offer so many examples. Although research is still quite recent in certain countries, several thousands have already been collected. Admittedly these belong to different categories: some come from architectural monuments (or tombstones); others are to be found on furniture and textiles as dedications but also for ornamental purposes (for the Arabs soon recognized the decorative value of their writing) and as official inscriptions on the *ṭirāz* cloths—a privilege of the ruler.

It is difficult to appreciate fully all that can be gained from a methodical study of epigraphical documents, for Muslim epigraphy as a scientific auxiliary discipline of history dates back only to the work of Max van Berchem (d. 1923) and has still been undertaken by only an extremely limited number of specialists. In consequence only provisional indications can be given.

It must be recognized with M. van Berchem that Arabic inscriptions (representing the vast majority of the epigraphical documents of the Muslim world) have considerably less documentary value than Greek or Latin inscriptions; almost all "are centered on one of the two predominant ideas in the Muslim world: divine power and absolute political authority. On the one hand, the Koran, invocations, and pious phrases, confessions of faith, mystical allusions, and prayers for the dead; on the other hand, the names of the sovereign, his titles, exploits, and his perpetual praise." Administrative inscriptions, which are of immediate value for the study of institutions, are too rare and are largely restricted to one or two centuries.

Moreover, the inscriptions cannot be compared with the numerous literary works already discussed: they obviously cannot give as much detail. Nevertheless, their very great importance should be fully recognized, for it gives rise to a method of research. Authentic, firsthand, and exempt from the accidental mistakes that frequently occur in the copying of literary works, they constitute documents that are perfectly reliable for what they are. They give exact dates, undistorted by the carelessness of copyists, and proper names in their correct official form; they complete genealogies and lists of officials. A study of the titles used in them allows us to determine the political status of a dynasty or the rank of a particular person within it. Official decrees permit a more accurate knowledge of administrative, and especially financial, practice; hundreds of deeds of vanished *waqf*s survive at least in summary, graven on stone. Lastly, the inscriptions fit the date of the monuments and objects on which they are found and thus form landmarks for the art historian and the archaeologist. They enable us to identify those of obscure nature and provide a sound basis for the historical topography of towns. Certain inscriptions on movable objects (stamps on weight, trade-marks of caliphal factories) are essentially official documents. No doubt the profit may seem slight, the waste enormous. But Islamic epigraphy is by no means exhausted, and inscriptions are far too often dismissed as "ordinary"; an authentic document is never really ordinary unless it is used in an ordinary way.

The significance of the inscriptions can be fully realized only if literary and epigraphical sources are continually used in conjunction. The narrative sources have the advantage of variety, the epigraphical sources, of authenticity and exactitude of detail; they make it possible to verify the chronicles, and where an inscription and a historical work differ, it is the inscription that will always be the more acceptable. Similarly, the epigraphical texts are usually too brief to provide more than allusions and become completely intelligible only with the aid of the chronicles; the material they provide remains "potential" until they have been systematically compared with other inscriptions and their indications collated with literary sources. A practical application of this method can be found in M. van Berchem's INSCRIPTIONS ARABES DE SYRIE, *MIFAO*, III (1897), which every historian should read.

The texts of almost all the inscriptions noted so far may be found in one of the two following publications: the *Corpus Inscriptionum Arabicarum* (*CIA*) and the *Répertoire chronologique d'épigraphie arabe.*

The *Corpus,* which was given the modest title of *Matériaux pour un Corpus Inscriptionum Arabicarum* by its initiator and principal author, M. van Berchem, and which has been published (with the exception of volume one) in *MIFAO*, is organized on a topographical plan: country by country, and in each country, town by town; in each town, monument by monument, the inscriptions being classified chronologically and numbered successively in each volume. Unfortunately, it is most unlikely that the work will ever be completed, at least in its present form. The following have been published: Part One, *Egypt*, two volumes: Vol. I, M. van Berchem, *Le Caire*, Mémoires de la Mission Archéologique Française au Caire, XIX (1894–1903); Vol. II, G. Wiet, *Le Caire (suite)*, *MIFAO*, LII (1930). Part Two, *Syrie du Nord*, two volumes: Vol. I, M. Sobernheim, *'Akkār, Ḥiṣn al-Akrād, Tripoli*, in *MIFAO*, XXV (1909); Vol. II, E. Herzfeld, *Inscriptions et monuments d'Alep*, two volumes, *MIFAO*, LXXVI-LXXVIII (1954–1956); in this work Herzfeld was able to draw upon the work of predecessors, which he held in trust, but he himself died before reaching the end of his task, which explains the incomplete nature of the notes; [n.v.] M. van Berchem, *Syrie du Sud*, *Jérusalem*, three volumes, *MIFAO*, XLVIII-XLV (1922–1949). Part Three, *Asie Mineure:* Vol: I, M. van Berchem and H. Edhem, *Siwas et Diwrigi*, *MIFAO*, XXIX (1917).

The *Répertoire* was planned quite differently by its authors, E. Combe, J. Sauvaget, and G. Wiet. The aim was to furnish rapidly the text of all published inscriptions (and some unpublished ones) on both monuments and objects. Each inscription is transcribed and translated; but the notes are limited to bibliographical references, and when an inscription has not previously been the object of an adequate edition or study, this inadequacy is naturally reflected in the *Répertoire*. In any case, the *Répertoire* lists the inscriptions but does not dispense with the need for reference to the special studies. Additions and corrections inserted in the later volumes and relating to preceding volumes compensate for the haste in which they were published. This very rapidity has none the less rendered valuable service. The inscriptions are classified by year from west to east. Thus all the inscriptions can be seen synchronously. They are numbered consecutively. Fifteen volumes have appeared since 1931 with volume fifteen going as far as 746/1346 (volume sixteen is in press).

For Spain and the Maghrib, see below, p. 220.

Good examples of studies of inscriptions on objects will be found in G. Wiet, *Catalogue général du Musée arabe du Caire: objets en cuivre; L'exposition persane de 1931*, a publication of the Arab Museum (Cairo, 1933), and *Soieries persanes* (Cairo, 1948).

There is no treatise of Arab epigraphy (Persian and Turkish epigraphy is relatively less important). See J. Sourdel-Thomine, "Quelques étapes et perspectives de l'épigraphie arabe, " *SI*, XVII (1962), and the forthcoming article on epigraphy by the same author in *EI*²; the Russian journal, *Epigrafika Vostoka*, especially the studies by V. A. Krachkovskaia (these and other articles by the latter will be found listed in the index of J. D. Pearson, *Index Islamicus* [cited p. 70], *s.v.* Krachkovskaya); and G. I. Iusupov, [*Introduction to Bulgaro-Tatar Epigraphy*] (Moscow, 1960), in Russian.

NUMISMATICS

What applies to epigraphy is true for numismatics. There is no private mintage in Islam: the striking of coins is a privilege of the ruler. Compared with ancient numismatics, Muslim mintage is poor because the representation of figures—which has added so much to our knowledge of the institutions and cults of the ancient world—is not permitted by Islam. But it is informative on certain aspects of political and, of course, economic history. Variations in the types and legends of coins may reveal the religious leanings of a dynasty. The titles of sovereignty and the date and place of the mint afford reliable means of checking chronological data and precise indications for the locations of mints, that is, administrative centers. Study of the type and even more of the weight and alloy used—in theory determined once and for all but in fact considerably fluctuating—should be of profit to economic history if investigations along this line that have begun were multiplied; analysis of the composition of treasures and the places where they are found would also be of value; unfortunately, these are sometimes unknown because of carelessness. In particular, the history of international trade would benefit. Coins, like inscriptions, are unimpeachable, authentic official documents, useful for the reconstruction of dynastic succession and for certain periods where the chronicles are silent. Muslim numismatics could become a rich field for research.

But it must be emphasized that Muslim numismatics, even more than numismatics in general, can no longer be the concern of the amateur collector—for exhibition in a show case. Money is an instrument of political power; above all it is the instrument of economic exchange. It must be studied as such, not in the museums but in the historian's study. Unfortunately, the catalogues published up to now do not give the historian much help. For many countries they are still very incomplete, and those that are at our disposal bear the mark of the spirit in which they were conceived: they give the legend, image, size, and weight but not the metal composition, which it is impossible to deduce automatically from the information given; nevertheless that alone is of value for economic studies. On the other hand, the way in which the coins have been collected has led to great dispersion. There is an urgent need for catalogues arranged according to category—which one or two scholars have done, all too recently and with too few followers.

The principal catalogues of collections are the following:

London

S. Lane-Poole, *Catalogue of Oriental Coins in the British Museum*, ten volumes (1875–1890). Vol. I covers the Eastern caliphate; II, lesser Eastern dynasties; III, the Seljuks, Artuqids, and Zengids; IV, Egypt from the Fāṭimids to the Mamlūks; V, Spain, the Maghrib, and the Yemen; VI, the Mongols; VII, Bukhārā from Tamerlane to the present; VIII, the Ottomans; IX, additions to I–IV; X, additions to V–VII. For Persia and India, see R. Stuart-Poole, *The Coins of the Shahs of Persia* (1887), and S. Lane-Poole, *The Coins of the Moghul Emperors of Hindustan* (1892). Vol. I has now been entirely replaced by two works by J. Walker, *A Catalogue of the Arab-Sassanian Coins in the British Museum* (London, 1941) and *A Catalogue of the Arab-Byzantine and Post-Reform Umaiyad Coins* (London, 1956).

Istanbul

Müze-i humāyūn, Meskūkāt-i qadīmeyi islāmiye kataloghu, five volumes, four in Turkish and a fifth in French (Istanbul, 1311/1894)—rich collections, particularly valuable for the Ottoman countries, especially volume four by Ahmed Tevhid.

Paris

H. Lavoix, *Catalogue des monnaies musulmanes de la Bibliothèque nationale*, three volumes (1887–1891): Vol. I, *Khalifes orientaux;* II, *Espagne et Afrique;* III, *Égypte et Syrie*, the work being incomplete.

Leningrad

A. Markov, *Inventarny katalog musulmanskikh monet . . .*, one volume and two supplements (St. Petersburg, 1896–1904).

It may be useful to consult recent catalogues, even limited ones, because of the more up-to-date documentation they give; one of the best is D. Sourdel, *Inventaire des monnaies musulmanes anciennes du musée de Caboul* (Damascus, 1953).

The works of G. Miles, *The Coinage of the Umayyads of Spain*, two volumes (1950), and *The Numismatic History of Rayy* (1938), and O. Grabar, *The Coinage of the Tūlūnids* (1957), are models of systematic cataloguing.

On the use of coins for economic history, the works of A. S. Ehrenkreutz and in particular his article, "Studies in the Monetary History of the Near East," *JESHO*, II (1959) and VI (1963) must be cited as examples.

There is no proper treatise of numismatics. O. Codrington's *A Manual of Musulman Numismatics* (London, 1904), was already incomplete, imprecise, and unreliable when it first appeared.

The very scattered bibliography has been listed exhaustively in L. A. Mayer's *Bibliography of Muslim Numismatics, India Excepted* (London, 1939), second edition brought up to 1950 (London, 1954). See also the excellent reports on progress and future tasks of research by G. Miles, "Islamic and Sasanian Numismatics: Retrospect and Prospect," *Ve Congrès International de Numismatique, Paris, 1953*, Vol. I, *Rapports*, pp. 129–144, and "Islamic Numismatics," *VI. Congresso Internazionale di Numismatica, Roma, 1961*, Vol. I, *Relazioni*, pp. 181–192. But in practice, it is possible to obtain substantial information from the catalogues of the great collections without having recourse to all the publications on the subject.

ARCHAEOLOGY

The historian's use of epigraphy and numismatics is not, nor should it be, any more than the particular application of a method which ought to be extremely fruitful: it consists in treating archaeology as an auxiliary science of history, using it to compensate for the inadequacy of our authentic documentation. We have emphasized the documentary value of inscriptions and coins merely because their use in historical research is more or less well known; but, as a matter of fact, what has already been said can be applied in the main to all the monuments of the past. If it is true that archaeology has not afforded the historian all the help it might, this has been due to an all too frequent tendency to leave it exclusively in the hands of art historians; a vigorous reaction is called for, and the difference between the two disciplines should be clearly marked, though they should, of course, coexist and coöperate.

The art historian is concerned primarily with aesthetic values. He differs from the pure aesthetician—artist or philosopher—in attempting to trace the evolution of art in time. If he is truly a historian, he will place the object in its historical context, explaining it through its cultural and social environment as Émile Mâle has done in such a masterly manner for medieval Europe. Nevertheless, his immediate object, his principal aim, is the explanation of the beautiful work of art. The archaeologist, on the other hand, is not concerned with artistic values; what matters for him is the interpretation of nonliterary, tangible monuments of ancient civilizations: their technical characteristics are naturally important, but the wider aim of archaeology is—or should be, as we might remind many pure technicians—the explanation of a monument or an object through historical methods and for historical purposes. Essentially, then, what interests him is the use to which monuments are put. As a result, the archaeologist must be acquainted with all the monuments and objects of the past, not only those which have aesthetic value. They, in fact, play minor roles. Shapeless ruins and a tool for daily use are objects of study for him in exactly the same way as the most magnificent buildings or great works of art. In practice, of course, the limits between the two disciplines are not so clear-cut; and the work of the two types of specialists, many of whom invade both fields of study, are not so easily distinguished. Nevertheless, the fundamental approach is different, especially if one considers extreme cases; an awareness of the historian's definition of archaeology, with its rigorously objective, scientific methods and its concern for all the signs of human activity, should warn the beginner against an approach that would restrict him to the consideration of artistic monuments isolated from their contexts and lead him toward an appreciation of them based on subjective aesthetic criteria.

Like inscriptions and coins (which are, in fact, archaeological material of a particular kind), the monuments of the past studied by the archaeologist are not merely genuine but concrete, tangible documents that frequently prevent one from being led astray by the rhetoric or inexactitude of the literary texts. At the same time they may shed light upon certain features of Islamic civilization neglected in literature; in all cases they make for a clearer picture in the mind as an illustration illuminates a text. Archaeology should be subservient to history; no longer should it be purely descriptive or claim to be an autonomous science. Archaeological monuments should be studied for what they reveal of the men who fashioned them to satisfy certain needs, just as a shell is studied in order to learn something of the creature that inhabited it. For the historian, the actual archaeological data are less important than their interpretation.

With these stipulations, archaeology can be extremely useful; it can serve all the aspects of history that have left material traces, but two categories are especially important: architectural monuments, which form the setting for social life and whose structure depends on the characteristics of society, and pictorial representations, which give more precise detail on certain material aspects of a civilization than the vaguer descriptions of the literary sources. According to a persistent legend, reproductions of the human figure are the exception in Islam; such is not the case.

The archaeological monuments, however, rarely offer complete information in themselves; more often they pose a problem which cannot be solved by archaeology alone. Here again, as in the case of epigraphy, the literary sources must be consulted at the same time. The correct method consists in cross-checking the evidence presented by the two sources of information.

Unfortunately, not even the raw material that would permit the immediate application of this method is available at the present time (though what does exist may serve to guide research along certain lines). Until quite recently and over vast areas of Islam—in Iran, for example—only well-preserved monuments, almost all of which were works of art, had been studied and even these inadequately, while no excavation was undertaken even in those very regions where there actually were excavators who specialized in the archaeology of ancient times. The task is complicated by the fact that often the site to be investigated has been continuously occupied up to and including modern times; psychological difficulties may also arise. Even so, there is no doubt that the archaeology of Islam has not been considered of equal importance with the archaeology of ancient times; certain recent exceptions merely underline the disparity.

It is easy to understand why we possess no comprehensive work on Muslim archaeology. Too often works claiming to deal with Muslim archaeology envisage monuments solely from the point of view of the history of art, though even here there is no good general history of Muslim art (see below, p. 103 f.). Almost all the older works suffer not only from the absence of the historical approach outlined above but also—often in the case of works by amateurs—from a lamentable lack of technical precision and even a partial ignorance of standard terminology.

Although devoted to the period immediately preceding Islam, in a region which was shortly to be conquered by the Arabs, the excellent volumes on ancient villages in Northern Syria, *Villages antiques de la Syrie du Nord,* three volumes (Paris, 1953–1958), by G. Tchalenko, must be cited as examples of research conducted with a regard for all that archaeology can contribute to history in general. Rich too are the investigations of Soviet archaeologists in Central Asia on the pre-Islamic and Islamic periods, which are of very great interest whatever one's opinion of some of their interpretations may be. A semipopular account of their work has been given by S. Tolstov for Khwārizm, *Po sledam drevnekhorezmiiskoi tsivilizatsii* (Moscow and Leningrad, 1948), translated into German by O. Mehlitz, *Auf den Spuren der altchoresmischen Kultur* (Berlin, 1953). In the Muslim field, models of the combined use of texts and monuments can be found best in J. Sauvaget's works cited on pp. 92, 128, 129, and 181.

The bibliography of publications devoted to archaeology and the history of art, which are highly dispersed, can be found in the specialized journals that frequently publish important reviews and articles bringing questions up to date (*Ars Islamica* [*AI*] which became *Ars orientalis* in 1954) and in L. A. Mayer, *Annual Bibliography of Islamic Art and Archaeology*, three volumes (Jerusalem, 1936–1938), then in J. D. Pearson and D. S. Rice, *Islamic Art and Archaeology, A Register of Works Published in 1954* (London, 1956), which will probably be continued.

In addition, K. A. C. Creswell has drawn up a methodical bibliography from his extensive card index, published by the American University in Cairo as *A Bibliography of the Archaeology, Arts and Crafts of Islam* (1961). For Iran, see the four-volume *Āthār-é-Īrān, Annales du service archéologique de l'Iran* (Haarlem and Paris, 1936–1949).

For the history of art proper, see below, p. 103 f.

9

Contemporary Geographical and Ethnological Material

The historical past has handed down to us archaeological or written documents that, except for some wear and tear, are exactly the same as when they were produced. The past has also bequeathed to the present traditions and influences that can still be felt to various degrees in different sectors of modern society with which they are inextricably mixed. It would be unfair not to count as part of our historical material all that the present has preserved in this way; but since it is often difficult to distinguish between the old and the new, it would almost always be unwise to conclude automatically that what exists today existed in the past. The projection of contemporary data back into the past is legitimate only if conditions of living have remained unchanged. It is true that one often hears a legend of the "unchanging Orient," the only purpose of which would seem to be to promote laziness. But no society stands still; even partial and temporary immobility must be proved before it can be considered fact. It is true that the East of modern times has not evolved at the same pace as Europe; nevertheless the East of today is not that of the nineteenth century, nor is the East of the nineteenth century the same as that of the great Ottoman period or of the classicial age of Islam. It is necessary, therefore, to define how the study of the present can aid us in our discovery of the past.

Physical geography is to some extent another matter, for the evolution of physical geography is slower than that of human society. But, even within the limits of Muslim history, there are problems of deterioration of the climate or the desert vegetation that, if real, may be the result of changes in human activity. Moreover, certain geographical characteristics may vary in importance according to whether they affect a society at one or another stage of its technical evolution; for instance, the significance of distances and natural obstacles depends on the manner and speed of transport, the mineral resources on the quantity and nature of minerals that are useful. See L. Febvre, *La terre et l'évolution humaine* in *L'évolution de l'humanité*, IV (Paris, 1922), and F. Braudel, *La Méditerranée et le monde méditerranéen à l'époque de Philippe II* (Paris, 1949).

Human geography comes nearer to the historian's preoccupations because the facts with which it deals in the present are similar at least in part to those in the past that interest the historian. The same applies to ethnology, sociology, and other marginal disciplines that have not in all cases agreed upon the limits of their field of activity or defined their particular methods of research. In fact, these disciplines are or should be closely associated with history. Geographers, ethnographers, and sociologists realize more and more that they cannot account for facts observable in the present without establishing their antecedents; the geographer in particular almost always doubles as a historian. Inversely, the historian, who cannot hope to find in the past all the material he needs to satisfy his curiosity, notes the existence of facts in the present that he may find useful for the interpretation of the past. Obviously, so long as the proof of their existence in the past has not been established, they can only give rise to hypotheses, which are none the less admissible as part of a possible explanation. The greatest service that geography and sociology render the historian consists in the drafting of a questionnaire to be applied, so to speak, to ancient documents. If he knows nothing but the documents, the historian runs the risk of seeing only problems similar to those to which their authors addressed themselves, whereas in fact it is not impossible that information given by them incidentally and almost unconsciously may provide the means of answering partially questions of quite a different order. The choice of questions, of course, should not be arbitrary. Thus, in the case of the history of agriculture, for instance, the proper method consists not in deducing from the present conditions the state of agriculture in the past but in drawing from its present characteristics a number of questions to be answered, if possible, with the help of ancient texts. Naturally, those modern societies—or those sectors within a given society—that should be examined are those in which changes recently introduced through European influence are least evident. The study of intermediary periods (perhaps especially with the aid of travelers' accounts) can help to forge a link between modern conditions and those that prevailed in the period under study, justifying the choice of questions and making the questions asked more specific.

For the principal works, see below, pp. 76 ff.

PART II

Tools of Research and General Works

10

General Information

HISTORIES AND REFERENCE WORKS

In the initial stages of his work, the beginner will naturally turn to outstanding textbooks for help in planning his research and for a view of the facts in their wider historical framework; at the same time these textbooks will show him the gaps in our knowledge. Unfortunately, there is no good general textbook of Islamic history as yet; indeed, how could there be, when so many historical sources are still unpublished and so many questions remain unelucidated for want of critical study? Most of the old general surveys look at history from an almost exclusively political standpoint, basing their work on that of the chroniclers; often, in fact, they are no more than Arabic historiography—itself incompletely known—translated into a European language. It is in this sense especially that G. Weil's *Geschichte der Chalifen* (Mannheim, 1846–1851) has become dated; the same applies to A. Müller's *Der Islam im Morgen- und Abendland*, two volumes (Berlin, 1885–1887), in spite of a more intelligent attempt at synthesis, and to the more succinct account by W. Muir, *The Caliphate, its Decline and Fall* (1891, 2d ed. by T. Weir, 1915–1925), while C. Huart, *Histoire des Arabes*, two volumes (Paris, 1912–1913), is a hodgepodge of names whose success in its time is now difficult to understand and which should be avoided.

Today the student has available a few better general accounts that are often included in wide surveys of history. In French, in the collection *Peuples et civilisations* published under the direction of L. Halphen and P. Sagnac, Vol. V, *Les barbares des grandes invasions aux conquêtes turques du XI. siècle* (4th ed., Paris, 1940), and Vol. VI, *L'essor de l'Europe* (*XIe–XIIIe siècles*) (3d ed., Paris, 1946), both by L. Halphen, are extremely interesting because they see the Muslim world "in perspective" in the history of Europe and Asia as a whole. Volume VII of the *Histoire du monde* edited by E. Cavaignac, *Le monde musulman et byzantin jusqu'aux croisades* (Paris, 1931), by M. Gaudefroy-Demombynes and S. F. Platonov, offers an evocative analysis of the Umayyad and 'Abbāsid periods. In the *Histoire générale* initiated by G. Glotz, Vol. III of the *Histoire du moyen âge*, *Le monde oriental de 395 a 1081* (Paris, 1936), by G. Marçais, gives a clear and detailed account of Muslim history though somewhat abbreviated in comparison with the chapters on Byzantine history by C. Diehl.

More recently, a few general histories of the Muslim world have been published in various languages. In France, in the *Histoire générale des civilisations*, edited under the direction of M. Crouzet, which is not concerned with a detailed account of political events, Vol. III, *Le moyen âge* (Paris, 1955), edited by E. Perroy, contains chapters on Islam by C. Cahen, who has attempted to present the evolution of the Islamic society and spiritual culture from its origins to the formation of the Ottoman Empire in relation to Oriental history as a whole. A chapter on Islam by G. Wiet, which is good in spite of its brevity, is also to be found in the *Histoire universelle*, Vol. II of the *Encyclopédie de la Pléiade* (Paris, 1955). In England, Bernard Lewis, who has announced a more extensive work to appear later, has given a brief account that nevertheless shows an intelligent awareness of the new state of the problems involved in *The Arabs in History* (London, 1950), French translation, 1958; P. K. Hitti offers in his *History of the Arabs* (London, 1937; 8th ed., 1964), an account that is extremely interesting to read but superficial. In Germany, C. Brockelmann has produced a *Geschichte der islamischen Völker* (1939), that has few rivals for its treatment of modern times but is of less interest on the Middle Ages; an English translation, *History of the Islamic Peoples*, was published by J. Carmichael and M. Perlmann (1947); the French translation, *Histoire des peuples islamiques* (Paris, 1949), is not good. More recently, B. Spuler, in his *HO*, furnished a clear résumé on the basis of a wide knowledge of recent studies: *Geschichte der islamischen Länder*, *Die Chalifenzeit* and *Die Mongolenzeit*, cited p. 67 f.; English translation by F. Bagley, *The Muslim World: A Historical Survey* (1960), part 1, *The Age of the Caliphs*, part 2, *The Mongol Period.* See also C. E. Grunebaum, "Der Islam: seine Expansion im Nahen und Mittleren Osten, Afrika und Spanien," *Propyläen Weltsgeschichte* (Berlin, 1963), Vol. V, pp. 21–179. In Italy, F. Pareja has supervised the editing of a kind of "summa" of uneven quality, *Islamologia* (1952–1954); a good little introduction is to be found in F. Gabrieli, *Gli Arabi* (1957), English translation (1963). The historians of Soviet Russia have recently condensed their views in the collective *Istoriia stran zarubezhnogo vostoka v srednie veka* (Moscow, 1957). In Arabic, the most important undertaking, primarily of a cultural nature, consists in the three series of volumes by Aḥmad Amīn, *Fajr al-islām*, *Duḥā al-islām*, and *Ẓuhr al-islām*, seven volumes in all (Cairo, 1942–1949). Ḥasan Ibrāhīm Ḥasan, *Ta'rīkh al-islām*, two volumes (1945), may also be consulted.

These general histories can be complemented by histories of the chief countries concerned. The best are:

G. Wiet, *L'Égypte arabe . . . 642–1517*, in *Histoire de la nation égyptienne*, edited by G. Hanotaux, IV (1937); a shorter account by the same author in the anonymously edited *Précis de l'histoire de l'Égypte* (1932–1935), II; in English, S. Lane-Poole, *A History of Egypt in the Middle Ages* (5th ed., 1936); H. Lammens, *La Syrie, précis historique* (1921), and P. K. Hitti, *History of Syria* (1951); M. Kurd 'Alī, *Khiṭaṭ al-shām*, four volumes (1920–1922); B. Spuler, *Iran in früh-islamischer Zeit, 633–1055* (1952), with English translation in preparation; V. Barthold, *Turkestan Down to the Mongol Invasion* (1902), in Russian with Persian texts, a revised English version but without the texts, *GMS*, n.s., V (London, 1928; reprinted, 1958), still remarkable and a basic work of reference; L. A. Stroieva and A. M. Belenitskii, *Istoriia Irana s'Drevneiskikh Vremen do Kontsa XVIII Veka* (Leningrad, 1958); C.-A. Julien, *Histoire de l'Afrique du Nord*, second edition, II, revised by R. Le Tourneau, to be supplemented by A. Basset, *Initiation à la Tunisie* (Paris, 1950), *Initiation au Maroc*, edited by Institut des Hautes Études Marocaines (Paris, 1932; 3d ed., 1945), and *Initiation à l'Algerie* by J. Alazard (Paris, 1957); also, by G. Marçais, *La Berbérie musulmane et l'Orient au moyen âge* (1946), and H. Terrasse, *Histoire du Maroc*, two volumes (1949–1950); E. Lévi-Provençal, HISTOIRE DE L'ESPAGNE MUSULMANE, three volumes (1944–1953), which go up to the eleventh century, to be supplemented by A. González Palencia, *Historia de la España musulmana* (4th ed., 1945), and the clear résumé, putting special emphasis on art, by H. Terrasse, *Islam d'Espagne* (1958), while awaiting the fifth volume of the collective *História de España*, edited by R. Menéndez Pidal; and lastly, M. Amari, *Storia dei musulmani di Sicilia*, new edition supervised by C. Nallino *et al.*, three volumes (1933–1939). On the question of Arabia and Yemen, the articles "al-'Arab" and "(Djazīrat al-) 'Arab" in *EI*[2] (see below, pp. 68 f. and 111) will serve as a guide, and for Yemen, the articles "Ṣan'ā'" and "Zabīd" in the *EI*. Lastly, on the subject of certain distinct peoples who, however, have never belonged to one particular state, see, for instance. G.-H. Bousquet. *Les Berbères* in the collection, Que sais-je?, no. 718 (1955)—a well-informed work but too negative—and B. Nikitine, *Les Kurdes* (1956), to be complemented for the Middle Ages by V. Minorsky's article in *EI*.

HANDBUCH DER ORIENTALISTIK (*HO*) in progress under the overall direction of B. Spuler will, when completed, cover the whole field of Oriental studies. Although the work in some cases goes beyond Islamic studies, its outstanding importance justifies the full outlining of the first section: I. Abteilung, *Der Nahe und der Mittlere Osten*, edited by Spuler and H. Kees

(Leiden and Cologne, 1952——): I. Bd., *Ägyptologie* (1952——); II. Bd., *Keilschriftforschung und alte Geschichte Vorderasiens* (1959——); III. Bd., *Semitistik* (1953–1954), particularly part 3, *Arabisch und Äthiopisch*, especially the chapters by C. Brockelmann, Spuler, M. Höfner, and J. W. Fück; IV. Bd., *Iranistik* (1955——) of which part 2, on literature, in preparation, plans chapters of special interst by T. Gändschäi and Spuler; V. Bd., *Altaistik* (1963——), particularly part 1, *Turkologie*, especially the chapters by A. von Gabain, A. Zeki Velidi Togan, F. Taeschner, and O. Spies, and part 5, in preparation, on history; VI. Bd., *Geschichte der islamischen Länder* (1952–1959), part 1, *Die Chalifenzeit*, and part 2, *Die Mongolenzeit*, both by Spuler, and part 3, *Neuzeit*, especially the contributions by H. J. Kissling, H. Scheel, H. Braun, E. Klingmüller, and H. Hartel; VII. Bd., *Armenische und Kaukasische Sprachen* (1963); VIII. Bd., *Religion* (1961——), particularly part 2, *Religiongeschichte des Orients in der Zeit der Weltreligionem*, especially the chapters by Spuler, Fück, A. J. Arberry, and R. Strothmann; Erg. Bd. I., *Islamische Masse und Gewichte umgerechnet ins metrische System* by W. Hinz (1955); and in preparation for inclusion in the I. Abteilung are supplementary volumes (II) on Arabic chronology, papyrology, and paleography by A. Grohmann; (III), on Oriental law; (IV), on Oriental music; (V), on cuneiform documents; and (VI), on Islamic philosophy, medicine, natural sciences, and Islamic geography.

The student of Muslim history should learn how to use the indispensable ENCYCLOPAEDIA OF ISLAM (*EI*), an invaluable work that the beginner may find a little difficult to handle. A second edition (*EI*²) is in the course of publication; but, as progress is slow, the volumes of the old edition that have not yet been replaced will have to be consulted for some time to come. The first edition (*EI*), four volumes and *Supplement* (Leiden, 1913–1942), is in the style of a dictionary; the beginner will find it difficult at first to know where to look for the information he needs, all the more so as the system of cross references is inadequate, and, apart from a few unexpected exceptions, the original Oriental forms and words are used for the entries: thus, donkey is to be found under "ḥimār," Tripoli under "Ṭarābulus," but Cairo under "Cairo." One learns one's way around this rather loose classification with practice, for there is no index but continued use makes it possible for the user to find his way through the maze.

The articles are of varying quality. Interrupted by World War I, the undertaking was finished according to a broader plan than that initially conceived. In general, the articles of the first volume (*A–D*) are not only old but superficial. In the three subsequent volumes, the articles attempt to give a strict summary of all that is known on the subject and a basic bibliography; many of them are good examples of sound scholarship that cannot be equaled elsewhere and that will not easily be superseded.

The *Encyclopaedia of Islam* was published simultaneously in German, English, and French; as the pagination could not be identical in the three editions, references must be made to entries and not to page numbers. An Arabic translation was made later, and an enlarged Turkish edition, *Islam Ansiklopedisi* (see below, p. 153) is now being issued.

During World War II, a *Handwörterbuch des Islams* was published (1943) of those articles of *EI* pertaining specifically to religion brought up to date, especially in the bibliography. An English edition, *Shorter Encyclopaedia of Islam*, appeared in 1946, continuing the revision up to that date.

Lastly, in 1954, a second edition (EI^2) was undertaken under the supervision of J. H. Kramers (succeeded by J. Schacht), H. A. R. Gibb (replaced by Bernard Lewis), and E. Lévi-Provençal (succeeded by C. Pellat). Letters *A* and *B*, forming a bulky volume of 1,359 pages in the English edition, were completed by 1960; and letters *C* to *F* (in progress) have subsequently been issued. This second edition, in French and English, is naturally superior to the corresponding parts of the first edition; not only have the topics been brought up to date, but an attempt has also been made to follow a more logical plan and to fill in a number of serious gaps.

The *EI* takes precedence as a work of reference over all others.

However worthy of praise the *EI* may be, it cannot in itself meet all the necessary requirements. Many essential reference works have yet to be undertaken and it will be some time before they are available. Oriental studies are still too recent a development, and there are not enough Orientalists at work to furnish the publications that would supply rapidly the answers to those questions of detail constantly confronting the research worker when he consults historical documents: the precise meaning of a technical term, the exact form of a proper name, the identification of a person, the location of a place on the map, or the verification of a point concerning some institution; many such questions require long research because of the inadequacy or unsuitability of our works of reference. To avoid being caught off one's guard and losing time following false trails, one must know which books should be consulted in different cases. As a consequence, we list here the principal technical works of reference available and the works dealing in a more general way with the main problems of Muslim history, while those concerned with particular periods of Islamic history will be dealt with in Part III.

The old *Bibliographie des ouvrages arabes ou relatifs aux Arabes* (Liège, 1892) by V. Chauvin and even the *Handbuch der Islam-Literatur* by G. Pfannmüller (Berlin, 1923) are no longer of much use. There is no complete general bibliography of the Muslim world (compiling one would be an enormous undertaking). The selective bibliographies in F. Pareja's *Islamologia* (cited p. 66), being recent, may be of use in research work in spite of their lack of order and critical judgment. The same applies to R. Ettinghausen, *A Selected and Annotated Bibliography of Books and Periodicals in Western Languages Dealing with the Near and Middle East* . . . (Washington, 1954). The systematic lists, albeit limited to publications for the years 1937 to 1953, by B. Spuler and L. Forrer, *Der Vordere Orient in islamischer Zeit, Wissenschaftliche Forschungsberichte, Geisteswissenschaftliche Reihe,* XXI, *Orientalistik,* Teil 3 (Bern, 1954), published by K. Hönn, are more complete in spite of excusable gaps. J. D. Pearson with the assistance of J. F. Ashton has produced INDEX ISLAMICUS, *1906–1955, A Catalogue of Articles on Islamic Subjects in Periodicals and other Collective Publications* (Cambridge, 1958), which is invaluable although the method of classification is naturally somewhat arbitrary and not always to be trusted. The first supplement of this work, for the years 1955 to 1960, appeared in 1962. All publications in Arabic up to 1930 have been reviewed in J. Sarkis, *Mu'jam al-maṭbū'āt al-'arabiyya,* two volumes and one supplement (Cairo, 1928–1930), continued after this date by U. R. Kaḥḥāla, *Mu'jam al-mu'allifīn* (Damascus, 1957——), two volumes of which have appeared.

In addition to these works there are regional bibliographies that are generally somewhat out of date and limited in scope but which may be of use for lack of anything better. The only really good bibliography of this kind does not deal exclusively with Islam: P. Thomsen, *Die Palästina-Literatur,* continued periodically, six volumes (1938–1955), covering publications between 1895 and 1944.

For other countries the following are still useful: for Persia, A. T. Wilson, *A Bibliography of Persia* (1930), an alphabetical list; M. Ṣabā, *Bibliographie française de l'Iran* (1936), methodical; A. Guillou, *Essai bibliographique sur les dynasties musulmanes de l'Iran,* published by the Egyptian Institute (Madrid, 1957), covering the years 1900 to 1957. One should also consult V. Minorsky, "Les études historiques et géographiques sur la Perse," *AO,* X (1932), XVI (1937), and XXI (1951). See also the important work by I. Afshar, *Bibliography of Persia,* three volumes (1955–1958), covering the years 1900 to 1957. For current Turkish publications, see *Türkiye Bibliografyası* (since 1939), and Enver Koray, *Türkiye Tarih Yayınları Bibliografyası* (Ankara, 1952), and a new, considerably enlarged edition (Istanbul, 1959), a bibliography of Turkish history. For North Africa, see R. Le Tourneau, cited p. 67, periodically brought up to date in the "Bibliographie marocaine" in the journal *Hespéris.* On Arabia, *A Bibliography of the Arabian Peninsula* (1958) and a *Bibliography on Yemen and Notes on Mocha* (1960), both by E. Macro, have recently been published.

PERIODICALS

An inevitable drawback to all bibliographical works is that they naturally stop at their date of publication. For this reason, periodicals must be consulted both for their original articles and for their bibliographies, which are brought up to date as new works are published; in some cases also, their critical book reviews provide information about the content and value of books and occasionally point out and correct errors.

The purely bibliographical review, *Orientalistische Literaturzeitung*, which gives monthly information with detailed reviews on current productions, appeared in Leipzig from 1898, suspended publication in 1944, and was revived in 1953. The entire field of Oriental studies is covered by this review. A similar journal, the *Bibliotheca orientalis*, published at Leiden (Holland), since 1943, appears every two months.

French

In France, the *Revue des études islamiques* (*REI*), quarterly, which replaced the *Revue du monde musulman* (*RMM*) that appeared in several volumes annually between 1906 and 1926, has published since 1926, in addition to its articles, a separately paginated bibliographical bulletin entitled *Abstracta Islamica* with titles systematically classified, brief summaries in some cases, and cross references to the more important book reviews. These *Abstracta*, formerly published irregularly are now organized in such a way as to render them even more useful: their publication is more rapid with less likelihood of gaps in documentation. Also in France, *Arabica*, quarterly, the journal first published in 1954, issued up to 1958 a bibliographical bulletin providing detailed analyses at more frequent intervals. This has been abandoned, although the book reviews have been retained, in order to concentrate all efforts of French Islamic scholars on the *Abstracta*. The *Bulletin des études arabes* (*BEA*), bimonthly (Algiers, 1941–1952) should also be consulted for the years covered.

Besides *Arabica*, now the chief organ of French Arabists, and the *Revue des études islamiques* (*REI*), the French periodicals that should be consulted are:

Annales de l'Institut d'Études Orientales (*AIEO*), annually, Algiers 1934——; published by the University of Algiers.

Bulletin d'études orientales (*BEOD*), irregularly, Damascus, 1931——; published by the Institut Français.

Bulletin de l'Institut Français d'Archéologie Orientale (*BIFAO*), annually, Cairo, 1901——.

Cahiers de Tunisie (*CT*), semiannually, Tunis, 1953——; published by the Institut des Hautes Études, Tunis, replacing *Revue tunisienne* (*RT*).

Hespéris, quarterly, Paris, 1921——; published by the Institut des Hautes Études Marocaines, Rabat; gives periodically a very complete bibliography concerning Morocco.

Journal asiatique (*JA*), quarterly, Paris, 1822——; organ of the Société Asiatique; covers all branches of Orientalism and publishes reviews.

Mélanges de l'Institut Dominicain d'Études Orientales (*MIDEO*), annually, Cairo, 1954——.

To these journals should be added a collection of studies of the greatest interest, *Studia Islamica* (*SI*) published irregularly, Paris, 1953—— (nineteen numbers published through 1963).

Outside France one should mention first of all two international journals:

International

Journal of the Economic and Social History of the Orient (*JESHO*), triennially, Leiden, 1957——; published with the intention of developing studies of Oriental economic and social history, too often neglected.

Oriens, semiannually, Leiden, 1948——; official journal of the International Society of Oriental Studies; publishes not only articles on various branches of Orientalism but also reviews and is especially valuable for listings of the contents of Near Eastern and in particular Turkish periodicals.

English and American

Bulletin of the School of Oriental Studies, annually in four parts, London, 1917——; since 1938 continued as *Bulletin of the School of Oriental and African Studies* (*BSOAS*), annually in three parts since 1952; publishes frequent book reviews.

Islamic Culture (*IC*), quarterly, Hyderabad, Deccan, 1927——.

Islamic Quarterly (*IQ*), London, 1954——.

Islamic Studies (*IS*), quarterly, Karachi, 1962——.

Journal of the American Oriental Society (*JAOS*), quarterly, New Haven. 1843——.

Journal of Near Eastern Studies, quarterly, Chicago, 1942——; replacing the *American Journal of Semitic Languages* (*AJSL*).

Journal of the Royal Asiatic Society (*JRAS*), annually in four parts, London, 1834——.

Middle East Journal, quarterly, Washington, D. C., 1947——.

Muslim World (*MW*), quarterly, Hartford, Conn., 1911——.

German

Der Islam, annually in one to four fascicles, Strasbourg, 1910–1919; Berlin and Leipzig, 1920–1938; Berlin, 1938——; important book reviews.

Mitteilungen des Seminars für Orientalische Sprachen (*MSOS*), annually in three parts: Eastern Asiatic Studies, Western Asiatic Studies, and African Studies, Berlin, 1898–1938; suspended since World War II.

Die Welt des Islams (*WI*), originally a German publication, 1913—— (suspended 1920–1922, 1944–1950); new series, four issues a year, irregularly, Leiden, 1951——.

Zeitschrift der Deutschen Morgenländischen Gesellschaft (*ZDMG*), four issues a year, irregularly, Leipzig, 1847——; important book reviews.

Italian

Annali. Istituto Universitario Orientale, Naples, mostly annually 1929–1937; new series, 1943——.

Orientalia, irregularly, Rome, 1920–1930; annually in four fascicles, 1930——; a publication of the Pontifical Biblical Institute, which prints articles and reviews in various languages.

Rivista degli studi orientali (*RSO*), annually in two to four fascicles, Rome, 1907——.

Spanish

al-Andalus, semiannually, Madrid, 1933——.

Scandinavian and Dutch

Acta Orientalia (*AO*) quarterly, Leiden, 1922——.

Eastern European

Acta Orientalia Academiae Scientiarum Hungaricae (*AOASH*) triennially; Budapest, 1950——.

Archiv orientální (*ArO*), annually in four numbers, Prague, 1929——; in all languages; important.

Przegląd orientalisticzny, quarterly, Warsaw, 1960——.

Rocznik orientalistyczny (*RO*), annually or biannually, Warsaw, 1914–1940, 1948——.

Russian and Soviet

Mir Islama, two volumes, St. Petersburg, 1912–1914.

Zapiski Vostochnago Otdieleniia Imperatorskago Russkago Arkheologicheskago Obshchestva, St. Petersburg, 1886–1921.

In addition to its *Izvestiia* (bimonthly, Moscow and Leningrad, 1836——)—which contains, among others, articles that are of interest to the study of the Muslim East—the Russian and later the Soviet Academy of Sciences (Akademiia Nauk SSSR) publishes the following special journals dealing with the subject:

Epigrafika Vostoka (*EV*), irregularly, Moscow, 1947——.

Kratkie Soobshcheniia Instituta Vostokovedeniia (*KSIV*), irregularly, Moscow, 1951——.

Narody Azii i Afriki, bimonthly, Moscow, 1959——; supersedes *Sovetskoe Vostokovedenie* (1955–1958) and *Sovestkoe Kitaevedenie* (1958); title, 1959–1961, *Problemy Vostokovedeniia*.

Palestinskii Sbornik, annually, Moscow, 1954——; continues as no. 63 of *Pravoslavnyi Palestinskii Sbornik*, St. Petersburg, 1881–1917.

Sovetskoe Vostokovedenie (*SV*), irregularly, Moscow, 1940–1949.

Uchenye Zapiski Instituta Vostokovedeniia (*UZIV*), annually, Moscow and Leningrad, 1950——.

Zapiski Kollegii Vostokovedov pri Aziatskom Muzae Rossiiskoi Akad. Nauk, 1925——.

The academies of Adharbaijan, the Uzbek SSR, and Armenia have their own publications, and from time to time the University of Leningrad publishes a volume of researches on the Near East.

The journals of the Muslim countries, which in the past have been of little value from the point of view of historical research, are beginning to demand more attention.

Arabic

Revue de l'Académie Arabe de Damas, quarterly, Damascus, 1921——.

Loghat el-'Arab, monthly, Baghdad, 1911–1931 (suspended 1914–1926).

Majallat al-Majma' al-'Ilmī al-'Irāqī, annually, irregular, Baghdad, 1950——.

Sumer, A Journal of Archaeology in Iraq, semiannually, Baghdad, 1945——.

Revue de l'Institut des Manuscrits Arabes (*RIMA*), semiannually, Cairo. 1955——.

al-Mashriq, bimonthly, Beirut, 1898—— (suspended 1943–1946); Christian Arabic journal.

Bulletin de l'Institut d'Égypte, semiannually, Cairo, 1857——; in various languages, mainly French.

Bulletin of the Faculty of Arts, annually, Alexandria, 1943——; in various languages; published by the University of Alexandria.

Bulletin of the Faculty of Arts, semiannually, Cairo, 1933——; published by Cairo University.

Turkish

Milli Tetebbüler Mecmuası, only two issues, Istanbul, 1915——.

Tarih-i Osmani Encümeni Mecmuası (*TOEM*), six issues published, Istanbul, 1911–1931; title changed to *Türk Tarihi Encümeni Mecmuası*, vols. 5 and 6, 1924–1931.

Tarih Vesikaları, irregularly, Ankara, 1956——.

Türk Hukuk Tarihi Dergisi, only one volume, Istanbul, 1944.

Türk Hukuk ve Iktisat Tarihi Mecmuası, only two volumes, Istanbul, Vol. I, 1931, Vol. II, 1939.

Türk Tarih Kurumu Belleten (*Belleten*), quarterly, Ankara, 1927——.

Türkiye Bibliografyası, quarterly, Ankara, 1934——; since 1953, Istanbul; index fascicle annually, see p. 70.

Vakıflar Dergisi, irregularly, Ankara, 1938—— (suspended 1943–1945).

Ankara Üniversitesi

Ankara Üniversitesi Dil Tarih ve Coğrafya Fakültesi Dergisi, quarterly, Ankara, 1942——.

Ilâhiyat Fakültesi Dergisi, quarterly, 1952–1957; annually, 1957——.

Ilâhiyat Fakültesi Yıllık Araştırmalar Dergisi, annually, 1956——.

Dâr ül-funun, Istanbul

Edebiyat Fakültesi Mecmuası, Vols. I–IX, Istanbul, 1916–1933.

Ilâhiyat Fakültesi Mecmuası, Vols. I–IV, Istanbul, 1925–1933.

Istanbul Üniversitesi

Edebiyat Fakültesi Tarih Dergisi (*TD*), annually, 1949——.

Iktisat Fakültesi Mecmuası (*IFM*), annually, 1939——.

Islam Tetkikleri Enstitüsü Dergisi, irregularly, 1958——.

Ṣarkiyat Mecmuası, irregularly, 1956——; published by *Ṣarkiyat Enstitüsü*.

Tarih Semineri Dergisi, only two volumes, Vol. I, 1937, Vol. II, 1938.

Türkiyat Mecmuası, annually, 1925—— (suspended 1940–1944); published by *Türkiyat Enstitüsü*.

Persian

Revue de la Faculté des Lettres de l'Université de Tabriz, quarterly, Tabriz, 1948——.

Revue de la Faculté des Lettres de l'Université de Teheran, four fascicles a year, Teheran, 1955——.

11

Special Disciplines

GEOGRAPHY, HISTORICAL TOPOGRAPHY, AND ETHNOLOGY

Knowledge of the geography of countries whose history one wishes to study is indispensable, but always bear in mind that in some cases geographical conditions may have changed.

A general view of the geographical situation of Islam will be found either in the volumes devoted to this question in the *Géographie universelle*, edited by P. Vidal de la Blache and L. Gollais, fifteen volumes (Paris): Vol. VIII (1929), *Asie occidentale* by R. Blanchard, and *Haute Asie* by F. Grenard; Vol. XI (1937), *Afrique septentrionale et occidentale* by A. Bernard, part 1, "Généralities—Afrique du Nord"; and Vol. XII (1938), *Afrique équatoriale, orientale, et australe* by F. Maurette; or better still in these more recent publications: J. Dresch and P. Birot, *La Méditerranée et le Moyen Orient*, two volumes (Paris, 1953–1956), Vol. I including North Africa and Vol II, the Middle East, both by J. Dresch; J. Despois, *L'Afrique du Nord* (Paris, 1949), Vol. I of *L'Afrique blanche française*. In German, the *Handbuch der geographischen Wissenschaft* edited by F. Klute includes Vol. IX (1936), on Africa, by F. Klute, L. Witteschell, and A. Kauffmann; and Vol. VII (1943), on the Middle East (Turkey to Arabia and India), by U. Frey, O. von Niedermeyer, P. Rohrbach, *et al.* In English, see a textbook by W. B. Fisher, *The Middle East* (London, 1950, 4th rev. ed., 1961).

The geography of Arabia is particularly interesting for the study of the origins of Islam and also because of the interest that memories of Arabia have always aroused in Muslims. Long inaccessible, the field has now been opened by a series of explorations of which the beginnings can be seen in Jacqueline Pirenne, *À la découverte de l'arabie* (1958), or R. Kiernan, *The Unveiling of Arabia* (1949); it is well to be acquainted with the principal accounts or results of these explorations through the following works:

C. Doughty, *Travels in Arabia Deserta*, two volumes (1888); abridged French translation, 1949.

A. Musil, *Arabia Petraea*, three volumes (1907–1908); *Arabia Deserta* (1927); *Northern Neǧd* (1928); *Northern Heǧaz* (1926); and *Palmyrena* (1928).

B. Thomas, *Arabia Felix: Across the Empty Quarter of Arabia* (1932).

H. Philby, *Arabian Highlands* (1952); *Sa'udi Arabia* (1955); *The Land of Midian* (1957); and *A Pilgrim in Arabia* (1943).

W. Thesiger, *Arabian Sands* (1959).

R. H. Sanger, *The Arabian Peninsula* (Ithaca, N. Y., 1954).

For Southern Arabia:

A. Grohmann, *Suedarabien als Wirtschaftsgebiet*, two volumes (1922–1933).

C. Rathjens and H. von Wissmann, *Von Wissmannsche Südarabien-Reise*, especially Vol. III, *Landeskundliche Ergebnisse* (1934).

H. Philby, *Sheba's Daughters* (1939).

W. Ingrams, *Arabia and the Isles* (1942).

H. Scott, *In the High Yemen* (1942).

See also the articles "'Arabiyya" and "Badw" (Bedouin), in *EI*². The same authors have also helped to collect material for the ancient history of Arabia, see below, p. 109 ff.

A satisfactory map of all the Muslim countries does not exist, nor can one be expected at the present time. The only geographical map that covers the Muslim world completely is the International Map of the World (scale 1/1,000,000), published in London, and it varies in quality from one country to another. Practice will show which maps are best to consult in each case; we will simply single out for mention here the magnificent French maps of Syria and Morocco (scale 1/50,000) and the surveys of the rest of North Africa on the same scale, almost as remarkable. There are also detailed maps of Palestine, the Egyptian valley, and the delta of the Nile.

Important for our particular purposes is a knowledge not only of the geography of the Middle East in general, but more especially of its geography in the past. Naturally, some time will elapse before a good historical atlas of the Muslim world can be produced. Beginners, however, can refer profitably to the *Historical Atlas of the Muslim Peoples* by R. Roolvink, S. El Ali [al-'Ālī], H. Mones [Mu'nis], and M. Salim (Djakarta and Amsterdam, 1957; also an edition published by Harvard University Press in 1958), which is attractive and well suited for teaching purposes. A historical atlas is announced as an appendix to *EI*².

The following works are of varying usefulness: H. Hazard and H. Lester

Cooke, *Atlas of Islamic History* (3d ed., Princeton, 1954), need not be consulted as it is artificially schematic and would be misleading for the inexperienced reader. To a certain extent, an account of the historical geography of the Muslim East will be found in G. Le Strange, *The Lands of the Eastern Caliphate* (excepting Syria-Palestine and Egypt) (2d ed., Cambridge, 1930), which groups usefully, but without further study or criticism, the data given by ancient geographers from the Arab conquest to Tamerlane. The same author published a similar *Palestine under the Moslems*, including Syria (1890).

The much-discussed question of a change in climate in the Middle East, since ancient times, may be approached with the help of the recent restatement of the question by K. Butzer, "Der Umweltfaktor in der arabischen Expansion," *Saeculum*, VIII (1957).

We need for our purposes not only a general knowledge of former geographical aspects of the land, but also, more technically, the identification and localization of ancient place names that have often disappeared or changed completely. The model here is R. Dussaud, *Topographie historique de la Syrie antique et médiévale* (Paris, 1927), which unfortunately does not go beyond the boundaries of the former French mandate (present-day Syria and Lebanon). For Palestine, efforts have been almost exclusively concentrated on ancient times.

For other countries, the following selection can be used with profit: on Egypt, J. Maspero and G. Wiet, *Matériaux pour servir à la géographie de l'Égypte*, *MIFAO*, XXXVI (1914–1919); on Iraq, M. Streck, *Die alte Landschaft Babylonien nach den arabischen Geographen* (1900–1901); on Iran, P. Schwarz, *Iran im Mittelalter nach arabischen Geographen*, nine volumes (1896–1936), unfortunately incomplete and without an index, and A. C. Barbier de Meynard, *Dictionnaire géographique, historique et littéraire de la Perse et des contrées adjacentes* (1861); on Arabia, A. Sprenger, *Die alte Geographie Arabiens als Grundlage der Entwicklungsgeschichte des Semitismus* (1875); H. von Wissmann and M. Höfner, *Beiträge zur historischen Geographie des vorislamischen Südarabiens* (1953); and Chaim Rabin, *Ancient Westarabian* (1951). A. Sprenger's *Die Post- und Reiserouten des Orients* (1864) can still be used. But very often the simplest procedure is to consult the geographical dictionary of Yāqūt (see p. 39), which was written precisely to meet the same kind of requirements as ours.

The ethnological documents are naturally very scattered, and will be found in studies of a particular region or subject, some of which are excellent.

The way of life of the Arabian Arabs (and those of the regions bordering on Arabia) is particularly interesting. In addition to the geographical works cited on p. 76 f. and an introduction to the subject by R. Montagne, *La civilisation du désert* (1947), there should above all be mentioned M. von Oppenheim, *Die Beduinen*, three volumes (1939–1952), completed by E. Bräunlich and W. Caskel, a general encyclopedia and inventory of the Bedouin tribes. Then see the more specialized studies: A. J. Jaussen, *Coutumes des Arabes au pays de Moab* (1908); A. Musil, *The Manners and Customs of the Rwala Beduins* (1928); J. J. Hess (von Wyss), *Von den Beduinen des innern Arabiens* (1938); Aref el-Aref, *Beduin Love, Law, and Legend* (1944); H. Dickson, *The Arab of the Desert . . . in Kuwait and Sa'udi Arabia* (1949); E. Bräunlich, "Beiträge zur Gesellschaftsordnung der arabischen Beduinenstämme," *Islamica*, VI (1934); A. de Boucheman, *Matériel de la vie bedouine* (1935); J. Henninger, *Die Familie bei den heutigen Arabiens und seiner Randgebiete* (1943).

For other traditional Muslim societies, see: R. and H. Kriss, *Volksglaube im Bereich des Islam*, Vol. I, *Wallfahrtswesen und Heiligenverehrung*, Vol. II, *Amulette und Beschwörungen* (1960–1962). For Egypt, see: E. W. Lane, *Manners and Customs of the Modern Egyptians* (many editions since 1836); H. Winckler, *Aegyptische Volkskunde* (1936); H. Ayrout, *Moeurs et coutumes des fellahs* (1938), English translation, *The Egyptian Peasant* (1963); J. Besançon, *L'homme et le Nil* (1957); J. Berque, *Histoire sociale d'un village égyptien au XXe siècle* (1957); and H. Ammar, *Growing Up in an Egyptian Village* (1954). On Palestine, which has been subjected to detailed investigation because of its special interest, consult G. Dalman, *Arbeit und Sitte in Palästina* (1928), and various studies by T. Canaan, such as *Mohammedan Saints and Sanctuaries in Palestine* (1927). On North Africa, much research has been done; a good introduction to the question may be obtained from J. Bourrilly, *Éléments d'ethnographie marocaine* (1932), and H. Pérès and G.-H. Bousquet, *Coutumes, institutions et croyances des indigènes de l'Algérie*, I (1939), which is the translation of an Arabic original of the same title written by J. Desparmet (Algiers, 2d ed., 1913); among many others, to be cited especially: A Hanoteau and A. Letourneux, *La Kabylie et les coutumes kabyles* (2d ed., 1893), used today as a statute book; E. Ubach and E. Rackow, *Quellen zur ethnologischen Rechts-Forschung . . .*, Vol. I, *Sitte und Recht in Nordafrika* (1923); R. Maunier (a jurist), *Mélanges de sociologie nord-africaine* (1930); A. Demeerseman, *La Tunisie, terre d'amitié* (1955); J. Berque, *Structures sociales du Haut-Atlas* (1955)—important; G. Boris, *Documents linguistiques et ethnographiques sur une région du sud tunisien* (1951); L. Brunet, *Les coutumes et les relations sociales chez les Marocains* (1950); A. Goichon, *La vie féminine au Mzab* (1927). On religious questions, see: A. Bel, *La religion musulmane en Berbérie* (1938) and E. Doutté, MAGIE ET RELIGION DANS L'AFRIQUE DU NORD (1909), of first importance, but compare his interpretations with E. Westermarck, *Pagan Survivals in Mohammedan Civilization* (1933), French translation, *Survivances païennes dans la religion mahométaine* (1935), and *Ritual and Belief in Morocco* (1926); E. Dermenghem, *Le culte des saints dans l'Islam maghrébin* (1954); G.-H. Bousquet, *L'Islam maghrébin* (2d ed., 1955). Craft techniques have been studied, for instance, by A. Bel, *Les industries de la céramique à Fès* (1918), and by R. Le Tourneau in various studies worked into his monograph on Fez (see below, p. 92); and textiles have been studied by L. Golvin, especially in *Les arts populaires en Algérie*, four volumes (1950–1953), and *Aspects de l'artisanat en Afrique du Nord* (1957). For Syria, see J. Weulersse, *Paysans de Syrie et du Proche Orient* (Paris, 1946).

We know less about Iran and Turkey. Besides Ann K. S. Lambton's *Landlord and Peasant in Persia* (1953), one should mention above all H. Massé, *Croyances et coutumes persanes*, two volumes (1938), English translation, *Persian Beliefs and Customs* (1954); Pertev Boratav and W. Eberhard, *Typen türkischer Volksmärchen* (1953).

Certain studies in human geography should be cited at the same time as the ethnographical studies, such as: C. Parain, *La Méditerranée. Les hommes et leurs travaux* (1935); J. Brunhes, *Étude de géographie humaine. L'irrigation . . . dans la péninsule ibérique et dans l'Afrique du Nord* (1902)—cf. G. S. Colin, "La noria marocaine . . . ," *Hespéris*, XIV (1932), 22–61; R. Thomin, *Géographie humaine de la Syrie centrale* (1936); J. Dresch, *Commentaires des cartes sur les genres de vie de montagne dans le massif central du Grand Atlas* (1941); X. de Planhol, *De la plaine pamphylienne aux lacs pisidiens (géographie humaine)* (Paris, 1959); to which should be added a few words of general regional geography such as J. Weulersse, *Le pays des Alaouites* (1940), and J. Lozach, *Le delta du Nil* (1935).

CHRONOLOGY

The establishing of chronologies is made difficult by the variety of methods of dating in use in the East alongside the era of the Hijra and the lunar calendar of the Arabs. In texts one may find dates calculated according to solar calendars for astronomical, agricultural, and financial needs. To illustrate, years may be reckoned according to the Seleucid era and the Syrian solar calendar (in Christian authors), or the era of the martyrs and the Coptic calendar—as in connection with the annual rising of the Nile—according to the era of Yazdagird and the Persian solar calendar (in Persian authors), the Julian calendar (Greek Orthodox and Spain), or the cycle of the twelve animals (Mongols). All necessary information on the different Christian calendars will be found in the masterly *Traité d'études byzantines* (1955) edited by P. Lemerle, Vol. I, *La chronologie* (Paris, 1958), by V. Grumel, which also gives a concordance, month by month, between the Byzantine calendar and the Muslim.

For many years the most trustworthy work for help in establishing a concordance between the official Islamic calendar and the Gregorian has been F. Wüstenfeld, *Vergleichungs-Tabellen der muhammedanischen und christlichen Zeitrechnung* (Leipzig, 1854), third edition revised by B. Spuler in collaboration with J. Mayr (1961), which also gives a table for converting the Ottoman financial (solar) years. For Spanish, there is M. Ocaña Jiménez, *Tablas de conversión de datas islámicas a cristianas y viceversa* (Madrid, 1946). But the most practical works are, in French, H. Cattenoz, *Tables de concordance des ères chrétienne et hégirienne* (Rabat, 1954), and, in English, T. W. Haig, *Comparative Tables of Muhammedan and Christian Dates* (London, 1932), but careful note should be taken of the list of errata that has been added at the beginning in the form of a loose leaf; owing to its small size, this book can be slipped into the epigraphist's pocket for use on the spot.

On other calendars, see, for example, H. Taqizadeh, "Various Eras and Calendars Used in the Countries of Islam," *BSOAS*, IX (1937–1939), 903–922, X (1940–1942), 107–132. For the Jewish calendar, see I. Loeb, *Tables du calendrier juif depuis l'ère chrétienne* ... (Paris, 1886), and E. Mahler, *Handbuch der jüdischen Chronologie* (Leipzig, 1918).

12

Dynastic Series and Tribal Genealogies

The large number of dynasties that have reigned over various parts of the Muslim world and the extreme confusion characteristic of so many periods of political history of Islam make it necesary for the student to consult handbooks giving the genealogy of each royal family and the dates of the beginning and the end of the reign of each sovereign.

The best of these is by E. von Zambaur, MANUEL DE GÉNÉALOGIE ET DE CHRONOLOGIE POUR L'HISTOIRE DE L'ISLAM (Hanover, 1927; reprinted, 1955), and is indispensable. Based on a systematic study of chronicles and of works of Orientalists as well as of inscriptions and coins, this very rich collection deals not only with ruling families but also with the great families playing a role in politics—such as viziers and provincial governors—from the beginnings of Islam to our own day. The titles and names are often given in their complete form, the tables are grouped according to a convenient geographical classification, and it provides a good system of cross references, index and maps, explanatory notes, and bibliographical indications.

Although it is older and less detailed, S. Lane-Poole, *The Mohammedan Dynasties* (London, 1894; reprinted, Paris, 1925), can still be used for its historical surveys and synoptical tables, especially in the form given it by Halil Edhem, *Düvel-i islamiye* (Istanbul, 1927), which is considerably augmented on the subject of the Turkish dynasties.

The importance that Arab groups have always attached—even within Islam—to genealogical descent makes it impossible to neglect this traditional point of view; though historically unreliable, it has influenced the formation of social structures. For the study of tribal genealogies, we have two good guides in F. Wüstenfeld, *Genealogische Tabellen der arabischen*

Stämme und Familien (1852–1853), and Amīn al-Suwaidī, *Sabā'iq al-dhahab fī ma'rifat qabā'il al-'arab* (Baghdad, A.H. 1296), an adaptation of a fifteenth-century work.

Certain family genealogies can be traced or completed with the aid of the old genealogical treatises published by E. Lévi-Provençal, see below, p. 123.

PERSONAL NAMES

For Arabic proper names, an *Onomasticon arabicum, ossia repertorio alfabetico dei nomi di persona e di luogo contenuti nelle principali opere storiche...* was begun by G. Gabrieli, but unfortunately not finished (Rome, 1915). For practical purposes one may consult the medieval Arabic works written to meet the same need, such as the *Kitāb al-ansāb* by al-Sam'ānī (twelfth century), facsimile edition by D. S. Margoliouth (1912); *al-Lubāb fī tahdhīb al ansāb* by Ibn al-Athīr, edited by Ḥusām al-Dīn al-Qudsī, three volumes (Cairo, 1357–1369/1938–1949); or the *Lubb al-lubāb* by Suyūṭī, edited by P. Veth (Leiden, 1830–1832).

We do not have at our disposal a complete repertory of Persian and Turkish names but much can be found in F. Justi, *Iranisches Namenbuch* (1895). For Turkish J. Sauvaget has drawn up a list of the principal Turkish names in the Mamlūk state, "Noms et surnoms de Mamelouks," *JA* (1950), 28–58; many others can be found in G. Moravcsik, cited on page 153.

METROLOGY

Islam inherited from preceding civilizations several systems of weights and measures that continued to be used throughout the Middle Ages, though their evolution varied according to different periods and countries, often even according to different towns; the same denomination may refer in different places to different standards; it is almost impossible, in the present state of our knowledge, to give an accurate current equivalent of a measure mentioned in a document.

A practical statement of the essential facts has recently been published by W. Hinz, *Islamische Masse und Gewichte*, *HO*, Erg. Bd. I, Heft I (cited p. 67 f.), practically superseding the obscure and unreliable *Traité pratique des poids et mesures des peuples anciens et des Arabes* by J. Decourdemanche (Paris, 1909) as far as the Muslim world is concerned. The "Matériaux pour servir à l'histoire de la numismatique et de la métrologie musulmane," by H. Sauvaire, *JA* (1879–1885), remains an invaluable mine of information drawn from historical sources (but one should not accept the conversions into the metrical system without verifying them).

Indications derived from sources from the Islamic domain may be supplemented by information given by Portuguese and Italian travelers, such as, for instance, B. Pegolotti (fourteenth century), *La pratica della mercatura*, edited by A. Evans with a good glossary.

We possess genuine measures dating from the first centuries of Muslim history. See, for instance, S. Lane-Poole, *Catalogue of Arabic Glass Weights in the British Museum* (1891), and G. Miles, *Early Arabic Glass-Weights and Stamps*, Numismatic Notes and Monographs, CXI (1948) and CXX (1951), and *Contributions to Arabic Metrology* by the same author, *ibid.*, CXLI (1958) and CL (1963).

QUOTATIONS

It is necessary to be able to identify rapidly the frequent quotations from the Koran and the *ḥadīth* that are found in texts of all kinds. On this subject, see the collections cited on pp. 28 and 117.

13

The Main Outlines of Muslim History

INTRODUCTION

Since the Muslim world stretches from the Atlantic Ocean to Mongolia and Java, and its history spans thirteen centuries, it must be studied by regions and periods; the essential bibliography will therefore be classified according to period and, in certain cases, according to region. But there are also works of a more general nature that deal with the Muslim world as a whole or, though devoted to questions of more limited scope, cover several periods and fall into our field of study. The bibliography of these chief aspects of Muslim history will be given here first before embarking on the detailed descriptions of the historical bibliography proper.

After what has been said of the gaps in our knowledge, it will not be surprising that we do not yet have a reliable and complete guide to Muslim society and culture. Much detailed research is still necessary before the compiling of such a work can be undertaken. The only general work to have such an aim—and it was deserving of the highest praise at the time of its composition—the *Culturgeschichte des Orients unter den Chalifen* by A. von Kremer, two volumes (1875–1879), English translation, unannotated by S. Khuda Bukhsh, *The Orient under the Caliphs* (Calcutta, 1920), seems to us now to have been a premature attempt at a synthesis, although certain sections, not yet superseded, may still be useful; Jurjī Zaidān, *Ta'rīkh al-tamaddun al-islāmī*, two volumes (4th ed. 1935), also deserves praise; the *Institutions musulmanes* by M. Gaudefroy-Demombynes (latest ed., 1946), English translation by J. MacGregor, *Muslim Institutions* (1950), provides a rapid introduction and is full of information but is nevertheless too succinct to serve as a work of reference after the initial stages. A sound and evocative account largely concerned with the modern world will be found in L. Gardet, *La cité musulmane* (1954). Above all, G. E. von Grunebaum, MEDIEVAL ISLAM (2d ed., 1953; French translation, 1962; enlarged German translation, 1963), without aiming at a detailed picture of the institutional or cultural facts, offers a rich and provocative general view of Muslim culture and the predominating conceptions that it expresses or implies. The collective work, *Unity and Variety in Muslim Civilization*, edited by the same author (Chicago, 1955), should be added to this, together with A. Mez, *Die Renaissance*, cited p. 137. Among the shorter studies we may mention C. H. Becker, "Der Islam als Problem," *Islam*, I (1910), also in his *Vom Wesen und Werden der Islamischen Welt, Islamstudien*, two volumes (Leipzig, 1924–1932), Vol. I, and H. A. R. Gibb, "An Interpretation of Islamic History," *JWH*, I (1953), republished in *MW*, XLV (1955), and also in his *Studies on the Civilization of Islam* (London, 1962). See also S. D. Goitein, "The Unity of the Mediterranean World in the 'Middle' Middle Ages," *SI*, XII (1960).

The close interpenetration in the Muslim world of religion and social affairs, with the same law governing both, makes it difficult at times to distinguish clearly even among modern works those which deal with religion from those devoted to social affairs. With these reservations in mind, we shall discuss first the material aspects of Muslim society and then its cultural life.

ECONOMIC AND SOCIAL LIFE

Economic and social history is a particularly neglected branch of Islamic studies. A good deal of specialized investigation is still required before an adequate general account can be written. An economic and social history of the East is in preparation under the direction of an international committee; but as things stand, the Muslim section, under the direction of C. Cahen, will be more a plan for study than a true summing up of the question. *The Social Structure of Islam* by R. Levy (1957), a new edition of his earlier *An Introduction to the Sociology of Islam*, two volumes (1931–1933), something of a modernized adaptation of A. von Kremer, cited on p. 85, does not fulfill the promise of its title and presents little of interest.

A few reflections on the present state of research and brief suggestions on the approach to certain problems will be found in C. Cahen, "L'histoire économique et sociale de l'Orient musulman médiéval," *SI*, III (1955), and "L'évolution sociale du monde musulman face à celle du monde chrétien jusqu'au XIIe siècle," *Cahiers de civilisation medievale*, II (1959); see also J. H. Kramers, "La sociologie de l'Islam," *AO*, XXI (1950–1953).

LAW

Given the present state of information and research, it is often impossible to approach the study of social entities other than indirectly through works on law. Nevertheless, few of the works devoted to Muslim law are able as yet to meet and satisfy completely the varied demands of the historian's curiosity. Some are devoted mainly to the study of the fundamental premises of the law rather than its positive content, and they generally touch on an aspect of the religious development of Islam that we shall return to when we come to study its cultural life. Others are intended primarily to meet the practical needs of modern administrators so that they are completely indifferent to questions of origin and progressive development or the possible variations of the law. As a result we shall cite only a few of these studies as examples, in addition to other works of a nonlegal nature that are capable of providing information on the physical aspects of the Muslim community.

The principal general accounts of Muslim law, each devoted essentially to one legal school, are by T. Juynboll, *Handbuch des islāmischen Gesetzes nach der Lehre der schāfi'itischen Schule*, a German translation (1910) from the Dutch (1903), and by E. Sachau, *Muhammedanisches Recht* (1897) on Shāfi'ite law; and D. Santillana, *Istituzioni di diritto musulmano malichita con riguardo anche al sistema sciafiita*, two volumes (Rome, 1925–1938), a masterly work with comparisons between Mālikite law and that of other schools, that of Shāfi'ī in particular. On the Ḥanbalite school, see *G. Bergsträsser's Grundzüge des islamischen Rechts* edited by J. Schacht (1935), a useful summary; and see L. Van den Berg, *Principes du droit musulman*, translated from the Dutch (1896), on the Ḥanafite and Shāfi'ite schools. E. Bussi, *Principi di diritto musulmano* (1943) is a more general study; likewise López Ortiz, *Derecho musulmān* (1932); L. Milliot, *Introduction à l'étude du droit musulman* (1953), of uneven originality and reliability, is especially sound on the question of modern Mālikite law in North Africa; for Mālikite law in Algeria, see also G.-H. Bousquet, *Précis de droit musulman*, two volumes (2d ed., n.d.), the second volume of which contains a number of texts. On India, see S. Vesey-Fitzgerald, *Muhammadan Law: An Abridgement according to its Various Schools* (1931), and A. A. A. Fyzee, *Outlines of Muhammadan Law* (2d ed., 1955), with modern laws. On the Shī'ites, see A. Querry, *Droit musulman: Recueil de lois concernant les musulmans schyïtes*, two volumes (1871–1872).

We have already described the spirit in which the legal works were written (see above, p. 40 ff.) dealing with their documentary value and also, to some extent, the conditions in which this legal system was formed. We would simply remind the reader here of the significant *Origins* by J. Schacht, cited p. 41. The same author has written an excellent account of another question—the survival in Muslim law of elements of the preëxisting legal systems of populations conquered by the Arabs and gradually converted to Islam—in his "Droit byzantin et droit musulman," *ALFAV*, XII (1957). In a more general way, the student will find information on many questions concerning the formation and content of Muslim law in the articles by C. Nallino collected in Vol. IV of his *Raccolta di scritti editi e inediti* (1946), in which Christian law in the East is also discussed, and in the articles by C. Snouck Hurgronje collected in Vol. II (1923) of his *Verspreide Geschriften*, six volumes. I–V (Bonn and Leipzig, 1923–1925), VI (Leiden, 1927); the essential elements of Vol. II, partly in Dutch, are to be found in translation (French and English) in the volume of *Selected Works* edited by G.-H. Bousquet and J. Schacht (Leiden, 1957). See also the new work by N. J. Coulson, *A History of Islamic Law* (1964).

But the legal works not only see reality through their own particular lens but also altogether neglect certain sectors of social and economic life and in any case are not concerned with describing all the aspects. For these we are obliged to draw upon all kinds of complementary documents which must be checked against one another.

FAMILY LIFE; SLAVERY; RELIGION; RACES

We have no history of the Muslim family; but an interesting introduction to certain problems will be found in the article by J. Lecerf, "La famille dans le monde arabe et islamique," *Arabica*, III (1956), dealing especially with the problem of its origins. This should be compared with the ethnographical studies cited on p. 79; the work of W. Robertson Smith, cited p. 112; R. Brunschvig, "De la filiation maternelle en droit musulman," *SI*, IX (1958); and G. Stern, *Marriage in Early Islam* (1939). Among the jurists we may cite M. Yusoof, *Mohammedan Law Relating to Marriage . . .*, two volumes (1895–1898), on India; M. Morand, *Études de droit musulman algérien* (1913), pp. 7–109; W. Marçais, *Des parents et alliés successibles en droit musulman* (1898); O. Pesle, *Le Testament dans le rite malikite* (Rabat, n.d.) and *La donation dans le droit musulman* (*rite malikite*) (Rabat, 1933); and the general treatises.

There is no history of slavery in Muslim society, but a good introduction can be obtained from the important article "'Abd" by R. Brunschvig in *EI*²; and many facts concerning one country in particular will be found in C. Verlinden, "L'esclavage dans l'Espagne musulmane," *Anuario del derecho español*, XII (1935), and in his book *L'esclavage dans l'Europe médiévale* (1955), which makes use of the same material.

There is no general history of interfaith relations in countries governed by Muslims, nor even studies on all the religious groups individually. But we have at least two lucid and richly documented works on Judeo-Muslim relations: S. D. Goitein, *Jews and Arabs* (1955) and S. W. Baron, A SOCIAL AND RELIGIOUS HISTORY OF THE JEWS, eight volumes, Vols. III–VIII, *High Middle Ages, 500–1200* (1957–1958), which differ from previous works on Jewish history by giving considerable attention to the East and to the social environment. On the more complex question of Islamic-Christian relations, one should refer to the histories of the Oriental churches and to studies on religious polemics (see below, p. 97 f.), or to what are essentially incomplete legal studies, such as A. Tritton, *The Caliphs and their non-Muslim Subjects* (1930), and A. Fattal, *Le statut légal des non-Musulmans en pays d'Islam* (1958).

On Islam and the racial problem, see the article "L'Islam et le problème des races," *RMM*, L (1922), by C. Snouck Hurgronje.

Nonreligious solidarity groups existing in certain milieux in the Muslim world have been studied especially in connection with Ibn Khaldūn's theory of *'aṣabiyya* (see below, p. 226); see, for example, H. Ritter, "Irrational Solidarity Groups," *Oriens*, I (1948).

TECHNOLOGY AND WARFARE

The technology of the Muslim world as it affected social life remains practically unstudied, and in the general histories of the subject Islam is almost completely a blank between Europe and the Far East. One may consult, however, *A History of Technology*, edited by C. Singer, five volumes (1954–1958). As to what Islamic civilization invented, handed down, and practiced, there are a few brief traditional assertions—nothing else. This very deficiency makes all the more interesting the résumés that G. Wiet has given in "L'évolution des techniques dans le monde musulman au moyen âge," *JWH*, VI/1 (1960), and in *L'Histoire générale des techniques*, Vol. I (Paris, 1963). Descriptions of artistic techniques may be found in the histories of art cited on p. 103 ff.; on textiles, apart from the texts collected by R. Serjeant in "Material for a History of Islamic Textiles up to the Mongol Conquest," *AI*, XI (1942), X (1943), XI (1946), XIII–XIV (1948), we can cite among others the articles, "Ṭirāz," by A. Grohmann in *EI* and *Supplement* and the posthumous article by U. Monneret de Villard, "Tessuti e ricami mesopotamici da tempi degli Abbasidi e dei Selgiukidi," *Atti della Accademia Nazionale dei Lincei, Memorie, Classe di scienze morali,* . . . Ser. VIII, Vol. VII/4 (1955). Certain techniques connected with warfare have also been the object of study; see, for example, K. Huuri, *Zur Geschichte des mittelalterlichen Geschützwesens aus orientalischen Quellen*

(1941), to be supplemented by C. Cahen's notes in his edition of "Un traité d'armurerie composé pour Saladin," *BEOD*, XII (1947–1948); A. Zeki Velidi [Togan], "Die Schwerter der Germanen (sic)," *ZDMG*, XCI (1936); M. Mercier, *Le feu grégeois* (1952), investigated in the Muslim world more than in the Byzantine; and best of all, J. R. Partington, *A History of Greek Fire and Gunpowder* (1960), but see D. Ayalon, "A Reply to Prof. J. R. Partington," *Arabica*, X (1963), 64–73. See also G. Scanlon's *A Muslim Manual of War* (Cairo, 1961), an edition and translation of a fourteenth-century Mamlūk text. A good example of a technical study in a more popular field is found in the article "Araba" by M. Rodinson in *EI*[2]. See also the treatises on the history of the sciences, cited on p. 100 ff., and modern ethnographical studies.

LAND TENURE, *Iqṭā'*, AND *Waqf* OR *Ḥubus*

Muslim society, or the military aristocracy within it, has often been called feudal. On this question one should read A. Poliak, "La féodalité islamique," *REI*, X (1936), in which interesting ideas are to be found amidst a good deal of vagueness and confusion. It will be worthwhile reflecting on the conditions in which conceptions and labels like that of feudalism can be transposed from one society to another with the help of the introduction and the chapters of comparative history by R. Boutruche, *Seigneurie et féodalité* (1959), with the commentary by C. Cahen in *JESHO*, III (1960). R. Coulborn and others, *Feudalism in History* (Princeton, 1956), is theoretical and does not deal with the Muslim world.

These questions are naturally bound up with the question of the type of land tenure and the form of combined land and tax concession called *iqṭā'*. On these questions one may still usefully consult S. de Sacy, "Nature et révolutions du droit de propriété en Égypte," *Mémoires de l'Institut Royal de France*, I, V, VII; M. van Berchem, *La propriété territoriale et l'impôt foncier* (1886); C. H. Becker, "Steuerpacht und Lehnwesen," *Islam* (1914), and "Die Enstehung von 'Ušr- und Ḫarāğland in Ägypten," *Islamstudien*, I, cited p. 86, interesting but actually refers mainly to the special conditions prevailing in Egypt. But all these studies need to be thoroughly revised; for this consult A. Poliak, "Classification of Lands in Islamic Law," *AJSL*, XLVII (1940); C. Cahen, "L'évolution de l'iqṭā'," *AESC*, VIII (1953), and "Fiscalité, propriété, antagonismes sociaux ... au temps des premiers 'Abbāsides," *Arabica*, I (1954); Ann K. S. Lambton, LANDLORD AND PEASANT IN PERSIA (1953); F. Løkkegaard, cited below, p. 95.

The *waqf* or *ḥubus* (a religious foundation) has been studied mainly from a legal standpoint, in view of the problems it poses for modern administrations, e.g., E. Clavel, *Droit musulman. Le waqf ou habous ...*, two volumes (Cairo, 1896); E. Mercier, *Le code du habous ou ouakf ...* (1899); J. Luccioni, *Le habous ou wakf ...* (1942); O. Pesle, *La théorie et la pratique des habous dans le rite malékite* (193?). But no work as yet has dealt with the history, let alone the economic history, of the *waqf;* all one can refer to are the remarks on the primitive doctrine of *waqf* by J. Schacht, "Early Doctrines on Waqf," *MK* (1953), and C. Cahen, "Réflexions sur le waqf ancien," *SI*, XIV (1961); one should also consult M. F. Köprülü [Köprülüzāde Meḥmed Fu'ād] "L'institution de vakf ... ," *Vakıflar Dergisi*, I (1938), in both French and Turkish.

In a more general way, legal studies have been devoted—but never in historical perspective—to various questions touching on the system of landownership. See, for instance, F. Schmidt, "Die occupatio im islamischen Recht," *Islam*, I (1910); F. Arin, "Essai sur les démembrements de la propriété foncière en droit musulman," *RMM*, XXVI (1914); Y. Linant de Bellefonds, "Un problème de sociologie juridique: Les terres 'communes' en pays d'Islam," *SI*, X (1959); and see E. Pröbster, "Privateigentum und Kollektivismus im Maghrib," *Islamica*, IV (1931). On the idea of ownership, see L. Gardet, "La propriété en Islam," *IBLA*, X (1947).

In Muslim society there is an immense difference between town dwellers and the rest of the population, and the nonurban population is not yet well known. On Iran, see p. 172, below, and Ann K. S. Lambton, cited above, p. 90. C. Cahen, "Le régime rural syrien pendant l'occupation franque," *Bulletin de la Faculté des Lettres de Strasbourg*, n.v. (1951), points out that the lack of Muslim sources of information must be compensated for by other sources (in this case, sources from the Latin East). Any questions must be formulated with the help of modern sociological and economic studies of the modern peasantry in those places where it has retained a traditional structure; see above, p. 79. On farming, a few specialized investigations prove that others would be worth making: in particular, D. Müller-Wodarg, "Die Landwirtschaft Ägyptens in der frühen Abbāsidenzeit," *Islam*, XXXI–XXXIII (1953–1958); M. Canard, "Le riz dans le Proche-Orient aux premiers siècles de l'Islam," *Arabica*, VI (1959). See also below, p. 219, on agronomy.

The essential distinction to be made among the various types of nonurban population is between farmers and nomadic shepherds; the latter have been studied in pre-Islamic Arabia and in modern times, but we lack studies on the intermediary periods except for the Hilālians (see below, page 221).

URBAN DWELLERS

The theories of urban sociology that have been developed during the last thirty years have yet to take note of a number of problems and they are not always free of error in historical method. The best general studies of the

Muslim town are G. Marçais, "La conception des villes dans l'Islam," *Revue d'Alger*, I (1945), and G. E. von Grunebaum, "Die islamische Stadt," *Saeculum*, VI (1955), English translation, "The Structure of the Muslim Town," in his *Islam*, cited p. 96. See the discussion of viewpoints by C. Cahen, "Zur Geschichte der städtischen Gesellschaft im islamischen Orient des Mittelalters," *Saeculum*, IX, I (1958), and his article in *Arabica*, cited below. See also E. Ashtor-Strauss, cited on p. 166. [E. Ashtor-Strauss is the transitional name taken by E. Strauss when he changed his name to Ashtor ("Strauss" translated into Hebrew).]

Historical monographs of various towns are indispensable; the best are J. Sauvaget on Aleppo, *Alep* (1941), which gives considerable attention to the social aspect of town life, and R. Le Tourneau, *Fès avant le protectorat* (1949)—a more sociological study, inevitably limited in its treatment of the Middle Ages by the lack of documents. But we have only a poor study of Cairo—such as *Le Caire*, two volumes (1934), by M. Clerget—nothing on Baghdad, and mere sketches on Damascus—K. Wulzinger and C. Watzinger, *Damaskus, die islamische Stadt* (1924), and J. Sauvaget, "Esquisse d'une histoire de la ville de Damas," *REI*, VIII (1934), essentially urban in outlook.

Interesting information may be drawn from legal works on questions of the city and the neighborhood by R. Brunschvig, "Urbanisme médiéval et droit musulman," *REI*, XVI (1947), and O. Spies, "Islamisches Nachbarrecht nach schafiitischer Lehre," *Zeitschrift für vergleichende Rechtswissenschaft*, XLIV (1928).

On professional organization, the restatement of the question by Bernard Lewis, "Islamic Guilds," *Economics History Review*, VIII (1937), which is good and clear as such, naturally does not deal with problems that had not received attention at that date. On the so-called *futuwwa* community organizations, the first important studies are by H. Thorning, cited p. 158; and the essential work at the present time is by F. Taeschner, whose latest statement of the question is to be found under the title, "Futuwwa, eine gemeinschaftbildende Idee . . . ," in *Schweizerisches Archiv für Volkskunde*, LII (1956); some complementary information and different points of view will be found in L. Massignon, "La 'Futuwwa' ou 'pacte d'honneur artisanal,' " *Nouvelle Clio*, IV (1952), and C. Cahen, "Mouvements populaires et autonomisme urbain dans l'Asie musulmane du moyen âge," *Arabica*, V–VI (1958–1959). On the bourgeoisie, see S. D. Goitein, cited p. 140.

On daily life, the all-too-accessible work by A. Mazahéri, *La vie quotidienne des Musulmans au moyen âge* (1951), is mentioned here only to point out its hasty generalizations and its superficial documentation. On one particular aspect, see M. Rodinson, "Recherches sur les documents arabes relatifs à la cuisine," *REI*, XVII (1949).

TRADE

The history of trade has been more widely studied but usually by historians of European trade and only from their standpoint. The basic work, the author of which has translated and analyzed a considerable number of Oriental texts, is still that by U. Heyd, which should be read in the French translation by F. Raynaud, completed by the author, *Histoire du commerce du Levant au moyen âge*, two volumes (1885; reprinted, 1923), which may be brought up to date on certain points by the more methodical *Handelsgeschichte der romanischen Völker des Mittelmeergebiets bis zum Ende der Kreuzzüge* by A. Schaube (1906) and Archibald Lewis, *Naval Power and Trade in the Mediterranean (500–1100)* (1951). The Orientalist should be aware of the controversy arising out of H. Pirenne's *Mahomet et Charlemagne* (6th ed., 1937), English translation by B. Miall, *Mohammed and Charlemagne* (1939), on the role of the Arab conquests and Muslim expansion on the economy of Europe; the interpretation of the Belgian scholar who saw in them a cause of decline for Europe is opposed by M. Lombard, "L'or musulman du VIIe au XIe siècle," *AESC*, II (1947), who on the contrary takes them to be stimulating factors. There is a good statement of the question in E. Perroy, "Encore Mahomet et Charlemagne," *RH*, CCXII (1954). More recent is J. Duplessy, "La circulation des monnaies arabes en Europe occidentale du VIIIe au XIIIe siècle," *Revue Numismatique*, XVIII (1956). See also *The Pirenne Thesis*, edited by A. Havighurst in *Problems in European Civilization* (Boston, 1958), and C. Cahen's lecture at the Settimana di Studi del alto Medioeva, Spoleto, 1964, in press.

A history of trade from the Oriental point of view has not yet been written. M. Lombard has published only extremely fragmentary conclusions drawn from long years of research, such as (in addition to the article cited above) "Arsenaux et bois de marine dans la Méditerranée musulmane (VIIe–XIe siècle)," *Le Navire. Actes du deuxième colloque d'histoire maritime* (1957). Valuable indications are given by W. Heffening in the article "Tidjāra" in *EI*; and M. J. de Goeje's observations, "International Handelsverkeer en de Middeleuwe," *Verslagen en Mededeelingen . . . Akad. v. Wetenschappen*, Afd. Lett; ser. 4, Vol. IX (1909), can still be read with interest. On the Indian Ocean, the forthcoming volume on the Geniza documents (see above, p. 18) with an important introduction by S. D. Goitein will completely alter the state of our knowledge; meanwhile, see G. Hourani, *Arab Seafaring in the Indian Ocean* (1951), to which A. Fahmy's *Muslim Seapower in the Eastern Mediterranean* (1950) somewhat corresponds. See also above, p. 38, the paragraph on geography.

A few questions relating to trade organization have been touched on by W. Björkman, "Kapitalentstehung und Anlage in Islam," *MSOS* (1929);

R. Brunschvig, "Coup d'oeil sur l'histoire des foires à travers l'Islam," *Recueils de la Société Jean Bodin*, V (1953); W. Hinz, "Lebensmittelpreise im mittelalterlichen Vorderen Orient," *WO*, II (1954); E. Ashtor-Strauss is preparing a work that summarizes articles on history of prices and salaries to be published in 1964 by l'École des Hautes Études, Paris; in W. Fischel's studies of more limited periods, see below, pp. 140 and 182; and in the study of M. Talbi on the trade agents, cited on p. 219.

A few aspects of trade law have given rise to studies that may be mentioned here: W. Heffening, *Das islamische Fremdenrecht* . . . , Beiträge zum Rechts- und Wirtschaftsleben des islamischen Orient I (1925)—some historical aspects of Muslim international law: R. Grasshof, *Das Wechselrecht der Araber* (1899); F. Arin, *Recherches historiques sur les opérations usuraires et aléatoires en droit musulman* (Paris, 1909); O. Spies, "Das Depositum nach islamischem Recht," *Zeitschrift für vergleichende Rechtswissenschaft*, XLV (1930); E. Bussi, "Del concetto di commercio e di commerciante nel pensiero giuridico musulmano," *Studi in memoria di Aldo Albertoni*, III (1938); A. d'Emilia, "Il *bai' al-ḫiyār*," *RSO*, XXIV (1949); C. Cardahi, "Les conditions générales de la vente en droit comparé occidental et oriental," *AEDB*, I (1945). See also the articles "'Aḳd," by C. Chehata, and "Bay'," by J. Schacht, in *EI*².

POLITICAL AND ADMINISTRATIVE INSTITUTIONS

The forms of government in Muslim society have naturally changed in the course of time and in the different regions. Most of the studies on this subject are either limited to one particular regime or else, when less restricted in scope, deal primarily with the period during which the institutions of the whole of the Muslim world were formed and from which all later regimes derive: that of the Umayyads and 'Abbāsids. For these studies, therefore, the reader is referred to Part III, the historical bibliography.

On the question of Muslim public institutions, no detailed general study exists except for the brief accounts to be found in the general works already mentioned. E. Tyan has undertaken the task of publishing the *Institutions du droit public musulman*, Vol. I, *Le califat* (1954), Vol. II, *Sultanat et califat* (1957), to be continued; but these, in spite of information that is of use to the specialist, seem to have been premature, not fully thought through methodologically, and so could mislead the beginner. *Al-Nuẓum al-islāmiyya* by 'Abd al-'Azīz Dūrī, I (Baghdad, 1950) is more limited in scope; but its concrete descriptions, practically centered on the 'Abbāsid period, are more reliable. We should also mention Ḥasan Ibrāhīm Ḥasan and 'Alī Ibrāhīm Ḥasan, *al-Nuẓum al-islāmiyya* (Cairo, 1959). Ann K. S. Lambton's articles on the general conception of government in Persia under the titles

"Quis custodiet custodes?," *SI*, V–VI (1956) and "Justice in the Medieval Persian Theory of Kingship," *SI*, XVII (1962) actually deal with the whole of the Muslim world.

The apex of the Muslim political structure—in practice during the early centuries and in legal theory later on—is the caliphate. On this question, after the superficial introduction by Sir T. W. Arnold, *The Caliphate* (1924), the reader may profitably consult the following: V. Barthold's articles "Khalif i Sultan," *Mir Islama*, I (1912), in Russian, German adaptation by C. H. Becker in *Islam*, VI (1915–1916); P. Wittek, "Konstantinopel, Islam und Kalifat," *Archiv für Sozialwissenschaft und Sozialpolitik*, LIII (1925); A Siddiqi, "Caliphate and Kingship in Medieval Persia," *IC*, IX–XI (1935–1937); and H. A. R. Gibb, "Some Considerations on the Sunni Theory of the Caliphate," *Archives d'histoire du droit oriental*, III (1947), and his *Studies on the Civilization of Islam* (cited p. 86). For the *Succession to the Rule of Islam*, see also the study under this title by A. Chejne (Lahore, 1960).

For questions of central administration and the forms of state government, see especially D. Sourdel, cited p. 139 ;and the other works concerning the 'Abbāsid period; and the good studies in the articles "Dīwān," by A. A. Dūrī, H. L. Gottschalk, and others, and "Daftar," by Bernard Lewis, in *EI*². On fiscal organization, an introduction will be found in the articles "Bayt al-Māl," "Ḍarība," "D͟jizya," (with "Kharād͟j," still to come) in *EI*²; see also pp. 134 and 90; D. Dennett (p. 126); and A. Grohmann and C. Leyerer (p. 139). The general study by F. Løkkegaard, *Islamic Taxation in the Classical Period* (1950), is rather difficult for the beginner and while containing much information and many judicious and useful ideas is neither complete nor reliable. See also *Arabica*, I (1954), 346–354; and, for an expression of points of doctrine, C. Snouck Hurgronje, "Le zakāt," *Verspreide Geschriften*, II, or *Selected Works*, cited p. 88. On currency, see the articles "Dīnār" and "Dirham" by G. Miles in *EI*² and the treatise published by Ḥ. Mu'nis, cited p. 218.

For the army, see pp. 125 and 139, and the articles "'Aṭā'," by C. Cahen, and "D͟jays͟h," by C. Cahen and E. Kedourie, in *EI*².

We now have an important general work on the Islamic judiciary by E. Tyan, *Histoire de l'organisation judiciaire en pays d'Islam*, two volumes (Paris, 1938–1943; 2d ed., 1961), complemented by M. Gaudefroy-Demombynes, "Notes sur l'histoire de l'organisation judiciaire ... ," *REI*, XIII (1939), to which should be added "Le notariat et le régime de la preuve par écrit en droit musulman," *AEDB*, II (1945), by the same author. Among other fairly general studies one should mention R. Brunschvig, "Théorie générale de la capacité chez les hanafites médiévaux," *Revue internationale des droits de l'antiquité*, II (1949), and E. Dib, "Essai sur une théorie des mobiles en droit civil hanafite," *AEDB*, n.v. (1952). Attention has already been drawn to various studies on law in application in the sections dealing with the appropriate aspect of social life. One should add, on the question of penal law, for example, L. Bercher, *Les délits et les peines de droit commun* ... (1926), and J. N. D. Anderson, "Homicide in Islamic Law," *BSOAS*, XIII/4 (1951).

Besides W. Heffening, cited p. 94, consult, on the question of Muslim international law, M. Khadduri, *War and Peace in the Law of Islam* (1955); J. Hatschek, *Der Musta'min* (1919); J. Castagna, "Études sur la notion islamique de souveraineté," *RMM*, LIX (1925); from a more historical point of view, M. Canard, "La guerre sainte dans le monde islamique et dans le monde chrétien," *RA*, LXXIX (1936).

CULTURAL LIFE

Simple readable introductions can be found in B. Carra de Vaux, *Les penseurs de l'Islam*, five volumes (1921–1926); see also: the collective work, *The Legacy of Islam* (1931) edited by Sir T. W. Arnold and A. Guillaume; its companion, another collection, *The Legacy of Persia* (1953) edited by A. J. Arberry (essays of uneven value); another collection, *The Arab Heritage* (1944) edited by N. A. Faris; De Lacy E. O'Leary's not entirely satisfactory *Arabic Thought and its Place in History* (rev. ed., 1954). We should also pay tribute to A. von Kremer, *Geschichte der herrschenden Ideen des Islams* (1868). The summary on science and philosophy in preparation by M. Plessner, H. Braun, and R. Walzer, for *HO* (cited p. 67 f.) Erg. Bd. VI will certainly be of great value.

On the general spirit of Muslim culture, in addition to the indispensable *Medieval Islam* by G. E. von Grunebaum, cited p. 86, read by the same author: "Idéologie musulmane et esthétique arabe," *SI*, III (1955); "The Spirit of Islam as Shown in its Literature," *SI* (1953); "An Analysis of Islamic Civilization and Cultural Anthropology," *Colloque sur la Sociologie musulmane, 11.–14. Septembre 1961, Actes* (Brussels, 1962); "Self-Image and Approach to History," *Historians of the Middle East* (cited p. 22); and various articles collected in *Islam, Essays in the Nature and Growth of a Cultural Tradition* (2d ed., 1961). And see: G. Levi Della Vida, "Dominant Ideas in the Formation of Islamic Culture," *Crozer Quarterly*, XXI (July, 1944), in Italian in his *Aneddoti e svaghi arabi e non arabi* (1959); F. Rosenthal, "The Technique and Approach of Muslim Scholarship," *Analecta Orientalia*, XXIV (1947); and, although inadequate, R. Jockel, *Islamische Geisteswelt von Mohammed bis zur Gegenwart* (1954). The participants at the Bordeaux Symposium of 1956 considered the causes and modalities of the gradual paralysis of Muslim culture: *Classicisme et déclin culturel dans l'histoire de l'Islam* (Paris, 1957) edited by R. Brunschvig and G. E. von Grunebaum; along the same lines, see also Brunschvig, "Perspectives," *SI*, I (1953), also in *Unity and Variety*, cited p. 86, dealing among other subjects with the rhythms of evolution of the Muslim world.

On the methods by which Muslim culture was transmitted and spread, see: M. Weisweiler, "Das Amt des Mustamli' in der arabischen Wissenschaft," *Oriens*, IV (1950–1951); A. Tritton, *Materials on Muslim Education in the Middle Ages* (1957); and B. Dodge, *Muslim Education in Medieval Times* (Washington, 1962).

RELIGION

On religious questions, the epoch-making work that must still be consulted as the starting point of contemporary scholarly research is I. Goldziher's VORLESUNGEN ÜBER DEN ISLAM (1910; 2d ed., 1925); French translation by F. Arin, *Le dogme et la loi de l'Islam* (1920). Despite the fact that recent developments in our knowledge occurred after its publication, it has never really been superseded. Also important are C. Snouck Hurgronje, "Der Islam," in Vol. I of *Lehrbuch der Religionsgeschichte*, two volumes, edited by A. Bertholet and E. Lehmann (Tübinnge, 1925), English translation by J. Schacht in the *Selected Works*, cited p. 88. Among the introductions from which the student may choose, the most practical is H. Massé, L'ISLAM (5th ed., 1948), English translation by H. Edib, *Islam* (1938); but also recommended are H. Lammens, *L'Islam, croyances et institutions* (rev. ed., Beirut, 1941); A. Tritton, *Islam* (1951); L. Gardet, *Connaître l'Islam* (1958), English translation, *Mohammedanism* (1961); E. Abd-eljalil, *Aspects intérieurs de l'Islam* (1950); A. Guillaume, *Islam* (Penguin Books, 1954). Above all see H. A. R. Gibb, MOHAMMEDANISM (1949), and the lectures in French, *La structure de la pensée religieuse de l'Islam* (1950), also in *MW*, XXXVIII (1948), and in his *Studies on the Civilization of Islam*, cited p. 86. A modern Muslim point of view is found in *Introduction to Islam* edited by M. Hamidullah (Paris: Centre Culturel Islamique, 1958). As a reminder the *Handwörterbuch* and the *Shorter Encyclopaedia*, cited p. 69, should be mentioned.

On the Koran, see below, p. 117 ff; on the *ḥadīth*, see above, p. 25 ff.

On Muslim theology in general are two works inspired by the desire to compare Islam and Christianity, even to give rise to discussion between them: L. Gardet and M. Anawati, *Introduction à la théologie musulmane, essai de théologie comparée* (1948), and W. Sweetman, *Islam and Christian Theology*, two volumes (1954–1957), concerning the ancient period; less reliable is A. Tritton, *Muslim Theology* (1947), a collection of material. Other studies are: A. J. Wensinck, *The Muslim Creed* (1932), a study of creeds from the early centuries; the works of M. Horten, such as *Die philosophischen Probleme der spekulativen Theologie im Islam* (1910), somewhat dated but not yet replaced; D. Macdonald, *Development of Muslim Theology, Jurisprudence and Constitutional Theory* (1903; reprinted, Beirut, 1964), more cursory; still deserving of mention are Macdonald's *The Religious Attitude and Life in Islam* (Chicago, 1906; 2d ed., 1912; reissued, Beirut, 1964), and *Aspects of Islam* (New York, 1911); and also W. Montgomery Watt, *Islamic Philosophy and Theology* (1962). See also below, p. 141 ff., the bibliography of Mu'tazilism; p. 143 ff., the bibliographies of important theologians and religious thinkers; and A. J. Arberry, *Revelation and Reason in Islam* (1957). The viewpoint of a modern Muslim is found in F. Rahman, "The Concepts Sunna, Ijtihād and Ijmā' in the Early Period," "Sunnah and Ḥadīth," and "The Post-Formative Development in Islam," all in *IS*, I (1962), and "Social Change and Early Sunnah," *IS*, II (1963). A. Jeffery has prepared two collections of texts illustrating the development of Islamic thought, the first entitled *Islam* (1958), and the second, *Reader on Islam* (1962). The small volume by Alden Williams (1961) is on the same lines, and there is a reader in German by J. Schacht, *Der Islam mit Ausschluss des Qor'āns*, Vol. XVI of *Religionsgeschichtliches Lesebuch*, edited by A. Bertholet (2d ed., Tübingen, 1931).

On the forms of worship, see, for example, C. H. Becker, "Zur Geschichte des islamischen Kultus," *Islam*, III (1913), also in *Islamstudien*, I, cited p. 86. For the Pilgrimage, consult M. Gaudefroy-Demombynes, LE PÈLERINAGE À LA MEKKE (1923), which also gives information on the primitive meaning of rites preserved by Islam. On the subject of Muslim feast days, there is an introduction by G. E. von Grunebaum, *Muhammadan Festivals* (1951). A number of questions concerning forms of worship and even Muslim teaching are dealt with by J. Pedersen in the article "Masdjid" (mosque) in *EI*. On a particularly important point, one may refer to the evocative article by S. D. Goitein, "Le culte du vendredi musulman: son arrière-plan social et économique," *AESC*, XIII (1958); also in English, "The Origin and Nature of the Muslim Friday Worship," *MW*, XLIX (1959).

On the heterodox sects, after reflecting on the ideas expressed by Bernard Lewis, "Some Observations on the Significance of Heresy in the History of Islam," *SI*, I (1953), and C. Cahen's remarks on the changing social significance of heterodox movements in *L'élaboration de l'Islam. Colloque de Strasbourg, 12–13–14 juin 1959*, Bibliothèque des centres d'études supérieures specialisées (Paris, 1961), the student may turn for information on Shī'ism in general to D. Donaldson, *The Schi'ite Religion* (1933), which, however, gives only a superficial introduction. For more detailed study of the particular sects, see Part III, for the bibliographies of the different periods concerned. There are a number of works by E. Blochet, fairly wide in scope but of uneven quality: *Études sur l'ésotérisme musulman* (1910); *Le messianisme dans l'hétérodoxie musulmane* (1903); "La pensée grecque dans le mysticisme oriental," *ROC*, XXVII–XXIX (1929–1934). On the "confessions of faith," see the article by W. Montgomery Watt, "'Aḳīda," in *EI*[2].

On the question of Ṣūfism, an introduction will be found in A. J. Arberry, *Sufism* (1950), French translation (1952); and see L. Gardet and M. Anawati, *Le mystique musulmane* (1961); but R. Nicholson, *The Mystics of Islam* (1914), is still indispensable; see also by the same author, *Studies in Islamic Mysticism* (Cambridge, 1921); E. Dermenghem, *Vie des saints musulmans* (2d ed., 1956); and the works cited on pp. 142 and 157. The fundamental works are L. Massignon, *al-Ḥalladj*, cited p. 142, and the *Essai sur les origines du lexique technique de la mystique* (2d ed., 1954). See also the philosophical discussions by H. Corbin, such as "Sympathie et théopathie chez les 'Fidèles d'Amour' en Islam," *Eranos-Jahrbuch*, XXIV (1955), and F. Meier, *Vom Wesen der islamischen Mystik* (1943). More recently by Meier, see *Die Fawā'iḥ al-ǧamāl wa-fāwatiḥ al-galāl des Naǧm ad-Dīn al-Kubrā; eine Darstellung mystischer Erfahrungen im Islam aus der Zeit um 1200 n. Chr.*, Mainz Akademie der Wissenschaften und der Literatur. Orientalische Kommission. Veröffentlichungen, Bd. 9 (Wiesbaden, 1957).

On the religious expansion of Islam we have only the superficial study by Sir T. W. Arnold, *The Preaching of Islam* (1913).

On the relations between Islam and other religions, see first the bibliographical collection by M. Steinschneider, "Polemische und apologetische Literatur in arabischer Sprache zwischen Muslimen, Christen und Juden," *AKM*, VI/3 (1877); and then E. Fritsch, *Islam und Christentum im Mittelalter. Beiträge zur Geschichte der muslimischen Polemik . . .* (1930); also on the question of the part played by polemics and contacts with other religions in the development of Islam itself, see various articles by A. Abel, such as "Baḥīra" in *EI*[2] and his contribution to *L'élaboration de l'Islam*, cited p. 98; and C. H. Becker, "Christliche Polemik und islamische Dogmenbildung," *ZA*, XXVI (1912), also in his *Islamstudien*, I, cited p. 86.

On the meaning of the *umma*, the Community of Believers, see C. A. O. van Nieuwenhuijze, "The *Umma*, an Analytic Approach," *SI*, X (1959).

PHILOSOPHY AND SCIENCE

The history of philosophy, naturally linked to the study of religious history, is in the process of radical revision thanks to recent studies (see below, pp. 141–143), and we therefore do not possess an up-to-date general statement on the subject. A general outline and bibliography is available in J. de Menasce, *Arabische Philosophie* (Berne, 1948); among recent concise syntheses, one may note R. Walzer's chapter, "Islamic Philosophy," in the *History of Philosophy East and West*, II (London, 1953), reprinted in *Greek into Arabic* (Oxford, 1962), a collection of Walzer's major studies on Arab and Greek philosophies. The more extended of the older works are T. de Boer, *Geschichte der Philosophie im Islam* (Stuttgart, 1901), English translation, *The History of Philosophy in Islam* (2d ed., London, 1933), and M. Horten, *Die Philosophie des Islams* (1924). G. Quadri, *La filosofia degli arabi nel suo fiore* (1939), French translation. *La philosophie arabe ...* (Paris, 1947), beginning with a broad general picture of Arab philosophy, is neither clear nor reliable. We should call attention to M. Cruz Hernandez, *Historia de la filosofia hispano-musulmana*, two volumes (1957). A larger work by H. A. Wolfson is expected.

The relationship between Muslim and Jewish thought in the Middle Ages is such that a knowledge of the latter is indispensable. A basis for study and references will be found in G. Vajda, *Introduction à la pensée juive du Moyen Age* (Paris, 1947); and see the general histories of the Jews, above, p. 89.

On a few special aspects of Muslim thought, see, on ethics: M. Talbi, "Les bida'," *SI*, XII (1960), H. Bauer, *Islamische Ethik* (1953), a translation from al-Ghazālī; D. M. Donaldson, *Studies in Muslim Ethics* (1953); and in *EI*[2] the article "Akhlāḳ" by R. Walzer; on politics: E. Rosenthal, *Political Thought in Medieval Islam* (1958), a collection of studies on a certain number of thinkers; on economics: M. Plessner, *Der Oikonomikos des Neupythagoreers Bryson* (1933), the transmission of this Hellenistic author in Muslim thought.

The history of science, still in the preparatory stages because of the technical difficulty of the texts, has been the subject of a premature and inadequate study by A. Mieli, *La science arabe et son rôle dans l'évolution scientifique mondiale* (Paris, 1938). But some invaluable preliminary considerations and a clear albeit provisional synthesis will be found in the chapters by L. Massignon and R. Arnaldez in *Antiquité et moyen âge* (1957), Vol. I of *Histoire générale des sciences*, edited by R. Taton. See also J. H. Kramers in his posthumous *Analecta*, II (1956), and G. Wiet, cited p. 89. A good inventory with a bibliography (within the general framework of a universal chronological account of science) will also be found in G. Sarton, *Introduction to the History of Science*, three volumes, Vol. I (up to the eleventh century), II (twelfth-thirteenth), III, in two parts (fourteenth) (1927–1948).

In addition there are a few works of uneven quality on the history of particular disciplines:

Mathematics

H. Suter, *Die Mathematiker und Astronomen der Araber* (1900), a repertory that may be usefully complemented by M. Cantor, *Vorlesungen über Geschichte der Mathematik*, three volumes (1880–1898), and the article "D̲jabr" by W. Hartner in EI^2.

Astronomy and astrology

C. Nallino, *Astrologia, Astronomia,...* Vol. V of *Raccolta di scritti editi e inediti* (1946); G. Ferrand, *Introduction à l'astronomie nautique arabe* (1928).

Physics and natural sciences

No good general account; many special technical studies by E. Wiedemann in *Sitzungsberichte der Physikalisch-medizinischen Sozietät in Erlangen* (1920–1928) summarized in such articles in *EI* as "Kīmiyā'" (chemistry) and "Mīzān" (balance). *La chimie au moyen âge* by M. Berthelot (Paris, 1893) is now out of date; a brief account, up to date and with references, is to be found in E. J. Holmyard, *Alchemy* (1957). On agronomy, see pp. 136 and 220.

Medicine

The old *Histoire de la médecine arabe* by L. Leclerc (Paris, 1876) is still the only detailed repertory; a superficial introduction to the subject may be found in E. G. Browne, *Arabian Medicine* (1921), French translation and revision, H. P. J. Reinaud, *La médecine arabe* (1932); D. Campbell, *Arabian Medicine and its Influence on the Middle Ages* (1926); C. Elgood, *A Medical History of Persia and the Eastern Caliphate* (1951).

A good picture of various recent avenues of research may be obtained from the bibliography of the works of specialists, e.g., Uri Ben-Horin. *The Works of Max Meyerhof* (1944), or "J. Ruska und die Geschichte der Alchemie," *Abhandlungen zur Geschichte der Medizin und Naturwissenschaften*, XIX (1937).

History and geography

See above, pp. 29 ff. and 37 ff. Travelers' discoveries are studied chronologically (within the framework of a general study of the discoveries of all peoples) by R. Hennig, *Terrae incognitae*, four volumes (2d ed., 1950–1956); Arab maps are published by K. Miller, *Mappae Arabicae*, three volumes (1926–1927). See also Yūsuf Kamāl, *Monumenta cartographica Africae et Aegypti*, five volumes (1926–1951) and *Quelques éclaircissements épars sur mes Monumenta cartographica Africae et Aegypti* (1953).

Music

H. Farmer, *A History of Arabian Music* (1929); R. d'Erlanger, *La Musique arabe*, six volumes (1930–1960)—both are mainly theoretical because of the lack of actual musical examples.

See also below, p. 143.

To keep in touch with current developments, consult the periodicals devoted to the history of science, especially *Isis* and the bibliographies furnished since 1956 in *al-Andalus*, covering from 1945 on; also J. D. Pearson, *Index Islamicus* (cited p. 70) pp. 142–191 (beware of the arbitrary division between science and philosophy) and 269–279 (geography); also the *Abstracta*, cited p. 71.

LITERATURE

A definitive history of Arabic literature does not exist. A brief practical account is given in French by C. Pellat, *Langue et littérature arabe* (Paris, 1952), to which may be added the indications contained in J.-M. 'Abd el-Jalīl, *Brève histoire de la littérature arabe* (Paris, 1946). In English we have the excellent *Arabic Literature: An Introduction* by H. A. R. Gibb (London, 1926; rev. ed., 1963), to which must be added the well-informed and richly documented *A Literary History of the Arabs* by R. Nicholson, second edition with bibliography (Cambridge, 1930). In Italian there is the excellent little *Storia della letteratura araba* by F. Gabrieli (2d ed., Milan, 1956). In Arabic, Ḥannā al-Fākhūrī, *Ta'rīkh al-adab al-'arabī* (Harrissa, 1951). All these works base their information to a large extent on C. Brockelmann's inventory, in German, in *GAL*, cited p. 49.

A true *Histoire de la littérature arabe* with all the historical and literary detail expected of histories of our European literatures has been undertaken by R. Blachère. The first volume, devoted to methodological generalities and pre-Islamic literature, has appeared (Paris, 1952); and the second volume, on the first century of the Hijra, was published in 1964.

On Persian literature, four works are up to date: E. Bertels [*History of Persian Literature*], published posthumously (1959), in Russian, concerned only with ancient literature; *Dějiny perské a tadžické literatury* (*History of Persian and Tajik Literature*), edited by J. Rypka (Prague, 1956; 2d ed., 1963), in Czech; German translation, *Iranische Literaturgeschichte* (Leipzig, 1959); an English translation is announced. In English, A. J. Arberry, *Classical Persian Literature* (1958), is recent; and in Italian, A. Pagliaro and

A. Bausani, *Storia della letteratura persiana* (1960). E. G. Browne, *A Literary History of Persia*, four volumes (Cambridge, 1928–1930; reissued 1956–1959), for a long time was the standard work, and although it reflects the knowledge of half a century ago, it provides many useful details and a wealth of translations.

On Turkish literature, in addition to the general view to be found in the article "Turk" in *EI*, we now have an excellent account, though limited in length: A. Bombaci, *Storia della letteratura turca* (Milan, 1956); see also the *Fundamenta*, cited on p. 153, and *HO* (cited p. 67 f.) I, V/1.

Some idea of Muslim literature in translation may be obtained from the general anthologies, such as: in French, E. Dermenghem, *Les plus beaux textes arabes* (Paris, 1951), and H. Massé, *Anthologie persane* (Paris, 1950); in English, among others, S. Hillelson, *Week-end Caravan* (1947), R. Nicholson, *Translations of Eastern Poetry and Prose* (1922), and E. Schroeder, *Muhammad's People* (1955).

HISTORY OF ART

As we have already seen, the history of art has frequently received more attention than archaeology, but we still do not possess a good general history of Muslim art. The old *Manuel d'art musulman* (2d ed., 1927), by G. Migeon and H. Saladin no longer corresponds to the present development of the discipline. A work in several volumes according to region was intended to replace it; but the volumes that have appeared—those by Migeon on plastic and industrial arts and by G. Marçais on Muslim architecture in the West—must now themselves be replaced: the former by M. Dimand, *A Handbook of Muhammadan Art* (3d ed., New York, 1958), the latter by G. Marçais, cited p. 104. The only fairly detailed general account at the present time is by J. Pijoan, in *Arte islamico*, Vol. XII of *Summa artis* (Madrid, 1949), in Spanish; it is not without defects both in its plan and its descriptions. An initial introduction may be found in the good little *L'art de l'Islam* by G. Marçais (Paris, 1946), or in G. Wiet's article in R. Huyghe, *L'art et l'homme* (1958), and see J. Sourdel-Thomine in *Encyclopédie du Pleiade, Histoire de l'Art.* In German, see E. Kühnel, *Die Kunst des Islams* (1963). See also E. Lambert, *Art Musulman et art chrétien dans la péninsule ibérique* (1958). See also H. Glück and E. Diez, *Die Kunst des Islam* (2d ed., 1929).

To some extent the gap created by the lack of a good general history of Muslim art can be bridged by regional histories. The most important is A. U. Pope, A SURVEY OF PERSIAN ART, six volumes (New York, 1938–1939), with a separate index (London, 1958), a magnificent collection of documents but unevenly exploited. See also *Ars hispaniae*, eighteen volumes (Madrid,

1946–1962), Vol. III, M. Gómez-Moreno, *El Arte Árabe Español hasta los Almohades; Arte Mozárabe* (1951); Vol. IV, L. Torres Balbás, *Arte Almohade, Arte Nazarí, Arte Mudéjar* (1949).

On archaeology see also p. 57 ff.

On some examples of questions relating the history of art to history in the wider sense, see: E. Kühnel, "Kunst und Volkstum im Islam," *WI*, I (1951), and *Kunst und Kultur der arabischen Welt* (Heidelberg, 1942); F. Gabrieli, "Correlations entre la littérature et l'art" in *Classicisme*, cited p. 96 f.; R. Ettinghausen, "Introduction and Integration in Islamic Art" in *Unity and Variety*, cited p. 86, and in particular the same author's *The Unicorn* (Washington, 1950); G. Marçais, "La question des images dans l'art musulman," *Byzantion*, VII (1932); L. Massignon, "Les méthodes de réalisation artistique des peuples de l'Islam," *Syria*, II (1921). To certain branches of art, a number of studies have been devoted, some significant, others at least useful. In the case of architecture, the outstanding books are confined to a single area: G. Marçais, *L'architecture musulmane d'Occident* (1954) (but H. Terrasse, *L'art hispano-mauresque des origines au XIIIe siècle* [1932] should still be consulted), and K. A. C. Creswell, *The Muslim Architecture of Egypt*, I (1952), including the Fāṭimids, II (1959), including the early Baḥrīs, which may be supplemented with the help of L. Hautecoeur and G. Wiet, cited p. 183; see also Creswell's *Fortification in Islam before A.D. 1250* (1952), a useful booklet; and L. Golvin, *La mosquée* (1960). D. Hill and O. Grabar are preparing a study of Islamic architecture and its decoration.

For the other branches of art, see above all E. Kühnel, *Islamische Kleinkunst* (1925); M. Dimand, *A Handbook of Mohammedan Decorative Arts*, fourth edition (1944); Arthur Lane, *Early Islamic Pottery* (1947), and *Later Islamic Pottery* (1957); R. Ettinghausen, *Arab Painting* (1962); on Oriental carpets, K. Erdmann, *Der orientalische Knüpfteppich* (1955); on the art of bookmaking, Sir T. W. Arnold and A. Grohmann, *The Islamic Book* (1929), and J. Pedersen, *Den arabiske bog* (1946). See above, the section on archaeology, and below, various chapters on the different periods and countries.

L. A. Mayer inaugurated a new genre with the study of *Islamic Architects and Their Works* (Geneva, 1950), and *Islamic Woodcarvers and Their Works* (1958).

PART III

Historical Bibliography

14

The Near East and Arabia on the Eve of the Advent of Islam

THE NEAR EAST (EXCLUDING ARABIA)

The history of the Muslim world is essentially the history of the encounter between certain traditions of the Arab society within which Islam came into being and the traditions of a series of societies of ancient civilization that were conquered by Islam and the Arabs. Some idea of these societies is therefore necessary before approaching the history of Islam itself. We shall deal with the Arabs and Arabia in more detail since they have been neglected in the standard works on the ancient world; but we shall refer the reader to the latter for information on the other societies in question. This does not mean that the history of Islam can be founded on the Arab substratum alone, and a few reminders of the state of the Near East and of the Mediterranean countries in general on the eve of the Muslim conquest are necessary. At the same time it must be stressed that the documentary gap separating the seventh century—on which we are well informed through Byzantine sources—and the ninth—when we can begin to make use of the Arabic sources—makes the history during this period particularly difficult to reconstruct. Egypt is the only exception to this rule, thanks to the papyri; her exceptional position, however, precludes automatic application of what we observe in her to the other countries.

The basic works to be consulted for the study of the Near East from the fifth to the seventh centuries are the following:

The Sassanian Empire

A. Christensen, *L'Iran sous les Sassanides* (2d ed., Copenhagen and Paris, 1944), which scarcely conceals from the attentive reader the sharp gaps in documentation, is largely based on writers of the Muslim period whose view of the Persian past was colored by their new perspectives. It must be supplemented by N. V. Pigulevskaya, *Les Villes de l'État Iranien*, translated from the Russian (Paris, 1963), which puts to best account the important Syriac sources for the period; French translation, 1963, *Les villes de l'état iranien aux époques parthe et sassanide.* See also R. Ghirshmann, *L'Iran des origines à l'Islam* (1951); English translation, *Iran from the Earliest Times to the Islamic Conquest* (1954).

The Byzantine Empire

The masterly *Geschichte des byzantinischen Staates* by G. Ostrogorsky (2d ed., 1952); French translation, *Histoire ...* (1954); English, *History of the Byzantine State* (1956); Italian (1956). See also N. Baynes, *The Byzantine Empire* (1925 and reprints), and Baynes and H. Moss, *Byzantium. An Introduction to East Roman Civilization* (1948). Important information on the religious situation may be supplemented by *Histoire de l'eglise*, edited by A. Fliche and V. Martin (Paris, 1934——), Vol. IV, *De la mort de Théodose à l'élection de Grégoire le Grand* by P. de Labriolle *et al*, (1937), and Vol. V, *Grégoire le Grand, les états Barbares et la conquête Arabe* by L. Bréhier and R. Aigrain (1938); and, on Armenia and Georgia see R. Grousset, *Histoire de l'Arménie, des origines à 1071* (1947), and W. E. D. Allen, *A History of the Georgian People* (1932). The study of the provinces of the Byzantine Empire that the Arabs were about to conquer is as important as that of its history in general and of its central government. It is a particularly unproductive task in the case of Syria, on which studies at present in progress in Paris will shed much light; for Egypt, see especially A. C. Johnson and L. West, *Byzantine Egypt: Economic Studies* (Princeton, 1949), E. Hardy, *Christian Egypt* (1952), and H. Bell, *Egypt from Alexander the Great to the Arab Conquest* (1948); for North Africa, C.-A. Julien, *Histoire de l'Afrique du Nord*, second edition, Vol. I, rewritten by C. Courtois (1951), will suffice; for Sicily and southern Italy, in addition to the general histories of Italy, such as the recent collective *Storia politica d'Italia* edited by A. Solmi (Milan, 1938–1955) in twelve volumes, the following studies are still valid: C. Diehl, *Études sur l'administration byzantine dans l'Exarchat de Ravenne* (1889), and L. Hartmann, *Untersuchungen zur Geschichte der byzantinischen Verwaltung in Italien* (1889).

Spain under the Visigoths

História de España, edited by R. Menéndez Pidal, Vol. III, cited p. 67.

PRE-ISLAMIC ARABIA

Pre-Islamic Arabia should be studied by the historian of Islam not merely because acquaintance with it constitutes a preface to his work but because a knowledge of the earlier Arab society determines that of Muslim society itself more than is usual in the case of other cultures. In spite of the apparent paradox, accounted for by a kind of racial mysticism and the fact that a knowledge of the language and tradition of pre-Islamic Arabic is indispensable for the understanding of the sacred texts of Islam, Muslims have always considered the time of "Ignorance" as the golden age of Arabism, during which the traditional virtues of the race flourished to a degree unrivaled since. Moreover, as many pre-Islamic customs were sanctioned by Muḥammad, many of the characteristics of the old pagan society survived after paganism disappeared. A knowledge of these customs is important. Just as important is the knowledge of customs to which the Prophet objected.

Our knowledge of pre-Islamic Arabia is undergoing modification at the present time with the discovery, in the course of the gradual exploration of the territory, of a considerable number of inscriptions. Their value on the average is slight, save in the case of South Arabia, but, as a whole they acquire considerable significance in view of the scarcity of information from more traditional sources, most of which, moreover, come from outside Arabia. For this reason, the old general accounts are of limited value today even though a recent synthesis has yet to replace them.

The inscriptions are usually divided into four groups: the Southern Arabian, the Central Arabian (usually called Thamudean), the Northern (Safaitic), and those of the Syro-Mesopotamian borders (Nabatean). The Nabateans make use of an alphabet of their own (related to the Aramaic), which was destined to become the classical Arabic alphabet, whereas the Thamudeans and the Safaites use the South Arabian alphabet with their North Arabian dialect. The inscriptions may be found in the *Corpus Inscriptionum Semiticarum*, of which have appeared six volumes of South Arabian inscriptions (4th section, 1889–1932) and a first volume of Safaitic inscriptions (5th section, 1950–1951). They are also available, more succinctly and with only brief reference to earlier editions, in the *Répertoire d'épigraphie sémitique*, edited by C. S. Clermont-Ganneau and J. Chabot, seven volumes (1900–1950). "The Safaitic Inscriptions," by E. Littmann, in *Syria. Publications of the Princeton Univ. Archaeological Expeditions to Syria in 1904–05 and 1909. Division IV/3* (Leiden, 1943), should be consulted for the sake of the introduction. To this should be added F. Winnett,

Safaitic Inscriptions from Jordan (1958). The Thamudean inscriptions have been collected by A. Van den Branden (1950), but his interpretation should be reëxamined in the light of J. Ryckmans, "Aspects nouveaux du problème thamoudéen," *SI*, V (1956), 5–17. On the language, see W. Caskel, *Lihyan und Lihyanisch* (Cologne, 1954). For those acquainted with the language and the script, there is an introduction of the South Arabian inscriptions in C. Conti Rossini, *Chrestomathia Arabica meridionalis epigraphica* (1931), which also provides the texts of ancient authors on the subject of Arabia; the voluminous work by J. Ryckmans, *Les noms propres sud-sémitiques*, three volumes (1934–1935), is also extremely useful. For the Nabatean inscriptions, see the works cited on p. 113. There is also an *Altsüdarabische Grammatik* by Maria Höfner (1943).

The extremely difficult archaeological exploration of the territory has hardly begun in spite of the importance of the South Arabian ruins, which run the risk of being destroyed by modern civilization before they can be protected. See R. le Baron Bowen and W. F. Albright, *Archaeological Discoveries in South Arabia* (Baltimore, 1958).

For the reasons already indicated the Muslim writers tried to gather the traditions of their Arab past, and they have for a long time provided us with a unique source of material. For South Arabia, particular mention should be made of *al-Iklīl* by al-Ḥamdānī, the geographer and historian, of which the following volumes have been found to date: Vol. I, edited by O. Löfgren in Bibliotheca Ekmaniana Universitatis Regiae Upsaliensis (1954); Vol. II, unpublished; Vol. VIII, edited by F. Anastase-Marie, O. Carm. (Baghdad, 1931), and by N. A. Faris, Princeton Orientalt exts, VII (Princeton and London, 1940), of which he made an English translation, *The Antiquities of South Arabia*, Princeton Oriental texts, III (Princeton and London, 1938); and Vol. X, edited by Muḥibb al-Dīn al Khaṭīb (Cairo, 1949). Note also a recent work in Russian by A. Lundin, ["South Arabia in the Sixth Century"] *Palestinski Sbornik*, VIII (Moscow and Leningrad, 1961). On the subject of pre-Islamic deities, see Ibn al-Kalbī, *K. al-Aṣnām*, second edition by A. Zakī Pasha (1924), German translation by R. Klincke-Rosenberger (1941), English translation by N. A. Faris, *The Book of Idols* (1952). We can no longer regard with the confidence of our predecessors the data derived from the so-called pre-Islamic poetry, since Ṭāhā Ḥusain demonstrated, in his *Fi 'l-shi'r al-jāhilī* (1926), the doubtfulness of their authenticity. They cannot, nevertheless, be rejected altogether, since this very uncertainty results precisely from the conservatism of their form and subject matter; see R. Blachère, *Histoire de la littérature arabe*, cited p. 102.

The data obtained from contemporary ethnographical studies are particularly important here, for which see p. 79.

From A. Caussin de Perceval, *Essai sur l'histoire des Arabes avant l'Islamisme*, three volumes (1847–1848), to M. Guidi, *Storia e cultura degli Arabi fino alla morte di Maometto* (1951), the general history of pre-Islamic Arabia has been the subject of various accounts to which the articles "'Arab" and "'Arab (Djazīrat al-)" in *EI*², and Y. Moubarac, "Éléments de bibliographie sud-sémitique," *REI*, XXIII (1955), will act as guides. A short but up-to-date summary by S. Moscati may be found in his *Storia e civiltà dei Semiti* (1949), French translation (1955), in English (London, 1957); also in the chapter, "L'Arabie avant l'Islam," by M. Rodinson in Vol. II of *Histoire universelle* in the *Encyclopêdie de la Plêiade* (1957); and in the chapter, "Pre-Islamic Arabia," by G. Levi Della Vida in *The Arab Heritage*, edited by N. A. Faris *et al.* (New York, 1946). See also A. Grohmann, *Arabien* in *Handbuch der Altertumswissenschaft*, edited by W. Otto, 3. Abt., 1.Teil, 3. Bd. 3. Abschnitt, 4 (1963). I. Guidi, *L'Arabie antêislamique* (1921), and De Lacy E. O'Leary, *Arabia before Mohammed* (1927), may also be consulted provided they are brought up to date by comparison with other sources, which also applies to the articles by C. Nallino collected in the third volume of his *Raccolta* cited on p. 88. In Arabic there has recently been published by Jawād 'Alī, *Ta'rīkh al-'arab qabl al-islām* (Baghdad, 1951–1956). F. Altheim and R. Stiehl are preparing a five-volume study on *Die Araber in der alten Welt*, Vol. I of which appeared (1963).

On certain aspects of the general history of pre-Islamic Arabia one may also consult F. Hommel, *Ethnologie und Geographie des alten Orients*, in *Handbuch der Altertumswissenschaft*, III/I/1 (1926); G. Ryckmans, "Les religions arabes pré-islamiques," which was reprinted from Vol. IV of the *Histoire des religions*, by M. Gorce and R. Mortier (Paris, 1947), and which lists facts mainly based on epigraphical material; N. V. Pigulevskaia, *Vizantiia na putiakh v Indiu* (*Byzantium on the Routes to India*) (1951), which will help to place the Arabs, on the eve of Islam, within the context of the economic and political conflicts between the neighboring empires. On the political history of the peninsula during the same period, see S. Smith, "Events in Arabia in the VIth Century," *BSOAS*, XVI (1954).

The first and only published volume of the *Handbuch der altarabischen Altertumskunde* by D. Nielsen (1927), is devoted entirely to South Arabia, indeed a whole world in itself. The contribution by N. Rhodokanakis on public life is, even now, especially useful. The accepted chronology was recently challenged, on the basis of considerations of interest at least from a methodological point of view, by Jacqueline Pirenne, *La Grèce et Saba*

(1955), and *Des origines à l'époque himyarite*, Vol. I of *Paléographie des inscriptions sud-arabiques* (1956).

On the question of religion: consult A. Jamme, *La religion sudarabique pré-islamique*, Vol. IV of *Histoire des religions* (1953), edited by M. Brillant and R. Aigrain; W. F. Albright, "Islam and the Religions of the Ancient Orient," *JAOS*, LX (1940); H. von Wissmann and M. Höfner, *Beiträge zur historischen Geographie des vorislamischen Südarabien* (1953); and N. V. Pigulevskaia, "Les rapports sociaux à Nedjran au début du VIe siècle," *JESHO*, III-IV (1960–1961). See also, by A. Grohmann, "Göttersymbole und Symboltiere auf südarabischen Denkmälern," *Denkschrift der Akademie der Wissenschaften, Wien*, vol. 58 (1914), and *Arabien*, cited on p. 111.

Most of the works devoted to the general history of pre-Islamic Arabia ignore South Arabia completely and concentrate mainly on the area and milieu in which Islam was to appear. The beginner may approach these questions through the introductions to most of the works on Muḥammad, such as those by M. Gaudefroy-Demombynes and W. Montgomery Watt, cited p. 117. The most important general survey, despite a certain amount of exaggeration of fact, is still that by H. Lammens, who, on the basis of literary works, undertook the description of the cradle of Islam in all its physical and human aspects in *Le berceau de l'Islam*, of which only the first volume has appeared (1914). Important complementary studies, however, have been published by him: "La Cité arabe de Taif à la veille de l'hégire" and "La Mecque à la veille de l'hégire," *MFO*, VIII (1922) and IX (1924), and also a group of studies collected under the title *L'Arabie occidentale à la veille de l'hégire* (1928). On the subject of the Bedouins in particular—who differ in many respects from the urban societies, even in Arabia—see the surveys by H. von Wissmann and others *s.v.* "Badw" in *EI*², which are uneven, and by J. Henninger *et al.* in *L'Antica società beduina*, a collection published by F. Gabrieli (1959); also W. Caskel, "Zur Beduinisierung Arabiens," *ZDMG*, CIII (1953), 28–36, or in *Studies in Islamic Cultural History*, edited by G. E. von Grunebaum (Chicago, 1954), expresses a number of ideas that have not received general assent. For the sociological point of view, see J. Chelhod, *Introduction à la sociologie de l'Islam* (1958), which is interesting but too theoretical and insufficiently supported by factual evidence.

Among the older works devoted to more specific questions, note: J. Wellhausen, *Reste arabischen Heidentums*, Vol. I of his *Skizzen und Vorarbeiten* (2d ed., 1897), dealing with pre-Islamic religion as described by Islamic writers or as manifested in the Muslim religion itself; on the family as an institution, W. Robertson Smith, *Kinship and Marriage in Early Arabia* (2d ed., 1903), on which see the article by J. Lecerf cited on p. 88; on weapons of war, F. W. Schwarzlose, *Die Waffen der alten Araber* (1886); among more recent works, B. Farès, *L'Honneur chez les arabes avant l'Islam* (1932); J. Henninger, "La sacrifice chez les arabes," *Ethnos*, XIII (1948), more reliable than J. Chelhod, *La sacrifice chez les arabes* (1955); H. Ringgren, *Studies in Arabian Fatalism* (1956), which also touches on Islam; and M. Hamidullah, "Les rapports économico-diplomatiques de la Mecque," *Melânges Louis Massignon* (1956–1957), II, 293–311.

On Christianity in pre-Islamic Arabia, the essential background material is still to be found in the article "Arabie" by R. Aigrain in the *Dictionnaire d'histoire et de géographie ecclésiastique* (1912–1924); and see R. Bell, *The Origins of Islam in its Christian Environment* (1926) and the bibliography on Muḥammad in chapter 15.

The Arabs spread very early beyond Arabia proper; in particular they came into contact with the Byzantine and Sassanian empires. Although the influences to which they were there exposed set them apart from the other Arabs, the information which we possess of them, which is frequently superior to what we know of the peninsular Arabs, can yet contribute to the understanding of what accounts we have of the latter. Considerable information has been brought together in R. Dussaud, *La pénétration des arabes en Syrie avant l'Islam* (1955). Petra and Palmyra were the two main centers of Arab settlement in contact with Byzantine Syria. Petra is the subject of a general study by A. Kammerer, *Pétra et la Nabatène*, two volumes (1929–1930), inadequate, but not yet superseded. On Palmyra, J. Fevrier, *Essai sur l'histoire politique et économique de Palmyre* (1931), published prior to recent discoveries, should be supplemented and brought up to date with the help of the following: H. Seyrig, *Antiquités syriennes*, five volumes (1934–1958); D. Schlumberger, *La Palmyrène du nord-ouest* (1951); J. Starcky, *Palmyre* (1952) and the chapter "Palmyréniens, nabatéens et arabes du nord avant l'Islam," in *Histoire des religions*, IV (Paris 1956) edited by M. Brillant and R. Aigrain.

Two principalities, the Ghassānids on the borders of Syria and the Lakhmids of Ḥīra on the borders of Iraq, were established in this period, the former by the Byzantines and the latter by the Sassanians. As far as the Lakhmids are concerned, the account by Th. Nöldeke, *Geschichte der Perser und Araber zur Zeit der Sasaniden* (1879), itself entirely based on Ṭabarī, has never been surpassed, and the subject remains little known, although some interesting remarks have been made by W. Seston, "Le roi sassanide Nersès, les arabes et le manichéisme," in *Mélanges syriens ... R. Dussaud* (1939), 227–234. The Ghassānids are better known, and to Nöldeke, *Die Ghassanischen Fürsten* (1887), should be added, especially with respect to their religious life and their relations with Byzantium,

F. Nau, *Les arabes chrétiens de Mésopotamie et de Syrie du VIIe au VIIIe siècle* (1935); H. Charles, *Le christianisme des arabes nomades sur le Limes* (1936); R. Devreesse, "Arabes perses et Arabes romains," *Vivre et penser*, second series (1942), 263–307, and *Le patriarcat d'Antioche depuis la paix de l'église jusqu'à la conquête arabe* (1945), and the research done by I. Kawar, for example in *Arabica*, III (1957) and V (1958), and by Roger Paret, *ibid.*

Finally, a knowledge of the history of the Red Sea and of Arabian-Ethiopian relations is necessary. A. Kammerer, *Essai sur l'histoire antique de l'Abyssinie et ses voisins d'Arabie* (1926) and *La Mer Rouge, l'Abyssinie et l'Arabie depuis l'antiquité* (up to the sixteenth century), five volumes (1929–1949), though insufficiently critical, will be of use, as will be the histories of Ethiopia such as that by C. Conti Rossini, *Storia d'Etiopia*, I (1928), and by J. Coulbeaux, *Histoire politique et réligieuse d'Abyssinie* (1929).

Aramaic loanwords in ancient Arabic have been provisionally studied by S. Fränkel, *Die aramäischen Fremdwörter im Arabischen* (1886).

15

Muhammad

THE MAN

In comparison with most founders of religions, Muḥammad appears to us as a truly historical character. It does not follow, however, that a really reliable biography of him can be established. His message can be found in the Koran, but it would be useless to expect it to provide us with information about his life or his role as the head of a state. All our information on these aspects of his personality comes from the *ḥadīth*, the limitations of which, from a historical point of view, have already been noted. No amount of historical criticism—in any case, not easy to apply here—can transform this mass of anecdotes into a reliable source of information. Moreover, Muḥammad, already legendary in his lifetime, belongs as much to the field of hagiography as to that of history, if not more so. But to restrict research to an exact assessment of the man would neglect an important aspect of the question, since the idea subsequently formed of him—one of the principal sources of inspiration in Islamic thought—also deserves to be known. In addition, the traditional data concerning the life of the Prophet are the key to many later events. A biography of Muḥammad can only be written with both the firm intention of critically establishing the historical facts and the awareness of a kind of perpetual oscillation between an almost intangible reality and an interpretative legend, which is at once distorting and enlightening. Needless to say, whether one subscribes to the Muslim faith or not, one should study the life of Muḥammad with the sympathy due all great and sincere efforts on the part of man to attain a higher mode of life.

A study of the sources for the life of Muḥammad and his immediate successors must rely mainly on the ANNALI DELL'ISLAM by L. Caetani, ten volumes (1905–1926), which supplies for each event in the texts, all the versions in chronological order together with a detailed critical analysis: Vol. I: A.H. 1–6: II: 7–12; III: 13–17; IV: 18–22; V: 23; VI: index for I–V; VII: 24–32; VIII: 32–35; IX: 36–37; X: 38–40.

The *ḥadīth* material (see above, p. 28) relating to the life of the Prophet was collected and made usable mainly by Ibn Isḥāq in his SĪRA in the recension of Ibn Hishām (early ninth century), edited by F. Wüstenfeld, two volumes (1858–1860), and also edited in Cairo by M. Saqqā and I. Ibyārī (1936) and by M. Muhyī al-Dīn (1937); English translation by A. Guillaume (1955), who also made a study of a recently discovered recension by Ibn Bukair, *New Light on the Life of Muhammad* (1960). The *Kitāb al-Maghāzī* by al-Wāqidī was edited by J. Wellhausen (1882), in Cairo (1948), and by J. B. M. Jones (1964), and the *Ṭabaqāt* by his disciple, Ibn Sa'd (d. 845), which gives biographies of the "companions" and "successors," generation by generation, was edited by E. Sachau *et al.* in fifteen volumes (1905–1940). On how to make use of this material, see Levi Della Vida's article "Sīra" in *EI*, and concerning H. Lammens' studies C. H. Becker, "Prinzipielles zu Lammens' Sīrastudien," *Islam*, IV (1913), 263–269, or in his *Islamstudien*, I, cited p. 86.

The life of Muḥammad has given rise to a large number of scholarly publications, not to mention works of fiction and polemical or popular apologetic works that the historian should obviously regard with suspicion. An introduction to the principal problems involved will be found in R. Blachère, *Le problème de Mahomet* (1952), in the article "Muḥammad" by F. Buhl in *EI*, and in R. Paret, *Mohammed und der Koran* (1957).

One should also mention the older biographies of Muḥammad by A. Sprenger, *Das Leben und die Lehre des Mohammed nach bisher grösstenteils unbenutzten Quellen bearbeitet*, three volumes (Berlin, 1861–1865) and H. Grimme, *Mohammed*, two volumes (Münster I. W., 1892–1895), even though their fundamental concepts belong to another age. A readable version of the traditional material is found in W. Muir, *The Life of Mohammed* (1858–1861), revised edition by T. Weir (1923), and better still in E. Dermenghem, *La vie de Mahomet*, (2d ed., 1950), English translation (1930). For a more detailed account, see F. Buhl, *Das Leben Muhammads* (1903), revised edition in Swedish (1953), German translation (1930; reissued 1955). The works that form the basis of our more recent understanding of Muḥammad are by Tor Andrae, MUHAMMAD, HIS LIFE AND DOCTRINE, in Swedish (1930), English translation (1936, New York, 1957), German translation (1936), French translation (1945), Italian (1934), and *Die Person Muhammeds in Lehre und Glauben seiner Gemeinde* (1918). More recently, K. Ahrens, *Muhammad als Religionsstifter* (1935), gives a usable account of the teachings of the Prophet of Islam.

The main work of recent years has been done by M. Gaudefroy-Demombynes and W. Montgomery Watt. In MUHAMMAD AT MECCA (1953), French translation (1957), MUHAMMAD AT MEDINA (1956), French translation (1959), and *Muhammad, Prophet and Statesman* (1961), the latter has given us a new understanding of the meaning of Muḥammad's activity within the particular social environment in which he lived. The work entitled MAHOMET, Vol. XXXII in the collection *L'évolution de l'humanité* (Paris, 1957), completed by M. Gaudefroy-Demombynes at the age of ninety-four, is not always abreast of more recent research (and beware of misprints), but it deserves to be mentioned as an example of the way in which scientific objectivity can be combined with human sympathy in the study of a man endowed with a strong personality, when the author is equipped with a knowledge of his social background. The life of Muḥammad is dealt with first, then his message, providing a wealth of information not to be found in other works. More recently M. Rodinson (1961) has produced a simpler but careful study on the subject.

It is interesting to compare these accounts with that of a contemporary educated Muslim, M. Hamidullah, *Mahomet, le prophète de l'Islam*, two volumes (1959), which concerns itself especially with Muḥammad's activity as the head of an emergent state.

On Muḥammad's family, see N. Abbott, *Aïsha, the Beloved of Mohammed* (1942), and H. Lammens, *Fatima et les filles de Mahomet* (1912).

THE KORAN

The Koran is the message transmitted by Muḥammad. The edition most used in Europe is that by G. Flügel, *Corani textus Arabicus* (1881), because Flügel also prepared the *Concordantiae Corani Arabicae* (2d ed., 1925), an index of all words including conjunctions and prepositions, as an easy means of placing all the verses in the text and identifying the constantly recurring quotations found in Arabic texts of all kinds. One should note, however, that the verse numbers given by Flügel do not correspond to those of the official Egyptian edition (1347/1928), which is used by Muslims, to which there now exist two concordances by M. Barakāt, *al-Murshid ilā āyāt al-Qur'ān al-karīm* (Damascus, 1358/1939), and by Muḥammad 'Abd al-Bāqī, *al-Mu'jam al-mufahras* (Cairo, 1364/1945).

Probably no translation of the Koran into a European language can ever render both its outstanding literary merit and its rigorously exact sense, still often the subject of controversy. Of the older translations one should mention J. Rodwell (1876) and E. Palmer (1880). The translation that comes closest to satisfying the critical exigencies of the historian is that by R. Blachère, *Le Coran* (1947–1950), in which he reconstructs the probable order of the suras, while in another edition (1957), which is easier to use, he returns to the traditional order without comment. The same spirit at work is to be found in the English version by R. Bell, *The Qur'an*, two volumes (1937–1939). A. J. Arberry, *The Koran Interpreted* (1955), aims at rendering in English the spirit and flavor of the Koranic original.

The study of the Koran is made difficult by the fact, recognized by all commentators, that the original official edition by the caliph 'Uthmān was made without any reference to the chronological order of the chapters. Many of these, in turn, probably contain originally independent passages that have been grouped together. The Koranic commentaries (*tafsīr*) by the great ancient Muslim scholars, of which one of the most important and oldest is that by Ṭabarī, are still indispensable. For modern study, however, the basic work is the GESCHICHTE DES QORÂNS by Th. Nöldeke, of which the second edition was completed by F. Schwally and G. Bergsträsser, three volumes (1909–1938). This should be supplemented with the following: A. Jeffery, *Materials for the History of the Text of the Qur'ān* (1937) and his *The Qur'ān as Scripture* (1952); the introduction by R. Blachère to his own translation; R. Bell, *Introduction to the Qur'ān* (1953); and R. Paret, *Grenzen der Koranforschung* (1950).

Attempts to understand the Koran have always led both believers and scholars to study its vocabulary. Studies such as R. Blachère, "Note sur le substantif nafs, 'souffle vital,' 'âme,' dans le Coran," *Semitica*, I (1948), 69–77, or I. Goldziher, "Muruwwa und Dīn," in his *Muhammadanische Studien* (1889–1890), I, discussed by M. Bravmann in "On the Spiritual Background of Early Islam and the History of its Principal Concepts," *Le Muséon*, LXIV (1951), 317–365, can be mentioned as examples. A. Jeffery has discussed the important problem of foreign loanwords in *The Foreign Vocabulary of the Qur'ān* (1938), and J. Horovitz has discussed foreign proper names in his *Koranische Untersuchungen* (1926), partly translated into English in the *Hebrew Union College Annual*, II (1925). R. Brunschvig, "Simples remarques négatives sur le vocabulaire du Coran," *SI*, V (1956), 19–32, shows the value of the study of the Koran from the point of view of words missing that one might expect to find there.

Among studies on the various aspects of Koranic teaching, should be mentioned: T. O'Shaughnessy, "The Development of the Meaning of Spirit in the Koran," *Analecta Christiana Orientalia*, CXXXIX (1953) (cf. R. Blachère above, p. 117); P. Eichler, *Die Dschinn, Teufel und Engel im Koran* (1928); H. Ringgren, "The Conception of Faith in the Qoran," *Oriens*, IV (1951), 1–20; and interestingly, although drawing conclusions which have not been widely adopted, P. Casanova, *Mohammed et la fin du monde* (1911–1924). See also H. Birkeland, *The Lord Guideth. Studies in Primitive Islam* (Oslo, 1956). There is also a study by R. Roberts, *The Social Laws of the Qoran* (1925).

The study of the origins of Islam has long included, in Western research, not only the character and work of Muḥammad, but also the influence of neighboring religions. Muḥammad's contacts with the Jews and the influence of Judaism on him have been dealt with by A. Geiger, *Was hat Muhhammad aus den Judenthume aufgenommen* (1893, reprinted 1902); A. J. Katsh, *Judaism in Islam, Biblical and Talmudic Backgrounds of the Koran and its Commentaries* (1954); A. J. Wensinck, *Mohammed en de Joden te Medina* (2d ed., 1928), partly translated by G.-H. Bousquet in *RA*, XCIX (1955); Z. Hirschberg, *Israel in Arabia* (1946), and S. D. Goitein, *Jews and Arabs* (New York, 1955), See also H. Speyer, *Die biblischen Erzählungen im Qoran* (reissued, 1961). Concerning the Christian environment, which may be studied for its relationship to the Koranic message, see Tor Andrae, *Der Ursprung des Islam und das Christentum* (1926), of which there is a French translation, *Les origines de l'Islam et le Christianisme* (1955), and R. Bell, *The Origin of Islam in its Christian Environment* (1926). And concerning the combination of both influences as a source of Muslim legend, see D. Sidersky, *Les origines des légendes musulmanes dans le Coran et dans les vies du prophète* (1933).

The tendency today is to look less for precise textual borrowings than to try to reconstruct the ideological atmosphere and the general religious evolution characteristic of the conditions under which the Prophet of Islam developed in contact with the Jewish and Christian faiths then penetrating Arabia. In this connection, attention has recently been drawn to the necessity of reconsidering the Arab milieu itself, a consideration of major importance. This has been facilitated by archaeological discoveries such as those surveyed by Y. Moubarac, "Les études d'épigraphie sud-sémitique et la naissance de l'Islam," *REI*, XXV (1957). For Semitic connections see G. Widengren, *Muḥammad, The Apostle of God and his Ascension* (1955), which places the twin concepts of "apostle" and "ascension" in the common stock of Semitic ideas, and for ancient Oriental links, see C. Dubler, "Survivances de l'ancien orient dans l'Islam," *SI*, VII (1957), 47–75. See also the interesting suggestions by R. Serjeant, "Ḥaram and Ḥawtah, the Sacred Enclave in Arabia," *Mélanges Taha Husain* (Cairo, 1962). Y. Moubarac, *Abraham dans le Coran* (1958), J.-M. 'Abd el-Jalīl, *Marie et l'Islam* (1950); J. Jomier, *Bible et Coran* (1959); D. Masson, *Le Coran et la révélation judéo-chrétienne* (1959); and M. Hayek, *Le Christ de l'Islam* (1959), are inspired by a concern for Muslim-Christian contacts and exchanges. Data and comparisons—correct in themselves—are given an emphasis, however, they do not have within the perspective of Islamic history.

Finally, an interest is being shown in the sociological aspect of the origins of Islam. Concerning the various opinions on this question, see the account by M. Rodinson, "La vie de Mahomet et le problème sociologique des origines de l'Islam," *Diogène*, XX (1957). The same author has compiled a general bibliographical review of recent works dealing with Muḥammad, man and teaching, in *RH*, 229 (1963), 169–220.

16

The Rāshidūn (Rightly-Guided) and Umayyad Caliphs and the Arab Conquests

SOURCES

The chief difficulty in studying the first century of Muslim history, which saw the conquest of an empire and the early organization of the caliphate, lies in the fact that, with the exception of the Egyptian papyri (see above, p. 16 ff.), the indigenous (Syriac) and the Byzantine sources are very scanty. Arabic sources appear late and despite quotations from earlier narrators are corrupted not only by the passage of time but also by the selection and suppression of evidence carried out under the influence of the 'Abbāsid caliphs who were the adversaries and successors of the Umayyads.

The ANNALS of Ṭabarī are by far the most important source and reproduce versions of several of his predecessors, dealing mainly, however, with Mesopotamia and Iran and almost entirely neglecting the Muslim West including Syria, which was the seat of the Umayyad government.

It is preferable to follow the standard edition by M. J. de Goeje *et al.*, fifteen volumes (Leiden, 1879–1901), divided into three sections each with its own pagination: Vol. I, The Jāhilīya and the Beginnings of Islam; Vol. II, The Umayyads; Vol. III, The 'Abbāsids to A.H. 311. Each volume begins with a summary in Latin: the last volume contains an index and glossary. A useful summary by I. Guidi for the years 648–717 will be found in *RL*, I (1925), 352–407. The French translation by H. Zotenberg of an abridged Persian version (reprinted, 1958), naturally cannot replace the original. See also a translation into English by E. Marin, *The Reign of al-Mu'taṣim*, American Oriental series, XXXV (1951).

The other chronicles are not as detailed as Ṭabarī, but as their inspiration and sources are different, they may serve to rectify and supplement his work. The most important general chronicles are by the Shī'ite, Ya'qūbī (called Ibn Wāḍiḥ and also known as a geographer, see p. 135), *Historiae*, edited by M. Th. Houtsma, two volumes (1883), and by Abū Ḥanīfa al-Dīnawarī, *al-Akhbār al-ṭiwāl*, edited by V. Guirgass (1888), with additions and corrections by I. I. Krachkovskii (Leiden, 1912), both dating from the third/ninth century. To these should be added a chronicle, which has not been preserved *in toto*, by an anonymous Northwest African author of the sixth/eleventh century, edited by M. J. de Goeje in *Fragmenta Historicorum Arabicorum*, I (1871), which contains some original information on the later Umayyads, that is from Walīd I, and the first 'Abbāsids. Halfway between the historical and the *adab* literatures are the *'Uyūn al-akhbār* by Ibn Qutaiba (d. 889), which are very valuable; they were partially edited by C. Brockelmann in four volumes (1900–1908), with a complete edition, in four volumes (Cairo, 1925–1930), and there is a partial translation by J. Horovitz in *IC*, IV–V (1930–1931). The MURŪJ AL-DHAHAB (*The Meadows—or Washings—of Gold*) by Mas'ūdī is a history in anecdote form of the various caliphs, edited and translated by A. J.-B. Pavet de Courteille and A. C. Barbier de Meynard, nine volumes (1861–1877), also in Baghdad (1938), and of which C. Pellat has begun a revised translation in French, the first volume of which appeared (Paris, 1962). P. Griaznevich, the Russian scholar, published a text by an anonymous author of the eleventh century that throws new light on the 'Abbāsid revolution, "Arabskii Anonim XI veka" (Moscow, 1950).

Some works are devoted to single events, such as the *K. al-Ridda* by Wathīma, on the revolt after the death of Muḥammad, while others deal especially with the great conquests, studied not only for their glory but also to record the precedents established at that time with regard to administrative procedure. The following works deserve to be mentioned: the FUTŪḤ AL-BULDĀN by al-Balādhurī, edited by M. J. de Goeje, *Liber expugnationis regionum* (1886), in Cairo (1932), and recently (1956–1957), and translated into English by P. K. Hitti and F. Murgotten, *The Origins of the Islamic State*, two volumes (1916–1925), and into German by O. Rescher, two volumes (1917–1923); the *Futūḥ Miṣr* by Ibn 'Abd al-Ḥakam, which includes the conquest of *al-Maghrib* and *al-Andalus*, edited by C. Torrey (1922), for which see R. Brunschvig, above, p. 26, and partially translated by A. Gateau, "La conquête de l'Afrique du Nord et de l'Espagne," *RT*, VI, IX, XXIII–XXV, XXIX, XXXIII–XXXIV, XXXVIII–XL (1931–1939). These works are valuable for Egypt and the West. Additional information on the conquests may also be obtained from Ibn A'tham al-Kūfī, for *Ifrīqiya*, H. Massé, "La chronique d'ibn A'tham et la conquête de l'Ifrīqiya," *Mélanges Gaudefroy-Demombynes* (1935–1945), and for Central Asia, A. Kurat in *AÜDTCFD*, VI–VII (1948–1949). The various accounts of the conquests attributed to al-Wāqidī are fictitious works of a later date.

Balādhurī was also the author of the *Ansāb al-ashrāf*, a voluminous collection of material concerning rulers and "nobles" classified by generations for the first two centuries of Islam, of which only fragments were known until recently. In 1883, in Greifswald, W. Ahlwardt published the section on 'Abdalmalik under the title *Anonyme arabische Chronik*. A partial edition was begun under the auspices of the Hebrew University, Jerusalem, of which the following volumes have been published: Vol. IV (on Yazīd I and Mu'āwiya II) by M. Schlössinger (1938); and Vol. V (on 'Uthmān, Marwān I, and 'Abdallāh b. al-Zubair) by S. D. Goitein (1936), and a complete edition is awaited by the Arab League, for which M. Hamidullah published Volume I (from Noah to Muḥammad) in Dhakhā'in al-'Arab, no. 27 (1958). G. Levi Della Vida translated the section on 'Alī in *RSO*, VI (1914–1915), and, together with O. Pinto, the section on Mu'āwiya under the title *Il Califfo Mu'āwiya* (Rome, 1939). See also M. Hamidullah's study, "Le Livre des généalogies d'al-Balādhurī," *BEOD*, XIV (1952–1954).

The history of particular categories of people connected with the government and the judiciary is the subject of *Ta'rīkh al-wuzarā'* by al-Jahshiyārī, of which incomplete manuscript a facsimile edition was published by H. von Mžik (1926) and an edition in Cairo (1947), and on which see D. Sourdel, "La valeur littéraire et documentaire du 'Livre des Vizirs' d'al-Ǧahšiyārī," *Arabica*, II (1955), 193–210; the *Akhbār al-quḍāt* (Cairo, 1947–1950), and the history of *The Governors and Judges of Egypt* by al-Kindī, edited by R. Guest (1912). See also: the *Sīrat 'Umar b. 'Abd al-'Azīz* by Ibn 'Abd al-Ḥakam (the brother of the historian), edited in Cairo (1927); the genealogical work of Mis'ab al-Zubayrī, *Nasab al-Quraysh*, edited by E. Lévi-Provençal (1954); and the *Jamharat al-ansāb* by Ibn Ḥazm, also edited by Lévi-Provençal (1948).

The *adab* works combine literary and historical information, a good example of which appears in the *Kitab al-'iqd al-farīd* by the Andalusian Ibn 'Abd Rabbihi (d. 940), edited in six volumes (Cairo, 1940–1950), for which M. Shafi compiled two volumes of *Analytical Indices* for Punjab University Oriental Publications, IX (Calcutta, 1935–1937), corresponding to the Cairo editon of A.H. 1321. The KITĀB AL-AGHĀNĪ by Abū 'l-Faraj al-Iṣfahānī (d. 967), is particularly valuable. This monumental collection of poetry set to music is a mine of information on the rulers, their courtiers, the poets and musicians, their milieu and the social life of the period; it was obviously conceived in the first place as a source of entertainment, but the documentation this made available is no less valid. Good editions at present being prepared in Cairo and Beirut are not yet complete, so that it is still necessary to consult the old edition made at Būlāq in twenty volumes (A.H. 1285) with a supplementary volume by R. Brünnow (1888), and the indispensable alphabetical tables by I. Guidi referring to the whole work (1895–1900).

One should not forget the collections of *ḥadīth* (see above, p. 28), the works of the heresiographers (see below, p. 136), and also certain poets involved in contemporary events who are often authentic—albeit hardly precise—witnesses of the Umayyad scene: al-Kumait, studied by S. Naja (1957); Kuthaiyir 'Azza, edited by H. Pérès in two volumes (1928–1930); Surāqa b. Mirdās, edited by S. Ḥusain in *JRAS* (1936); and the Christian al-Akhṭal, discussed by H. Lammens, "Le chantre des Omaiyades," *JA* (1894). On all these poets, see C. Nallino, cited p. 129, and R. Blachère, *Histoire de la littérature arabe*, II, cited p. 102.

For non-Muslim sources, note: the Byzantine annalist, Theophanes Confessor, *Chronographia* (up to the year 813), two volumes, critical edition by C. de Boor (Leipzig, 1883–1885); the Syriac chronicle under the name of Dionysios of Tell-Maḥrē, edited and translated by J. Chabot under the title *Chronique de Denys de Tell Maḥrê, quatrième partie*, Bibliothèque de l'École des Hautes Études. Sciences philologiques et historiques, fasc. 112 (Paris, 1895); the Copt, Johannes of Nikiou, contemporary of the Arab conquests, whose *Chronicle* is only known through an Ethiopic version, edited with translation by H. Zotenberg in *Notices et extraits de manuscrits de la Bibliothèque Nationale*, XXIV (1883), or better still, in English, by H. Charles (1916); and the Armenian, Sebeos, whose *Chronicle* has been translated by F. Macler (1905). To these should be added the general history of the patriarchs of Alexandria, which has become known as the work of Sawīrūs (Severus) b. al-Muqaffa', although he wrote only the beginning of the whole work, subsequently continued by several authors, of which the following editions exist: "History of the Patriarchs of the Coptic Church of Alexandria," edited with English translation by B. Evetts, *PO*, I/2 and 4, V/1, X/5, four volumes (Paris, 1904–1915); *Severus Ibn al-Muqaffa', Alexandrinische Patriarchengeschichte von S. Marcus bis Michael I*, edited by C. F. Seybold (Hamburg, 1912); *Historia Patriarcharum Alexandrinorum*, edited by C. F. Seybold, *CSCO*, Scr. Ar. Ser. III, tom. 9, fasc. 1, 2 (Beirut and Paris, 1904–1910; reprinted as Scr. Ar. 8, 9, Louvain, 1954); *History of the Patriarchs of the Egyptian Church*, edited by Yassā 'Abd al-Masīh, O. H. E. Khs-Burmester, and A. S. Atiya, Vol. II, pt. 1–3. Publications de la Société d'Archéologie Copte. Textes et Documents (Cairo, 1943–1959). The last edition is the continuation of Seybold's edition in *CSCO* and covers the years 849–1102. For later times (until 1243) use the Latin adaptation by E. Renaudot, *Historia Partiarcharum Alexandrinorum Jacobitarum* (Paris,

1713) who uses besides Sawīrus and his followers other Arabic historians and authors.

The imperfections of these sources are partly responsible for the gaps in our knowledge of the Umayyad period. A more enlightened and careful study of the nature of each type of source, a more precise reading of the texts, and the elucidation of the meanings of technical terms would have made possible a more rapid increase in our knowledge.

For the period as a whole, the *Chronografia Islamica* by L. Caetani (1912) provides a list of the main events, year by year (A.H.) and in topographical order, with detailed references to sources, forming a collection of notes which was to have been used for the continuation of the *Annali dell'Islam* (cited p. 115 f.): Vol. I: A.H. 1–22; II: 23–45; III: 45–65; IV: 66–85; V: 86–132.

THE ARAB CONQUEST

The history of the Arab conquests, especially on the Sassanian side, was extensively studied in *Prolegomena zur ältesten Geschichte des Islams* by J. Wellhausen in his *Skizzen und Vorarbeiten* VI (1899). It is also included in various works on the individual countries concerned. On Syria, see M. J. de Goeje, *Mémoire sur la conquête de la Syrie*, Vol. II of *Mémoires d'histoire et de géographie orientales* (2d ed., Leiden, 1900). For Egypt, see A. Butler, *The Arab Conquest of Egypt and the Last Thirty Years of the Roman Dominion* (1902), and E. Amélineau, "La conquête de l'Egypte par les arabes," *RH*, CXIX–CXX (1915). For Central Asia, see H. A. R. Gibb, *The Arab Conquests in Central Asia* (1923). See also a recent study by D. Dunlop, *The History of the Jewish Khazars* (1954). To these should, of course, be added the general histories of the various countries concerned, cited on p. 107 ff.

On relations with Byzantium and Armenia after the period of the great conquests, see: E. Brooks, "The Arabs in Asia Minor (641–750)," *Journal of Hellenic Studies*, XVIII (1898); M. Canard, "Les expéditions des arabes contre Constantinople dans l'histoire et dans la légende," *JA* (1926); M. Cheïra, *La lutte entre arabes et byzantins, la conquete et l'organisation des frontières aux VIIe et VIIIe siècles* (Alexandria, 1947); H. A. R. Gibb, "Arab-Byzantine Relations under the Umayyad Caliphate," *Dumbarton Oaks Papers*, XII (1958) reprinted in his *Studies on the Civilization of Islam*, cited p. 86, which contains some interesting suggestions; J. Laurent, *L'Arménie entre Byzance et l'Islam depuis la conquete arabe jusqu'en 886* (1919); and the works by R. Grousset and E. Honigmann, cited on pp. 108 and 138. The Muslim army has been studied by N. Fries, *Das Heereswesen der Araber zur Zeit der Omaijaden, nach Ṭabarī* (1921).

On the policy of the caliphs in the Mediterranean and on naval power, see:

Archibald Lewis, *Naval Power and Trade in the Mediterranean* (1951); E. Eichhoff, in a thesis for the University of Saarbrücken, *Seekrieg und Seepolitik zwischen Islam und Abendland (650–1040)* (1954); W. Hoenerbach, "Araber und Mittelmeer. Anfänge und Probleme arabischer Seegeschichte," *60. doğum yılı münasebetiyle Zeki Velidi Togan armağanı* (Istanbul, 1950–1955), and "La navigación omeya en el Mediterráneo y sus consecuéncias político-culturales," *Miscelánea de estúdios árabes y hebraicos [Univ. Granada]*, II (1953).

The financial and religious conditions attending the submission and organization of the conquered territories have been studied in a monograph by D. Dennett, *Conversion and the Poll-tax in Early Islam* (1950), that is flawless from the point of view of method. It calls into question many of the ideas put forward by M. van Berchem and C. H. Becker, cited p. 90.

THE RĀSHIDŪN AND UMAYYAD PERIODS

The domestic history of the period of the first four caliphs, called *rāshidūn*, is the subject of the following studies: E. Sachau, "Der erste Chalife Abu Bakr," *SBPA* (1903); H. Lammens, "Le triumvirat Abou Bakr, 'Omar, et Abou Obaida," *MFO*, IV (1910), controversial; Ṭāhā Ḥusain, *al-Fitnat al-kubrā*, two volumes (1947–1953), on 'Uthmān and 'Alī; L. Veccia Vaglieri, "Il conflitto 'Alī-Mu'āwiya e la secessione kharigita riesaminati alla luce di fonti ibāḍite," *Annali. Istituto Universitario Orientale di Napoli*, n.s., IV–V (1932), and in English, *Proceedings of the XXIInd Congress of Orientalists, 1951*, Vol. II (1947), and also by the same author "Sulla denominazione Ḫawāriğ," *RSO*, XXVI (1951); the biography of 'Alī by F. Buhl, in Swedish (1921); E. Petersen, "'Alī and Mu'āwiyah. The Rise of the Umayyad Caliphate," *AO*, XXIII (1959), 157–196; and R. Vesely, "Die Anṣār im ersten Bürgerkrieg, 36–40," *ArO*, XXVI (1958), 36–58.

The work which is still the pioneer among modern studies of the Umayyad period, in spite of a presentation that lacks clarity as well as certain ideas that need revision, is J. Wellhausen, DAS ARABISCHE REICH UND SEIN STURZ (1902), of which there is an English translation *The Arab Kingdom and its Fall* (Calcutta, 1927), with an index that is not in the original. This was based on a critical study of the sources of Ṭabarī and represents the first attempt at a reaction against the traditional 'Abbāsid presentation of Umayyad history.

The works of H. Lammens devoted to the Umayyad period are more attractive and well documented, although their interpretation is often rather loose. His chief works are as follows. *Études sur le règne du Calife Omaiyade Mo'āwiya Ier* (1908), is composed of a series of special studies originally published in *MFO*, I–III (1906–1908), hence is not a comprehensive survey of the reign as a whole. Similarly, *Le Califat de Yazīd Ier* (1921) originally appeared in *MFO*, IV–VII (1910–1921). "L'Avènement des Marwanides et le califat de Marwan Ier," *MFO*, XII (1927), is more reliable. ***Études sur le siècle des Omayyades*** (Beirut, 1930) is a collection of short studies on "Ziād b. Abīhi, vice-roi de l'Iraq," *RSO*, IV (1911–1912); see also "Un poète royal à la cour des Omayyades," *ROC*, IX (1903); "Le chantre des Omaiyades," *JA* (1895); "Le calife Walīd Ier et le prétendu partage de la mosquée des Omayyades à Damas," *BIFAO*, XXVI (1926); "Un gouverneur ... d'Egypte ... ," from the *Bulletin de l'Institut d'Egypte*, Sér. V, Vol. I, based on Arabic papyri; "La Bâdia et la Hīra sous les Omayyades," *MFO*, IV (1910), which is particularly hazardous; and "Mo'āwiya II," *RSO*, VII (1916–1918).

The monographs by F. Gabrieli on various reigns and episodes of the Umayyad period are more reliable: "Il califfato di Hisham," *Mémoires de la Société Archéologique d'Alexandrie*, VII (1935); "al-Walīd b. Yazīd, il califfo e il poeta," *RSO*, XV (1935); "La rivolta dei Muhallabiti e il nuovo Balāḏurī nel Iraq," *RL*, Ser. VI, Vol. XIV (1938); and "L'eroe eomayyade Maslama b. 'Abdalmalik," *ibid.*, Ser. VIII. Vol. IV (1950–1951). Similarly, see U. Rizzitano, "Abdalaziz b. Marwàn governatore d'Egitto," *ibid.*, Ser. VIII, Vol. II (1941). On 'Umar b. 'Abdal'azīz, see also an early monograph by C. H. Becker, "Omar II," *ZA*, XV (1900). J. Périer wrote *La vie d'al-Ḥajjaj ibn Yousof* (1904), a detailed study of limited outlook.

Since the works mentioned above dwell on the history of a particular prince or leader, they preclude any treatment of broader topics. There are several important studies at our disposal that do have wide scope, but they are antiquated and require revision in the light of recently published sources; the work of revision has but barely begun. The main works are: J. Wellhausen, "Die religiös-politischen Oppositionsparteien im alten Islam," *AGG*, V/5 (1901); G. van Vloten, *Recherches sur la domination arabe, le shi'isme et les croyances messianiques sous les Omayyades* (Amsterdam, 1894); on the political and religious struggles and administrative institutions, H. I. Bell, "The Administration of Egypt under the Umayyad Caliphs," *Byzantinische Zeitschrift*, XXVIII (1928). The works of C. H. Becker, also, are models of clear, logical reasoning and open up numerous new possibilities, even when they include a large measure of hypothetical interpretation (see D. Dennett, above, p. 126). The most important of these, such as "Die Entstehung von 'ušr- und ḫarāğland," *ZA*, XVIII (1904), and "Steuerpacht und Lehnswesen," *Islam*, V (1914), which are included in his *Islamstudien*, I (cited p. 86), opened up new issues in their time, but can now be used only as a source of material and as an indication of the problems involved. See also, in the same collection, "Grundlinien der wirtschaftlichen Entwicklung Aegyptens in den ersten Jahrhunderten des Islam," reprinted from *Klio*, IX (1909), a continuation of the *Beiträge zur Geschichte Aegyptens unter dem Islam*, two volumes (1902–1903), both of which use, to full advantage, the papyri first edited by C. H. Becker.

Among recent works, special note should be made of a variety of studies: H. A. R. Gibb, "The Evolution of Government in Early Islam," *SI*, IV (1955), 1–17, and "The Fiscal Rescript of Omar II," *Arabica*, II (1955), 1–16; on monetary history, P. Grierson, "The Monetary Reforms of 'Abd al-Malik," *JESHO*, III (1960), 241–264; J. Schacht, *Origins*, cited p. 41; Sāliḥ al-'Ālī, *al-Tanẓīmāt al-ijtimā'īya wa'l-iqtiṣādīya fī 'l-Baṣra fī 'l-qarn al-awwal* (Baghdad, 1953); L. Massignon, "Explication du plan de Baṣra," *Westöstliche Abhandlungen R. Tschudi* (1954); A. Launois, "Deux estampilles et un gros poids Omeyyades en verre," *JA* (1958), 287–311, which is actually a study of the fiscal policy of the later Umayyads; W. Montgomery Watt, "Kharijite Thought in the Umayyad Period," *Islam*, XXXVI (1961), which will be continued; E. Salem, *The Political Theory and Institutions of the Khawarij* (Baltimore, 1956); T. Lewicki, "Les Ibadites dans l'Arabie du sud," *International Orientalists Congress, XXIV* (Munich, 1957), 362–364, also in *Folia Orientalia* [Publications of] Académie Polonaise des Sciences, I (Cracow, 1959), 3–17; M. Hodgson, "How Did the Early Shī'a Become Sectarian?" *JAOS*, LXXV (1955); S. Moscati, "Per una storia dell'antica šī'a," *RSO*, XXX (1955), 257–267; W. Thomson, "The Character of Early Islamic Sects," in Vol. I of *Goldziher Memorial Volume*, two volumes (1948–1958); H. Ritter, "Studien zur Geschichte der islamischen Frömmigkeit, "*Islam*, XXI (1933), on Ḥasan al-Baṣrī and others; A. Vasiliev, "The Iconoclastic Edict of the Caliph Yazīd II, A.D. 721," *Dumbarton Oaks Papers*, IX–X (1955–1956), 23–47; M. Sprengling, "From Persian to Arabic," *AJSL*, LVI–LVII (1939–1940); and A. Poliak, "L'arabisation de l'orient sémitique," *REI*, XII (1938), on which see W. Marçais, below, p. 220. The settling of Arabs in conquered territory is also the subject of J. Sauvaget's work, "Remarques sur les monuments Omeyyades. I: Châteaux de Syrie," *JA* (1939), which he had intended to study in more detail. On this subject see also C. Cahen, "Histoire économico-sociale et islamologie: la question préjudicielle de l'adaptation entre les indigènes et l'Islam," *Colloque sur la Sociologie musulmane, 11.–14. Septembre 1961, Actes.* (Brussels, 1962). On the 'Abbāsid revolution see the *mise au point* and discussions in C. Cahen, "Points de vue sur la Révolution Abbaside," *RH*, CCVII (1963).

LITERATURE AND ART

On the literature, see above p. 102 and C. Nallino, *Arabic Literature from the Beginnings to the Umayyads*, lectures given in Arabic in Cairo (1910–1911), in Italian in his *Raccolta*, IV (cited p. 88), French translation (1950); R. Blachère, "Regards sur l'acculturation des Arabo-Musulmans jusque vers 40/661," *Arabica*, III (1956), 247–265, and "Les principaux thèmes de la poésie érotique au siècle des Umayyades de Damas," *AIEO*, V (1939–1941).

On art and archaeology, the chief descriptive work is by K. A. C. Creswell: *Early Muslim Architecture*, two volumes (1932–1940), with a summary by the author; *A Short Account of Early Muslim Architecture* (Pelican Books, 1958); and in the article "Architecture" in *EI*². Often there is more to be drawn from certain special studies such as these: D. Schlumberger, "Les origines antiques de l'art Islamique à la lumière des fouilles de Qasr el-Heir," *Syria*, XX (1939); J. Sauvaget, *La mosquée Omeyyade de Médine* (1947); R. Hamilton, *Khirbat al-Mafjar, an Arabic Mansion in the Jordan Valley* (1959), or even from the studies arising out of the dispute, now more or less obsolete, as to the origin of the castle of Mshatta, which is Umayyad and not pre-islamic (see *EI*, *s.v.*).

17

The ʿAbbāsid Caliphate and the Successor States

TO THE MIDDLE OF THE ELEVENTH CENTURY

SOURCES

Other than the necessarily brief chapters devoted to them in the general histories, we do not have a study in depth on the ʿAbbāsids. Even the requisite preliminary studies are far from complete. This is all the more surprising since this period is the most glorious of Muslim history and there exists, except for the early years, a remarkable corpus of documents some of which, it is true, have only recently been discovered. It must be reiterated, and particularly in this case, that research has too often been restricted either to the facts that were made accessible, more or less by chance, in the chronicles, or to a limited number of questions in which the nineteenth-century Orientalist was interested. Nowhere is the need more evident than here for serious thought on the period as a whole in order to reveal the basic problems and to fill in the most serious gaps.

There is no lack of source material. In addition to the Egyptian papyri that have been published—roughly half of which are concerned with Egypt before the Fāṭimid conquest in A.D. 969—some interesting Syrian papyri have been edited, such as by N. Abbott, "Arabic Papyri of the Reign of Ǧaʿfar al-Mutawakkil ʿala-llāh," *ZDMG*, XCII (1938). The chronicles and other works have also preserved a certain number of official letters, of which those prior to the fourth/tenth century are reproduced in the publication by A. Z. Ṣafwat, *Jamharat rasāʾil al-ʿarab*, four volumes (Cairo, 1937). Finally there are three collections of official correspondence, dating from the Būyid period, mixed with documents concerned with administrative activities as well as personal letters. The most famous of these is the collection of letters by the caliph's secretary, Abū Isḥāq al-Ṣābī, of which a small part has been published by S. Arslan (1898), while those by the "ṣāḥib" Ibn 'Abbād, a famous literary man and vizier, edited by 'Abd al-Wahhāb 'Azzām and Shawqī Ḍaif (Cairo, 1947, and Teheran, 1955), are even more useful for the historian. See C. Cahen, "Une correspondance buyide inédite," in *Studi orientalistici in onore di Giorgio Levi Della Vida*, I (Rome, 1956).

All the works cited for Umayyad history (see chap. 16) were written under the 'Abbāsids and can also be used for the early period of 'Abbāsid history as a means of checking Ṭabarī, the most important historian by far, although his account of the last years up to A.H. 311 is rather weak. Here we mention works concerned with the 'Abbāsid period exclusively especially those coming after Ṭabarī.

Ṭabarī's history, the history par excellence in the eyes of later Muslims, was continued by several authors. The Spaniard, 'Arīb, writing up to the year 320/923, was edited by M. J. de Goeje in 1897; the next most important is Thābit b. Sinān, a "Sabian" of Ḥarrān, and also a scholar and high-ranking official of Baghdad, writing up to the year 362/973, whose work was continued in turn by the Muslim member of a related family, Hilāl al-Ṣābī, who wrote up to the year 447/1055. Of their original work only a fragment, covering the period from the end of A.H. 388 to the beginning of A.H. 393, has come down to us. Essential information can be found, however, in later historical works, particularly in the TAJĀRIB AL-UMAM (*The Experiences of the Nations*) by Miskawaih, a philosopher, physician, and statesman, who died in 421/1030; also in the continuation of the *Tajārib* by the vizier, Abū Shujā' al-Rūdhrawārī, who died in 488/1095. In the manuscript containing the two latter works, they are connected to the three preserved years of the work by Hilāl al-Ṣābī that ends the history. The whole has been edited with an English translation by D. S. Margoliouth and H. Amedroz, *The Eclipse of the Abbasid Caliphate* (London, 1920–1921), consisting of three volumes of text, three volumes of translation, and a small volume containing an index, which also refers to Tanūkhī (see below, p. 133). The intelligence of the authors, their documentary and oral sources of information, and the government connections that they enjoyed make this an incomparably rich source—yet to be exploited.

A few years earlier, L. Caetani had published a facsimile edition of the first, fifth, and sixth volumes of the Istanbul manuscript of the *Tajārib*, *GMS*, VII/1, 5, 6 (Leiden and London, 1909–1917), Vol. I covering the years A.D. 622–657. M. J. de Goeje had also covered the reigns from al-

Ma'mūn to al-Musta'īn in his *Fragmenta Historicorum Arabicorum*, II (1871). In this period, however, Miskawaih adds little to Ṭabarī and is, therefore, not of great interest. H. Amedroz published a parallel table of passages of Miskawaih, *Tajārib al-Umam*, 'Arīb, *Tabarī Continuatus*, and Hilāl, *Kitāb al-Wuzarā'*, for the years A.H. 295–320 as an appendix to his article "The Tajārib al-Umam of Abū 'Alī Miskawaih," *Islam*, V (1914), and a study on "The Vizier Abū 'l-Faḍl Ibn al 'Amīd from the Tajārib al-Umam of Abū 'Alī Miskawaih," *Islam*, III (1912).

Among other authors of works of a historical nature, we should mention Ibn abī Ṭāhir Ṭaifūr, a fragment of whose *Kitāb Baghdād*, describing in detail the beginning of al-Ma'mūn's reign at Baghdad, has been edited with a German translation by H. Keller (1908), and also edited in Cairo (1949). A special place should be reserved for the *Kitāb al-Awrāq* (*The Book of Leaves*) by al-Ṣūlī (d. A.H. 946), edited by J. Heyworth-Dunne (Cairo, 1937), in which he relates, very simply, his lively memories of his life as a courtier in Baghdad. There is a French translation with very valuable notes by M. Canard with the title *Akhbār al-Rāḍī billāh wa'l-Muttaqī*, two volumes (Algiers, 1946–1950).

An Egyptian Christian, Yaḥyā al-Anṭākī, who lived in Antioch in the first half of the eleventh century, composed a most valuable chronicle, combining both Byzantine and Muslim history which is particularly well informed on the relations between the two empires. The best edition, together with a French translation, is by I. I. Krachkovskii and A. Vasiliev in *PO*, XVIII (1924) and XXIII (1932). The Nestorian chronicle by Mari, continued up to the twelfth century by 'Amr bar Ṣlībā, and edited by P. H. Gismondi (1903), is also useful.

Various local chronicles are also noteworthy for general history. The *Ta'rīkh-i Qumm*, a history of the little Iranian town of Qumm, by Ḥasan b. Muḥammad Qummī, is quite remarkable for the importance of the documents it preserves. It has come down to us through a Persian translation, edited by Jalāl al-Dīn Tihrānī, I–V (Teheran, 1934), on which see the article by Ann K. S. Lambton in *BSOAS*, XII (1947–1948), 580 ff. The Persian *Ta'rīkh-i Sīstān*, edited by Malik al Shu'arā' Bahār (1935), is also most valuable for Eastern Iran. For the history of Muslim Central Asia during the Ghaznawid period, much material is to be found in the apologia of Maḥmūd of Ghazna, by al-'Utbī, in Arabic, *al-Ta'rīkh al-yamīnī*, of which there is an English translation (based on a Persian adaptation by Manīnī) by J. Reynolds (1858), and in the extremely detailed *Ta'rīkh* by Baihaqī, in Persian and only partially preserved, dealing with the reign of Mas'ūd, the best edition of which is by S. Nafīsī, with two volumes of notes (Teheran, 1945–1953). Also, see the more limited *Zain al-akhbār*, a concise general history in Persian and valuable for Central Asia, by Gardīzī, edited by M. Nāẓim (Berlin, 1928), and by S. Nafīsī (Teheran, 1954); and the *Ta'rīkh-i Bukhārā* by Narshakhī, handed down through a Persian adaptation, edited by C. Schefer (1892), and translated into English with notes by R. Frye (Cambridge, Mass., 1954).

Among the local chronicles of the rest of the Eastern Muslim world, we shall only note here those of the Yemen, which are still only partially catalogued, and *Die Chroniken der Stadt Mekka*, edited by F. Wüstenfeld, four volumes (1857–1861).

Of the works devoted to particular categories of people we mention especially the work on viziers, *Tuḥfat al-umarā' fī ta'rīkh al-wuzarā'* by Hilāl al-Ṣābī, an outstanding work containing genuine documents, only partially preserved, which is a continuation of al-Jahshiyārī; it has been edited by H. Amedroz, *Three Years of Buwaihid Rule in Baghdad 389–393 A.H.* (London, 1901).

The collection of short stories, *Nishwār al-Muḥāḍara*, only partially preserved, by the qāḍī, al-Tanūkhī (d. A.D. 994), contains some interesting suggestions. The first volume was edited and translated by D. S. Margoliouth, *The Table-Talk of a Mesopotamian Judge* (London, 1921), while the second volume was edited by the same author in the *Revue de l'Académie Arabe de Damas*, X (1930) and XIII (1932), and translated in *IC*, III–VI (1929–1932; offprint, 1934). In *Abulkasim, ein Bagdader Sittenbild von Muḥammad b. Aḥmad al-Muṭahhar al-Azdī*, edited by A. Mez (Heidelberg, 1902), the *Kitāb al-muwaṣhshā* by Washshā', edited by R. Brünnow (1886), and by K. Muaṣṭfā (Cairo, 1953), and in the *Maqāmāt* (*Assemblies*) by Badī' al-Zamān al-Hamadhāni (d. 1008), of which extracts were translated by R. Blachère and P. Masnou (1957), we have small romances on manners.

Among the literary productions of the great writer, al-Jāḥiẓ, there are several small works containing substantial historical material, such as *Manāqib al-atrāk*, devoted to the virtues of Turkish soldiers, *Dhamm akhlāq al-kuttāb*, devoted to the satirizing of public officials, edited by G. van Vloten, in *Tria Opuscula* (Leiden, 1903), and, in similar vein, *Dhamm 'amal al-sulṭān*, which was included in the *Majmū'āt rasā'il* (Cairo, 1324/1906), pp. 155–180. Of importance to the historian are also the treatises concerned with commerce, such as "al-Tabaṣṣur bi'l-tijāra," edited by Ḥ. Ḥ. 'Abdulwahhāb in the *Revue de l'Académie Arabe de Damas*, XII (1932), and in Cairo (1935), and on the Jews and Christians, *al-Radd 'alā 'l-naṣārā wa'l-yahūd*, edited by J. Finkel in *Three Essays of . . . al-Jāḥiẓ* (1926), translated by him into English in *JAOS*, XLVII (1927), and into French by I. S. Allouche in *Hespéris*, XXVI (1939). The *Kitāb al-diyārāt* by al-Shābushtī, edited by G. 'Awad (1951), supplies information on the Christians from a rather special point of view.

Useful information can also be gleaned from certain later works by poets or literary men such as Abū Ḥayyān al-Tawḥīdī and al-Tha'ālibī, not to mention the military romances discussed by M. Canard, above, p. 24.

It was during the 'Abbāsid period that the basic legal works were written as well as works on administrative procedure. These include, for instance, the KITĀB AL-KHARĀJ by Abū Yūsuf, edited in Cairo (A.H. 1352), and translated into French by E. Fagnan, *Le livre de l'impôt foncier* (1921), which should be compared with the work of Yaḥyā b. Ādam, edited by T. Juynboll (1896), and translated into English by A. Ben Shemesh, *Yaḥyā ben Ādams Kitāb al-Kharāj* (*Taxation in Islam*), I (Leiden, 1958), with a useful concordance of traditions, and also with the *Kitāb al-amwāl*, a collection of *ḥadīth*, by Abū 'Ubayd b. Sallām, edited in Cairo (1353).

Various works were written on the bureaucracy of *kuttāb*, one of the first being the *Kitāb al-kuttāb* by al-Baghdādī, edited by D. Sourdel, *BEOD*, XIV (1952–1954). Corresponding more exactly to administrative needs was the *Kitāb al-kharāj* by the writer and civil servant, Qudāma b. Ja'far, which embraced nearly all branches of the administration, and of which only the second half has been preserved. Even this has been only partially published. The Arabic text is available in an unpublished doctoral thesis by A. Makki at the Sorbonne, Paris. The chapters giving a description of the fiscal system in the provinces of the empire have been edited and translated in *BGA*, VI, cited p. 135. The *Mafātīḥ al-'ulūm* by al-Khwārizmī, edited by G. van Vloten (1895), a small practical encyclopedia-like work giving the terminology of the various sciences, professions, and intellectual pursuits, draws upon similar material for the articles on institutions. Outside the field of "orthodox" jurisprudence, see Zaid b. 'Alī, above, p. 43, and R. Serjeant, "A Zaidi Manual of Ḥisbah of the IIIrd Century," *RSO*, XXVIII (1953), 1–34. Finally, there exist scientific treatises, especially on mathematics, designed for the use of administrative and tax officials, such as the *Kitāb al-hāwī*, which has been studied and partially edited by C. Cahen in various articles, in particular in "Quelques problèmes économiques et fiscaux de l'Iraq Buyide," *AIEO*, X (1952). The treatise published by M. Hamidullah, cited on p. 147, is based on inventories of the treasury.

On Māwardī, see above, p. 44.

Most of the works described as geographical are also closely related to administrative affairs. In fact, several are descriptions of what civil servants and governors needed to know about the Muslim world. The 'Abbāsid period is the golden age of a type of geographical writing that was seldom used again in later centuries.

As an introduction one may cite the accounts of travelers such as Ibn Faḍlān, the secretary to the embassy of the Bulgars of the mid-Volga, who was an extraordinary observer of a country of which we would know almost nothing but for him. His account, for a long time known only through incomplete translations, has now been edited and translated into German from a manuscript closer to the original by its discoverer, Zeki Velidi Togan, *Ibn Faḍlans Reisebericht* (1939); also edited and translated into Russian by I. Kovalevsky (Leningrad 1939; 2d ed., Kharkov, 1956); also edited by S. Dahhān (Damascus, 1959), and in French by M. Canard, *AIEO*, XVI (1958), 41–146. Of the same kind are the accounts of sea voyages on the Indian Ocean, such as that by the merchant, Abū Zaid Ḥasan al-Sīrāfī, of which there is an edition with translation and commentary by J. Sauvaget, *Relation de la Chine et de l'Inde*, Collection Arabe de l'Association G. Budé (Paris, 1948). The Spanish Jew, Ibrāhīm b. Ya'qūb al-Ṭurṭūshī, known only through translations which were wrongfully attributed to two separate authors, seems to have taught the Muslims the little they knew about Christian Europe before al-Idrīsī, on whom see below, p. 219, just as the prisoner, Hārūn b. Yaḥyā, was their unique source of information on Constantinople; his report is discussed by M. Izzeddin in "Un prisonnier arabe à Byzance au IXe siècle," *REI*, XV (1941–1946). One should add to these accounts, which are mainly informative on the non-Muslim world, the Persian *Sefer-nāmeh* by Nāṣir-i Khusrav, edited and translated by C. Schefer (1881), which is useful for the countries between Khurāsān and Egypt at the very end of our period.

Most of the geographical texts that are of importance for the 'Abbāsid epoch have been edited by M. J. de Goeje, although not in chronological order, in *BGA* (see next paragraph). The work of Ibn Khurdādbeh (Khurradādhbih), a postmaster, of which there is a French translation together with a fragment of Qudāma in the fourth volume, belongs to the ninth century and mainly provides information on the state of roads. Other ninth-century authors, such as Ibn Rusteh, of whom a French translation is now available by G. Wiet, *Les atours précieux* (1955), and al-Ya'qūbī (see p. 122 on his history), also translated by G. Wiet, *Le livre des pays* (1937), will be found in *GBA*, VII. Finally, the *Kitāb al-buldān* by Ibn al-Faqīh al-Hamadhānī, of which only an abridged version has survived, appears in *BGA*, V.

The first three volumes of BIBLIOTHECA GEOGRAPHORUM ARABICORUM (*BGA*) are devoted to three fundamental and related geographical works of the eleventh century. The first volume presents al-Iṣṭakhrī's work which derives from the lost work of al-Balkhī, the founder of this kind of research, under the title *Viae regnorum*. The second volume contains the work of Ibn Ḥawqal, perhaps a Fāṭimid agent, of which J. H. Kramers published a new edition in two volumes (1938–1939), with reproductions of the original maps and based on more complete manuscripts than those used by M. J. de Goeje. A French translation by G. Wiet is in preparation. His *Opus geographicum* in part reproduces, in part completes, the work of al-Iṣṭakhrī. Finally, a third volume offers al-Muqaddasī, *Descriptio imperii moslemici* (2d ed., 1906), which makes use of the foregoing authors and goes considerably beyond them. The chapter on Maghreb was translated by C. Pellat (1950), the one on Syria and Palestine by P. Miguel (1964).

These works constitute a description of the Muslim world, province by province, from various standpoints. Al-Muqaddasī, in particular, has produced a quite extraordinary piece of work. With his untiring curiosity, broad-mindedness, and human interest, the author provides very accurate, personal information, drawing a general picture of each region together with a wealth of detail on local custom, language, economy, and any pecularities that may exist with regard to roads and so forth.

The eighth volume of *BGA* contains the *Kitāb al-Tanbīh* by al-Mas'ūdī, which cannot be classified under any particular heading; it was translated into French by B. Carra de Vaux, *Le Livre de l'avertissement et de la revision* (Paris, 1896). The fourth volume of *BGA* is the glossary and index for Volumes I–III, while the end of the eighth volume provides the glossary and index for Volumes V–VIII.

A few works, discovered later, have not been incorporated into *BGA*. Of special interest for Central Asia, both Muslim and non-Muslim, are two sources that in part derive from the lost book of the Sāmānid vizier al-Jaiḥānī. Both have been edited, translated, and expertly commented on by V. Minorsky: the anonymous *Ḥudūd al-'ālam*, a Persian work of the end of the fourth/tenth century, appears in the *GMS*, n.s., XI (1937) (Addenda in *BSOAS*, XVII [1955]), and, the other, Marvazī, was published in 1942, *On China, the Turks and India*.

On the practices and theories relating to agriculture, the *Kitāb al-filāḥa*, the so-called *Nabatean Agriculture*, attributed to Ibn Waḥshīya, provides considerable information. On this question see M. Plessner, "Der Inhalt der nabatäischen Landwirtschaft," in *Zeitschrift für Semitistik und verwandte Gebiete*, VI (1928).

Finally, the 'Abbāsid period saw the appearance of the basic theological and philosophical works, also of the first substantial accounts of sects and heresies, in particular, the *Maqālāt al-islāmiyyīn* by al-Ash'arī, edited by H. Ritter in two volumes (1929–1930), and the *Firaq al-shī'a*, under the name of al-Nawbakhtī, also edited by H. Ritter (1931), of which a French translation by M. J. Mashkūr appears in the *Revue de l'histoire des religions*, CLIII–CLV (1958–1959).

The state of modern studies does not fulfill the expectations raised by such a corpus of source material. Apart from the handbooks, no general account of 'Abbāsid history exists. The student may take note, provisionally, of certain questions raised in the *Leçons d'histoire musulmane* by C. Cahen, duplicated by the *Centre de Documentation Universitaire*, in three parts (Paris, 1957–1958), which covers the period from the eighth to the eleventh centuries. See also the article "'Abbāsids" in *EI*², by Bernard Lewis.

A general account of the civilization and institutions in the fourth/tenth century will be found in DIE RENAISSANCE DES ISLAMS by A. Mez (Heidelberg, 1922), translated into English (1937), Spanish (1936), and Arabic (1947), the last two of which provide a complete index and bibliography that are lacking in the original and in the English translation. This is a basic work—it draws on a multitude of sources, particularly literary, from which it extracts a mass of information, but still remains a little confused, superficial, and on certain points behind the present state of research. Moreover, arbitrarily limited as it is to the tenth century, it omits on the one hand the history of the first century of 'Abbāsid history, but at the same time touches on the history of the independent states, which in certain respects altered the facts of Muslim life in the course of the tenth century, without clearly indicating this duality or the historical evolution involved. The word "Renaissance" in the title, while obviously chosen to evoke the Renaissance of the sixteenth century, can only refer to the brilliant cultural development resulting from the infusion and diffusion of Hellenistic ideas. In Arabic, students may read, by 'Abd al-'Azīz Dūrī (A. A. Duri) *al-'Aṣr al-'abbāsī al-awwal* (Baghdad, 1945), and some useful hints may be found in R. Levy, *A Baghdad Chronicle* (1929).

GENERAL AND POLITICAL HISTORY

The political history of individual reigns, periods, or episodes of the 'Abbāsid caliphate has been the subject of a number of studies, all with a limited objective, among which the following may be cited: S. Moscati, "Studi su Abū Muslim," *RL*, VIII/4 (1949–1950); Th. Nöldeke, "Al-Mansūr," in *Sketches from Eastern History* (London, 1892), German edition, *Orientalische Skizzen* (Berlin, 1892); to be supplemented by A. Dietrich, "Das politische Testament des zweiten abbasiden Kalifen, al-Mansūr," *Islam*, XXX (1952); S. Moscati, "Studi sul califfato di al-Mahdī," *Orientalia*, n.s., XIV–XV (1945–1946) and "Le califat d'al-Hādī," *Studia orientalia*, XIII (1946); N. Abbott, *Two Queens of Baghdad, Mother and Wife of Hārūn al-Rashīd* (Chicago, 1946) [there is no satisfactory biography of Hārūn himself, the most famous of the 'Abbāsid caliphs]; L. Bouvat, *Les*

Barmécides (1912), outdated; F. Gabrieli, "La successione di Hārūn al-Rashīd e la guerra fra al-Amīn e al-Ma'mūn," *RSO*, XI (1928), 26–28, and *al-Ma'mūn e gli Alidi*, Vol. II/1 of *Morgenländische Texte und Forschungen* (1929); O. Pinto, "al-Fatḥ b. Khāqān, favorito di al-Mutawakkil," *RSO*, XIII (1931–1932); also on al-Mutawakkil, N. Abbott, "Arabic Papyri," cited p. 130; W. Hellige, *Die Regentschaft al-Muwaffaqs* (Berlin, 1936); and H. Bowen, *The Life and Times of 'Alī b. 'Īsā, the Good Vizier* (1928). All political history of the Samarra period which concerns the government of the caliphate will be found in E. Herzfeld, *Geschichte der Stadt Samarra* (1947), published in connection with the excavations of that town.

The military and diplomatic history of the caliphate consists essentially of the relations between the 'Abbāsids and the Byzantines, for the early stages of which see E. Brooks, "Byzantines and Arabs in the Time of the Early Abbasids," *English Historical Review*, XV (1900). For the ninth century and the beginning of the tenth, we have at our disposal an important work, as well informed on Byzantium as on Islam, in A. Vasiliev, BYZANCE ET LES ARABES, first edition in Russian (1902). It should be consulted in the new French edition, publication of which it not yet complete. The Russian text has been entirely recast and greatly improved by H. Grégoire, M. Canard, and M. Nallino in *Corpus Bruxellense Historiae Byzantinae* (Brussels, 1935–1950); Vol. I, *La dynastie d'Amorium (820–867)* (1935; reprinted 1959); II, *La dynastie macédonienne* (867–959) in two parts of which only part two has appeared: it consists of extracts from Arabic sources translated by M. Canard (1950); in connection with these volumes there is an extremely valuable third volume in German by E. Honigmann, *Die Ostgrenze des byzantinischen Reiches (363–1071)* (1935), which deals with historical geography and gives virtually a history of the military campaigns. Add to these the studies of individual events by M. Canard, such as "Deux épisodes des relations diplomatiques arabo-byzantines au Xe siècle," *BEOD*, XIII (1949–1951), and "Quelques 'a côtés' de l'histoire des relations entre Byzance et les arabes," *Studi orientalistici in onore di Giorgio Levi Della Vida*, I (1956). See also the texts translated by M. Hamidullah in "Nouveaux documents sur les rapports de l'Europe avec l'orient musulman au moyen âge," *Arabica*, VII (1960), 281–301. On Muslim Crete, see I. Papadopoulos, *He Krete hypo tous Sarakenous* (*Crete under the Saracens*) (Athens, 1948), and G. Miles, "Coins of the Amirs of Crete" *Kretika Chronika* (1956).

Western scholars have studied the relations between the 'Abbāsids and the Carolingians or their successors, despite their comparative lack of importance from the Oriental point of view. See for instance, F. Buckler, *Hārūn al-Rashīd and Charles the Great* (1931); the latest treatment of the problem is by G. Musca, *Carlo Magno ed Harun al Rashid* (Bari, 1963); on an embassy brought to light by M. Hamidullah in the *Journal of the Pakistan Historical Society*, I (1953), see G. Levi Della Vida, "La corrispondenza di Berta di Toscana col califfo Muktafī," *Rivista storica italiana*, LXVI (1954), and "Aneddoti e Svaghi" (1959), and also the observations by C. Mor in "Intorno ad una lettera di Berta di Toscana al califfo di Baghdad," *Archivio Storico Italiano*, CXII (1954). On the so-called protectorate of Charlemagne in the Holy Land, the importance of which has been exaggerated, an objective restatement of the question will be found in S. Runciman, "Charlemagne and Palestine," *English Historical Review*, L (1935).

On the 'Abbāsid state, see the general works mentioned on p. 94 ff., but primarily for the origins and conception of the regime, see the important considerations discussed by S. D. Goitein in "A Turning-point in the History of the Muslim State, à propos of ibn al-Muqaffa''s Kitāb al-ṣaḥāba," *IC*, XXIII (1949). For a description of the institutions and the changing character of the vizierate, we now have an essential work by D. Sourdel, LE VIZIRAT ABBASSIDE, two volumes (1959–1960), that supersedes almost all previous publications and presents a picture very different from the traditional image that has been accepted for too long. By the same author, lastly see "La politique religieuse du calife 'abbaside al-Ma'mun," *REI*, XXX (1962), 27–48.

On the army, see W. Hoenerbach, "Zur Heeresverwaltung der Abbasiden, Studie über Abulfarağ Qudāma," *Islam*, XXIX (1950).

ECONOMIC AND SOCIAL INSTITUTIONS

Concerning fiscal organization, the general works cited above, p. 95, deal mainly with the 'Abbāsid period. They may be supplemented by the articles by C. Cahen, cited pp. 90 f. and 134, and especially by A. von Kremer, "Über das Einnahmebudget des Abbasidenreiches," *Denkschriften der Akademie der Wissenschaften in Wien, Phil.-Hist. Kl.*, XXXVI (1888). More particularly for Egypt, supplement these with studies on the papyri by A. Grohmann, especially in *ArO*, VII (1935), on which "Die Verrechnung und Verwaltung von Steuern im islamischen Aegypten," *ZDMG*, CIII (1953), by C. Leyerer, is based, and in which he announced the future publication of a more general financial history.

On the capital of the 'Abbāsid caliphs, Baghdad, see the relevant article by A. A. Duri in *EI*², where the essential information required is provided, and the special issue of *Arabica*, IX (1962).

The economic life can be studied mainly with the help of the general works mentioned above, p. 93 f. They may be supplemented by the excellent article by S. D. Goitein, "The Rise of the Near Eastern Bourgeoisie," *JWH*, III (1956), 583–604. And see: 'A. 'A. Dūrī, *Ta'rīkh al-'Irāq al-iqtiṣādī fī 'l-qarn al-rābi'* (1948), a valuable collection of facts, methodically presented; the provocative article by L. Massignon, "L'influence de l'Islam au moyen âge sur la fondation et l'essor des banques juives," *BEOD*, I (1931); the elaborate technical work by W. Fischel, "The Origin of Banking in Medieval Islam," JRAS, LIII (1933), also included in *Jews in the Economic and Political Life of Medieval Islam* (1937); H. Gottschalk, *Die Māḏarā'iyyūn, Studien zur Geschichte und Kultur des islamischen Orients*, 6. Heft (Berlin and Leipzig, 1931), on an influential family of financiers; A. Yakubovsky, "Ob ispolnikh arendakh v Irake v III v.," *SV*, IV (1947), on agrarian contracts, and also A. S. Ehrenkreutz, cited above, p. 56.

For social and economic history, almost everything of importance has been mentioned on pp. 86 ff. and 91 ff.; also add Th. Nöldeke, "Ein Sklavenkrieg . . . ," in his *Skizzen*, cited p. 137; on the Zanj, Faiṣal al-Sāmir, *Thawrat al-Zanj* (Baghdad, 1945); C. Cahen, "Notes pour l'histoire de la ḥimāya," *Mélanges Louis Massignon*, I (1956), on a form of "commendation" and protection, which may usefully be compared with a similar Byzantine usage; and M. F. Ghāzī, "Un groupe social, 'les Raffinés'," *SI*, XI (1959), 39–71, for an interesting indication of how to deal with documents thought to be too exclusively literary.

On commerce, to the works mentioned on p. 93, add R. Hennig, "Der mittelalterliche arabische Handelsverkehr in Osteuropa," *Islam*, XXII (1935), for its discussion, albeit inconclusive, of the questions raised by the extensive discoveries of Muslim coins in Russia and the Baltic territories, among other subjects.

NATIONAL MOVEMENTS AND SUCCESSOR STATES

On the question of "national" resistance, M. 'Azīzī, *La domination arabe et l'epanouissement du sentiment national en Iran* (1938), is slightly partisan but well informed. On the various dynasties that grew up at the expense of the caliphate in the third and fourth centuries of the Hijra, see: Z. M. Hassan, *Les Tulunides* (Paris, 1933), which does not make superfluous C. H. Becker, "Die Stellung der Tuluniden," in the *Beiträge*, II, cited p. 128; M. Canard, *Histoire de la dynastie des Hamdānides*, I (1951), on historical geography and political history, the second volume of which is awaited; on the Būyids (or Buwaihids), the short study by V. Minorsky, *La domination des Daylamites* (1932); G. Wiet, *Soieries*, cited p. 145; B. Spuler, *Iran*, cited p. 67; C. Cahen, *EI²*, *s.v.*; H. Bowen, "The Last Buwayhids," *JRAS* (1929); on the Ṣaffārids, Th. Nöldeke in his *Skizzen*, cited p. 137, together with W. Barthold's contributions in *Orientalische Studien Theodor Nöldeke . . .* (1906); on the Sāmānids, Barthold, *Turkestan*, cited p. 67; also the recent special studies by Russian scholars, discussed by R. Frye in his "Soviet Historiography on the Islamic Orient," *Historians of the Middle East*, cited p. 22; on the Ghaznawids, M. Nazim, *The Life and Times of Sultan Maḥmūd of Ghazna* (1931); S. Nafīsī's notes in his *Baihaqī*, cited p. 132; C. Bosworth, "Ghaznevid Military Organisation," *Islam*, XXXVI (1960), 37–77, "The Imperial Policy of the early Ghaznawids," *IS*, I/3 (Karachi, 1962), and now his comprehensive *The Ghaznavids. Their Empire in Afghanistan and Eastern Iran* (Edinburgh, 1963). On the South Caspian provinces, see Rabino di Borgomale, "Les dynasties de Mazandéran," *JA* (1936) and "L'histoire du Mazandéran," *JA* (1943–1945); on northwestern Iran, A. Kasravi, *Shahriyārān-i gumnām*, in Persian (1928–1930); V. Minorsky, *Studies in Caucasian History* (1953) and *A History of Sharvan and Darband* (1958); for the Zaidites of the Yemen, see p. 142; for the Fāṭimids, p. 146 ff.; for the Maghrib, p. 220 ff.; for Spain, p. 222 ff.

RELIGIOUS LIFE

The religious movements, which are almost inseparable from political, social, and national history, have been studied more often, although sometimes from too exclusively religious a viewpoint and, in the case of older works, without the resources and methodological safeguards of more recent research. The Iranian movements, both non-Muslim and heretical, are the subject of a good study by G. Sadighi, *Les mouvements religieux iraniens au IIe et au IIIe siècles de l'hégire* (1938). The chief among them, the Babek movement, is discussed in a monograph, in Persian, by S. Nafīsī, *Bābek Khurramdīn* (1955), comprehensively documented. The struggle of Islam against Manicheanism and the *zindīqs* is discussed by M. Guidi in the introduction which precedes his edition of a treatise by al-Qāsim b. Ibrāhīm against Ibn al-Muqaffa' in *La Lotta tra l'Islam e il Manicheismo* (Rome, 1927), on which subject see also G. Vajda, "Les zindīqs en pays de l'Islam au début de la période abbaside," *RSO*, XVII (1938), and F. Gabrieli, La "Zandaqa" au Ier siècle abbaside," in *L'élaboration de l'Islam*, cited p. 98.

An introduction to the question of Mu'tazilism, the rise of which is linked, among other things, with the struggle against the *zindīqs*, will be found in the article by H. Nyberg in *EI*, to whose discoveries we are indebted for the real advances made in this field. See also W. Montgomery Watt, *Free Will and Predestination in Early Islam* (1948), on a question of fundamental importance to the Mu'tazilites, and A. Nader, *Le système philosophique des mu'tazilites* (Beirut, 1956); also D. Sourdel, cited above, p. 103. The struggle against Mu'tazilism, together with the origin of the important Ḥanbalite movement, forms the subject of the study by W. Patton, *Aḥmad b. Ḥanbal and the Miḥna* (1897), still particularly useful for the texts published in it. On Aḥmad b. Ḥanbal himself, see first the article by H. Laoust in *EI*², of major importance.

On the later Khārijites, especially in the East, see L. Veccia Vaglieri, "Le vicende del ḫarigismo in epoca abbaside," *RSO*, XXIV (1949), which suffers from the fact that it ignores the fundamental *Ta'rīkh-i Sīstān*, and T. Lewicki, "Les sub-divisions de l'Ibadiya," *SI*, IX (1958). See also Veccia Vaglieri, "L'imamato ibādito dell Oman," *Annali. Istituto Universitario Orientale di Napoli*, n.s., III (1949). For the Maghrib, see below, page 220.

On Zaidism, the most important of the various Shī'ite movements before and contemporary with the Ismā'īlī movement (on which see p. 146 ff.) the main works are by R. Strothmann, starting with an introduction in his article "Zaidiyya" in *EI*, See also C. van Arendonk, *Les débuts de l'imamat zaydite au Yemen* (1919; reissued 1960), and for the origins of Nuṣairism, dating back to the same period, see the article "Nuṣairiya" by L.Massignon in *EI*.

On Ṣūfism (see p. 99), and more generally on the religious atmosphere of Iraq in the second 'Abbāsid century, there is the masterly work by L. Massignon, LA PASSION D'AL-HALLAJ, two volumes (1932), of which a second edition has been announced, combining extraordinary documentation with a rare gift of sympathetic insight. On the religious atmosphere prevailing in the following century, we now have a valuable study by H. Laoust in the introduction to his translation, *La profession de foi d'Ibn Baṭṭa* (1958). On a significant point of detail, there is an interesting study by C. Pellat, "Le culte de Mu'āwiya au IIIe siècle de l'hégire," *SI* (1956), 53–66.

Concerning Ṣūfism in particular, one may study al-Muḥāsibī, with the aid of the important books by M. Smith, *An Early Mystic of Baghdad; a Study of the Life and Teaching of Ḥārith b. Asad al-Muḥāsibī* (London, 1935); J. van Ess, *Die Gedankenwelt des Ḥāriṯ al-Muḥāsibī* (Bonn, 1961); and al-Kāzarūnī in the light of F. Meier's comments in his edition of the biography by Maḥmūd b. 'Uthmān, *Die Vita des Scheich Abū Isḥaq al-Kāzarūnī* (Leipzig, 1948).

Several studies have recently been devoted to the sect of the Yazīdīs and also its connection to the cult of the Umayyads. As an introduction see the article in *EI*, then see: M. Guidi, "Origine dei Yazīdī e storia religiosa dell'Islam e del dualismo" and "Nuove ricerche sui Yazīdī," both *RSO*, XIII (1931–1932); G. Furlani, "L'antidualismo dei Yezīdī," *Orientalia*, n.s. XIII (1944); and F. Meier, "Der Name der Yazīdī's," *Westöstliche Abhandlungen R. Tschudi* (1954).

On the formation of *fiqh*, see p. 40 ff.

On Sunnite theology, see J. Schacht, "New Sources for the History of Muhammadan Theology," *SI*, I (1953). On the publications concerning al-Ash'arī, an introduction may be found in the article in *EI*[2] by W. Montgomery Watt; see also G. Makdisi, "Ash'arī and the Ash'arites in Islamic religious history," *SI*, XVII–XVIII (1962–1963), and the general works cited p. 97. In this connection, note R. McCarthy's editions of al-Bāqillānī, *Kitāb al-tamhīd* (Beirut, 1957) and *Kitāb al-bayān* (Beirut, 1958), and also his book, *The Theology of al-Ash'arī* (1953).

CULTURAL LIFE, LITERATURE, AND ART

On the literary and intellectual life of the first 'Abbāsid century we have C. Pellat's impressive work, *Le milieu baṣrien et la formation de Djāḥiz* (1953). See also his article "Djāḥiẓ" in *EI*[2]. Important research has also been devoted to the interesting personality of Ibn al-Muqaffa', especially F. Gabrieli, "L'opera di Ibn al Muqaffa'," *RSO*, XIII (1931–1932), and D. Sourdel, "La biographie d'Ibn al-Muqaffa'," *Arabica*, I (1954). On the literary and social movement of rivalry between the adherents of Arabism and the supporters of the traditions of other peoples, see the relevant recent remarks of H. A. R. Gibb, "The social significance of the Shu'ūbīya," *Studia Orientalia . . . Joanni Pedersen septuagenario . . . dicata* (1953).

It was during the 'Abbāsid period that Islam came into possession of a large part of the classical heritage, producing in its turn great works under its fertilizing influence. On the question of translations, see M. Steinschneider, *Die arabischen Übersetzungen aus dem Griechischen* (Graz, 1960), the contents of which originally appeared in *Beihefte zum Centralblatt für Bibliothekswesen*, 5 (1889) and 12 (1893), *Virchows Archiv*, CXXIV (1891), and *ZDMG*, L (1896), still the basic work despite the number of additions and corrections necessary. Among recent special works should be mentioned the articles by R. Walzer on "Aflaṭūn" (Plato) and "Arisṭūṭalīs" (Aristotle) in the Muslim world in *EI*[2], and among his other articles, "The Rise of Islamic Philosophy" *Oriens*, III (1950), all of which are included in his *Greek into Arabic* (1962); M. Plessner, "Hermes Trismegistus and Arab Science," *SI*, II (1954); S. Pines, *Beiträge zur islamischen Atomenlehre* (1936), and the fundamental study, far reaching in its implications, by P. Kraus in his work, *Jābir ibn Ḥayyān. Contribution à l'histoire des idées scientifiques dans l'Islam*, in *MIE*, XLIV (1933) and XLV (1942); a third volume on Jābir's religious position was never finished. A. Badawi has published numerous Arabic translations from the classical languages, and the publication of a *Plato Arabus*, begun by R. Klibansky, is in progress. M. Gaudefroy-Demombynes discusses in *Revue de l'histoire des religions*, CXXIV (1941), the present status of the problems surrounding the person and the works of al-Rāzī that had previously been studied by P. Kraus, M. Meyerhof, J. Ruska, and others. See also A. J. Arberry, *The Spiritual Physick of Rhazes* (1950). On al-Kindī, there is a good recent study by F. Rosenthal, "Al-Kindī and Ptolemy," *Studi orientalistici in onore di Giorgio Levi Della Vida*, II (Rome, 1956); on al-Fārābī, note I. Madkour, *La place d'al-Fārābī dans l'école philosophique musulmane* (1934). To Avicenna (Ibn Sīnā), an introduction is provided by A. Goichon, *La philosophie d'Avicenne et son influence en Europe* (2d ed., 1951) and *Lexique de la langue philosophique d'Avicenne* (1938). The specialists have not been able to agree on all aspects of the great man's work and several important studies have been published more recently, particularly for the millenary of his birth, such as *Mémorial Avicenne* (Cairo, 1952–1954); L. Gardet, *La pensée réligieuse d'Avicenne* (1951) and "L'humanisme gréco-arabe, Avicenne," *JWH*, II (1954–1955); H. Corbin, *Avicenne et le récit visionnaire* (Teheran, 1954), translated into English by W. R. Trask, *Avicenna and the Visionary Recital* (New York, 1960); S. Pinès, "La 'philosophie orientale' d'Avicenne," *Archives d'histoire doctrinale et littéraire du Moyen Âge*, XXVII (1952); and a more general work by S. Afnan, *Avicenna, His Life and Works* (1958). See also A. J. Arberry, *Avicenna on Theology* (1951) and G. Wickens (ed.), *Avicenna* (1952). The millenary of al-Bīrūnī also gave rise to several publications, such as D. Boilot, "L'oeuvre d'al-Beruni, essai bibliographique," *MIDEO*, II (1955), with addenda and corrigenda, III (1956). See also, on Bīrūnī, S. Tolstov (ed.), *Bīrūnī* (Moscow, 1950), in Russian. In general, see S. Grigorian [*Studies in the History of Philosophy in Central Asia and Iran in the VII–XII Century*] (Moscow, 1960), in Russian.

The general works cited on p. 102 f. may be used for the study of literature to which should be added G. E. von Grunebaum, *Kritik und Dichtkunst* (1955); A. Traboulsi, *La critique poétique des arabes jusqu'au Ve siècle de l'hégire* (1955); the outline by H. Pérès, "Le roman dans la littérature arabe," *AIEO*, XVI (1958); M. F. Ghāzī, "La littérature d'imagination en arabe du VIIIe au XIe siècle," *Arabica*, IV (1957), indicating a line of research too often neglected; G. E. von Grunebaum, "Aspects of Arabic Urban Literature," *al-Andalus*, XX (1955), in addition to his studies already cited on p. 96; R. Blachère, *Un poète arabe ... abou ṭ-Tayyib al-Motanabbî* (Paris, 1935); al-Yāsīn, *Al-Ṣāhib Ibn 'Abbād* (Baghdad, 1956); I. Keilani, *Introduction à l'œuvre d'abū Ḥayyān al-Tawhīdī, un essayiste arabe* (1950); H. Laoust, "La vie et la philosophie d'Abū'l-'Alā' al-Ma'arrī," *BEOD*, X (1943–1944), and R. Nicholson, *Studies in Islamic Poetry* (1921).

On Persian literature, see H. Massé, *Firdausi et l'épopée nationale* (1935), and the general works cited on p. 102.

On education, see A. Tritton cited on p. 97, and A. Tibawi, "Muslim Education in the Golden Age of the Caliphate," *IC*, XXVIII (1954).

In the field of art; it is all important to keep in touch with archaeological developments. The excavations at Samarra, the second 'Abbāsid capital, the findings of which have never been completely published, are essential in view of the fact that medieval Baghdad has disappeared, practically without trace. A general view can be obtained from E. Herzfeld, *Erster vorläufiger Bericht über die Ausgrabungen von Samarra* (1912), with plans; his *Geschichte*, cited p. 138; F. Sarre, "Die Kleinfunde von Samarra," *Islam*, V (1914); see also A. Susa, *Rayy Sāmarrā'*, two volumes (Baghdad, 1948–1949), on irrigation. On Baghdad, see above, p. 139.

Outside Iraq, the most important results have been obtained on the outer borders of Iran, both in Afghanistan by D. Schlumberger, "Le palais ghaznévide de Lashkari Bazar," *Syria*, XXIX, (1952), and by J. Sourdel-Thomine, "Les stèles arabes de Bust," *Arabica*, III (1956), and in Central Asia by Russian archaeologists such as S. Tolstov, cited on p. 59. On the Būyid period there is a good study by E. Kühnel, "Die Kunst Persiens under den Būyiden," *ZDGM*, CVI, n.s., 31 (1956).

On the minor arts, important discoveries of materials have gradually helped to close the gaps in our knowledge. See especially G. Wiet, *Soieries persanes* (1948), and also the bibliography in J. D. Pearson, *Index Islamicus* (cited p. 70), page 221 ff.

18

The Ismāʿīlīs and Fāṭimids

SOURCES

For the history of the period extending from the end of the third/ninth century to the beginning of the sixth/twelfth, a special chapter must be devoted to the Ismā'īlī movement—at that time far more important than the other branches of non-Sunnite Islam—and to the Fāṭimid dynasty arising out of it, which ushered in an epoch of independence and exceptional brilliance in Egyptian history.

As already pointed out, the history of Ismā'īlism and the Fāṭimids is being entirely rewritten as a result of the discovery and publication, mostly by W. Ivanow, of the principal works of the sect, long buried in various hiding places in Central Asia, the Yemen, and particularly India. For this reason, almost all the studies at present at our disposal have become obsolete. Much remains to be done, since, of necessity, research has been devoted mainly to the direct interpretation of the works discovered and, to some extent, to the doctrinal aspects of the movement rather than to its general historical context.

L. Massignon's bibliography, "Esquisse d'une bibliographie qarmate," in *A Volume of Oriental Studies . . . E. G. Browne* (1922), of course outdated, is still useful, while W. Ivanow, *A Guide to Ismā'īlī Literature* (1933) (2d ed., 1958), is an annotated edition of an ancient bibliographical handbook.

Almost all the documents relating to the Ismā'īlī movement in our possession, in addition to the general chronicles already noted, belong to the period after the Fāṭimid dynasty took over the movement, so they are not always easy to interpret accurately. A certain number of archives and some official correspondence of the Fāṭimid period have survived: for example, *al-Sijillāt al-mustanṣiriyya* by the fifth Fāṭimid caliph of Egypt, the ninth of the dynasty, which consist of letters to his Yemenite vassals, edited by A. Mājid (Magued) (Cairo, 1954); the autobiographical correspondence of the *dā'ī* or missionary, al-Mu'ayyad al-Shīrāzī, edited by K. Ḥusain (1949); and, of course, the documents reproduced in chronicles and other works emanating from the chancelleries, such as by G. Shayyāl, *Majmū'āt al-wathā'iq al-fāṭimiyya*, I (1958), and the Jewish documents cited on p. 18; see also S. M. Stern, "A Fāṭimid Decree of the Year 524/1120," *BSOAS*, XXIII (1960), and his work cited on p. 21.

Of the Fāṭimid chronicles nothing has survived except indirectly, for instance in Ibn Ẓāfir, whose works are unpublished; in Ibn Muyassar, a Sunnite of the thirteenth century, whose *Annales d'Égypte*, which are incomplete, were edited by H. Massé (1919); especially in Maqrīzī, either in the *Khiṭaṭ*, cited on p. 178, or in his history of the Fāṭimids, of which only the beginning has been edited by H. Bunz (1909), or still better by G. Shayyāl (1948), and the rest of which is preserved in a single unpublished manuscript mentioned in *REI*, X (1936), 352. The general history of the Ismā'īlīs, composed in the ninth/fifteenth century by the *dā'ī*, Idrīs, still unpublished, is disappointing. On Fāṭimid Syria, see Ibn al-Qalānisī, below, p. 163. On the early years of the dynasty in the Maghrib, see below, p. 221 f. M. Hamidullah has brought to light and edited the *Kitāb al-dhakhā'ir wa'l-tuḥaf* (1959) by Ibn al-Zubair, which belongs mainly to the Fāṭimid period and is concerned with the diplomatic exchange of gifts, dealing also with the 'Abbāsids (see above, p. 137). The information on institutions given by the chronicles, often based on Ibn al-Ṭuwair (end of the twelfth century), may be supplemented or verified with the aid of Ibn al-Ṣairafī, *Code de la chancellerie d'état*, edited and translated by H. Massé in *BIFAO*, XI (1914), on which see also A. Mukhlis, *ibid.*, XXV (1925) and XXVI (1926), and of Ibn al-Mammātī and al-Makhzūmī, cited on p. 165. C. Cahen has written an article, "Quelques chroniques anciennes relatives aux derniers Fatimides," *BIFAO*, XXXVII (1937–1938).

The discoveries recently made have been especially fruitful in the field of doctrinal writings, although their content also has general historial implications. Theological works have been published, such as Abū Ya'qūb al-Sijistānī, *Kashf al-maḥjūb*, edited by H. Corbin (1949); al-Kirmānī, *Rāḥat al-'aql*, edited by K. Ḥusain (1952); Nāṣir-i Khusrav, *Jāmi' al-ḥikmatain*, edited by H. Corbin and M. Mu'īn (1953) (on the *Sefer-nāmeh* by the same author, see above, p. 135); and the anonymous *Umm al-kitāb*, edited by W. Ivanow, *Islam*, XXIII (1936), have been published, as were also juridical works, such as Qāḍī al-Nu'mān (on whom see below, p. 217), *Da'ā'im al-Islām*, edited by A. A. A. Fyzee, two volumes (Cairo 1951–1960); and *Kitāb al-iqtiṣār*, edited by M. Mirza for the Institut Français of Damascus (1957). See also the list of his other (mostly unpublished) works in A. A. A. Fyzee, "Qāḍī an-Nu'mān. The Fāṭimid Jurist and Author," *JRAS* (1934). An anonymous encyclopedia, *Rasā'il ikhwān al-ṣafā'* or *The Epistles of the Sincere Brethren*, edited in Beirut (1950), has been known for a longer time, and the precise nature of its relationship to the Ismā'īlī movement has been the subject of much discussion, on which see A. Tibawi, "Ikhwān al-ṣafā' and their Rāsā'il, A Critical Study of a Century and a Half of Research," *IQ*, II (1955). More "popular" works are W. Ivanow, *A Creed of the Fāṭimids* (1936); *al-Hidāyat al-āmiriyya, being an Epistle of the Tenth Fatimid Caliph*, edited by A. A. A. Fyzee (1938), a doctrinal encyclical by al-Āmir; and *al-Majālis al-mustanṣiriyya*, edited by K. Ḥusain, undated, which consists of the doctrinal sessions of the caliph, al-Mustanṣir. Writings by the Syrian Ismā'īlīs have also been published, such as Muḥammad b. 'Alī al-Ṣūrī, *al-Qaṣīda al-ṣūriyya*, edited by 'A. Tāmir for the Institut Français of Damascus (1955).

The small commercial treatise, *Maḥāsin al-tijāra*, has been studied and partially translated by H. Ritter, *Islam*, XII (1921), and recently studied by C. Cahen, "A propos et autour d' 'Ein arabisches Handbuch der Handelswissenschaft'," *Oriens*, XV (1962), 160–171.

Poets, or rather their commentators, have also helped to establish points of history, as for example the information which M. J. de Goeje has extracted from the commentator on Ibn al-Mukarram, and used in "La fin de l'empire des Carmathes du Bahrayn," *JA* (1895), or H. Dérenbourg from 'Umāra of Yemen, cited on p. 150.

GENERAL HISTORY: ISMA'ĪLĪSM; THE FĀṬIMID STATE; SECTS; THE YEMEN

On the origins of the Ismā'īlī movement, Bernard Lewis, *The Origins of Isma'ilism* (1940), is a clear and stimulating demonstration of the principal problems, although his conclusions have been contested on certain points by W. Ivanow, *The Alleged Founder of Isma'ilism* (1946; 2d ed., 1956), and H. F. Al-Hamdānī, *On the Genealogy of the Fatimids*, Publications of the American University of Cairo, School of Oriental Studies, Occasional Papers, I (1956).

On the Qarmaṭians, who were the first Ismā'īlīs to organize open opposition to the 'Abbāsid regime, and on their relations with the Fāṭimids, nothing yet entirely replaces M. J. de Goeje, "Les Carmathes du Bahrayn et les Fatimides," in Vol. I of his *Mémoires d'histoire et de géographie orientales* (2d ed., 1886). One should mention, however, W. Ivanow, "Isma'ilis and Qarmatians," *JBBRAS*, n.s., XVI (1940), and especially S. M. Stern, a paper, under the same title, given at the colloquium on the theme *L'élaboration de l'Islam*, cited p. 98, in which he announced a work on early Ismā'īlīsm to be published shortly. A study by W. Madelung, "Fatimiden und Baḥrainqarmaṭen," has been published in *Islam*, XXIV (1959).

We have no history of the Fāṭimids to replace the old *Geschichte der Fatimiden-Califen* by F. Wüstenfeld (1880), which merely analyzes the data of the chronicles. The general studies, less voluminous and more readable, by De Lacy E. O'Leary, *A Short History of the Fatimid Caliphate* (1923), G. Wiet in the *Histoire*, cited on p. 67, Ḥasan Ibrāhīm Ḥasan, *al-Fāṭimiyyūn fī Miṣr* (1932), and the article "Fāṭimids" in *EI*, were all written before the recent discoveries. An analysis providing, in a more widely known language, the substance of Zāhid 'Alī's *Ta'rīkh-i Miṣr-i Fāṭimiyyīn*, Osmania University Series, No. 371 (Hyderabad-Deccan, 1948), the work in Urdu of an Ismā'īlī author, would be useful.

On the Fāṭimids in the Maghrib, see p. 221.

There exists no good monograph on any of the Fāṭimid caliphs, and even on the most famous of them, al-Ḥākim, there are only the books by M. 'Inān (Cairo, 1937), in Arabic, and by B. Bouthoul (1950), in novel form. More reliable but incomplete is the article on al-Ẓāhir by C. H. Becker in his *Beiträge*, I, cited p. 128.

The more recent studies deal with the politico-religious aspects of the Fāṭimid regime and with Ismā'īlī doctrine. While none of them could afford to ignore the textual discoveries made by W. Ivanow, his rather complicated exposition of many aspects of Ismā'īlī history cannot generally be accepted without question. A brief and incomplete synthesis will be found in his *A Brief Survey of the Evolution of Isma'ilism* (1952). S. M. Stern's studies are more reliable: "Isma'ili Propaganda and Fatimid Rule in the Sind," *IC*, XXIII (1949), "Heterodox Isma'ilism in the Time of al-Mu'izz," *BSOAS*, XVII (1955), and "The Succession to the Fatimid Imām, al-Āmir, The Claims of the Later Fatimids to the Imamate and the Rise of Tayyibī Isma'ilism," *Oriens*, IV (1951). On questions of doctrine, the works of H. Corbin, such as "De la gnose antique à la gnose isma'ilienne," *ALFAV*, XII (1957), are attractive and original. See also W. Madelung, "Das Imamat in der frühen ismailitischen Lehre," *Islam*, XXXVII (1961). See also E. Bertels, *Nasir-i Khosrov i ismailizm* (Moscow, 1959).

On the institutions, A. Mājid (Magued), in his *Nuẓūm al-Fāṭimiyyīn wa-ru'ūmu-hum*, two volumes (1953–1955), does not distinguish clearly enough between what is peculiarly Fāṭimid and what is common to the Muslim states as a whole. The works of M. Canard are more detailed, such as "Le cérémonial fatimite et le cérémonial byzantin," *Byzantion*, XXI (1951); "L'impérialisme des Fatimides et leur propagande," *AIEO*, VI (1942–1947);

"Un vizir chrétien à l'époque fatimite," *AIEO*, XII (1954), and the same author's supplementary article, "Notes sur les Arméniens en Égypte à l'époque fāṭimite" *AIEO*, XIII (1955); and his more recent work on Qalqashandī, *Les institutions des Fatimides en Égypte* (Algiers, 1957). See also P. Vatikiotis, *A Reconstruction of the Fatimid Theory of State* (1957) and "The Syncretic Origins of the Fatimid Da'wa," *IC*, XXVIII (1954); I. Hrbek, "Die Slawen im Dienste der Fatimiden," *ArO*, XXI (1953); and C. Cahen, "Contribution à l'étude des impôts dans l'Égypte fatimide," *JESHO*, V (1962).

On the Fāṭimid missions, see W. Ivanow, "The Organisation of the Fatimid Propaganda," *JBBRAS*, n.s., XV (1938), and H. F. Al-Hamdānī, "The History of the Ismā'īlī Da'wat and its Literature during the Last Phase of the Faṭīmid Empire" *JRAS* (1932).

On economic life, see R. al-Barawī, *Ḥālāt Miṣr al-iqtiṣādiyya fī 'ahd al-Fāṭimiyyin* (1948); also the suggestive observations by Bernard Lewis, "The Fatimids and the Route to India," *IFM*, XI (1949–1950); and the article by S. D. Goitein, "New Light on the Beginnings of the Karimi Merchants," *JESHO*, I (1958); on the pending publication of a book by the same author, see above, p. 93. C. Cahen has prepared a paper on trade, forthcoming in *JESHO*.

Though extremely commendable, J. Mann, *The Jews in Egypt and Palestine during the Fatimid Caliphate* (1920), will have to be completed and revised when the Geniza documents are published.

On the Druzes, a sect that broke away from the Fāṭimids, the masterly account by S. de Sacy, *Exposé de la religion des Druzes*, two volumes (1853), includes correspondence dating from the early years of the sect and still holds good, while P. K. Hitti, *The Origins of the Druze People and Religion* (1928), is a good general survey.

On the Assassins, another sect descended from Ismā'īlīsm, all the necessary documentation has been collected by M. G. S. Hodgson, *The Order of the Assassins* (1955); on the Ṣyrian Assassins, there is a study of sources by Bernard Lewis, "The Sources for the History of the Syrian Assassins," *Speculum*, XXVII (1952).

On the Ṣulaiḥids, Yemenite vassals of the Fāṭimids, see H. Hamdānī, *al-Ṣulaiḥiyyūn* (Cairo, 1955); H. Dérenbourg, *Oumara du Yemen*, two volumes (1897–1904); and H. Kay, *Yaman, Its Early Medieval History . . .* (London, 1892), consisting essentially of translations from 'Umāra al-Ḥakamī, Ibn Khaldūn, and Bahā' al-Dīn al-Janadī.

On Fāṭimid art, we now have the monumental work by K. A. C. Creswell on architecture, cited p. 104.

19

Seljuks and Their Descendants

ELEVENTH TO THIRTEENTH CENTURY

Islam and the Crusades

THE ADVENT OF THE TURKS

The history of the Turks—that is, of the peoples speaking Turkic languages—in Islam, like that of the earlier Arab expansion, has something of the character of a great adventure, and their appearance marks a decisive turning point in the evolution of the East. A primitive people when they arrived from the steppes of Asia, they imposed their rule upon the whole of the Near East, supplanting both Arabs and Iranians in the political arena. When the Mongol onslaught, which swept many Turkic elements along with it, had passed over, they recovered to found an empire—which was to last for many centuries—stretching from the borders of Persia to those of Morocco and from the Crimea to the Yemen, bringing with it the final downfall of Byzantium, and becoming the strongest and most stable of all the political structures in Islam. They are now, finally, for all to see, building a nation on the remains of this empire that is resolutely coming to grips with new ways of life. The founding of the Seljuk Empire, the first link in this extraordinary chain of events, is thus of special interest.

The evolution of the "Eastern question" in the nineteenth century resulted in a strong and long-lasting prejudice in the West against Turkey and things Turkish. With understandable reaction, some contemporary Turkish scholars have perhaps exaggerated the importance of the Turkish contribution in certain fields. All the historian can do is to distinguish as objectively as possible between what, in the history of the Near East, is Turkish and what is common to the Muslim East as a whole. It is certain, however, that the appearance of the Turks is linked with the transformation of Muslim civilization. On one hand, the Turks introduced into the states they founded certain traditions of their own, which belonged to their past in Central Asia, mingled with those they had inherited from their Iranian predecessors that spread with them to the Mediterranean, to say nothing of the innovations arising out of the entirely new situations they faced. On the other hand, whereas the inherent tendencies of the Muslim East favored Turkish ascendancy, the times themselves generally encouraged the diffusion, under their aegis, of new modes of thought and ways of life, which spread as far as Egypt. From then on, despite some convergence of trends, the civilization of the Near East presents certain characteristics that distinguish it from the Maghrib; it remained for a long time, and in some respects always, free from Turkish influence. The Seljuk period is the key to the history of the Near East from the eleventh century onward, and is thus a necessary, albeit remote, introduction to the understanding of certain aspects of the modern Islamic world. Even European history is affected by the Seljuks, since it was their descendants who led the struggle against the Crusaders until their ultimate expulsion. All these considerations combine to make it a period particularly worthy of the historian's attention.

In spite of all the interest this period presents, it had nevertheless been almost completely neglected by historians until quite recently. This is because European Orientalists have allowed themselves to be mesmerized by the so-called classical period of Muslim history. They therefore concentrated their studies on Egypt (not reached by the great movement until a much later date) or on the Maghrib (where it was practically without effect), when, in fact, the roots lie in Persia, Mesopotamia, and Syria, all countries which have not been open to scientific research long enough to have furnished the material for definitive works. Not infrequently, historians have restricted their studies too narrowly, both in time and space, thus passing over a major problem often without a cursory glance.

It must be admitted that the scattered documentation is particularly difficult to handle. In addition to the Latin and French chronicles, which are easy to consult but often useful only as a means of checking data, it will be necessary simultaneously to employ Arabic, Persian, even Greek, Armenian, Syrian, and Georgian sources. It must be said that several Muslim chronicles relating to this period are often vitiated by an excess of rhetoric, since the author, anxious to display the wealth of his vocabulary in endless periods of rhymed prose (*saj'*), wrote page after laborious page, and it is not always apparent whether or not a detail was used merely to provide a sonorous rhyme. The Seljuk period does offer a good opportunity for applying the systematic exploitation of the archaeological sources recommended above. Interesting inscriptions, collections of coins, and monuments are known in sufficient numbers to afford a basis for serious study, and experience has shown that a substantial contribution can be made to our knowledge of the period, especially with regard to its institutions.

TOOLS OF RESEARCH IN OLD TURKISH HISTORY

A few works are common to the whole field of Turkology and, though Turkish does not become the language of the historical sources, except in Central Asia, until the fourteenth century, and then only partially, a knowledge of modern Turkish is practically indispensable for the study of all periods of Turkish history because of the contributions Turkish scholars have made to the history of their people. First one should mention the *Islam Ansiklopedisi*, which in 1963 has completed the letter R. It is a Turkish translation of the *Encyclopaedia of Islam* (*EI*) but with the addition of original, often important, articles on Turkish subjects. Of the *Philologiae Turcicae Fundamenta*, initiated by J. Deny, V. Grønbech, H. Scheel, Z. V. Togan, similar in pattern to the old *Grundzüge der iranischen Philologie*, only the first volume, devoted to language, has appeared (1959). Other volumes are planned on history and literature (the latter in press), as well as one on auxiliary sciences. In the meantime, the best comprehensive introductions to Turkish studies are the article "Turk" in *EI* and *Turkologie* in *HO*, cited p. 67 f., I, V/1. In Turkish, Zeki Velidi Togan, *Umumī türk tarihine giriş* (Istanbul, 1946), and *Tarihde usul* (Istanbul, 1950), may profitably be used provided they are read critically. For the bibliography, see above, p. 70. G. Moravcsik has published an inventory with ample notes of all the information on the Turks—taking the term in its broadest sense—to be gleaned from Byzantine authors, entitled *Byzantino-Turcica*, two volumes (Berlin, 1958).

The invasion of Muslim territory by the Turks is partly the result of a series of events that had taken place earlier on the steppes of Asia. A quick introduction is available in the clear account by J. Deny, "L'expansion des Turcs en Asie jusqu'au XIe siècle," in *En terre d'Islam* (1939), 191–215; there is also a brochure by P. Pelliot, *La Haute-Asie* (Paris, 1931); and more recently L. Hambis, *La Haute-Asie* (Paris, 1953), in the series Que sais-je?, no. 573. But the best general survey is that by W. Barthold, first published in Turkish, *Orta Asia Türk tarihi hakkinda dersler* (Istanbul, 1927), translated into German, *Zwölf Vorlesungen über die Geschichte der Türken Mittelasiens* (Berlin, 1935), and into French, *Histoire des turcs d'Asie Centrale* (Paris, 1945). See the forthcoming *HO* (cited p. 67 f.), I, V/5 on the history of the Turks in Asia. Further details can be obtained from a work by R. Grousset, with the attractive title *L'empire des steppes* (Paris, 1939). More especially on the Oghuz, the forebears of the Seljuks, see A. Iakubovskii, "[The Seljuk Movement and the Turcomans,]" in Russian, in *Izvestiia Akad. Nauk SSSR* (1937); Faruk Sümer, "X yüzyılda Oğuzlar," *AÜDTFD*, XVI (1958); and O. Pritsak, "Der Untergang des Reiches des oguzischen Yabgu," *MK* (1953), 397–221. See also the commentaries by V. Minorsky in his editions of geographical works, cited on p. 136.

We lack a general survey of the institutions and customs of the Old Turks necessary if we are to find out what was retained of them after their migration into Western Asia. A general work of this kind will be well-nigh impossible for some time as the scarcity and distribution of the information demand a knowledge of many languages. For the student of Islam, one of the most noteworthy items for a general picture of this kind is provided by the *Divanü lûghat-it-Türk* by Maḥmūd Kashgharī, edited by K. Rifat, two volumes (A.H. 1333), an eleventh-century Turkish-Arabic dictionary that is astonishingly rich in information of every kind, and to which an incomplete but practical introduction may be found by C. Brockelmann, *Mitteltürkischer Wortschatz* (1928).

GENERAL SOURCES AND SOURCES ON SELJUK HISTORY

Two general histories of the Muslim world should head this section: the *Kāmil* by Ibn al-Athīr (thirteenth century), edited by C. J. Tornberg, fourteen volumes (Leiden and Upsala, 1851–1876), an intelligent and remarkably well-informed work, although the author sometimes disguises his genuine information by his method of handling it; and the *Mir'āt al-zamān* by Sibṭ b. al-Jawzī, of which only the part covering the twelfth and thirteenth centuries, to 1253, has been published, in facsimile, by J. R. Jewett (1907), and, following him, at Hyderabad, two volumes (1951–1952), a less well-informed work, except on Mesopotamia and Syria, but faithfully preserving important sources that have not always survived elsewhere.

The history of the Karakhānids, the first Turkish dynasty in Central Asia and not well known, is excellently described in W. Barthold, *Turkestan*, cited p. 67, which may be supplemented or verified in some details by O. Pritsak, "Die Karachaniden," *Islam*, XXXI (1954), 17–68.

The narrative sources for the history of the Seljuks form the subject of a paper by C. Cahen contained in *Historians of the Middle East*, cited p. 22. Apart from the Mesopotamian sources, mainly accessible through the *Mir'āt al-zamān* by Sibṭ b. al-Jawzī, for the fifth/eleventh century, unpublished, and the *Kāmil* by Ibn al-Athīr just cited, above, the principal sources are the *Histoire des Seldjoucides de l'Iraq* by 'Imād al-Dīn al-Iṣfahānī, based on al-Bundārī's slightly abridged version, edited by M. Th. Houtsma, *Histoire des Seldjoucides de l'Iraq*, Vol. II (1889) of *Recueil de textes relatifs a l'histoire des Seldjoucides*, four volumes (Leiden, 1889–1902); the *Akhbār al-dawla al-saljūqiyya*, attributed to 'Alī b. Nāṣir, edited by M. Iqbāl (Lahore, 1933); and, in Persian, the *Seljūqnāmeh* by Ẓahīr al-Dīn Nīshāpūrī, edited by G. Khāwar (Teheran, 1963), of which there is an arrangement by Rāwandī in the *Rāḥat al-ṣudūr*, edited by M. Iqbāl, *GMS*, n.s., II (1927). The part concerning the reign of Sanjar has been edited and translated by C. Schefer as *Tableau du règne de Mouïss-eddin Aboul Harith Sultan Sindjar* in Publications de l'École des Langues Orientales Vivantes, Sér. II, XIX (Paris, 1886). (*Storey* [cited p. 51], I, 257, warns of Schefer's translation as full of grave errors that entirely alter the sense.) Among the local chronicles, M. Th. Houtsma, *Histoire des Seldjoucides du Kermân par Muḥammad b. Ibrahîm*, Vol. I of *Recueil* (Leiden, 1886), analyzed by the same author in *ZDMG*, XXXIX (1885), 362–401, is in fact based on the *Badī' al-zamān* by Afḍal al-Dīn Kirmānī, of which it has been possible to reconstruct the text by collation of the various compilations, edited by Mahdī Bayānī (Teheran, 1947). On the other hand G. Makdisi has published an interesting "diary" by a citizen of Baghdad in the time of Alp Arslan, "The Autograph Diary of an XIth Century Historian," *BSOAS*, XVIII-XIX (1956–1957). The enormous *Muntaẓam*, in which Ibn al-Jawzī (twelfth century) was the first to collect, year by year, notes on events and about deceased people of importance, is no more than a Mesopotamian, or even Baghdadian chronicle, written from a Ḥanbalite point of view, and though somewhat careless, is very useful within its limited scope. It has been edited at Hyderabad in ten volumes (1939–1940), five of which are devoted to the text and five to the index, wisely omitting the portion dating from before the fourth/tenth century.

The historicopolitical memoirs, in Persian, of the famous vizier Niẓām al-Mulk, *Siyāsatnāmeh*, were edited with a French translation by C. Schefer (Paris, 1891–1893), in English by H. Darke (London, 1960), in German by K. E. Schabinger von Schowingen (Freiburg, 1960), and in Russian by B. Zakhoder (Moscow, 1949).

We also possess, for the Seljuk period, correspondence and official documents, owing particularly to the collection by Muntakhab al-Dīn Badī', *'Atabat al-kataba*, edited by M. Qazwīnī and A. Eghbāl (1950), the usefulness of which can be appreciated from Ann K. S. Lambton, "The Administration of Sanjar's Empire as illustrated in the 'Atabat al-kataba," *BSOAS*, XIX (1957).

On the last of the Ghaznawids and their successors, the Ghūrids, who were eastern contemporaries of the Seljuks, the principal source is Jūzjānī, *Ṭabaqāt-i Nāṣirī*, edited by W. N. Lees (Calcutta, 1864), of which there are other Oriental editions, translated by H. Raverty, two volumes (London, 1881).

On the chief Iranian epigones of the Seljuks, the Khwārizmshāhs, the most important special sources are: in Persian, the second volume of the *Tārīkh-i Jahāngushā* by 'Aṭā-Malik Juwainī, edited by M. Qazwīnī, *GMS*, XVI/2 (1916), translated into English by J. Boyle, *The History of the World Conqueror* (Manchester, 1958), from Vol. I, page 277, to Vol. II, page 78; and in Arabic, for the end of the dynasty, the *Vie de Jalal al-din Manguberti* by Nasawī, edited with French translation by O. Houdas in two volumes (Paris, 1891), and also edited in Cairo (1953). We also have a very valuable collection of official documents in Bahā' al-Dīn al-Baghdādī, *al-Tawaṣṣul ilā 'l-tarassul*, edited by A. Bahmanyār (Teheran, 1936). The *Mu'jam al-buldān* by Yāqūt (above, p. 39) and the *Guide des lieux de pèlerinage* by 'Alī al-Harawī, edited by J. Sourdel-Thomine (Damascus, 1957), also belong to the same period. On Idrīsī, see p. 219.

THE SELJUKS OF THE EAST, MODERN WORKS

The history of the Seljuk period has only been treated generally in works of a wider scope, and then very inadequately. The most recent works on the early years are by C. Cahen, "Le Maliknameh et l'histoire des origines seldjoucides," *Oriens*, II (1949), and by C. Bosworth, cited on p. 141. Elements for a general survey of the great Seljuks may be found, by the same author, in the chapter, "The Turkish Invasion: the Selchükids," in Vol. I of *A History of the Crusades*, edited by K. Setton (Philadelphia, 1955), of which the second volume appeared in 1962. On Malikshāh one may consult I. Kafesoglu, *Sultan Melikşah devrinde Büyük Selçuklu Imperatorluğu* (Istanbul, 1953). On their expansion to the West, see C. Cahen, "La première pénétration turque en Asie Mineure," *Byzantion*, XVIII (1948), 6–68 (which also deals with Syria and Upper Mesopotamia). On their decadence, see M. Köymen, *Büyük Selçuklu İmperatorluğu tarihi*, Vol. II of *Ikinci imperatorluk devri* (Ankara, 1954), Vol. I of which did not appear, and F. Sanāullāh, *The Decline of the Seljukid Empire* (Calcutta, 1938). Information on the institutions will be found in A. Eghbāl [*The Vizirate in the Age of the Great Seljuks*], in Persian, (1959); V. Barthold and A. Siddiqi, cited p. 95; Ann K. S. Lambton, cited pp. 90 and 94; and C. Cahen, [*La tughrā*], *JA* (1943–1945). On Niẓām al-Mulk, see the article by H. Bowen in *EI*, the studies by K. E. Schabinger von Schowingen in *Historisches Jahrbuch*, LXIX (1942–1949) and LXXI (1952), and on the subject of his death, K. Rippe in *MK* (1953).

On the policy of official support for orthodox teaching, one of the chief characteristics of the regime, an introduction will be found in the article "Masdjid" in *EI* by J. Pedersen, Section F of which contains an account of the madrasas. On the most important of these, A. Talas, *La Madrasa Nizamiyya et son histoire* (1939), is a small and superficial work.

On the economic life of the Seljuk empire, there is little worthy of mention besides Jean Aubin's article, "La ruine de Siraf et les routes du golfe persique," *Cahiers de civilisation médiévale*, II (1959).

More has been written concerning the spiritual temper of the times, which was heavily oriented toward Ṣūfism. On Ghazālī, the philosopher who represents the passing from the age of scholasticism to the age of mysticism, the main outlines will be found in A. J. Wensinck, *La pensée de Ghazali* (1940); the more detailed but controversial research by M. Asín Palácios, *La espiritualidad de Algazel*, four volumes (1934–1941); and G.-H. Bousquet's analysis, in French, of his main work, the *Iḥyā' 'ulūm al-dīn* (Paris, 1955). See the new book by W. Montgomery Watt, *Muslim Intellectual* (1963), on Ghazālī. On the mystics, the principal works are concerned with al-Suhrawardī, discussed by H. Corbin in a series of studies to which his small general work, *Suhrawardi d'Alep* (1939), forms an introduction; Najm al-dīn Kubrā, whose *Fawā'iḥ al-jamāl* have been studied and annotated by F. Meier (Wiesbaden, 1957); and 'Abd al-Qādir al-Jīlānī, on whom the article by W. Braune in *EI*² gives the general outline.

On the Assassins, see above, p. 150.

On the growth of a Turco-Muslim literature alongside Arabic and Persian literature, the standard work is still M. F. Köprülü, *Türk Edebiyatinda ilk Mutasavvıflar* (*The Early Mystics in Turkish Literature*), (Istanbul, 1918), of which an analysis by C. Huart will be found in the *Journal des savants* (1922).

On art and archaeology, see, in addition to the general works: E. Diez, *Iranische Kunst* (1944); J. Sauvaget, "Observations sur quelques mosquées seldjoukides," *AIEO*, IV (1938); J. Sourdel-Thomine, "Deux minarets d'époque seldjoukide en Afghanistan," *Syria*, XXX (1953); A. Godard, "Historique du Masjid-e-Djuma d'Ispahan," *Athār-ē Īrān* (1936); and the review by O. Grabar in *Ars orientalis*, II (1957), 545–547, of a book by A. M. Pribitkova (Moscow, 1955) on recent Russian excavations.

Little has been written on the Ghūrids, although the study made by A. Maricq and G. Wiet on the Jam minaret, discovered on the site of the former Ghūrid capital, entitled *Le minaret de Djam* (Paris, 1959), with a historial introduction, is worthy of attention. On the Khwārizmshāhs, see I. Kafesoglu, *Harezmşahlar Devleti Tarihi* (*485–617/1092–1229*) (1956).

THE CALIPHATE AFTER THE REIGN OF THE SELJUKS

It was during the period of Seljuk decline that the caliphate regained political independence. For the history of the caliphate at this stage, after the *Muntaẓam* (above, p. 155), the principal source would have been Ibn al-Sā'ī, *al-Jāmi' al-mukhtaṣar*, but only one volume has survived, covering the years A.H. 595–606, edited by F. Anastase-Marie, O. Carm. (1934).

From the year A.H. 626 onward, we have a work that draws much of its inspiration from the Mongol period by Ibn al-Fuwaṭī, *al-Ḥawādith al-jāmi'a*, edited by M. Jawād (Baghdad, 1932).

The most interesting personality is the caliph al-Nāṣir, one of whose activities—and that which has been most studied—was the reform of the *futuwwa* (see p. 92). On this subject one should consult, in addition to F. Taeschner's account, cited on the same page, his earlier and more detailed studies, in particular "Islamisches Ordensrittertum zur Zeit der Kreuzzüge," *Welt als Geschichte*, IV (1938) and "Das Futuwwa-Rittertum des islamischen Mittelalters," *Beiträge zur Arabistik, Semitistik und Islamwissenschaft*, edited by R. Hartmann and H. Scheel (Leipzig, 1944); also P. Kahle, "Die Futuwwa-Bündnisse des Kalifen en-Nasir," an improved edition in his *Opera Minora* (1956); the study and translation, by H. Thorning, of a most important text that he brought to light in the course of a wider study, *Beiträge zur Kenntniss des islamischen Vereinswesens* (1913), which came before the edition of Ibn al-Mi'mār al-Baghdādī's *Kitāb al-futuwwa* by al-Hilālī, M. Jawād, A. al-Najjār, and A. Nājī al-Qaisī (Baghdad, 1960), and which although of uneven quality, is valuable; C. Cahen, "Les débuts de la futuwwa d'an-Nacir," *Oriens*, VI (1953); the article "Mouvements populaires ... ," cited p. 92; and A. Gölpınarlı, in the work cited on p. 159. See also the article by A. Salinger, "Was the Futuwwa an Oriental Form of Chivalry?" in *Proceedings of the American Philosophical Society* (1950).

TURKISH ASIA MINOR

The history of the first Turkish dynasty in Asia Minor is of special interest as the ancestor of modern Turkey, owing its originality to the fact that it grew up, not in ancient Muslim territory, but in a country of Byzantine tradition. The only general statement on the question is by V. Gordlevskii, *Gosudarstvo Seldzhukidov Maloi Azii* (Moscow, 1941), now in his *Selected Works*, I (1960), written, unfortunately, before the recent publication of several important documents. A brief general outline will be found in the chapter by C. Cahen, "Turks in Iran and Anatolia before the Mongol Invasion," in Vol. II of *A History of the Crusades* (1962). The same author hopes to publish a general work on the subject later.

The oldest Muslim historiographical source for Asia Minor dates back no further than the second half of the thirteenth century; the *el-Evāmirü 'l-'Alā'iyye fī 'l-umūri 'l-'Alā'iyye* by Ibn Bībī, edited by A. Erzi and N. Lugal, Vol. I (Ankara, 1957), the second volume of which has not yet been published, but is available in a photostat edition by A. Erzi (1956); a slightly abridged version was published much earlier by M. Th. Houtsma in the fourth volume of his *Recueil* (cited p. 154), *Histoire des Seldjoucides d'Asie Mineure d'après l'abrégé du Seldjouknāmeh d'Ibn-Bībī* (1902), in Persian, as was also the Turkish adaptation by Yaziji-Oghlu (fourteenth century) in the third volume, *Histoire des Seldjoucides d'Asie Mineure d'apres Ibn-Bībī* (1902); a German translation of the Persian abridged version has been published by H. Duda, *Die Seltschukengeschichte des Ibn Bibi* (1959), with additional material from the original. For the first half of the thirteenth century, add to Ibn Bībī the following authors who supplement, or after 1280 continue, his work: Kerīm ül-dīn Maḥmūd (Aqsarāyī), *Müsâmeret ül-ahbār*, edited by O. Turan (1944), with a detailed analysis in German by F. Işiltan, *Die Seltschukengeschichte des Aksarāyī* (1943), and the anonymous work edited by F. Uzluk under the title *Anadolu Selçuklulari devleti tarihi* (Ankara, 1952).

The hagiographical treatises are also increasingly important for this period, and in particular Eflākī on the Mevlevi dervishes, translated into French by C. Huart with the title *Les saints des derviches tourneurs*, two volumes (1918–1922), which can be supplemented by the correspondence of the founder, Jalāl al-Dīn Rūmī, edited by F. Uzluk, *Mevlananın mektubları* (Istanbul, 1937). On Rūmī, see R. Nicholson's small volume, *Rūmi* (1950). In a similar way, the treatises on *futuwwa*, of which the most important has been published in facsimile, translated into Turkish, and analyzed in French by A. Gölpınarlı, "Islām ve türk illerinde futüvvet teşkilātı ve kaynakları," *IFM*, XI (1949), 3–345, for the Turkish and French edition of which, see *ibid.*, XVII (1956). One of the most important was published by F. Taeschner, *Der anatolische Dichter Nasiri und sein Futuvvetname* (1944). See also such poets as Sultan Veled. For the thirteenth century we also have foundation deeds of *waqf*s, several of which have been edited by O. Turan in *Belleten*, XI (1947) and XII (1948); also other archives or collections of *inshā'* in various languages assembled by the same author in his *Türkiye Selçukları Hakkında Resmî Vesikalar* (Ankara, 1958). There is also the important general study on sources of all kinds by M. F. Köprülü, "Anadolu Selçukları tarihinin yerli kaynakları," *Belleten*, VII (1943).

For the eleventh and twelfth centuries, the only sources are either Arabic, secondarily Persian, or Greek works by authors such as Georgios Kedrenos, Johannes Skylitzes, Michael Attaliates, Nikephoros Bryennios, Anna Komnena, Johannes Kinnamos, and Niketas Choniates, all edited in *Corpus historiae Byzantinae* (Bonn, 1828–1897), though a better edition of Anna Komnena is *Alexias* edited with translation by B. Leib, three volumes (Paris, 1937–1945); there is also an English translation by E. Dawes (1928). There are also sources in Armenian (see below, p. 165), Georgian (see p. 51),

Latin (p. 165 f.), and most of all in Christian Syriac (p. 165). Nor should one altogether neglect Turkish epic literature, especially the *Dānishmend-nāmeh*, edited by Irène Mélikoff, *La geste de Mêlik Danishmend*, two volumes (1960). See also a work in Russian by V. Garbuzov, *Kissa-e Melik-Danishmend* (1959).

The inadequacy of the sources makes the Arabic inscriptions reproduced in the *Répertoire*, cited p. 53 f., particularly valuable. Thesewere published earlier, above all in Ismā'īl Ḥakkı [Uzunçarsılı]; *Kitabeler ve Sahip Saruhan Aydın Menteşe, İnanç, Hamit oğulları hakkında malûmat*, two volumes (Istanbul, 1927–1929), in the *Corpus*, cited p. 53 f., and in certain of the monographs on towns, mentioned below. For currency, see the catalogues, cited p. 55, and P. Casanova, "Numismatique des Danishmendites," *Revue Numismatique*, Sér. III, Vols. XII-XIV (1894–1896).

The history of events in Turish Asia Minor should be studied on the basis of the articles in the *Islam Ansiklopedisi*, cited p. 153, and in *EI*[2]. The period of the conquests has been studied by J. Laurent, *Byzance et les Turcs seldjoucides jusqu'en 1081* (1931), but vitiated by the author's ignorance of Arabic and Persian; M. Halil Yınanç, *Türkiye Tarihi. Selçuklular devri*, Vol. I of *Anadolu'nun fethi* (1st ed., 1934; 2d ed., 1944); and C. Cahen, "La première pénétration turque en Asie Mineure," *Byzantion*, XVIII (1948) and "La campagne de Mantzikert," *Byzantion*, IX (1934). For the twelfth century an aspect of Turkish history is treated from the Byzantine point of view, in F. Chalandon, *Les Comnènes*, two volumes, the first of which is on Alexis (1900), and the second on John and Manuel (1912). P. Wittek, "Von der byzantinischen zur türkischen Toponymie," *Byzantion*, X (1935), deals with the history of Western Asia at the end of the century.

The conflict of forces dominating this period of history has been well defined by P. Wittek in "Deux chapitres de l'histoire des Turcs de Rum," *Byzantion*, XI (1936). An introduction to other problems may be found in two articles by C. Cahen, "Le problème ethnique en Anatolie" and "Le régime de la terre et l'occupation turque en Anatolie," *JWH*, II (1954) and III (1955), and also by the same author in "Le commerce anatolien au début du XIIIe siècle," *Mélanges ... du Moyen Âge ... Louis Halphen* (Paris, 1951), 91–101; also see O. Turan, "Le droit terrien sous les Seldjoukides de Turquie," *REI*, XVI (1948), 25–49, and "Les souverains Seldjoukides et leurs sujets non-musulmans," *SI*, I (1953), 65–100. Concerning the Anatolian form of the *futuwwa*, the *akhi*, see the article by F. Taeschner, cited on p. 158 f., and his article "akhi" in *EI*[2], both of which refer to his earlier studies, in particular in *Islamica*, IV (1929). See also A. Gölpinarli, cited p. 159. Finally, on the economic life of the Seljuk-

Mongol period (end of the thirteenth century), there is an important article by A. Zeki Velidi [Togan], "Moğollar devrinde Anadolu'nun iktisadî vasiyeti," in *Türk Hukuk ve İktisat Tarihi Mecmuası*, I (1931), and see also M. Akdağ, "Türkiye'nin iktisadî ve ictimaî tarihi, I, 1243–1453," *AÜDTCFYay*, CXXXI (1953).

There has been much discussion on the probable origin of the Turks of Dobruja, followers of the Seljuk ruler, Kaikā'ūs II. The latest study is by P. Wittek, "Les Gagaouzes, Les gens de Kaykaus," *RO*, XVII (1951–1952), 12–24, and "Yazıjıoghlu on the Christian Turks of the Dobruja," *BSOAS*, XIV (1952), 639–668, providing a complete picture of that controversy; see also P. Mutafciev, "Die angebliche Einwanderung von Seldschuk-Türken in die Dobrudscha im XIII. Jahrhundert," *Spinasie na Bulgarskata Akademia na Naukite i Izkustvata*, LXVI/1 (1943); F. Babinger, *Beiträge zur Frühgeschichte der Türkenherrschaft in Rumelien, XIV.–XV. Jhdt.* (1944); and H. Duda, "Balkantürkische Studien," *SBAW, Phil.-Hist. Kl.*, CCXXVI/1 (1949).

The historical geography of Asia Minor has been the subject of general study only for the Ottoman and Byzantine periods, such as E. Honigmann, cited p. 138, and W. Ramsay, *The Historical Geography of Asia Minor* (1890). Archaeology has been the subject of more numerous works: the magnificent compendia by A. Gabriel, *Monuments turcs d'Anatolie*, two volumes (1931–1934) for Central Asia Minor; and *Voyages archéologiques dans les provinces orientales de la Turquie*, with a study on inscriptions by J. Sauvaget (1940). They do not render redundant the special studies on towns by European or Turkish scholars, such as F. Sarre, *Qonya* (1913), Halil Edhem, *Qaisariye Shehri* (A.H. 1328), Ismā'īl Ḥakkı [Uzunçarsılı] and R. Nafid, *Sivas Shehri* (1925), and T. Yaman, *Kastamonu Tarihi* (1935), which are general histories of the towns and deal fully with the local archaeological material. On the art of the Seljuk period, see also K. Erdmann, "Beobachtungen auf einer Reise in Zentralanatolien," *Jahrbuch des Deutschen Archäologischen Instituts, Archäologischer Anzeiger*, LXIX (1954), and K. Yetkin, *L'architecture turque en Turquie* (Paris, 1962), whose views are disputable.

On the cultural life, the basic works are in Turkish: M. F. Köprülü, *Türk Edebiyat Tarihi* (1926) and "Selçukîler zamanında Anadoluda Türk medeniyeti," *Milli Tetebbüler Mecmuası*, II (A.H. 1331), who has provided a stimulus for this branch of research; from the linguistic standpoint, M. Mansuroğlu, "The Rise and Development of Written Turkish in Anatolia," *Oriens*, VII (1954); A. Bombaci, cited p. 103; and by M. F. Köprülü, the article "Türk" in *EI*, and "Anatolische Dichter in der Seldschukenzeit," *Körösi Csoma-Archivum*, I (1921–1925) and II (1926–1932).

On the chief poet in the Turkish language, see A. Gölpınarlı, *Yunus Emre* (1936). It is well known that most of the literary works were written not in Turkish but in Persian, which is discussed by A. Ateş, "Hicre VI-VIII asırlarda Anadolu'da farsça eserler," *Türkiyat Mecmuasi*, VII-VIII (1945). Concerning the greatest poet in the Persian language in Anatolia, who was also its greatest mystic and founder of the Mevlevi order, see A. Gölpınarlı, *Mevlana Celalüddin* (2d ed., 1952), H. Ritter, "Philologika XI. Maulānā Ğalāladdīn Rūmī und sein Kreis," *Islam*, XXVI (1940–1942), and the article "Djalāl ad-Dīn Rūmī" in *EI*[2] by A. Bausani. On religious life see O. Turan, "Selçuk Türkiyesi din tarihine dair bir kaynak," *MK* (1953), and various of M. F. Köprülü's articles, of which one may form some impression from his study, in French, "Les origines du bektachisme," for the *4e Congrès International d'histoire des religions* (1923).

See also the works relating to the origins of the Ottoman Empire, cited p. 202.

THE CRUSADES

The history of the Syrian, Mesopotamian, and Egyptian states which sprang up under the aegis of the Seljuks has suffered neglect, owing especially to the marked bias in favor of the study of the history of the Crusades from a predominantly European or Christian point of view. In order to acquaint oneself with their history, one must have recourse to the general histories of the Crusades and of the so-called Latin East, particularly to those that attempt to assess the Muslim reaction, such as W. Stevenson, *The Crusaders in the East* (Cambridge, 1907); S. Runciman, *A History of the Crusades*, three volumes (London, 1951–1954); *A History of the Crusades*, cited p. 156, and, in French, R. Grousset, *Histoire des croisades et du royaume franc de Jérusalem* (1934), which is spoiled by excessive sentimentality. All these works are strictly limited to political history; an attempt at a wider understanding will be found in C. Cahen, *La Syrie du Nord à l'époque des croisades* (Paris, 1940), an early work written before the author was sufficiently aware of the true nature of Islam. On the Muslim reaction and the mutual influence exerted by Islam and the Latin East, a few useful suggestions may be found in A. S. Atiya, "The Crusades. Old Ideas and New Conceptions," *JWH*, II/2 (1954–1955), and C. Cahen, "L'Islam et la croisade," in the *Relazioni del X Congresso Internazionale di Scienze Storiche*, III (Florence, 1955), 625–635, or his article "Crusades" in *EI*[2].

The Latin East may be studied with profit even by the student of Islamic history, on the one hand for that which it retained of its Muslim past, and on the other for its comparatively rich documentation, which is of assistance in the reappraisal of certain factors in the general history of Syria and Palestine: see for example, C. Cahen, "La féodalité et les institutions politiques de l'Orient Latin," *ALFAV*, XII (1957), and "Le régime rural syrien pendant l'occupation franque," *Bulletin de la Faculté des Lettres de Strasbourg*, XXIX (1951). A rich bibliography for the Crusades and for the Latin East has been provided, in German, by H. Mayer, *Bibliographie zur Geschichte der Kreuzzüge* (Munich, 1960). Less up to date is A. S. Atiya's *The Crusade: Historiography and Bibliography*, companion volume to the author's *Crusade. Commerce and Culture* (both Bloomington, Indiana, 1962). It offers, however, a detailed outline of the major monumental collections of sources and documents related to the history of the Crusades such as *RHC*, *Palestine Pilgrim's Text Society Library*, *Archives de l'Orient Latin Exuviae Sacrae Constantinopolitanae*, *Bibliothèque des Croisades*, *Records of Civilization*, and *BGA*.

On the Muslim states themselves, a review of sources will be found in the introduction, by C. Cahen, to his *La Syrie du Nord àl'époquedescroisades* (Paris, 1940), and in some valuable critical notes on some of them by H. A. R. Gibb, "Notes on the Arabic Materials for the History of the Early Crusades," *BSOAS*, VII (1933–1935), 739–754, and "The Arabic Sources for the Life of Saladin," *Speculum*, XXV (1950), of which selected excerpts have been translated into Italian by F. Gabrieli, *Storici arabi delle crociate* (1957, 2d ed., 1963). The Arabic sources relating to the history of the Near East about the time of the Crusades have been collected in the *Recueil des historiens des croisades* (*RHC*) (Paris, 1841–1906); there five volumes are devoted to Frankish sources (*RHCHoc*, 1844–1895); two to Greek (1875–1881); two to Armenian sources (*RHCArm*, 1869–1906); five to extracts from Arab chronicles, (*RHCHor*, 1872–1896); and two further volumes are devoted to the laws of the Crusades states (1841–1843); Syriac sources are not included. Its excellent presentation and imposing size do not, unfortunately, exclude a number of serious defects. The standard of editing and translation is uneven, cuts have been made arbitrarily without notation, and the choice of works published is uncritical. At the present time the principal published sources are: for the mid-twelfth century, in particular the *History of Damascus* by Ibn al-Qalānisī, edited by H. Amedroz (Leiden, 1908), translated into English, for the period of the Crusades only, and with a few omissions, by H. A. R. Gibb, *The Damascus Chronicle of the Crusades* (London, 1932), which has an excellent introduction, and into French by R. Le Tourneau, *Damas de 1075 a 1154* (Damascus, 1952); for Saladin and his times, in the absence of the complete history by 'Imād al-Dīn al-Iṣfahānī, of which only three unedited fragments (one of them in Morocco) have survived, see a work which uses it in combination with other sources, by Abū Shāma, *Le livre des deux jardins,* of which there are substantial extracts edited and translated by A. C. Barbier de Meynard in *RHCHor,* IV (1898) and V (1906), printed in full in Cairo (1287/1872) and currently being edited by A. Hilmy of which the first volume appeared (Cairo, 1957). See also the biography of Saladin by Ibn Shaddād in *RHCHor,* III (1884), of which there is an English translation by C. R. Conder, *The Latin Kingdom of Jerusalem* (1897).

ZENGIDS AND AYYŪBIDS: SOURCES

The thirteenth-century authors are represented by the following: Ibn al-Athīr, cited p. 154, in extracts in *RHCHor,* I (1872) and II (1876), and in the "Histoire des Atabeks de Mossoul," *RHCHor,* II; Sibṭ b. al-Jawzī, cited p. 154; Ibn Wāṣil, *Mufarrij al-kurūb,* being edited by G. Shayyāl (1953——), of which three volumes, extending to the reign of al-Kāmil, have been published; Kamāl al-Dīn b. al-'Adīm, *Zubdat al-ḥalab min ta'rīkh Ḥalab,* edited by S. Dahhān, two volumes published thus far (Damascus, 1951——); extracts have been edited and translated by A. C. Barbier de Meynard in *RHCHor,* III (1848) for the years 1096 to 1146; there is a mediocre translation of the years following 1146 by E. Blochet in *Revue de l'Orient latin,* III-VI (1895–1898); al-Makīn b. al-'Amīd, edited by C. Cahen, "La chronique d'al-Makin des Ayyoubides," *BEOD,* XV (1955–1957); and reference may also be made to Abū 'l-Fidā''s history, modeled on that of Ibn Wāṣil, in the first volume of *RHCHor.* Certain important chronicles are, however, still unpublished. See below for the first of the Mamlūks.

To the chronicles should be added: the memoirs of Usāma b. Munqidh, edited by H. Dérenbourg, in the Publications de l'École des Langues Orientales Vivantes, Sér. II, Vol. XII (Paris, 1886–1889), reëdited by P. K. Hitti (Princeton, 1930) and translated by him, *An Arab Syrian Gentleman* (New York, 1929), and of which there is a French translation by H. Dérenbourg in *Revue de l'Orient latin,* II (1894), a German translation by G. Schumann (Innsbruck, 1905), and a Russian translation by M. Sale (Moscow, 1958); also the travel accounts, in particular the *Riḥla* by the Andalusian Ibn Jubair, edited by W. Wright, second edition revised by M. J. de Goeje, *GMS,* V (Leiden, 1907; reprinted, 1949), of which there is an Italian translation by C. Schiaparelli (Rome, 1906), an English translation by R. Broadhurst (1952), and a French translation by M. Gaudefroy-Demombynes in three parts in Vols. IV–VI of *Documents relatifs à l'histoire des croisades* (Paris, 1949–1956); published by the Académie des Inscriptions et Belles-Lettres; and a work on administrative and historical geography, *al-A'lāq al-khaṭīra fī dhikr umarā' al-Shām wa'l-Jazīra* by 'Izz al-Dīn b. Shaddād, of which there is an edition of the section on Aleppo by D. Sourdel (Damascus, 1959), of the sections on Damascus and on Palestine by S. Dahhān (Damascus, 1956).

Several works relating to institutions and also technical works of importance for general history were produced under the Ayyūbids; C. Cahen has published, translated, and annotated "Un traité d'armurerie composé pour Saladin," *BEOD*, XII (1948); for the *muḥtasib*s, who were municipal and commercial police, works on *ḥisba* were composed, the prototype of which appears to have been the *Nihāyat al-rutba fī ṭalab al-ḥisba* by 'Abd al-Raḥmān b. Naṣr al-Shaizarī, edited by al-Sayyid al-Bāz al-'Arīnī (1946) and studied and translated earlier by W. F. A. Behrnauer, who called the author "Nebrawī" in "Les institutions de police ... ", *JA* (1861); an enlarged version by Ibn al-Ukhuwwa (d. 1329) was published by R. Levy, *Ma'ālim al-qurba* (1938). Finally, and most important of all, the reign of Saladin is noteworthy for the remarkable accounts of the Egyptian fiscal and economic systems by Ibn Mammātī, *Qawānīn al-dawāwīn*, edited by A. S. Atiya (1943), and by al-Makhzūmī, for which latter see two articles by C. Cahen, *JESHO*, 5 (1962), which correspond to various small works at the end of the Ayyūbid period by 'Uthmān b. Ibrāhīm al-Nābulsī, such as the *Kitāb luma' al-qawānīn*, edited by C. Cahen, *BEOD*, XV (1955–1957). See also the description of Fayyūm by C. Cahen, below, p. 166.

Among the Oriental Christian authors, special mention must be made of those writing in Syriac, who are omitted in *RHC*, such as Michael the Syrian, edited by J. Chabot, three volumes (1899–1910); *Anonymi auctoris chronicon ad annum Christi 1234 pertinens*, edited by J. Chabot in *CSCO*, Sér. III, vols. 14–15 (Paris, 1916–1920), of which a translation of the part concerning the first half of the twelfth century was published by A. Tritton in *JRAS* (1933), and *Chronography* by Gregory Abū 'l-Faraj, called Bar Hebraeus, edited and translated by E. A. Wallis Budge, two volumes (1932). The chief Armenian author is Matthew of Edessa, edited and translated in *RHCArm*, I (1869). The principal Latin author is William of Tyre, who appears with his successors, in French, in *RHCHoc*, I and II, of which there is an annotated English translation by F. Babcock and A. Krey (1943). For the thirteenth century, see also *Les gestes des Chiprois. Recueil de chroniques françaises écrites en Orient au XIIIe et XIVe siècles*, edited by G. Raynaud (Paris, 1887), while for Egypt, the "History of the Patriarchs," cited p. 124, and by Abū Ṣāliḥ the Armenian, a work on the churches of Egypt, edited by B. Evetts (1895). See also E. Butcher, *The Story of the Church of Egypt*, two volumes (1897).

There are also various deeds and commercial agreements between the merchant cities of the Mediterranean and the Muslim states, a list of which appears in the analytical compilation by R. Röhricht, *Regesta regni Hierosolymitani* (1898) and supplement (1901), which covers a much wider field than the title would suggest.

MODERN WORKS

The history of the Muslim states of Syria and Mesopotamia during the Crusades has not received adequate attention. On Nūr al-Dīn, we shall soon have N. Elisséeff's thesis, but in the meantime, see his articles, such as "La titulature de Nur al-din d'après ses inscriptions," *BEOD*, XIV (1952–1954), 155–196. The best general account of the period is in the two chapters by H. A. R. Gibb in the first volume of *A History of the Crusades*, cited p. 156, entitled "Zenghi and the Fall of Edessa," and "The Career of Nūr-al-dīn," to which should be added the chapter by Bernard Lewis on the Syrian Assassins in the same work, "The Ismā'īlites and the Assassins," to be compared with M. Hodgson, cited on p. 150. See also in the second volume, the chapter "The Ayyūbids," by H. A. R. Gibb (1962). On the Artuqids (or Ortukids), the position adopted by C. Cahen, in *EI*², reveals a wider outlook than the earlier and more detailed study by the same author, "Le Diyar Bakr au temps des premiers Urtuḳides," *JA* (1935). There are many useful suggestions in the epigraphical works of M. van Berchem and J. Sauvaget, cited p. 54, especially in *Alep*, cited p. 92. Interesting views on social and institutional history are expressed by E. Ashtor-Strauss, "L'administration urbaine en Syrie mediévale," *RSO*, XXXI (1956), on which see C. Cahen cited on page 92.

The Ayyūbid period is a little better served, although there are still considerable gaps. C. Cahen has provided a general outline in his article "Ayyūbids" in *EI*². On Saladin there is an interesting study by H. A. R. Gibb, "The Achievement of Saladin," *Bulletin of the John Rylands Library*, XXXV (1952) and his chapter "The Rise of Saladin," in Vol. I of *A History of the Crusades* and his general chapter on the Ayyūbids in Vol. II, cited p. 156. The biography of Saladin by S. Lane-Poole, *Saladin and the Fall of the Kingdom of Jerusalem* (1898; 2d ed., 1926), though superficial, is preferable to A. Champdor, *Saladin, le plus pur héros de l'Islam* (Paris, 1956). See also the work by L. Slaughter, *Saladin* (1955). The most interesting of Saladin's successors is the subject of a detailed study by H. Gottschalk, *al-Malik al-Kāmil* (Wiesbaden, 1958). The economic aspects of the Ayyūbid regime have been studied by C. Cahen, "Le régime des impôts dans le Fayyūm ayyūbide," *Arabica*, III (1956), and above all by A. S. Ehrenkreutz, applying the method of the economic history of currencies, new to the history of the East, in articles such as "Contributions to the

Knowledge of the Fiscal Administration of Egypt in the Middle Ages," *BSOAS*, XVI (1954), "The Crisis of the Dinar in the Egypt of Saladin," *JAOS*, LXXVI (1956), and "The Place of Saladin in the Naval History of the Mediterranean Sea in the Middle Ages," *JAOS*, LXXV (1955). Problems of population have been treated very methodically by J. Sourdel-Thomine, "Le peuplement de la région des 'villes mortes' (Syrie du Nord) à l'époque ayyubide," *Arabica*, I (1954). See also the article by H. Gottschalk, "Die Aulād Šaiḫ aš-šuyūḫ (Banū Ḥamawiyya)," *WZKM*, LIII (1956).

The spiritual life of the period, though lacking the richness of the classical period, should not be neglected: on law, H. Laoust, *Le précis de droit d'ibn Qudāma* (1951); on poetry, J. Rikabi, *La poésie profane sous les Ayyubides* (1949), and K. Ḥusain, *al-Shi'r fī 'aṣr al-Ayyūbiyyīn* (1957); on mysticism, A. Affifi, *The Mystical Philosophy of Muhyīd Dīn-Ibn al 'Arabi* (1939), and Asín Palácios, *El Islam cristianizado* (1931), while on the mystical poet see the article "Ibn Fāriḍ" in *EI*. On the scholar Ibn al-Nafīs, the discoverer of the lesser circulation of the blood, see M. Meyerhof, "Ibn al-Nafīs and seine Theorie des Lungenkreislaufs," *Quellen und Studien zur Geschichte der Naturwissenschaften und der Medizin*, IV (1935), of which there is a summary in English in *Isis*, XXIII (1935); and in French in *BIFAO*, XVI (1934); A. Chehade, *Ibn al-Nafīs* (1955); and J. Schacht, "Ibn al-Nafīs et son Theologus Autodidactus," *Homenaje a Millás-Vallicrosa*, II (1956). See also the study by D. Sourdel, "Les professeurs de Madrasa à Alep aux XIIe–XIIIe siècles," *BEOD*, XIII (1949–1951).

The Zengid-Ayyūbid period produced some fine artistic achievements, and a study on the military architecture has been published by K. A. C. Creswell, *Fortification*, cited p. 104, to be supplemented by A. Abel, "La citadelle eyyubite de Bosra Eski Cham," *Annales archéologiques de Syrie*, VI (1956), which may profitably be compared with the results of a study of the architecture of the Crusades by P. Deschamps, *Les châteaux des Croisés en Terre Sainte*, two volumes (1934–1939). Of a more general nature is the *Monuments ayyubides de Damas*, published by the Institut Français de Damas, of which the first three volumes are by J. Sauvaget (1948), and the fourth is by J. Sourdel-Thomine (1938–1955). For Aleppo, the book by J. Sauvaget, cited p. 92, will provide all the necessary information. On Egypt, see the general work by K. A. C. Creswell, cited p. 104, of which the second volume appeared in 1959. In the field of the minor arts, D. S. Rice, "Studies in Islamic Metalwork," *BSOAS*, XIV-XVII (1952–1955), deserves special praise.

Mention should be made of Ayyūbid Yemen, on which O. Löfgren has published an important study, *Descriptio Arabiae Meridionalis* (1951), by Ibn al-Mujāwir.

20

The Muslim World under the Mongols and the Timurids

The founding of the Mongol Empire, the beginnings of which were outside Islamic territory, was to have the gravest effects upon the Muslim world. In the Muslim countries overrun by the Mongols, the systematic destruction during the period of invasion and the development of nomadism completely upset the social balance of Arabo-Muslim culture, while the partial break from tradition that resulted from the domination by a people completely foreign to Islam, on its arrival, widened the gap that had already begun to form between the Irano-Turkish and the Arab worlds.

In time, however, the Mongols of Western and Central Asia and of Eastern Europe themselves became converts to Islam and, unlike their kinsmen in Eastern Asia, come within the scope of this book for their own sakes, and not merely because of their influence upon their Muslim subjects. It is clear that a complete study of the Mongol states, including their governmental institutions and their peculiarly Mongol customs, cannot be made without a general knowledge of Mongol history and culture, which in turn presupposes a knowledge of the Mongol language and Chinese. In this respect the student of Islam can only refer to the works of his colleagues, the specialists in Far Eastern studies, of which those in Russian are particularly important. It would nevertheless be an exaggeration to conclude that the student of Islam cannot study this period of Iranian and Turkish history, since it remains, after all, primarily the history of the Muslim populations already settled before the arrival of the Mongols, and is based on sources, the majority of which are written in Persian.

SOURCES

The Arabic sources are all of Mamlūk origin (see p. 176) except Ibn al-Fuwaṭī, above, p. 158.

The Persian sources for the history of the period of the Ilkhāns (the title of the Mongol rulers of Iran) are essentially Juwainī, *Ta'rīkh-i jahān-gushā*, cited p. 156, first volume, and Rashīd al-Dīn, *Jāmi' al-tawārīkh*, an immense compilation of uneven quality, by the famous vizier who attempted to cover not only the whole history of Islam, dynasty by dynasty, but also that of the Turks and the Mongols, the Chinese and the Franks, and so on: in short, producing the only example, in the Muslim Middle Ages, of a universal history such as might be conceived by the masters of an empire claiming to be universal. The portions relating to the conquest and the Ilkhānids have been published by E. Quatremère, *Histoire des Mongols de la Perse* (1836), together with a translation in French up to the year 1265; K. Jahn, *Ta'rīkh-i Mubārak-i Ghāzānī, Geschichte der Ilkhane Abaqa bis Gaiḫatu (1265–1295)*, in *Abhandlungen der Deutschen Gesellschaft der Wissenschaften und Künste in Prag*, Phil.-Hist. Abt., I. Heft (Prague, 1941), and *Geschichte Gāzān-Ḫāns*, *GMS*, n.s., XIV (London, 1940), with analytical tables. The whole of these parts has also been translated into Russian by K. Arends, *Sbornik Letopisei*, III (Moscow and Leningrad, 1946). K. Jahn has also edited and translated (Leiden, 1951) the section covering the Franks, translated from Martinus Polonus, which may be read for curiosity, being of no real interest for our purpose.

More profit will be derived from the geographical part of the *Nuzhat al-qulūb*, by Ḥamdullāh Mustawfī Qazwīnī, edited and translated by G. Le Strange (1919), than from the inadequate collection of abbreviated dynastic histories, *Ta'rīkh-i Guzīdeh*, by the same author, edited with a French translation by J. Gantin (Paris, 1903), only one volume of which has appeared, and in English by E. G. Browne and R. Nicholson, *GMS*, XIV/1–2 (Leiden and London, 1910–1913). The overrated *Ta'rīkh-i Waṣṣāf* was edited and partly translated by J. von Hammer-Purgstall (1856), and edited in full in Bombay (1853) and in Teheran (1959).

The Persian and Arabic sources may be completed by Bar Hebraeus (cited p. 165); the Georgian authors in M. Brosset's collection (p. 51); Western historians of the Latin East (p. 164 f.); and especially Armenian authors, such as Giragos of Kantzag, extracts of whose work have been edited and translated by E. Dulaurier in *JA* (1858); Gregory of Akner (or Aknac'), *The History of the Nation of the Archers*, formerly attributed to Malachy the Monk, has been edited by R. Blake and R. Frye in the *Harvard Journal of Asiatic Studies*, XII (1949), reprinted (Cambridge, Mass., 1954); Stephen Orbelian, *Histoire de Siounie*, translated by M.

Brosset (1864–1866); and Hétoum (Hayton), "La flore des éstoires de la terre d'Orient," *RHCArm*, II (1869).

The great Western travelers in Mongol lands did not cross much Muslim territory; we mention here only Ricoldo da Montecroce, *Il libro della peregrinazione*, edited by U. Monneret de Villard (1948), in our view the most important as it is exclusively concerned with the description of Muslim countries. On the other hand, the Syriac account of an embassy to Phillipe le Bel, *History of Mar Jabhallaha IIIrd*, edited and translated into French by J. Chabot (1895), into English by J. Montgomery (1927), and into Russian by N. V. Pigulevskaia (1958), makes interesting reading. Ibn Baṭṭūṭa's *Travels*, edited with French translation by C. Defrémery and B. Sanguinetti, in five volumes (1853–1879), and translated into English by H. A. R. Gibb, for the Hakluyt Society, in four volumes (1958——), of which two have thus far been published, are extremely informative on the fourteenth-century Muslim world in general, and even on the Far East. For the fifteenth century see the writings of the Russian Nikitine of Tver, translated into English by Count Wilhorsky in "The Travels of Athanasius Nikitin," *India in the Fifteenth Century*, edited by R. H. Major (London, 1857); Russian edition and translation, *Afanasii Nikitin, Khozhenie za tri moria 1466–1472 gg.*, by D. N. Butorin and B. M. Nemtinov (Moscow, 1960), has the text in Old Slavic, Hindi, and English.

Among the epigraphical documents, special mention should be made of the Persian inscription in the Manūchihr mosque at Ani, discussed in Russian, by V. Barthold and translated into German by W. Hinz in *ZDMG*, CI (1951).

On Timur, the study by W. Hinz, "Quellenstudien zur Geschichte der Timuriden," *ZDMG*, XC, n.s., XV (1936), is still useful but out of date. The main work at our disposal is the history of Timur's conquests by his official historian, Niẓām al-Dīn Sāmī, edited by F. Tauer, Vol. I (1937), Vol. II (1957), supplemented by the *Ẓafar-nāmeh* by Sharaf al-Dīn 'Alī Yazdī, edited by M. 'Abbāsī (Teheran, 1957). These should be compared with the accusations of his victim, Ibn 'Arabshāh, in his history, in Arabic, of which there are many editions including an old but still valid French translation by P. Vattier, two volumes (1658), and a poor English translation by H. Sanders (1936). The personalities of the chief participants lend interest to the account by Ibn Khaldūn, cited p. 226, of his interview with Timur, in his *Ta'rīf*, recently discovered, and edited by M. b. Tāwīt al-Ṭanjī (1951), and also translated and studied by W. Fischel, *Ibn Khaldun and Tamerlane* (1952). See also the Armenian account by Thomas of Metsop, translated by F. Nève, *Exposé des guerres de Tamerlan et de Schakh-Rokh*, (1860–1870), and discussed by V. Minorsky, "Thomas of Metsop on the

Timurid-Turkman Wars," in the *Mohammad Shafi Presentation Volume* (1956). For the Timurid period we also have Western travelers' accounts, the most important being that by Clavijo, the Spanish ambassador in Samarqand, edited by F. López (1943), and translated into English by G. Le Strange (1928).

In the universal histories, the parts covering the fourteenth and fifteenth centuries are the most reliable. These histories, known for a long time, are by Mīrkhwond, *Rawḍat al-ṣafā'*, edited, in five volumes (London, 1891–1894), of which there are many partial translations and editions for which see *Storey* (cited p. 51), Vol. I, pp. 95–98; and Khwondamīr, *Ḥabīb al-siyar*, edited (Teheran, 1954), of which the extracts on Turkestan have been translated by C. Defrémery in *JA* (1852). These draw essentially on other chronicles made available more recently, such as that by Ḥāfiẓ Abrū, edited and translated clumsily into French by Khān-Bābā Bayānī (1939), and the work by 'Abdurrazzāq Samarqandī, *Maṭla' al-sa'dain*, edited by M. Shafi (1950).

The value of other types of sources—regional chronicles and chronicles devoted to a limited period of time—is only just being realized. Examples may be found in the *Ta'rīkh-i Shaikh Uwais* (fourteenth century) edited by J. B. Van Loon (The Hague, 1954); the anonymous writer of Iskandar, often thought to be Mu'īn al-Dīn Naṭanzī, of whom J. Aubin has published extracts, *Muntakhab* (1957); Tāj al-Salmānī, *Shams al-ḥusn* (beginning of the fifteenth century), edited by H. R. Roemer (1956); Ẓahīr al-Dīn Mar'ashī, *Ta'rīkh-i Ṭabaristān*, published by B. Dorn in his *Beiträge zur Geschichte der kaukasischen Länder*, two volumes (1850–1858); the anonymous history of the Ayyūbids of Ḥiṣn Kaifā analyzed by C. Cahen, "Contribution à l'histoire du Diyar Bakr au XIVe siècle," *JA* (1955); chronicles of towns, such as the *Ta'rīkh-nāmeh-i Herāt* by Saif b. Muḥammad b. Ya'qūb al-Harawī, edited by Muḥammad Zubair al-Ṣiddīqī (1944); the biographies of saintly persons, such as the *Ṣafwat al-Ṣafā'*, on the ancestors of the Ṣafavids, analyzed by B. Nikitine in *JA* (1957); and for the fifteenth century, those which J. Aubin has shown to be of wide interest in his "Deux Sayyids de Bamm," *Abhandlungen der Akademie der Wissenschaften, Mainz*, VII (1956) and in his *Matériaux pour la biographie de Shah Ni'matullāh Kirmānī* (1956).

There are also interesting treatises dating back to those two centuries, concerned with institutions and finance, such as the unpublished *Dastūr al-kātib* by Hindūshāh Nakhjavānī, an administrative handbook of the Jalā'irid dynasty of the mid-fourteenth century; the *Resāla-ye falakiyyä* [Risāla-i falakiyya] by 'Abdullāh al-Māzandarānī, edited by W. Hinz (1952), a treatise on fiscal accounting in the fourteenth century; the *Shams al-siyāq* by 'Alī Shīrāzī, yet another financial treatise, on which see Hinz, "Ein orientalisches Handelsunternehmen im XV. Jahrhundert," *WO*, I (1947–1952).

Finally, certain official documents have come down to us in collections, the diversity of which may be deduced from the *Mukātabāt* by Rashīd al-Dīn, edited by M. Shafi (1947), and for the fifteenth century, H. R. Roemer, *Der Sharafnāmeh des 'Abdullāh Marwārīd* (1952).

GENERAL HISTORY

On the Mongols in general, the works by A. d'Ohsson, *Histoire des Mongols*, four volumes (2d ed., 1852), and H. Howorth, *History of the Mongols*, five volumes (1876–1927), are now quite inadequate, but have not yet been replaced. More recent but shorter accounts will be found in R. Grousset, *L'empire des steppes* (1939); *L'empire Mongol*, first part by R. Grousset (1941), second part by L. Bouvat (1927), in Vol. VIII/3 of *Histoire du monde*, edited by E. Cavaignac; B. Spuler, "Geschichte Mittelasiens" in *Geschichte Asiens*, by E. Waldschmidt *et al.*, in *Weltgeschichte in Einzeldarstellungen* (Munich, 1950), pages 309–360, and in *HO* (cited p. 67 f.) I, Bd. III/2, and in French, *Les Mongols dans l'histoire* (Paris, 1961); and also J. Auboyer's chapter in *Le Moyen Âge* by E. Perroy, Vol. III (1955) of *Histoire générale des civilisations*, edited by M. Crouzet (Paris, 1953–1957).

On the Ilkhāns, a detailed general account will be found in B. Spuler, *Die Mongolen in Iran* (2d ed., 1955), with bibliography. Recent Russian works by I. Petrushevskii and others, dealing with the social history of Ādherbaijān in the Ilkhānid period or during the Mongol or post-Mongol periods in general, should be especially noted. A synthesis of these may now be found in A. Ali-Zade, *Sotszial'no-economicheskaia i politicheskaia istoriia Azerbaizhana XIII-XIV vv.* (1956), and, above all, I. Petrushevskii, *Zemledelie i agrarnye otnosheniia v Irane XIII-XIV vv.* (Moscow, 1960), on land and agriculture, with a rich bibliography, especially of Russian works. Ann K. S. Lambton, cited p. 90, is also important on this question. On the Serbedars, see Petrushevskii in *UZIV*, XIV (1956).

On the Timurid period, an introduction may be found in V. Minorsky, "La Perse au XVe siècle," in *Orientalia Romana*, I (Rome, 1958). Although we have no good general study of the period, there are valuable special studies, among which the first that should be mentioned is V. Barthold, *Mir Ali Shir* (1928), translated into English by T. and V. Minorsky in the *Four Studies on the History of Central Asia*, III (1962), and into German by W. Hinz, *Herat unter Husain Baiqara* (1938); a work on Ulugh Beg and his times, translated into German by the same author (1935), and into English by T. and V. Minorsky, *Four Studies*, II (1956–1958). Among recent works are A. Boldyrev, "A Sketch of the Life of Herat Society in the XV-XVI Centuries," *Trudy Otdela Vostoka Leningrad. Gosudarstvennye Ermitazh*, IV (1947), in Russian with an English summary, and, on the towns, V. Lavrov, *Gradostroitelnaia kultura srednei Azii* (1950), of which an analysis in English will be found in the *Central Asian Review*, LV (1956).

On Iraq from the Mongol conquest to the Ottomans, 'Abbās al-'Azzāwī, *Ta'rīkh al-'Irāq baina 'l-iḥtilālain*, four volumes (Baghdad, 1935–1956), of which the first volume was translated into English (Teheran, 1936), and which is an outdated annalistic presentation, but rich in information. See also, by the same author, *Ta'rīkh al-ḍarā'ib al-'irāqiyya* (1959), on taxation.

On the Persian Gulf, see J. Aubin, "Les princes d'Ormuz du XIIIe au XVe siècle," *JA* (1953).

On cultural life, see H. Massé, *Essai sur le poète Sa'ḍi* (1919), and H. R. Roemer, *Probleme der Hafizforschung* (1951), dealing with two of the greatest thirteenth- and fourteenth-century poets. For the period immediately following, see H. Aubin, "Le mécénat timouride à Chiraz," *SI*, VIII (1957), where it is discussed in relation to the times and in its true proportions. On Turkish literature, see M. F. Köprülü, cited p. 161, and E. Bertels [Ali Shir] *Navoi* (1948), in Russian. On science, see T. Kary-Niyazov, in Russian, on the school of astronomy of Ulugh Beg (1950), and A. Sayili, *The Observatory in Islam* (Ankara, 1960). On the religious life, see J. Aubin, cited p. 171, and R. Strothmann, *Die Zwölfer-schī'a* (1926), which deals mainly with this period, devoting considerable space to Naṣīr al-Dīn Ṭūsī, who is also discussed for his work as a scholar.

On art, after A. U. Pope's inventory (cited p. 103) see especially D. Wilber, *The Architecture of Islamic Iran. The Ilkhanid Period* (1955), the collection *Persian Painting of the XVth Century*, edited by R. Pinder-Wilson (1959), and the work by I. Stchoukine, *La peinture iranienne sous les derniers Abbassides et les Ilkhans* (1936) and *Les peintures des manuscrits timourides* (1954).

ASIA MINOR

On the Western borders of the countries sharing in the Mongol heritage, the qāḍī, sultan, and poet, Burhān al-Dīn of Sıvas, who ruled in the second half of the fourteenth century, found a historian in 'Azīz b. Ardashīr Astarābādī, whose *Bezm u rezm*, in Persian, is an important and almost unique source for the history of Central Asia Minor after the Seljuks and Ilkhānids, and has been edited by Mukrimin Halil [Yınanç] (Istanbul, 1928).

The importance for the later history of Persia and the Turko-Ottoman world of the two states of Aq-Qoyunlu and Qara-Qoyunlu, in Western Iran and Eastern Turkey, at the end of the fourteenth and in the fifteenth centuries, is now being realized. A few chronicles which deal with them specifically are now being brought to light and published, such as the first volume of the *Ta'rīkh-i diyārbakriyya* by Abū Bakr Tihrānī, edited by F. Sumer and N. Lugal, in *TTKYay*, Seri III/7 (Ankara, 1962), and the *Ta'rīkh-i Rūzbihān*, which has been translated, omitting the more lengthy literary passages, by V. Minorsky with the title *Persia in 1478–1490 A.D.* (1957).

In addition to the fiscal documents preserved in the Ottoman archives and used by W. Hinz in his "Das Steuerwesen Ostanatoliens im XV–XVI. Jahrhundert," *ZDMG*, C (1950), documents found in various collections, and in particular Armenian and Georgian, have also been published; on these see H. Busse, cited p. 185. Good examples of the use to which such texts may be put will be found in V. Minorsky, "A Civil and Military Review in Fars," *BSOAS*, X (1940–1942) and "A Soyurghal of Qasim Aqqoyunlu," *BSOAS*, IX (1939), and in J. Aubin, "Notes sur quelques documents Aq-Qoyunlus," *Mélanges Louis Massignon*, I (1956).

As examples of more recent studies, other than annotations to the texts mentioned, there is nothing of great interest except for a few works by V. Minorsky, such as *La Perse au XVe siècle entre la Turquie et Venise* (1933). On the same question compare B. Baykal, "Uzun Hasan'in osmanlılara karşı halı mücadeleye hazırlıkları," *Belleten*, XXI (1957), dealing with the foreign policy of the Aq-Qoyunlu, especially in the time of Uzun Hasan in the second half of the fifteenth century. V. Minorsky also wrote a series of articles, "Turcmenica," of which see especially no. 11: "The Aq-qoyunlu and Land Reforms," *BSOAS*, XVII (1955), for an interesting aspect of their domestic policy on the eve of the fall of the dynasty. See also the articles "Akkoyunlu" and "Karakoyunlu" in the *Islam Ansiklopedisi*.

THE GOLDEN HORDE

We shall speak only briefly on the state known as the Golden Horde founded by the Mongols of the steppes to the north of the Black and the Caspian seas, even though they became converts to Islam and survived to the sixteenth century. Owing to the lower level of culture of the Golden Horde, the sources concerning them are almost all non-Islamic. Those which were produced among the Muslims of Asia or Egypt have been collected by W. Tiesenhausen, *Sbornik materialov otnosiashchikhsya k istorii Zolotoi Ordy*, two volumes, vol. I (1884), vol. II, published posthumously

(1941). Their history is closely bound up with Russia. The reader is referred particularly to B. Grekov and A. Iakubovskii, *La Horde d'Or*, French translation (1939), and even more so to B. Spuler, *Die Goldene Horde* (1943), which provides all the available bibliographical material right up to the date of publication and of which a new edition has been announced.

21

The Mamlūks and the Arab East

TWELFTH TO FOURTEENTH CENTURY

SOURCES

The period of Syrian and Egyptian history during the Mamlūk regime has sometimes suffered unduly from the discredit brought upon it by the undisciplined behavior of its soldiers. It is a period for which we have—or could have—at our disposal a most remarkable corpus of material both in quality and quantity. If advantage is taken of the unique character of our sources, a degree of knowledge not attainable in other fields should be within our grasp. In fact, our knowledge of the Mamlūk period should, with the necessary reservations and verification, assist in the reconstitution of most points in the history of some of the Mamlūks' forerunners or neighbors.

We cannot, naturally, list here all the chronicles to which we may have recourse; indeed, not all of them have been published and those which were published first are not always the most worthy of our attention. The publication of the most interesting of them is at present an urgent necessity.

The basic work on the first Mamlūks, even though official, is by Ibn 'Abd al-Ẓāhir, on Baibars, Qalā'ūn, and Khalīl; later chroniclers and compilers relied on him for the bulk of their information. An edition of the complete *History of Baibars*, based on a recently discovered manuscript, is being prepared by A. A. Khowaitir, while the part which was previously accessible has been edited in an English translation by M. Sadeque, *Baybars the First of Egypt* (Dacca, 1956). The life of Khalīl was edited as early as 1902 with a Swedish translation by A. Moberg, and the life of Qalā'ūn has been edited by Murād Kāmil, *Tashrīf al-ayyām wa'l-'uṣūr fī sīrat al-*

Malik al-Manṣūr (Cairo, 1961). 'Izz al-Dīn b. Shaddād (cited p. 164 f.) is also the author of a life of Baibars, of which the second part, all that has been found to date, has been published in a Turkish translation by M. Yaltkaya (1941).

For the first Mamlūks, see also: al-Yūnīnī, who continued the work of Sibṭ b. al-Jawzī, the portion of whose work that covers the early years up to 670/1271 has recently been published (although badly) at Hyderabad (1954–1955); Jazarī, a fragment of whose work, covering the years A.H. 689–698, has been made available through a detailed study by J. Sauvaget, *La chronique de Damas de al-Jazari* (1949); Mufaḍḍal b. Abī 'l-Faḍā'il, a Christian who continued the work of al-Makīn (cited p. 164), whose work has been edited and translated poorly by E. Blochet in *PO*, XII, XIV, and XX (1919–1928); the work of an anonymous writer edited by K. Zetterstéen with the title *Beiträge zur Geschichte der Mamlukensultane* (1919), for the years 1291 to 1340; al-Dawādārī, whose volume on al-Malik al-Nāṣir Nāṣir al-Dīn Muḥammad b. Qalā'ūn has just been published by H. R. Roemer (1960); al-Nuwairī, whose chief interest for us lies in the historical part of his immense encyclopedia, in its seventeenth volume with publication only just begun; and al-Dhahabī, *Ta'rīkh al-Islām*, a huge chronographical and biographical compilation, which, in its fifth volume, has just reached the history of the 'Abbāsids. The biographical dictionary by his contemporary and friend, the Damascene, al-Ṣafadī, which is extremely valuable (see p. 34), should be compared with the biographical sections in al-Dhahabī. For a discussion of some of the more important sources for this period—yet unpublished—see E. Ashtor-Strauss, "Some Unpublished Sources for the Bahri Period," *Studies in Islamic History and Civilisation*, edited by U. Heyd (Jerusalem, 1961), Vol. IX of *Scripta Hierosolymitana* published by the Hebrew University.

There are also other great compilers, later in date, who are especially useful for the period in which they lived; for example: the Damascene, Ibn Kathīr, author of the *Bidāya*, on which see H. Laoust in *Arabica*, II (1955); the Egyptian, Ibn al-Furāt (beginning of the fifteenth century), whose work has only been preserved in part, of which the volumes concerning the years 1273–1296 and 1385–1397 have been published by C. Zurayk and N. Izzeddin (1936–1938 and 1939–1942); the Syrians Ibn Ḥajar al-'Asqalānī and Ibn Qāḍī Shuhba, for the first half of the fifteenth century, and al-'Aynī, unedited, to the middle of the fifteenth century; in Egypt, Maqrīzī, whose *History of the Mamluk Sultans*, extending to the beginning of the fifteenth century, is now being edited by M. M. Ziyāda, six volumes (1934–1958), up to the year A.H. 756. It has been partially translated (for the years 1250–1308), with notes that are still valuable, by E. Quatremère, four parts in two volumes (1837–1845), and was continued for the second half of the fifteenth century by Sakhāwī; Abū 'l-Maḥāsin b. Taghrībirdī, *al-Nujūm al-Ẓāhira;* of these, Vols. V–VII, for the years 1345 to 1467, have been edited by W. Popper (1909–1936), who also translated them into English, for the years 1382 to 1469 (1954–1960). Popper also edited *Ḥawādith al-duhūr* for the years 1441 to 1470, four volumes (1930–1942), and wrote the very informative *Egypt and Syria under the Circassian Sultans* (1955–1957).

The same Ibn Taghrībirdī was the author of a curious dictionary that contains, in particular, the names of the Mamlūk emirs; it has been studied by G. Wiet, *Les biographies du Manhal Ṣāfī* (Cairo, 1932). See, finally, Ibn Iyās, author of a diary of a citizen of Cairo up to the Ottoman conquest, of which the most important part, for the years 1468 to 1522 (Vols. III–V), has been edited in three volumes by P. Kahle, M. Muṣṭafā, and M. Sobernheim, and an index volume by A. Schimmel, in *Bibliotheca Islamica*, 5/c to f (Istanbul, 1931–1945). A large section was translated into French by G. Wiet under the title *Histoire des Mamlouks Circassiens*, Vol. II (*sic*) (Cairo, 1945), under the auspices of the Institut Français d'Archéologie Orientale du Caire, of which *Journal d'un Bourgeois du Caire*, Vol. I (Paris, 1955), Vol. II (Paris, 1960), published as part of the Bibliothèque Générale d l'École Pratique des Hautes Études, is the continuation. M. Mostafa [Muṣṭafā] recently reëdited Vols. IV and V, *Bibliotheca Islamica*, 5/d to e (Cairo, 1960–1961), and also edited *Unpublished Pages of the Chronicle of Ibn Iyās* (Cairo, 1951). For a useful introduction to Egyptian historians of the fifteenth century, see M. M. Ziyāda, *al-Mu'arrikhūn fī Miṣr fī al-qarn al-khāmis 'ashar* (2d printing, Cairo, 1954).

To these may be added a number of more limited chronicles, such as the unpublished diary of the Damascene, Birzālī, for the end of the thirteenth century to the beginning of the fourteenth, and the works of other Damascenes, Ibn Ṭūlūn, of which R. Hartmann edited a section covering the years 1480 to 1520, under the title *Das Tübinger Fragment der Chronik Ibn Tuluns* (1926, new Egyptian edition, 1964), and Ibn Ṣaṣrā, *A Chronicle of Damascus*, edited and translated by W. M. Brinner, two volumes (Berkeley, Calif., 1963); see also the translation by H. Laoust, *Les gouverneurs de Damas* (1952), with a continuation into the Ottoman period, and *Relation d'un voyage du sultan Qaitbay en Palestine et en Syrie*, translated by R. Devonshire in *BIFAO*, XX (1922) or (Cairo, 1921). In a special genre is *Histoire de Beyrouth* by Ṣāliḥ b. Yaḥyā, actually a history of the Gharb emirs that includes documents from family archives, edited by L. Cheikho (1902), with corrections by J. Sauvaget, *BEOD*, VII–VIII (1937–1938), 65–82.

To the chronicles should be added some important works on archaeology and institutions. In the former category, the chief work is al-Maqrīzī's *al-Mawā'iẓ wa'l-i'tibār fī dhikr al-khiṭaṭ wa'l-āthār*, a methodical description of Egypt and Cairo, of which an exemplary edition that unfortunately is not finished was begun by G. Wiet in five volumes in *MIFAO*, XXX (1911), XXXIII (1913), XLVI (1922), XLIX (1924), LIII/1 (1925). For the greater part we have to rely on the editions printed at Būlāq, two volumes (1270/1853), or Cairo (A.H. 1324), which are without index. The *Khiṭaṭ* is a mine of information on geography, archaeology, institutions, and history, and also useful for the period prior to the advent of the Mamlūks. The same author also produced a short work on coinage. *Shudhūr al-'uqūd fī dhikr al-nuqūd*, which was edited and translated by L. A. Mayer (London, 1933). For Damascus, see the *Description de Damas*, edited and translated by H. Sauvaire, *JA* (1894–1896), which is based especially on 'Almāwī (fifteenth century), with an *Index Général* by E. Ouechek (Damascus, 1954). For Aleppo, see Sibṭ b. al-'Ajamī, *Les Trésors d'Or*, edited by J. Sauvaget (1951).

The Mamlūk period also gave rise to voluminous official and administrative works, such as general surveys of the knowledge required by officials and models of letters based on genuine examples. The most famous of these are by Ibn Faḍlullāh al-'Umarī, al-Qalqashandī, and Khalīl al-Ẓāhirī. The *Masālik al-abṣār* by the first of these, written in the fourteenth century, was studied by E. Quatremère in the *Notices et extraits de manuscrits de la Bibliothèque du Roi*, XIII (1838), but badly edited in Cairo even as late as 1312/1924. The part concerned with administrative geography was translated into German by R. Hartmann, "Politische Geographie des Mamlukenreiches," *ZDMG*, LXX (1916); the chapter on the Maghrib into French by M. Gaudefroy-Demombynes, *L'Afrique moins l'Égypte* (Paris, 1927); and the part dealing with Asia Minor edited by F. Taeschner, *Al-'Umarīs Bericht über Anatolien* (Leipzig, 1929).

The *Ṣubḥ al-a'shā* by Qalqashandī contains a wealth of information and documents on the Mamlūk as well as preceding periods. A good edition was published in Cairo in fourteen volumes (1913–1919), and some idea of its contents may be obtained from F. Wüstenfeld, "Calcaschandi's Geographie und Verwaltung von Ägypten," *AGG*, XXV (1879), from W. Björkman, *Beiträge zur Geschichte des Staatskanzlei im islamischen Aegypten* (1928), and from 'Abdallaṭīf Ḥamza, *al-Qalqashandī fī kitābihi Ṣubḥ al-A'sha: 'arḍ wa taḥlīl* (Cairo, 1962). The *Zubda kashf al-mamālik* by Khalīl al-Ẓāhirī, gives an interesting picture of the Mamlūk state, court, and army; it has been edited by P. Ravaisse (1894); a translation by Venture de Paradis, dating back to the end of the eighteenth century, has been brought to light and published by J. Gaulmier (Beirut, 1950). On early Mamlūk customs, much information is to be had from the *Kitāb al-mudkhal* by

Ibn al-Ḥājj, a Maghribī, edited in Cairo in four volumes (1929), of which Vol. IV, on the corporative aspects of public life, is of particular interest.

Many works on the military arts, recreation, and sports lie untouched in libraries and deserve to be brought to light. One of these, *A Muslim Manual of War*, has recently been edited by G. Scanlon (see above, p. 90). There is also a cadastral survey of sorts of fifteenth-century Egypt by Ibn Jai'ān *al-Tuḥfa*, edited (Cairo, 1898). There are many smaller works on law, economics, and so forth, although most of them are not available. This applies, for example, to the work of the prolific writer, al-Suyūṭī (fifteenth century).

The foregoing list is a mere sketch of our resources. It should be supplemented by Abū 'l-Fidā''s *Geography*, edited by J. T. Reinaud (1848), and by the accounts of travelers and merchants who have described the country or provided information about it, both Muslim, such as Ibn Baṭṭūta (cited p. 170), and European, for instance, Bertrandon de la Broquière, an agent of Philip the Good, Duke of Burgundy, *Le voyage d'outremer*, edited by C. Schefer (1892). See also the *Reisebuch* by the Bavarian prisoner, J. Schiltberger, edited by V. Langmantel (Tübingen, 1885), who provides a full report on earlier editions, the edition in *Insel-Bücherei*, no. 219 (Leipzig, 1917), and *Hans Schiltbergers Reise in die Heidenschaft* (Hamburg, 1947), and an English translation by J. B. Telfer (London, 1897). Among the texts recently issued or reissued are Balducci Pegolotti, *La pratica della mercatura*, edited by A. Evans (1936); Emmanuel Piloti, *Traité du passage en Terre Sainte* edited by H. Dopp (Cairo, 1950; Louvain and Léopoldville, 1958), and the *Ascensus Barcoch* by Beltram de Mignanelli recently brought to light by W. Fischel in *Arabica*, VI (1959). The importance of the vast *Diarii* by Marino Sanuto of Venice (see below, p. 200), should also be noted. In the absence of more general works, a list of medieval travelers in the Orient may be obtained from R. Röhricht, *Bibliotheca geographica Palestinae* (Berlin, 1890) and *Deutsche Pilgerreisen nach dem Heiligen Lande* (Gotha, 1889). See also A. S. Atiya, *The Crusades in the Later Middle Ages* (London, 1938), and J. Ebersolt, *Constantinople byzantine et les voyageurs du Levant* (1918).

Add to these literary documents the archives in Italian, and subsidiarily in French and Spanish (cited p. 18), and the documents found in the Muslim world itself, such as the Sinai archives (cited p. 18), or the foundation deeds of *waqf*s such as those studied by L. A. Mayer, *The Buildings of Qaytbay* (1938), or A. Darrag, *L'acte de waqf de Barsbay*, as a thesis (Paris, 1955). Finally see those brought to light through epigraphical study, such as G. Wiet, "Répertoire des décrets Mamlouks de Syrie," *Mélanges syriens ... R. Dussaud*, II (1939); J. Sauvaget, "Décrets Mamelouks de Syrie," *BEOD*, II–III (1932–1933) and XII (1947–1948); G. Wiet, "Un décret du sultan mamlouk Malik Ashraf Sha'ban II à la Mecque," *Mélanges Louis*

Massignon, III (1957), an exemplary study; and A. S. Atiya, "An Unpublished Fatwa on the Status of Foreigners in Mamluk Egypt and Syria," *Studien . . . P. Kahle zum 60. Geburtstag* [Festschrift], edited by W. Heffening and W. Kirfel (Leiden, 1953).

HISTORY

The only good general survey of Mamlūk history we have (despite its limitations imposed by the collection and date of publication prior to several noteworthy studies) is that by G. Wiet in *L'histoire de la nation égyptienne*, cited p. 67. A rapid introduction to the subject, in English, may be found in the older study by W. Muir, *The Mameluke or Slave Dynasty of Egypt* (1896). The period of Baibars and Qalā'ūn–Nāṣir Muḥammad has been the subject of a number of appreciable studies recently done in Arabic by Jamāl al-Dīn Surūr, *Dawlat Banī Qalā'ūn fī Miṣr* (1947), which is better than his *al-Ẓāhir Baibars* (1938), and by 'Alī Ibrāhīm Ḥasan, *Dirāsāt fī ta'rīkh al-mamālīk al-baḥriyya* (1944). More recently see Sa'īd 'Abdalfattāḥ 'Āshūr, *al-Ẓāhir Baibars* (Cairo, 1963). For an introductory survey to the entire period see the same author's *Miṣr fī 'aṣr dawlat al-mamālīk al-baḥrīya* (Cairo, 1959), and Ibrāhīm 'Alī Tarkhān, *Miṣr fī 'aṣr dawlat al-mamālīk al-Jarākisa* (Cairo, 1960). The only reign to have been studied thoroughly and extensively is that of Barsbay (beginning of the fifteenth century) by A. Darrag, *L'Égypte sous le règne de Barsbay* (Damascus, 1961). See however Ṣehabeddin Tekindağ, *Berkuk devrinde memluk sultanliği* (Istanbul, 1961).

Information on the institutions of the period, based essentially on Qalqashandī, will be found in F. Wüstenfeld, cited p. 179; M. Gaudefroy-Demombynes, *La Syrie à l'époque des Mamelouks* (1923); particularly W. Björkman, cited p. 179; and on a special point, A. Schimmel, "Kalif und Kadi im spätmittelalterlichen Aegypten," *WI*, XXIV (1942; offprint, 1943). As the result of a meticulous study on the army and the fundamental constitution of the regime, D. Ayalon has published a number of essays, which are to be continued, such as "Studies on the Mamluk Army," *BSOAS* XV–XVI (1953–1954), "L'esclavage du Mamelouk," in *Oriental Notes and Studies* published by the Israel Oriental Society (1951), *Gunpowder and Fire-arms in the Mamluk Kingdom* (1956), and "The System of Payment in Mamluk Military Society," *JESHO*, I (1957–1958). J. Sauvaget, *La Poste aux chevaux dans l'empire des Mamelouks* (1941), offers an exemplary study illustrating the combined use of historical and archaeological sources. The same author is responsible for a provisional and incomplete, but nonetheless useful, "Noms et surnoms de Mamelouks," *JA* (1950).

The most important of the theorists of the Mamlūk period is the subject of a masterly study by H. Laoust, *Essai sur les doctrines sociales et politiques d'ibn Taymiya* (1939). Regarding various aspects of social and religious history, see on the *iqṭāʿ* the articles in Russian, by S. B. Pevzner, analyzed, in French, by M. Canard in *Arabica*, VI–VII (1960–1961), and A. Poliak, *Feudalism in Egypt, Syria, Palestine and the Lebanon (1250–1900)* (1939), "Les révoltes populaires en Égypte a l'époque des Mamelouks et leur causes économiques," *RIE*, VII (1934), and "Le caractère colonial de l'état mamelouk dans ses rapports avec la Horde d'Or," *REI*, IX (1935). On a particular aspect of religious life, see J. Jomier, *Le mahmal et la caravane égyptienne des pèlerins de la Mecque, XIIIe-XXe siècles* (1953). The two-volume work by E. Ashtor-Strauss [*The Jews under the Mamluks*], is in Hebrew, but see his article, in English, "The Social Isolation of the Ahl al-Dhimma," in *Études orientales à la mémoire de P. Hirschler* (1950). On interfaith relations, see M. Perlmann, "Notes on Anti-Christian Propaganda in the Mamluk Empire," *BSOAS*, X (1940–1942). On Palestine see E. Cerulli, *Etiopi in Palestine*, two volumes (1943–1947), which deals in fact, with many questions concerning Islamic-Christian relations in the Holy Land and is an excellent study covering a wider field than the title would suggest. On town life in Syria, E. Ashtor-Strauss, "L'urbanisme syrien à la basse-époque," *RSO*, XXX (1958), is the continuation of his work cited on p. 166; N. Ziadeh, *Urban Life in Syria under the Early Mamluks* (1953), is a general study rather than a monograph proper on the towns, well documented but not very profound.

On economic history proper, other than the works cited above and on p. 93, a number of interesting ideas and facts will be found in S. Y. Labib, "Geld und Kredit, Studien zur Wirtschafts-Geschichte Aegyptens im Mittelalter," *JESHO*, II (1959); W. Fischel, "Über die Gruppe der Kārimī-Kaufleute," *Analecta orientalia*, XIV (1937), with a revision by the same author in *JESHO*, I (1958); and on a broader aspect of the same subject, G. Wiet, "Les marchands d'épices sous les sultans Mamlouks," *Cahiers d'histoire égyptienne*, VII (1955). Valuable documentation will be found in E. Ashtor-Strauss, "Prix et salaires à l'époque mamlouke," *REI*, XV (1949).

The study of relations with the European powers should be based on A. S. Atiya, *The Crusades in the Later Middle Ages* (London, 1938). See also by the same author, "Egypt and Aragon," *AKM*, XXIII (1938), which may be supplemented by various studies that have appeared in *Estúdios de edad media de la corona de Aragón*, from VI (1956), particularly by A. López de Meneses, "Los Consulados Catalanes de Alejandria y Damasco en el Peinado de Pedro el Ceremonioso," VI (1956); see also H. Lammens, "Correspondences diplomatiques entre les Mamlouks et les puissances chrétiennes," *ROC* (1904) and "Les relations entre les Mamlouks et la cour romaine," *ROC* (1903); M. Canard, "Un traité entre Byzance et l'Egypte au XIIIe siècle," *Mélanges Gaudefroy-Demombynes*, (1935–1945); F. Dölger, "Der Vertrag Sultan Qalauns von Ägypten mit dem Kaiser Michael VIII," *Serta monacensia Franz Babinger . . .* (1952);

G. Wiet, "Les relations égypto-abyssines sous les sultans mamlouks," *Bulletin de la Société d'Archéologie Copte*, IV (1938); and lastly, G. Hill, the third volume of *A History of Cyprus* (1940–1952), which is well documented and sound. On the Italian cities, the works on commerce in the Levant cited on p. 93 may be used.

Somewhere between general history and archaeology, the works by L. A. Mayer, *Saracenic Heraldry*, two volumes (1933), *New Material for Mamluk Heraldry* (Jerusalem, 1937), and *Mamluk Costume* (Geneva, 1952), are extremely precise and well informed.

On art, see especially L. Hautecoeur and G. Wiet, *Les mosquées du Caire*, two volumes (1932).

For characteristic literary works, see H. Wangelin, *Der Baibarsroman* (1933) and *Das arabische Volksbuch vom König Aẓẓāhir Baibars*, Heft XVII of *Bonner Orientalistische Studien* (Stuttgart, 1936). For an encyclopedic survey of Mamlūk literature, see Maḥmūd Rizq Salīm, *'Asr salāṭīn al-mamālīk wa-nitājuhu al-'ilmī wa'l-adabī*, six volumes to date (Cairo, 1946——).

ARABIA

The history of Arabia, and especially that of the Yemen, cannot be dissociated from that of Egypt, even though from the thirteenth to the fifteenth century it has an importance of its own. Texts relating to medieval Aden have been published by O. Löfgren, *Arabische Texte zur Kenntniss der Stadt Aden* (1936–1950), and al-Khazrajī's chronicle on the Rasūlids has been indifferently published and translated by J. Redhouse and M. Asal, *The Pearl-Strings*, five volumes (1906–1915), while many others, of all kinds, discovered during the course of this century in the rich and original collections in the Yemen are still awaiting publication. On a customs list of the port of Aden, see C. Cahen and R. Serjeant, "A Fiscal Survey of the Medieval Yemen," *Arabica*, IV (1957). Various treatises by the navigator, Ibn Mājid, as important for economic history as for nautical science, have been edited by G. Ferrand, *Instructions nautiques et routiers arabes et portugais des XVe et XVIe siècles*, I–III (1921–1928). An edition including a good general study and a Russian translation by T. A. Shumovskii with a Portuguese translation by M. Malkiel-Jirmounskii was published under the title *Três roteiros desconhecidos de Aḥmad ibn-Mādjid, o piloto árabe de Vasco de Gama* (Moscow, 1957–1960) on which cf. Ritter's remarks in *Oriens*, XI (1958), 298–305. For the fourteenth century, see Ibn Baṭṭūṭa, cited p. 170. See also R. Serjeant, "New Material for the History of the Ḥadramawt," *BSOAS*, XIII (1950). The only recent studies to be mentioned are the articles "Aden" in *EI*², and "San'ā'," "Ẓufar" and "Shihāb al-Dīn Aḥmad" in *EI*. On the Portuguese intervention, see below, p. 190.

22

Iran and the Non-Ottoman Muslim East

FROM THE ADVENT OF THE ṢAFAVIDS TO THE BEGINNING OF THE NINETEENTH CENTURY

SOURCES

Iran opposed the Ottoman Empire throughout its history and—unless one includes the semi-Muslim empire of the Moguls of India and Morocco at the other extremity of the Muslim world—represents in modern times the only great Muslim state to remain independent of it. It is true that its unique character had long been well defined within the Muslim world and persisted while principalities were born and empires developed on its soil. Nevertheless it is only with the advent of the Ṣafavids that, for the first time since the Muslim conquest, a state was formed limited to the Iranian people, who now acquired a strong awareness of their national unity, expressed by their adoption of Shī'ite teachings. But perhaps, precisely because it was to some extent shut off from the rest of the Muslim world, its history has been studied very inadequately, and even then less for its own sake than for its connections with other, particularly European, countries who would often regard it as an ally against the Ottomans. In this context, see H. R. Roemer, "Die Safawiden, ein orientalischer Bundesgenosse des Abendlands im Türkenkampf," *Saeculum*, IV (1953).

There is no general account of the history of the Ṣafavids, unless we include the naturally quite inadequate general histories, such as that by Sir Percy Sykes, *A History of Persia*, two volumes (3d ed., 1930); and see the article in *EI*, *s.v.* There is no lack of source material, however: archive sources or collections of copies are useful mainly for the list of the publications provided, such as the introduction to H. Busse's *Untersuchungen zum islamischen Kanzleiwesen an Hand turkmenischer und safawidischer Urkunden*, Abhandlungen des Deutschen Archäologischen Instituts, Kairo, Islamische Reihe, I (1959), which is a model of good editing and supplies useful information on the diplomatic content of the deeds. The editions containing the greatest number of deeds are those obtained from Armenian and Georgian archives by M. Chubua, *Persidskie Firmany i ukazy Muzeja Gruzii* (1949) and A. D. Papazyan, *Persidskie documenty Matenadarana* (Erevan, 1956). See also I. Petrushevskii below, p. 186.

The most important chronicles do not extend beyond the seventeenth century. The only one to have been translated is by Ḥasan Rūmlū, *Aḥsan al-tawārīkh*, edited and translated into English by C. Seddon, two volumes (1931–1934). The most important is that by Iskander Munshī, *Ta'rīkh-i 'ālam-ārāy-i 'abbāsī*, written under Shāh 'Abbās, of which there is available a good edition by I. Afshār (Teheran, 1955), and a continuation (*dhail*) edited by S. Khwānsārī (1938–1939). Dealing more especially with the Kurds is Sharaf al-Dīn Bidlīsī's *Sharaf-nāmeh*, edited by V. Veljaminov-Zervov, two volumes (1860–1862), or M. 'Awnī (Cairo, 1930), and translated into French by M. Brosset, *Collection d'historiens arméniens*, I (1874–1876). The sources for the period of Nādir Shāh are studied in L. Lockhart's works, cited p. 186. The fairly recent regional histories are particularly interesting, such as the *Fārs-nāmeh-i Nāṣirī*, written in the middle of the nineteenth century and edited, two volumes (Teheran, 1895–1896).

The accounts of travelers, foreign ambassadors, and others, and the reports of the Indian companies become extremely important in this field. The *Voyages* by the French travelers, J. Chardin (1st ed., 1686) and J.-B. Tavernier (1st ed., 1677), are particularly important. To these may be added P. Della Valle, *Viaggi*, of which there are several editions and translations (Rome, 4 vols., 1650–1663; Venice, 4 vols., 1661–1663; German translation, 1 vol., Geneva, 1674; French translation, 8 vols., Rouen, 1745); Raphael du Mans (the father), *Estat de la Perse en 1660*, edited by C. Schefer (1890); N. Sanson, *Estat présent du royaume de Perse* (Paris, 1694), translated into English (1695); *A Chronicle of the Carmelites in Persia*, two volumes (London, 1939); and E. Kaempfer, *Amoenitatum exoticarum . . . fasciculi V* (1712), translated into German by W. Hinz (1940), almost all of which are listed in A. Gabriel, *Die Erforschung Persiens* (1952). For the archives of the India companies, see L. Lockhart (cited p. 186) and below, p. 190. On relations with Russia, see N. Veselovskii, *Pamiatniki diplomaticheskikh i torgovykh otnoshenii moskovskoi Rusi s Persiei*, three volumes (St. Petersburg, 1890–1898).

A very important administrative document, an anonymous composition of the seventeenth century resembling an abstract, of Ṣafavid institutions, has been published, annotated, and translated into English by V. Minorsky, *Tadhkirat al-mulūk*, in the *GMS*, n.s. XVI (1943).

HISTORY OF IRAN

Except for the rather poor general histories of Persia, the only recent general account of this period of Iranian history is the good introduction, with bibliography, by H. Braun, "Geschichte Irans seit 1500," in *HO*, (cited p. 67 f.) I/VI-3. The work of W. Hinz, *Irans Aufstieg zum Nationalstaat im fünfzehnten Jahrhundert* (1936), in spite of much sound information, requires a revision of its basic concepts. There is an important social study by J. Aubin, "Études safavides. I: Shāh Ismā'īl et les notables de l'Iraq persan," *JESHO*, II (1959). On the founder of the dynasty, there is G. Sarwar, *History of Shāh Ismā'īl Ṣafavī* (Aligarh, 1939); the study by W. Hinz, "Schah Esmā'īl II. Ein Beitrag zur Geschichte der Safaviden," *MSOS*, XXXVI (1933); on the events following his death, H. R. Roemer, *Der Niedergang Irans nach dem Tode Ismā'īls des Grausamen*, 1577–1581 (Würzburg, 1939); on the recovery and zenith of the dynasty's fortunes, only the superficial work by L. Bellan, *Chah Abbas Ier* (1932). The final downfall of the Ṣafavids at the beginning of the eighteenth century has been described reliably and in detail, especially from the political and military point of view, by L. Lockhart, *The Fall of the Safawi Dynasty and the Afghan Occupation of Persia* (1958), who also wrote an excellent work, *Nadir Shah* (1938), devoted to the founder of the succeeding dynasty. In addition there is the commendable work by the Iranian scholar, S. A. Kasravī Tabrīzī, *Daure-i Nādir Shāh* (Teheran, 1945).

On Ṣafavid administration, consult R. Savory, "The Principal Offices of the Safawi State during the reign of Isma'il Ist," *BSOAS*, XIII–XIV (1960–1961), and V. Minorsky's notes to his edition of the *Tadhkirat al-mulūk*, cited above. We have an important work on the social and economic institutions of Ādharbaijan by I. Petrushevskii, *Ocherki po istorii feodal'nyke otnoshenii v Azerbaidzhane i Armenii v XVI–nachale XIX cc.* (1949), which deserves to be translated. See also Ann K. S. Lambton, cited p. 90, and M. Dickson, *Shah Tahmasb and the Uzbeks* (1958).

On religious questions, there is only the exemplary study by H. Corbin, "Les confessions extatiques de Mir Damad," *Mélanges Louis Massignon*, I (1956), and more recently by the same author, *Terre céleste et corps de résurrection de l'Iran Mazdéen à l'Iran shi'ite* (1960). See also N. D. Miklukho-Maklai, "Shiizm i ego sotsial'noe litso v Irane na rubezhe XV–XVI vv.," *Pamyati Akademika . . . Krachkovskogo* (Leningrad, 1958).

On art, apart from A. U. Pope, cited p. 103, there is an excellent study of the Ṣafavid capital by A. Godard, "Iṣfahān," *Āthār-ê Īrān*, II (1937), and on painting by I. Stchoukine, *Les peintures des manuscrits safavis* (1959). On foreign relations, consult K. Bayani, *Les relations de l'Iran avec l'Europe à l'époque safavide* (1937); H. 'Alī, *Essai sur l'histoire des relations irano-ottomanes de 1722 à 1747* (1937); V. Pontecorvo, "Relazioni tra lo scià Abbas e i Granduchi di Toscana," *RL*, III (1949–1950); and D. M. Lang, *The Last Years of the Georgian Monarchy, 1658–1832* (New York, 1957).

On the history of Afghanistan during the same period, which was also its formative period, see P. Sykes, *A History of Afghanistan* (1940), with a bibliography complete up to that date, and the article in *EI²*.

CENTRAL ASIA AND THE RUSSIAN STEPPES

Central Asia and the steppes in the more southerly parts of Russia have remained up to recent times a region of Islamic states or peoples. In the sixteenth century the Timurids of Turkestan were replaced by the Shaibānids of the Uzbek people, whose principal historian was their own countryman, Abū 'l-Ghāzī Bahādūr Khān (seventeenth century), the author of the *Shajarat al-Atrāk*, in Chaghatay Turkish, edited and translated by J. Desmaisons (1871–1874); new Russian edition by A. N. Kononov (Moscow, 1958). The archives of Khiva, the capital of Khwārizm from the sixteenth century on, have yielded very valuable documents that have been employed in the remarkable publication by E. Bertels and V. Struve [*Documents . . . concerning Land Tenure and Trade in the XVIth Century*] (1938), in Russian. See also the paper by M. I. Iuldashov in *Papers presented by the Soviet delegation at the XXIII International Congress of Orientalists* (1954), and the article by H. R. Roemer cited on p. 16. Many texts have been translated into Russian in *Materialy po istorii Uzbekskoi, Tadzhikskoi i Turkmenskoi SSR*, I (Leningrad, 1952) and *Materialy po istorii Turkmen i Turkmenii*, Vol. XXIX/8 of *Trudy Instituta Vostokovedeniia*, two volumes (Moscow and Leningrad, 1938–1939).

The history of the Muslim people gradually incorporated into the Russian state may be obtained in part from the general histories of Russia and, better still, from the histories of the individual peoples of the USSR, such as by K. B. Trever, A. I. Iakubovskii, *et al.*, *Istoriia narodov Uzbekistana* (*History of the Uzbek People*) two volumes (Tashkent, 1947–1950), and B. G. Gafurov [*History of the Tajik People*] (3d ed., 1955), in Russian. By Tajik is meant the people from Central Asia, and in particular the present-day Tajikistan or upper Amu Darya, who are of Iranian and not Turkish background. See also two books in Russian, *Istoriia Uzbekskoi S.S.R.* (Tashkent, 1955) and *Istoriia Khazakhskoi S.S.R.* (Moscow, 1957). For the student who does not read Russian the only introduction is through such articles as "Tatar," "Uzbek," and "Bashkīr," in *EI*, or the Turkish *Islam Ansiklopedisi*, which is considerably augmented on these subjects; and more concisely W. Barthold, cited p. 153. See also E. Sarkisyanz, *Geschichte der orientalischen Völker Russlands bis 1917* (1961). For the peoples of the Caucasus, see also *EI*², which contains some good observations on these questions by H. Carrière d'Encausse and A. Bennigsen. On the Crimea, see below, p. 214. There is a bibliography up to 1952 in pages 104–112 of the work by B. Spuler and L. Forrer cited on p. 70, and at the end of the article by B. Spuler, "Wolga-Tataren...," *Islam*, XXIX (1949–1950). The history of these peoples is so closely bound up with the history of the Russian state that it is quite impossible to deal with them in detail in a work of this kind, but they should not be neglected, nor the importance of their role in the history of Islam and the Turks forgotten.

MUSLIM INDIA

Of the states governed by the Muslims in India, the greater number remained untouched by Islamic influence, yet in view of the fact that now Pakistan occupies territory in the north of the subcontinent where Islam has been well established for many centuries and where it represents almost the only existing religion, the subject cannot be bypassed.

Several of the Muslim sources have been translated or analyzed by H. Elliot and M. Dawson, *The History of India as Told by its Own Historians, The Muhammadan Period*, eight volumes (1866–1877; reissued Calcutta, 1953). Three of the sources have been studied by P. Hardy, *Historians of Medieval India* (1960). See also *Historians of India, Pakistan and Ceylon*, edited by C. Phillips (London, 1961). Among the most important should be mentioned the *History* by Firishta, four volumes, translated by G. Briggs (1829), which includes the pre-Mogul period, and that by Badā'ūnī (Badāōnī), translated by G. S. A. Ranking, T. W. Haig, and W. H. Lowe, three volumes (Calcutta, 1884–1925), which also touches on the empire of the Great Moguls; on the latter see the *Ṭabaqāt-i akbarī* by Niẓām al-Dīn Aḥmad, translated into English by B. De, three volumes (Calcutta, 1913–1939); the memoirs of Babur entitled *Babar-nāmeh* in Chaghatay Turkish, edited by A. Beveridge in *GMS*, I (Leiden and London, 1905), translated into English by the same author (London, 1921), and into French, from a Persian version, by A. J.-B. Pavet de Courteille (1871), and of which a Russian translation appeared (Tashkent, 1955); the *Akbar-nāmeh* by Abū 'l Faḍl 'Allāmī, edited by A. A. 'Alī and 'Abd al-Raḥīm (Calcutta, 1873–1887), English translation by H. Beveridge (Calcutta, 1897–1921); the *Ā'īn-i akbarī* (institutions) by the same Abū 'l-Faḍl 'Allāmī, edited by H. Blochmann (Calcutta, 1867–1877), which he and H. S. Jarrett translated into English, three volumes (Calcutta, 1868–1894), of which there are a revised edition by D. C. Phillott (Calcutta, 1927–1939) and a revised and further annotated edition of Vol. III by Sir Jadu-Nath Sarkar (Calcutta, 1948); and the *Aḥkām-i 'ālamgīrī* (institutional anecdotes) by 'Ināyat Allāh Khān Kashmīrī, not edited, but for MSS see *Storey* (cited p. 51) I, 597 and 1318. Almost all these editions, generally mediocre, are in the *Bibliotheca Indica.*

General information on Muslim India will be found in the *Cambridge History of India*, III–VI (1922–1937), or more briefly in the *Oxford History of India* (2d ed., 1958). See also the articles, "India" and "Mughal," in *EI*, which should be supplemented by the articles "Afghanistan," "Akbar," "Babur," "Bahmaniyya," "Dilhi," and so forth, in *EI*², which are more specialized. Among the various special but fairly comprehensive works, particularly on the Mogul period, see S. Edwards, *Babur* (1926), in English, or F. Grenard, *Babur* (1930), in French; V. A. Smith, *Akbar, The Great Mogul* (1917); W. H. Moreland, *From Akbar to Aureng-Zeb, a Study in Economic Indian History* (1923); J. Sarkar, *History of Aurengzib* (2d ed., 5 vols., 1912–1916), and *The Fall of the Mughal Empire* (*1739–1754*), I (1932–1950). On the institutions and society in general, see W. Irvine, *The Army of the Indian Moghuls* (1903); Abdulaziz, *The* manṣabdari *System and the Mughal Army* (Lahore, 1945); P. Tripathi, *Some Aspects of Muslim Administration* (1936); Ibn Hasan, *The Central Structure of the Mughal Empire* (1936); P. Saran, *The Provincial Government of the Mughals* (1941); W. H. Moreland, *The Agrarian System of Moslem India* (1929); T. Bailey, *A History of Urdu Literature* (1932); J. Fergusson, *History of Indian and Eastern Architecture*, revised and enlarged edition by J. Burgess and R. P. Spiers (London, 1910); P. Brown, *Indian Architecture, The Islamic Period* (1942–1943); and R. Grousset, *Les civilisations de l'Orient, l'Inde* (1930).

EXPANSION AROUND THE INDIAN OCEAN

The expansion of Islam in the form of coastal colonies all around the Indian Ocean, from East Africa to the Malayan Archipelago, dates back to the very earliest stages in its history; it is not until the fourteenth and fifteenth centuries that it began to penetrate more deeply, not only into India, but also Indonesia, today one of the most heavily populated Muslim areas. We cannot discuss the case of Java in detail, as it has not in fact become a truly Islamic society in the sense of a society similar in structure and institutions to that of the ancient Muslim countries. We would remind the reader of the pioneer work done by C. Snouck Hurgronje, *The Achehnese* (1906), and the later observations by C. C. Berg, "The Islamisation of

Java," *SI*, IV (1955), a general review of the facts and theories of the subject; see also G.-H. Bousquet, *Introduction à l'étude de l'Islam indonésien* (1938); G. Drewes, "Indonesia: Mysticism and Activism," in *Unity and Variety*, cited p. 86, concerned particularly with the modern aspects of the question; J. Crawford, *De indische Archipel* (1823–1825); F. Stapel, *Geschiedenis van Nederlandsch Indie*, five volumes (1938–1940); and F. Pareja, cited p. 66.

From the sixteenth century onward the traditional Muslim trade patterns were modified by Ottoman intervention (see below, p. 207 ff.) and especially by the victorious rivalry of the Portuguese and later of other European nationalities. In this regard Portuguese documents are most revealing: either the travel accounts, such as that by Pedro Texeira, English translation, *The Travels of Pedro Texeira* (1902), or the archive material of which a general survey is now being prepared by J. Aubin, *Mare Luso-Indicum.* See also R. Serjeant, *The Portuguese off the South Arabian Coast* (1962), consisting of an important introduction and translations of unedited sources from Ḥaḍramaut. A study of the various Dutch, English, and French India companies is recommended.

For East Africa, a bibliography will be found in the articles in *EI*, especially by G. Ferrand, *s.v.* "Madagascar," "Somali," "Waḳwaḳ," "Zanzibar," and so on. See also G. S. P. Freeman-Grenville, *The Medieval History of the Coast of Tanganyika with Special Reference to Recent Archaeological Discoveries* (London, 1962).

23

The Ottoman Empire

A complete bibliography of the Ottoman Empire alone would fill a volume this size. The most important aspect—the spirit in which Ottoman history should be approached—will be emphasized even though much must be omitted from this work.

The Ottoman Empire is still frequently regarded with an undeserved prejudice, that can be traced to the history of its relations with Europe from the end of the eighteenth century to the beginning of the twentieth. From the fifteenth to the eighteenth centuries the Ottoman Empire was one of the greatest powers in the Western world, and indeed, at times, the greatest. No multinational empire, since Rome, has lasted so long. Every Christian state in Europe had contact with it, through politics, war, or trade; even Sweden under Charles XII had its Ottoman adventure. The peoples of the Balkans, Asia, and Arab Africa, who for many centuries formed an integral part of the Ottoman Empire, cannot dissociate their own history from that of their conquerors. Histories of other nations could not therefore neglect the Turks, but the image of them that they depicted requires revision in many respects. They normally view the Ottomans from the only standpoint that Europe, in the period of its giddy ascension, could regard them: as the survivors of another age to be eliminated. The "Eastern question," Ottoman decadence, the "sick man of Europe," barbarity, and oppression are too frequently the themes of the manuals of the past. What they fail to point out is that the Ottoman Empire, at the time of the Renaissance, compelled the admiration of visiting Europeans for its military might, the devotion of its people, its administrative organization, and its culture, its very opponents being forced to respect it. Louis XIV, as F. Grenard reminds us, "so arrogant in claiming respect for his dubious privileges at the Holy See, allowed his ambassador at Constantinople to be beaten and imprisoned."

Even when an effort was made to understand the Ottoman Empire, its history was too often studied, not only entirely from the point of view of its relations with Europe, but based almost exclusively on European records, and written by scholars, one of the most distinguished of whom had no knowledge of Turkish. It is obvious that a revision of method and outlook is essential.

Today, both in Turkey and elsewhere, an attempt is being made to study the Ottoman Empire from within and for its own sake. Since the Ottoman Empire preserved archives similar in quality and quantity to those which European historians are accustomed to use, we should be able to achieve this successfully.

PERIOD OF ITS ORIGIN

The Ottoman principality was originally merely one of the many Turkish principalities, first neither in date nor importance and born of the disintegration of the Seljuk, Mongol, and Byzantine states in Western Asia Minor. The history of the other principalities, that were gradually absorbed by the Ottoman state has not however, been preserved. In order to piece it together we are reduced to drawing as much as we can from the scant information afforded by the scattered and heterogeneous sources, among which must be counted epigraphical sources, coins, and a few recently discovered archives. Besides these, there are the accounts of foreigners both Muslim—such as Ibn Baṭṭūṭa (above, p. 170) and al-'Umarī (above p. 179)—and Byzantine and Western—the historians of the Byzantino-Turkish wars of the fourteenth century.

The single exception, and for this reason the more valuable, is the *Düstürnāmeh* by Enveri (fifteenth century), which includes a Turkish historical poem of the fourteenth century and is remarkably well informed concerning the history of the wars waged against the Christians in the Aegean Sea by the Aydın Turks during the first half of that century; it should be consulted in the edition, with French translation and notes, by Irène Mélikoff, *Le Destān d'Umur Pacha*, Vol. II of *Bibliothèque byzantine. Documents* (Paris, 1954), which has been used by P. Lemerle in his model study, *L'émirat d'Aydin, Byzance et l'Occident* (1957); on this emirate, and in particular the internal aspects of its history, see, in Turkish, Himmet Akın, *Aydın oğulları tarihi hakkında bir araştırma* (1946). The older study, based on a more limited documentation, by P. Wittek, *Das Fürstentum Mentesche* (Istanbul, 1934), is still exemplary. From the Byzantine point of view, see A. Wächter, *Der Verfall des Griechentums in Kleinasien im XIV. Jahrhundert* (Leipzig, 1903). Concerning the history of the Turkoman principalities a discussion of the outstanding events will be found in Ismā'īl Ḥakkı Uzunçarşılı,

Anadolu Beylikleri (Istanbul, 1937). On the origins of some of them, see M. F. Köprülü, "Anadolu Beylikleri tarihine ait notlar," *Türkiyat Mecmuası*, II (1926), 1–33, and C. Cahen, "Notes pour l'histoire des Turcomans d'Asie Mineure au XIIIe siècle, " *JA* (1951), 335–354. Also consult the *Islam Ansiklopedisi*.

On art, see F. Diez and O. Aslanapa, *Karaman devri sanatı̆* (Istanbul, 1950), and R. Riefstahl, *Die Kunst Südwestanatoliens* (1931), of which there is an English translation, *Turkish Architecture in South Western Anatolia* (1931).

SOURCES OF OTTOMAN HISTORY: ARCHIVES, LITERARY, AND FOREIGN

On Ottoman history proper, the importance of the archives above all else should be stressed. A few figures will convey an idea of the extent of these archives: 600–1,000 cadastral registers and over 600 bundles of registers from the administration of *waqf*s have been preserved; apparently there remain on Turkish soil approximately a half million documents from the archives of the Sublime Porte, which have come down to us incomplete (J. Deny). Add to these the financial, judicial, and religious documents, the naval archives, and documents scattered throughout the provinces and former dependent territories of the Ottoman Empire, such as Egypt, Syria, or the Maghrib.

The classification and cataloguing of these resources, which has officially begun, will put a wealth of information at our disposal and some is already available. A general idea of the materials may be obtained from P. Wittek, "Les archives de Turquie," *Byzantion*, XIII (1936) and the article "Başvekalet Arşivi" by Bernard Lewis in EI^2; their importance for the history of the peoples forming a part of the Ottoman Empire may be gauged from the same author's "The Ottoman Archives as a Source for the History of the Arab Lands," *JRAS* (1951), 139–155. Two parts of a guide to the Saray Archives have been published, including an index of names and subjects, *Topkapı Sarayı Müzesi arşivi kılavuzu* (1938–1940). Tahsin Öz has published in *Belleten*, XIV (1950), a list of over a hundred documents, "Topkapı Sarayı Müzesi arşivinde Fatih II Sultan Mehmede ait belgeler."

Turkish documents in foreign countries, which are mainly of a diplomatic nature, or in the principal towns of the former Ottoman provinces, now independent states or European colonial territories, have been studied for a longer period of time. The studies based on these archives are of wider interest inasmuch as they aid in the understanding of Ottoman archives in general, whatever their origin. In "Documents d'archives turcs conservés à Marseille," *JA* (1931), and in the collection, *Histoire et historiens depuis cinquante ans* (1927), J. Deny has provided a list of collections and publications concerned with this material up to publication dates. His own descriptive catalogue of a collection of archives in *Sommaire des archives turques du Caire* (1930), together with a most important introduction on the administrative organization of the Ottoman Empire, is excellent and should be supplemented with Stanford J. Shaw, "Cairo's Archives and the History of Ottoman Egypt," in the *Report on Current Research of the Middle East Institute* (1956), 59–72. There is also an excellent recent work by R. Mantran, *Inventaire des documents d'archives turcs de Tunisie*, Publications de la Faculté des Lettres de l'Université de Tunis. Sér. Histoire, I (Tunis, 1961).

A certain number of extremely important texts have already been published. There is a series of *Qānūn-nāmehs*, cadastral and fiscal surveys, edited especially by O. Barkan, *XV ve XVI inci asırlarda Osmanlı Imparatorluğunda zirai ekonominin hukuki ve mali esasları. I: Kanunlar*, in İstanbul Üniversitesi Edebiyat Fakültesi. Yayinlar, CCLVI (1943), on regulations concerning agriculture, and the judicial and fiscal questions relating to it, by provinces. The part concerning Syria has been translated and annotated by R. Mantran and J. Sauvaget, with some additions and corrections, *Règlements fiscaux ottomans* (Beirut, 1951). Similar though less complete documents had already been found in the archives at Vienna, and used by J. von Hammer-Purgstall in his *Geschichte*, cited p. 201; of a similar nature is the anonymous publication, "Kanunname-i Al-i Osman," *TOEM*, I (1330/1914–1915), on Mehmed II; II (1329/1913–1914), on Sulaiman; and see F. von Kraelitz, "Ḳānūnnāme Sultan Meḥmeds des Eroberers," *Mitteilungen zur osmanischen Geschichte*, I (1921–1922); I. H. Uzunçarşılı, "Kanun-ı Osmanî mefhûm-ı Defter-i Hâkanî," *Belleten*, XV/59 (1951), 381–395, concerning a cadastral law of 1642; F. Babinger, *Sultanische Urkunden zur Geschichte der osmanischen Wirtschaft und Staatsverwaltung am Ausgang der Herrschaft Mehmeds II.*, first part (1956); R. Anhegger and H. Inalcik, "Kanunname-i Sultanî ber mûceb-i örf-i Osmani," *Belleten*, XXI (1957); and the annotated translation by N. Beldiceanu, *Les actes des premiers sultans ...*, I (1960). To these may be added certain documents stemming from various European sources, published with commentaries or notes, on diplomacy, paleography, or Ottoman institutions; for example: A. Kurat and K. Zetterstéen, *Türkische Urkunden* (1938), from Swedish archives; H. Duda, "Die osmanischen Staatschreiben des kgl. Reichsarchivs zu Kopenhagen," *Mitteilungen des Instituts für Österreichische Geschichtsforschung*, LVIII (1950); and L. Fekete, in the work on Hungary cited on p. 213. Mention should be made of the *Munsha'āt al-salāṭīn* by Ferīdūn, an ancient collection of imperial diplomas, which suffers from alterations of various kinds.

A number of documents relating to the European provinces of the Ottoman Empire consisting mainly of various old deeds and cadastral records have been published: on Albania, H. Inalcik, "Hicrī 835 tarihli sûret-i defter-i sancak-i Arvanid," *TTKYay*, XIV/1 (Ankara, 1954); on the Jugoslavian territories, *Prilozi*, I–IV (1950–1953); B. Durdev, in Serbo-Croatian, ["A Fiscal Register of the Sanjak of Montenegro in the Time of Skanderbeg,"] *Prilozi*, I (1950); H. Šabanovič, ["Turkish Documents as Sources for the History of Our People,"] *Prilozi*, I (1950), and an edition of the four ["Oldest Bosnian Deeds of Waqf, 1462–1518,"] *Prilozi*, III–IV (1952–1953, also in Serbo-Croatian); on Bulgaria, G. Elejovič, "Turski spomenici," *ArO*, XIX (1955), J. Kabrda, "Les anciens registres turcs de cadis de Sofia et de Vidin," *ArO*, XIX (1951), and "Les documents turcs relatifs aux impôts ecclésiastiques prélevés sur la population bulgare au XVIIe siècle," *ArO*, XXIII (1955); on Macedonia, I. Vasdravellis, *Historika arkheia Makedonias*, two volumes, Vol. I, *Arkheion Thessalonikes. 1695–1912*, Vol. II, *Arkheion Berroias-Naouses. 1598–1886* (Salonica, 1952–1954), Turkish documents translated into Greek, and *Makedonia vo XVI i XVII vek* (Skoplje, 1955); on Thrace, M. T. Gökbilgin, *15–16 asırlarda Edirne ve Paşa livāsı vakıflar, mülkler, mukataalar*, İstanbul Üniversitesi Edebiyat Fakültesi. Yayınlar, MVIII (1952). To this should be added the collection of documents published by A. Refik, [*Life in Istanbul*] (1931; 2d ed., 1932), in Turkish (1935), for the eleventh to the fourteenth century.

The non-European provinces are less favored. Documents relating to Bursa have been published by H. Dağlıoglu, on the fourteenth century, in Bursa Halkevi Neşriyatı, XL (1940–1943), and by H. Inalcik, "Bursa seri'ye sicillerinde Fatih Sultan Mehmed'in Fermanları," *Belleten*, XI (1947). On Palestine, Syria, and Salonika, see Bernard Lewis "Notes and Documents from the Turkish Archives, a Contribution to the History of the Jews," *Oriental Notes . . . Israel Oriental Society* (1952) and U. Heyd, cited p. 212; similarly, on Algiers, J. Deny, "Les registres de solde des janissaires," *RA*, LXI (1920), and M. Colombe, "Contributions à l'étude du recrutement de l'Odjaq d'Alger dans les dernières années de l'histoire de la Régence," *RA*, LXXXVII (1943).

A few recent works are helpful in understanding these texts which, for the uninitiated, present a number of difficulties. In particular, mention should be made of a long-standing specialist on Turkish documents in Hungary, L. Fekete, *Einführung in die osmanisch-türkische Diplomatik der türkischen Botmässigkeit in Ungarn* (1926), on which compare J. Deny, *JA* (1930), 338–352, and especially *Die Siyāqat-Schrift in der türkischen Finanzverwaltung* (1955), which was reviewed by E. Meriçli in *IFM*, XV (1953–1954), 330–343; A. Zajączkowski and J. Reichmann, *Zarys dyplomatiyki osmansko-tureckiej* (1955), English translation announced; M. Guboglu, *Paleografia si diplomatica turco-osmana* (1958), and especially on questions of accountancy and figures, S. Elker, "Divan Rakamları," *TTK*, VII/22 (Ankara, 1953). See also F. von Kraelitz, "Osmanische Urkunden in türkischer Sprache der 2. Hälfte des XV. Jahrhunderts, ein Beitrag zur osmanischen Diplomatik," *Abhandlungen der Akademie der Wissenschaften in Wien* (1921).

The archives of foreign countries naturally contain, in their respective languages, important pieces of diplomatic, and especially consular correspondence. The significant role played by France—politically, commercially, and culturally—in the external relations of the Ottoman Empire, and even to some extent in its domestic affairs, makes the French archives particularly valuable. Some of these are in the Marseilles Chamber of Commerce and even more in Paris, in the War Ministry, the National Archives, and, most of all, at the Foreign Ministry. For the War Ministry and the National Archives, see the *Catalogue Général des manuscrits des bibliothèques publiques de France*, especially *Bibliothèques de la Guerre* (Paris, 1911) and *Bibliothèques de la Marine* by C. de La Roncière (1907), *Supplement* (1924).

The Foreign Ministry records in Paris (also for Morocco, Tunisia, and Persia) contain correspondence with ambassadors from the sixteenth century onward; an *État numérique* (1936) exists, which is a catalogue classified according to countries. The National Archives preserve in 1,154 large volumes, of which there exists a typewritten list, consular corrrespondence coming from all the principal Eastern towns, mainly in the eighteenth century but sometimes dating back to the seventeenth century; also various documents from ministries and chambers of commerce and a varied collection of reports relating especially to the Levant for the seventeenth and eighteenth centuries. R. Mantran, *İstanbul dans la seconde moitié du XVIIe siècle. Essai d'histoire institutionelle, économique et sociale*, Bibliothèque archéologique et historique de l'Institut Français d'Archéologie d'Istanbul, XII (Paris, 1962), 659–661, gives a selective survey of the most important documents, and for a bibliography of the documents published, see *ibid.*, 666–667. Others are listed in the *Inventaire sommaire des archives du Département des affaires étrangères. Mémoires et documents*, three volumes (Paris, 1883–1896), particularly in Vol. II, *Fonds divers*, and Vol. III, *Fonds France et fonds divers. Supplément;* and finally documents brought back from the embassies and consulates where they had formerly been kept. Certain documents may also be found in the Bibliothèque Nationale (Paris), but they have not yet been officially catalogued.

The archives of other countries cannot all be listed here. Especially deserving of attention, however, are the documents in the Public Records Office in London, the Archives in the USSR, and the reports (*relazioni*) of

Venetian ambassadors (for those from the sixteenth century, see the next paragraph).

A certain number of important documents have been edited; for instance: by E. Charrière, *Négociations de la France dans le Levant*, four volumes, in *Documents inédits de l'histoire de France* (1848–1860); *Treaties . . . between Turkey and Foreign Powers, 1535–1855, compiled by the Foreign Office* (1855); G. Noradounguian, *Recueil d'actes internationaux de l'Empire Ottoman*, four volumes (1897–1903), the first volume devoted to the period before 1789; A. de Testa, *Recueil de traités de la Porte Ottomane avec les puissances étrangères*, ten volumes (1864–1910); and A. Gevay, *Urkunden und Aktenstücke zur Geschichte der Verhältnisse zwischen Österreich, Ungarn und der Pforte im 16. und 17. Jahrhundert*, two volumes (Vienna, 1838–1842). For the period during which the Ottoman power was at its height, the *relazioni* of the Venetian ambassadors and consuls are particularly valuable, such as the *Relazioni dei consoli veneti nella Siria*, edited by G. Berchet (1866); *Le Relazioni degli Stati Europei lette al Senato dagli Ambasciatori Veneziani nel secolo XVII*, edited by N. Barozzi and G. Berchet, ser. 5, *Turchia*, two volumes (Venice, 1866–1872); and E. Albertini, *Relazioni degli ambasciatori veneti ... durante il secolo XVI*, Ser. III, three volumes (1840, 1845, and 1855).

Documents have, of course, been published in several of the studies mentioned below, especially on p. 204.

The narrative historiographical sources have been listed by F. Babinger, cited p. 51. The Turkish historical and geographical manuscripts in the libraries of Istanbul have been partially catalogued in the *İstanbul Kütüphaneleri Tarih-Coğrafya Yazmaları Katalog* (Istanbul, 1943–1953), of which the first series has been published consisting of the following parts: 1, general histories; 2, Turkish history; 3, other countries; 4, Muslim law and pre-Islamic Prophets; 5, Muḥammad; 6, panegyrics and lives of the saints; 7, lives of the poets; 8, various biographies; 9, embassy records; and 10, political, administrative, and economic edicts. Consultation of these works is facilitated by the old alphabetical dictionary of all the persons quoted in the Ottoman political history by Mehmet Süreyya, *Sijill-i Osmānı*, four volumes (Istanbul, 1311/1892) and in the technical dictionary by M. Zeki Pakalın, *Osmanlı tarih deyimleri ve terimleri sözlügü*, three volumes (Istanbul, 1948–1956).

The Turkish chronicles are only rarely available to the non-Turkish reader. One of the few provided with a translation is the edition by F. Giese, "Altosmanische anonyme Chroniken," *AKM*, XVII/1 (1925). Among other important ancient sources for Ottoman history should be mentioned particularly *Die altosmanische Chronik* [*Tevārīkh-i Āl-i Osmān*] *des Aşik-*

paşazade, edited by F. Giese (Leipzig, 1929), and discussed by P. Wittek, "Zum Quellenprobleme der ältesten osmanischen Chroniken," *Mitteilungen zur osmanischen Geschichte*, I (1921–1922), on which see also *ibid.*, III (1923–1926), 147 ff., and *Orientalische Literaturzeitung*, XXXIV (1931); also Neşrī, *Cihān-nümā* (up to the death of Mehmed the Conqueror), of which there are two editions, one by F. Unat and M. Köymen, two volumes (Ankara, 1947–1957), on which see F. Taeschner in *Islam*, XXIX (1950), 307–317, and the other, based on a new manuscript, by F. Taeschner, I (1951), II (1955). To these should be added more sophisticated works, such as Idrīs Bitlīsī, *Hasht bihisht*, in Persian, not edited, but for MSS see *Storey* (cited p. 51), I, 413–415, and Mehmet Pasha Qaramānī, *Risāla fī tawārīkh al-Salāṭīn al-'Uthmāniyya* and *Risāla fī ta'rīkh Sulṭān Muḥammad b. Murād Khān min Āl 'Uthmān*, not edited but for translations, see Mükrimin Halil Yınanç, "Millî Tarihimize dâir eski bir vesikalar," *TOEM*, 3 (1924), 144. There are also Greek descriptions of the Ottoman conquests, not only from the Byzantine point of view, but also from that of those who rallied to the Turkish cause, dealing particularly with the victories of Mehmed the Conqueror; we shall merely cite here Kritobulos [Kritovoulos], *The History of Mehmed the Conqueror*, in an unannotated English translation by C. Riggs (1954). For the other Byzantine sources, as also for the Slav, Balkan, and Latin sources, see G. Ostrogorsky, cited p. 108. For Armenian sources, see A. Anasian, [*Armenian Sources for the Fall of Byzantium*] (Erevan, 1957), in Russian.

On the great period in the sixteenth century, the most outstanding historian is Kemālpashazāde whose *Tevārīkh-i Āl-i Osmān* was edited and partially translated into French by A. J.-B. Pavet de Courteille (Paris, 1859) and also edited by Ş. Turan in two volumes, *TTKYay*, I/5 and III/5 (Ankara, 1954–1957). One may add also: Luṭfīpasha, whose *Āṣaf-nāmeh* has been edited and translated into German by R. Tschudi in the series *Türkische Bibliothek*, XII (Berlin, 1910); Sa'dī, the author of a *Selīm-nāmeh*, which was the prototype of various other *Sulaymān-nāmehs*, edited by M. Speiser (Zürich, 1946); Sa'd al-Dīn, *Tāj ül-tevārīkh;* 'Alī, *Künh ül-akhbār*, Vol. III and part of Vol. IV of which have appeared, five volumes (Istanbul, A.H. 1277–1285); special accounts of particular campaigns such as the Djerba expedition, on which see A. Bombaci, "Le fonti turche della battaglia della Gerbe (1560)," *RSO*, XIX–XXI (1941–1943) and XXI (1946), or the biographies of outstanding persons, such as the memoirs of the famous pirate and conqueror of the Maghrib, Khair al-Dīn Barbarossa, which no doubt existed, and of which a Spanish adaptation has survived, the Arabic version having been lost. A history known in Europe through a Latin translation by Johann Löwenklau [Johannes Leunclavius] was written under similar circumstances. The great Arabic dictionary by Ṭāshköprüzāde dates back to the same period and gives the lives of the first ten Ottoman sultans with information on 522 ulemas and shaikhs of the brotherhoods classified according to *ṭabaqāt* up to the reign of Sulaiman, with his autobiography at the end. It was printed in the margin of Ibn Khallikān (Cairo, A.H. 1299), O. Rescher translated it into German, *Es-šaqā'iq en-no'mānijje von Ṭašköprüzade enthaltend die Biographien der türkischen und im osmanischen Reiche wirkenden Gelehrten, Derwisch-Scheiẖ's und Ärzte von der Regierung Sultân 'Oṯmâns bis zu der Sülaimân's des Grossen* (Constantinople-Galata, 1927).

In the seventeenth century there were several great historians writing in various languages, who concerned themselves to a much greater extent than their predecessors with universal history based on serious documentation and a real understanding of the conditions in which the empire existed. Ḥājjī Khalīfa, whom we have already met as a bibliographer, was also a geographer, as the author of the *Jihān-nūmā*, of which there is a Latin translation by M. Norberg (1818), and a historian, as the author of *Tühfet ül-kibār*, translated into English by J. Mitchell, *The History of the Maritime Wars of the Turks* (London, 1831); Munajjim Bāshı was the author of a universal history in Arabic, known for many years only through a Turkish summary (and still the only version published) containing fresh information on the minor dynasties of the Ottoman Empire. Lastly, Na'īmā, coming at the end of the century, was the author of a perceptive work, *Annals of the Turkish Empire from 1591 to 1659*, edited and translated into English by C. Fraser (London, 1832), to which there is a sequel by Rashīd of events up to 1721. There was no great Turkish historian in the eighteenth century, although the scholar may use accounts by such nineteenth-century Turkish writers as Resmī, Sa'dullāh Enverī, and Wāṣif Efendī.

There are such specialized works as an eyewitness account of the siege of Vienna in 1683, available in a German translation by R. F. Kreutel, *Kara Mustafa vor Wien*, Vol. I of *Osmanische Geschichtsschreiber* (Graz, 1955), and various travel or embassy reports, such as Evliyā Chelebi, *Im Reiche des Goldenen Apfels*, translated by the same author (Graz, 1957), containing the impressions of a stay in Vienna. Historicopolitical writings that are devoted to reflections on the causes of the decline of the empire and to the necessary reforms are also of interest, such as Waisī, *Khwāb-nāmeh* (Būlāq, A.H. 1252; Istanbul, A.H. 1263 and 1293), German translation by H. F. von Diez, *Ermahnung an Islambol* (Berlin, 1811); and Quci Beg (Kocabeg), *Risāla*, on which see W. F. A. Behrnauer, "Koğabegs Abhandlung über den Verfall des osmanischen Staatsgebäudes seit Sultan Suleiman dem Grossen," *ZDMG*, XV (1861), and the Russian translation by A. Tveritinova, "Vtoroi traktat Kochibeya," *UZIV*, VI (1953); and also Bernard Lewis, "Ottoman Observers of Ottoman Decline," *IS*, I (1962).

Ottoman geographical literature also boasts some very fine works. Apart from Sulaimān Mahrī, who continued the work of Ibn Mājid (cited p. 183), Pīrī Re'īs and Evliyā Chelebi, cited in the preceding paragraph, should be particularly noted. Their works are of different kinds: the former the author of a remarkable study, with equally remarkable maps, on navigation and the Mediterranean coasts at the beginning of the sixteenth century; his *Baḥrīye* has been edited by P. Kahle (Berlin, 1926–1927), who also began but unfortunately did not finish a translation (1926). Evliyā Chelebi, on the other hand, composed a number of extraordinarily detailed and valuable accounts based on his travels throughout the empire, and particularly on his observations of the human aspects of Constantinople, which have been translated in their essentials by J. von Hammer-Purgstall, *Narrative of Travels in Europe, Asia and Africa by Evliya Efendi*, two volumes (1834–1846); it was on the basis of the historical-topographical information and the road map of Asia Minor supplied by this work that F. Taeschner wrote his *Das anatolische Wegenetz*, in *Türkische Bibliothek*, XXII–XXIII (1924–1926). See also the description by the Armenian, Eremya Chelebi, in the İstanbul Üniversitesi Edebiyat Fakültesi. Yayinlar, MVI (1952).

To Ottoman literature proper should be added that of the non-Turkish provinces of the Empire, even though not as rich. The only really great work, of fundamental importance for the study of eighteenth- and early nineteenth-century Egypt, is by al-Jabartī, *'Ajā'ib al-āthār*, edited at Būlāq (1880), four volumes, with an index by G. Wiet, *Index de Djabarti* (Cairo, 1954); and see the articles by D. Ayalon, cited p. 211. A Russian translation has been started (1962). Other works are mentioned in *GAL*, cited p. 49.

An exhaustive list of sources should include the histories of all peoples who came into contact with the Ottoman Empire. For example, see the very important *Diarii* of Marino Sanuto, fifty-eight volumes (Venice, 1879–1903), for the beginning of the sixteenth century; also, for the importance of European commercial documents to the history of trade in the period of the great conquests, see, for example, the *Lettres Commerciales de Bembo*, studied by F. Thiriet in *Studi in onore A. Sapori*, II (1957); *Lettres d'un marchand vénitien, Andrea Berengo 1553–1556*, edited by U. Tucci in the collection *Affaires et gens d'affaires*, X, published by the École Pratique des Hautes Études, 6e sect. (Paris, 1957); or even works such as the famous book by J. Savary, *Le parfait négociant* (Paris, 1752).

Here innumerable reports by European travelers to the East naturally enter. It is not possible to give a full or even a selective account. There is no catalogue of such works, but the essential data may be found in J. Carré, *Voyageurs et écrivains français en Égypte*, Vol. I (*1517–1840*), *Du début à la fin de la domination turque* in the Publications de l'Institut Français d'Archéologie Orientale. Recherches d'archéologie, de philologie et d'histoire, IV (Cairo, 1932); H. Omant, *Missions archéologiques en Orient au XVIIe et au XVIIIe siècles*, two volumes (1902); and E. Charrière, cited p. 197. As examples see Ogier de Busbecq, *Itinera* ... (1881), translated into English, *Turkish Letters* (1927), I. Chesneau, *Le voyage de M. d'Aramon*, edited by C. Schefer (Paris, 1887), Paul Lucas, *Voyages* (1705, 1720, 1731; Paris, 1912), and C.-Fr. Volney, *Voyage en Égypte et en Syrie*, reëdited and studied by J. Gaulmier (1959).

The geographical information provided by travelers has been collected and will be found in the maps and text of *Die Erdkunde*, twenty-one volumes, by K. Ritter (1882–1859).

Finally, homage must be paid to the monumental DESCRIPTION DE L'EGYPTE, a most remarkable work in every way, compiled by various scholars at Napoleon's command during his Egyptian expedition, twenty-three volumes (Paris, 1809–1828; 2d ed., 24 vols., 1821–1829). This work is an inexhaustible source of all kinds of information on Egypt on the eve of its transformation through contact with European influences.

Ottoman numismatic material is mainly to be found in S. Lane-Poole's catalogues in the British Museum and in Halil Edhem in *Meskūkāt*, Vol. VI (both cited p. 56). For archaeology, see below, p. 215. On epigraphy, see the regional monographs cited on p. 211 ff.

GENERAL WORKS AND POLITICAL HISTORY

A bibliography of Ottoman history may be compiled with the aid of the general collections cited on p. 153. J. Birge, *A Guide to Turkish History* (1949), is not well informed on publications not in the English language. See R. Mantran, "Les études historiques en Turquie depuis 1923, éléments de bibliographie," *Anadolu*, I [= *Études orientales*, XII] (1952).

Since the larger works could not exploit fully the archive sources and even some of the more important literary sources, they are no longer as useful as we might wish, although they are far from superseded; for example, see: the *Geschichte des Osmanischen Reiches* (up to 1774) by J. von Hammer-Purgstall (2d ed., 10 vols., 1827–1835), reprinted in Veröffentlichungen der Hammer-Purgstall-Gesellschaft, Reihe A, Werke I (Graz, 1963——); French translation (based on the 1st ed.) by J. Hellert, eighteen volumes (1835–1843), and also by L. Dochez (based on the 2nd ed.), three volumes (1840–1844); J. W. Zinkeisen, *Geschichte des Osmanischen Reiches in Europa*, seven volumes (1845–1863; reprinted, 1963——); N. Iorga, *Geschichte des*

Osmanischen Reiches, five volumes (1908–1913). A rapid introduction, especially to the history of foreign relations, may be obtained from A. de la Jonquière, *Histoire de l'Empire Ottoman* (3d ed., 1914), or L. Lamouche, *Histoire de la Turquie Ottomane*, revised edition by J. Roux (1953). Wider in scope but necessarily elementary, is R. Mantran, *Histoire de la Turquie ottomane*, in the collection Que sais-je?, no. 539 (1952), and H. J. Kissling and H. Scheel in *HO* (cited p. 67 f.), I/VI, 3. In Turkey, considerable advances have been made in various articles of the *Islam Ansiklopedisi*, cited p. 153, and especially in the *Osmanli Tarihi* of the Turkish Historical Society, of which I. Ḥakkī Uzunçarşılı has published Vols. I, origins to 1453 (1947), II, 1453–1566 (1949), and III–IV, 1566–1789 (1951 and 1954–1956); and Enver Ziya Karal the three volumes for the years 1789 to 1876 (1947, 1954, and 1956). See also the chronological work by I. Danişmend, *Izahlı Osmanlı Tarihi Kronolojisi*, four volumes (1947–1956), to the year 1924, in which the references are particularly useful.

On geography, and more especially the geography of Asia Minor, see: K. Ritter (cited p. 201); F. Taeschner (p. 200); K. Mostras, *Dictionnaire géographique de l'Empire Ottoman* (1873); S. Fraschéry, *Dictionnaire universel d'histoire et de géographie* (1889–1898); the official publication *Köylerimiz*, a gazetteer; and the article "Anadolu" by F. Taeschner in *EI*², which refers to various important descriptions for the nineteenth century, of which only *La Turquie d'Asie* by V. Cuinet (1892–1894) is here listed.

On the atmosphere in which the early Ottoman regime was born and developed, we have two good general outlines that differ from each other without contradiction: M. F. Köprülü, *Les origines de l'Empire Ottoman* (Paris, 1935), and P. Wittek, *The Rise of the Ottoman Empire* (1938), to which may be added W. Langer and R. Blake, "The Rise of the Ottoman Turks and its Historical Background," *American Historical Review*, XXXVII (1932). On the early years of the Ottoman Empire, consult, with caution, H. Gibbons, *The Foundation of the Ottoman Empire* (1916), still the only correct account of events as a whole. On the question of relations with Byzantium and for information on Ottoman history to be obtained from Greek sources, see the work of the Byzantinists, a masterly synthesis of which may be found in the *Geschichte* by G. Ostrogorsky, cited p. 108; see for example, G. Arnakis, *Hoi Protoi Othomanoi* (*The First Ottomans*), Vol. XLI of Texte und Forschungen zur byzantinisch-neugriechischen Philologie (Athens, 1947). The Turks have devoted particular attention to the Qay tribe to which the Ottoman Turks belonged: M. F. Köprülü, "Osmanlı İmparatoluğunun etnik menşei mes'eleri," *Belleten*, VII (1943), 215–303, and F. Demirtaş, "Osmanlı devrinde Anadolu'da Kayılar," *Belleten*, XII (1948), 575–615, with a summary in French. P. Wittek and

F. Taeschner wrote a study, "Die Vezier-Familie der Ǧandarlyzade und ihre Denkmäler," *Islam*, XVIII (1929).

On the subject of the political and social crisis at the beginnings of the fifteenth century and the recovery before the taking of Constantinople, P. Wittek has defined the general development of the situation in "De la défaite d'Ankara à la prise de Constantinople," *REI*, XII (1938), while F. Babinger has studied the important social and religious movement of "Schejch Bedr ed-Din, der Sohn des Richters von Simaw," *Islam*, XI (1921), supplemented in *Islam* XVII (1928) and "Beiträge zur Frühgeschichte der Türkenherrschaft in Rumelien" in *Südosteuropäische Arbeiten*, no. 34 (Brünn, Munich, and Vienna 1934). Wittek has posed the problem of whether the levying of Christian children for the army was in accordance with Islamic Law, in "Devshirme and Shari'a," *BSOAS*, XVII (1955), and S. Vryonis has studied "Isidore Glabas and the Turkish Devshirme," *Speculum*, XXXI (1956). Wittek is also the author of an important article, "Notes sur la tughra ottomane," *Byzantion*, XVIII (1948) and XX (1950); and add I. H. Uzunçarşılı, "Tuğra ve Pençeler," *Belleten*, V (1941).

For the anti-Ottoman Crusades, see A. S. Atiya, above, p. 182, and F. Babinger, "Von Amurath zu Amurath, Vor- und Nachspiel der Schlacht bei Varna (1444)," *Oriens*, III (1950) with additional remarks in *Oriens*, IV (1951), 80. See also the histories of the Italian merchant towns and U. Heyd, cited above, p. 93.

On Muḥammad (Mehmet) II there is a large general work by F. Babinger, *Mehmed II. der Eroberer und seine Zeit* (1953), translated into French (1954), and into English (1956), which has aroused controversy. See also I. Ertaylan *Fātih ve fütuhatı*, İstanbul Fethinin 500. Yıldönümü Münasebetiyle Yapılan İstanbul Üniversitesi Edebiyat Fakültesi Yayınlarından (1953). The fifth centenary of the taking of Constantinople gave rise to a number of works, the bibliography of which has been begun by S. Özerdim and M. Mercanlıgıl "Fethin 500 yılönümü dolayısiyle çıkan eserler," *Belleten*, XVII/62 (1953), 413–428. A brief account of the various points of view on the event may be found in *The Fall of Constantinople. A Symposium held at the School of Oriental and African Studies, May 29, 1953* (London, 1955) with contributions by S. Runciman, Bernard Lewis, *et al.*

On the conquest of Albania, consult A. Gegaj, *L'Albanie et l'invasion turque au XVe siècle* (1937), and the article "Skander beg" in *EI*. See also I. Dujcev, "La conquête turque et la prise de Constantinople dans la littérature slave," *Byzantinoslavica*, XIV (1953) and XVI (1955).

On the reigns of Bayezid II and Selim II, see F. Gücüyener, *Yavuz Sultan Selim*, two volumes (Istanbul, 1945); on domestic policy in the time of Bayezid II, S. Fisher, "Civil Strife in the Ottoman Empire, 1481–1503,"

Journal of Modern History, XIII (1941); on foreign policy, by the same author, *The Foreign Relations of Turkey, 1481–1512* (1948), and H. Jansky, "Die Eroberung Syriens durch Sultan Selim I.," *Mitteilungen zur osmanischen Geschichte*, II (1923–1926). See also Hans Pfeffermann, *Die Zusammenarbeit der Renaissancepäpste mit den Türken* (1946), and M. Silberschmidt, *Das Orientalische Problem zur Zeit der Entstehung des Türkischen Reiches* (1923). There is also a Russian work by N. Smirnov, [*Russia and Turkey in the XVIth and XVIIth Centuries*] (1946).

On the history of Sultan Djem, the brother of Bayezid II who took refuge in Europe, see L. Thuasne, *Djem-Sultan, étude sur la question d'Orient à la fin du XVe siècle* (1892), and I. Ertaylan, *Sultan Cem*, İstanbul Üniversitesi Edebiyat Fakültesi Yayınlar (1951).

For the reign of Sulaiman Qānūnī (Sulaiman the Magnificent), which marked the zenith of the Ottoman Empire, the general outlines may still be found, albeit incompletely, in F. Babinger, "*Sulejman der Grosse*," in *Meister der Politik* (1923), and R. Merriman, *Suleiman the Magnificent* (1944), better than H. Lamb, with the same title (1951), which is more elementary. In this connection, see the chapter by V. Parry, "The Ottoman Empire, 1520–1566," in the second volume of the *New Cambridge Modern History* (1957——). On particular expeditions, consult F. Tauer, *Histoire de la campagne de Suleyman contre Belgrade en 1571* (Prague, 1924), and "Solimans Wiener Feldzug," *ArO*, VII–VIII (1935–1936) and XXIV (1956); A. J.-B. Pavet de Courteille, *Histoire de la campagne de Mohácz* (1859); A. Gabriel, "Les étapes d'une campagne dans les deux Iraks," *Syria*, IX (1928); M. Tayyib Gökbilgin, "Arz ve raporlarına göre Ibrahim Paşa'nın Irakeyn seferindeki ilk tedbirleri ve fütuhatı," *Belleten*, XXI/83 (1957), 449–482, dealing with documents concerning the organization of the "two Iraqs" after the campaign of 1534; Safvet, "Kıbrıs fethi üzerine vesikalar," *TOEM*, LV (1329/1913–1914), 1177–1193, documents concerning the conquest of Cyprus; H. Burski, *Kemal-Re'is, ein Beitrag zur Geschichte der türkischen Flotte* (1928); and on Khair al-Dīn Barbarossa and the conquest of North Africa, there is G. Fisher, *Barbary Legend; War, Trade and Piracy in North Africa* (1957).

For the end of the sixteenth century, a general acquaintance with a variety of problems concerned with the Mediterranean may be had in F. Braudel, *La méditerranée et le monde méditerranéen à l'époque de Philippe II* (1949), dealing with the historical geography, structure, and civilization, in all their aspects, of the Mediterranean countries, both Christian and Muslim, and finally with the political and actual history of international relations during the reign of Philip II in Spain. With respect to the Ottoman aspects of the work, considerable appreciation has been shown, especially in view of the fact that the author did not know Turkish, by O. Barkan in his review in *IFM*, XI (1949–1950).

The period extending from the end of the sixteenth to the beginning of the nineteenth century, is less glorious and has been studied less, and then too often from the standpoint of Christian Europe and its wars with the Empire. One may examine the question of the decline of the Empire, the rapidity of which should not be exaggerated nor its causes attributed entirely to internal weaknesses, with the aid of F. Grenard, *Grandeur et décadence de l'Asie* (1939), and Bernard Lewis, "Some Reflections on the Decline of the Ottoman Empire," *SI*, IX (1958). For the eighteenth century in particular, but generally for the institutions of the Ottoman Empire, it will be necessary to start with the valuable but uneven general survey by H. A. R. Gibb and H. Bowen in *Islamic Society and the West*, Vol. I, *Islamic Society in the Eighteenth Century* in two parts (London, New York, and Toronto, 1950–1957, Part I reprinted 1951, 1957, and 1960; Part II reprinted 1962). See also the opening pages of Bernard Lewis, *The Emergence of Modern Turkey* (1961); the interesting work by M. Shay, *The Ottoman Empire from 1720 to 1754 as Revealed in Despatches of the Venetian Baili* (Urbana, 1944); and the booklet by L. Stavrianos, *The Ottoman Empire* (1957).

The only sultan of the period studied is Selim III (end of eighteenth century), because of his personality, his attempts at reform, and his tragic fate. See especially E. Karal, *Selim III'ün Hatt-i humayunlari* (1942).

INSTITUTIONS

On the administrative institutions of the Ottoman Empire, the old surveys by J. von Hammer-Purgstall, *Des Osmanischen Reiches Staatsverfassung und Staatsverwaltung* (1815) and C. M. d'Ohsson, *Tableau général de l'Empire Ottoman*, seven volumes (1787–1824), whose authors saw the functioning of the traditional Ottoman government, still merit consultation, provided their statements are checked and verified. A more reliable account, though narrower in scope, is that by A. Lybyer, *The Government of the Ottoman Empire in the Time of Suleiman the Magnificent* (1913). A more recent work by I. H. Uzunçarşılı, "Osmanlı Devletinin merkez ve bahriye teşkilâtı," *TTKYay*, VIII/16 (Ankara, 1948), an abundant but uncritical collection of information, contains, in addition to a detailed presentation of the chief administrative services, a special study on the navy. On law in general, see A. Heidborn, *Manuel de droit public et administratif de l'Empire ottoman*, two volumes (Vienna and Leipzig, 1908–1912), especially on the nineteenth century, and N. E. Tornau, *Le droit musulman exposé d'après les sources* (1860).

One of the general questions most discussed is the comparison of the originality of Ottoman institutions with Byzantine institutions on the one hand, and with those of the older Muslim states on the other. M. F. Köprülü has shown that as far as government and administration are concerned, more was borrowed from the Muslim and Turkish past than from the Byzantine, and not the reverse, as former Byzantinists, such as N. Iorga, had too hastily concluded; see "Bizans müesseselerinin Osmanlı müesseselerine te'sire hakkında bâzı mülahazalar," *Türk Hukuk ve İktisat Tarihi Mecmuası*, I (1931), 165–298. The conclusions would obviously be different in the case of institutions directly concerned with the administration of non-Turkish populations, where the Ottomans sought above all to promote continuity and efficient functioning. In *Les institutions juridiques turques au Moyen Âge* (Istanbul, 1938), which was translated from *Belleten* II (1938), the same author tries to detect the continuity of a Turkish law as distinct from Islamic Law, but his conclusions here seem less significant. The *Osmanlı Devleti teşkilâtına medhal*, by I. H. Uzunçarşılı, in *TTKYay*, VIII/10 (Istanbul, 1941), which attempts to follow each institution separately throughout the states dominated by the Turks before the Ottoman Empire, is not sufficiently critical, although very useful as a reference work on the history of the institutions of these states, in which connection it has already been mentioned.

Among the more specialized works should be mentioned A. Alderson, *The Structure of the Ottoman Dynasty* (1956); on the palace, N. Penzer, *The Harem* (London, 1936), and B. Miller, *The Palace School of Muhammad the Conqueror* (1941); I. H. Uzunçarşili, *Osmanlı Devletinin Saray teşkilâtı* (Ankara, 1945), which also provides information on the installation of the first sultans at Bursa and Adrianopolis; W. Wright, *Ottoman Statecraft* (1935). On the sultanate and the caliphate, see the works cited on p. 94 f., and in particular H. A. R. Gibb and P. Wittek; R. Anhegger has studied a number of attempts at reform in the seventeenth century in "Hezarfen Hüseyin Efendi'nin Osmanlı devlet teşkilâtına dair mülahazaları," *Türkiyat Mecmuası*, X (1953), 365–393.

On the army there is an outline study on the Janissaries by T. Menzel, "Das Korps der Janitscharen," *Jahrbuch der Münchner Orientalischen Gesellschaft* (1902–1903), but a fuller account of military institutions, well informed and well written, will be found in I. H. Uzunçarşılı, *Osmanlı devleti teşkilâtından kapukulu ocakları*, two volumes (Ankara, 1943–1944), the first volume of which deals with the "ojak" of the 'ajamis and the Janissaries, while the second volume deals with the cavalry, the artillery, and all the specialized corps. Also of interest on the subject of the Janissaries is the book by A. Pallis, *In the Days of the Janissaries* (1951). On the Turkish army in North Africa, see below. On the *tīmār*, see p. 208.

On financial questions, apart from the treatises on institutions, we have N. Aghnidès, *Mohammadan Theories of Finance* (1916), and more specialized studies, such as that by N. Çağatay, "Osmanlı İmparatorluğunda reayadan alınan vergi ve resimler," *AÜDTCFD*, V (1947), 483–511, concerning the taxes imposed on the peasants; B. Nedgoff, *Die Ǧizya im Osmanischen Reich* (1942), of which there is a Turkish translation, "Osmanlı İmparatorluğunda cizye," *Belleten*, VIII (1944), 599–652; O. Barkan, "Hicri 933–934 [1527–1528] mali yılına ait bütçe örnegi," *IFM*, XV (1953–1954), 251–329, which also includes a study of Ottoman budgets, especially in the sixteenth century, and see also the article by the same author, *ibid.*, XVII (1960).

On the subject of currency, see A. Refik, "Osmanlı İmparatorluğunda meskûkât, 7–12 asır," *TOEM*, XIV (1340/1924) and XV (1341/1925), and 'Alī, "Le prime monete e i primi 'Aspri' dell'Imperio Ottomano," *Rivista italiana di numismatica e scienze affini*, XXXIX (1921), which is a translation of an article in Turkish in *TOEM*, VIII (1334/1917–1918), 356–375.

FOREIGN POLICY

The foreign policy of the Ottoman Empire has given rise only to fragmentary studies written from the standpoint of other states. It would be impossible to give even a short list here, but the reader is referred to D. Vaughan, *Europe and the Turk, 1350–1700* (1954), J. Deny in *Histoire et historiens* ..., cited p. 193 f., and P. Masson (p. 210). A few recent monographs should be quoted as examples of studies in which the Turkish point of view is considered, such as I. Soysal, "Türk-Fransız diplomasi münasebetlerin ilk devresi," *İstanbul Üniversitesi Edebiyat Fakültesi Tarih Dergisi*, III/5 (1951), 63–94, and 6 (1952), on the early stages of Franco-Turkish relations; A. Kurat, *Türk-Ingiliz münasebetlerinin başlangıç ve gelişmesi, 1553–1610*, in Ankara Üniversitesi Dil ve Tarih-Coğrafya Fakültesi Tarih Enstitüsü, XVI (1953), and *Isveç kıralı Karl'in Türkiye'de kalışı* (Istanbul, 1943), on Charles XII and Turkey; A. Refik, *Osmanlılar ve Büyük Frederik* (1333/1916–1918), on the Ottomans and Frederick II up to 1765; and A. Belin, cited p. 214.

ECONOMIC AND SOCIAL LIFE

On economic history in general, the older study by A. Belin, *Essai sur l'histoire économique de la Turquie d'après les écrivains originaux* (Paris, 1885), should still be consulted for the documents it contains. Concerning the documentation available, see H. Inalcik, "15 asır Türkiye iktisadı ve içtimaı tarihi kaynakları," *IFM*, XV (1953–1954), 51–55, which particularly stresses the importance of legacies, and M. Akdağ, *Türkiye'nin iktisadî ve ictimaî Tarihi, I, 1243–1453, AÜDTCFYay*, CXXXI (1953). On the general economic situation during the period of the Empire's development, the ideas and information in M. Akdağ, "Osmanlı İmparatorluğunun kuruluş ve inkişaf devrinde Türkiyenin iktisadî vaziyeti," *Belleten*, XIII–XIV (1949–1950), which deals, among other things, with the relationship between Ottoman and world economy, and is discussed by H. Inalcik, "Osmanlı . . . vaziyeti üzerinde bir tetkik münasebetiyle," *Belleten*, XV (1951), 629–684, can only be raised as interesting suggestions for future research. On economic development in the eighteenth century, see A. Hourani, cited p. 211.

On the history of the agricultural economy, the most comprehensive and well-documented studies are by O. Barkan, whose works on other topics are cited on pp. 194 and 207. An introduction to these works may be had from his own summary, "Les problèmes fonciers dans histoire Ottoman au temps de sa fondation," *Annales d'histoire sociale*, I (1939); the main studies have been published in Turkish and French in *IFM* of which he was the founder: "Les formes de l'organisation du travail agricole dans l'Empire Ottoman aux XVe et XVIe siècles," I/1 (1939), 2 and 4 (1940), and "Aperçu sur l'histoire des problèmes agraires des pays balkaniques," VII (1945–1946); also by the same author, "Türk-Islam toprak hukuku tatbikatının Osmanlı İmparatorluğunda aldığı sekiller, I: Malikâne-divani sistemi," *Türk Hukuk ve İktisat Tarihi Mecmuası*, II (1932–1939), on Ottoman land laws applying to large estates, and "Osmanlı İmparatorluğunda toprak vakıflarının idarî-malî muhtariyeti mes'elesi," *Türk Hukuk Tarihi Dergisi*, I (1941–1942), on the immunity of religious properties; I. Hüsrev, *Türkiye köy iktisadiyatı* (1934), a partly historical study on rural economy; and see also the works of X. de Planhol, cited p. 80. We would remind the reader of M. Worms, "Recherches sur la constitution de la propriété territoriale dans les pays musulmans et subsidiairement en Algérie," *JA* (1842–1844), although A. Gurland, *Grundzüge der muhammedanischen Agrarverfassung* (1907), is better. See also A. Belin, "Étude sur la propriété foncière en pays musulmans et spécialement en Turquie," *JA* (1861–1862).

For the *tīmār* (land concession to soldiers), the best account is by J. Deny in *EI*, *s.v.*; it may be supplemented for a specific Balkan region by N. Filipovič, "Bosna-Hersek timar sisteminin inkişafi," *IFM*, XV (1953–1954), 155–188. See also P. A. von Tischendorf, *Das Lehnswesen in den Moslemischen Staaten insbesondere im Osmanischen Reiche* (Leipzig, 1872).

On mining, the fundamental work is by R. Anhegger, *Europäische Türkei*, Vol. I of *Beiträge zur Geschichte des Bergbaus im Osmanischen Reich* (Istanbul, 1943); there are many documents in A. Refik, *Osmanlı devrinde Türkiye madenleri* (Istanbul, 1931), and N. Çağatay, "Osmanlı İmparatorluğunda maden hukuk ve iktisadiyatı hakkında vesikalar," *Tarih Vesikaları*, II/10 (1942) and II/12 (1943).

On domestic trade and the provisioning of towns, see L. Gücer, "Le commerce intérieur des céréales dans l'Empire Ottoman pendant la 2e moitié du XVIe siècle," *IFM*, XI (1949–1950), 397–416; and the documents presented by O. Barkan on the control of goods in certain towns, "Bazı büyük şehirlerde eşya ve yiyecek fiatlarının tesbit ve teftişi hususlarını tanzim eden kanunlar," *Tarih Vesikları*, I/5 (Feb., 1942), II/7 (June, 1942), II/9 (Oct., 1942). On the provisioning of Istanbul especially, it is still useful to consult A. Refik, "Sultan Süleyman kanuni'nin son senelerinde İstanbul'un usul-i iaşe ve ahvāl-i tüccariyesi," *TOEM*, IV (1332/1916–1917). See also R. Mantran, "La police des marchés a Istanbul au début de XVIe siècle," *CT*, IV (1956), annotated.

On the monetary aspect of economic history, N. Beldiceanu, "La crise monétaire ottomane au XVIe siècle et son influence sur les principautés roumaines," *Südöstliche Forschungen*, XV/1 (1957).

The organization of labor is bound up to some extent with that of the *akhi* and *futuwwa* communities, the bibliography for which will be found above, p. 160. The formation of these institutions preceded the Ottomans, and the height of the Empire coincides with their decline. From a general point of view our only choice is between the very comprehensive study by Bernard Lewis, cited p. 92, and the rather limited notes, on the condition of labor, by N. Çağatay, "Osmanli İmparatorluğunda maden işletme tarzlari hakkında tetkik tecrübesi," *AÜDTCFD*, II/1 (1943), 116–126, or by S. Ülgener, "La morale des métiers et les critiques qui leur ont été adressées," *IFM*, XI (1949–1950), 397–416, in Turkish and French. The work by F. Taeschner, "Das bosnische Zunftwesen zur Türkenzeit, 1463–1878," in *Festschrift Franz Dölger zum 60. Geburtstage gewidmet. Byzantinische Zeitschrift*, XLIV (1951), goes in fact beyond Bosnia.

The Empire's foreign trade, and more especially the trade of foreigners with the Empire, has been among the chief subjects for study, and while too often one-sided, much of the work done is still valid. A number of problems may be defined with the aid of F. Braudel, "Note sull'economia, ... " in *Economia e storia*, I/2 (1955), and later in French, "L'économie de la Méditerranée," *CT*, IV (1956). Most of the studies concern themselves with European enterprises, and are outside the scope of this work. For a general introduction to the question, the reader is referred to the histories of commerce as a whole, such as by J. Lacour-Gayet, *Histoire du commerce* (1950–1955); a few particularly noteworthy studies, more directly concerned with Ottoman history proper, or too recent to be included in other bibliographies, are given here: P. Masson, *Histoire du commerce français dans le Levant au XVIIe siècle* (1896), which may be supplemented with three volumes of *Histoire du commerce de Marseille;* III, by J. Billoud and R. Collier (1951), IV, by L. Bergasse and G. Rambert (1954), V, by R. Paris (1957); also by P. Masson, *Histoire ... au XVIIIe siècle* (1911); A. Wood, *A History of the Levant Company* (1935); H. Wätjen, *Die Niederländer im Mittelmeergebiet* ... (1909); H. Hassinger, "Die erste Wiener orientalische Handels-compagnie," in *Vierteljahrschrift für Sozial- und Wirtschafts-Geschichte*, XXXV (1942). Although exclusively based on European archives, N. Svoronos, *Le commerce de Salonique au XVIIIe siècle* (1956), is the first important attempt to study a port of the Empire, especially a Greek port, for its own sake, on which see the review by R. Mantran in *JESHO*, II/1 (1959). In another connection, the work by H. Kahane and A. Tietze, *The Lingua Franca in the Levant, Turkish Nautical Terms of Italian and Greek Origin* (1958), is also interesting. See further the article by I. H. Uzunçarşılı, "Osmanlı ... bahriye teşkilâtı," cited p. 205. On Russian trade with the Muslim world at this time, see N. Fekhner, [*Russia's Commercial Relations with Eastern Lands in the XVIth Century*] (1956). On foreign relations, see p. 207 ff.

Demographical problems have been studied mainly by O. Barkan: in particular, "Tarihi Demografi araştırmaları ve Osmanlı tarihi," *Türkiyat Mecmuası*, X (1953), 1–26, which should be supplemented by his article in French, "Essai sur les données statistiques des registres de recensement dans l'Empire Ottoman aux XVe et XVIe siècles," *JESHO*, I/1 (1957). Internal colonization as a method of occupation is the subject of two important articles by O. Barkan, "Osmanlı İmparatorluğunda bir iskan ve kolonizasyon metodu olarak vakıflar ve temlikler," *Vakıflar Dergisi*, II (1942), 279–387, which investigates the role of the *waqf* foundations in this regard, and "Les déportations come méthode de peuplement," *IFM*, XI (1949–1950), 534–569, in Turkish and French. On the special question of the settlement of nomads, M. T. Gökbilgin, *Rumeli'de Yürükler Tatarlar ve Evlâd-ı Fâtihân* (Istanbul, 1957). On the tribes of Asia Minor in the sixteenth century, see A. Refik, *Anadoluda türk aşiretleri* (1930).

Concerning the social life and other aspects of Constaninople in the seventeenth century, see p. 204 ff., and the important new work by R. Mantran, *Istanbul dans la seconde moitié du XVIIe siècle* (1962). The basic reference work is still Osman Ergin, *Mecelle-i Umur-u Belediye* (1337/1922), on municipal affairs. See also A. Schneider, "Türkische Literatur zur Geschichte und Topographie Konstantinopels," *Islam*, XXIX (1950).

PROVINCES

In the study of the provinces of the Empire, the Arab provinces take first place, although they produced the fewest scholarly works. Historians of the Arab world have too often set aside the Ottoman period, or dealt merely with those episodes which serve to bring into view the adversaries of the regime to which Europe was opposed. Apart from G. Stripling, *The Ottoman Turks and the Arabs, 1511–1574* (1942), which is inadequate, there are only a few studies, on specific places or incidents, or the elementary accounts in the general histories of individual countries.

This is true in the case of Egypt, although in the fifth volume of the *Histoire de la nation égyptienne*, cited p. 67, the Ottoman period has at least been treated independently by H. Dehérain as a special volume, *L'Égypte turque* (Paris, n.d., copyright 1931). The reader is also reminded of the important contribution by J. Deny, cited p. 193 f. Among the rare recent works are D. Ayalon, "Studies in al-Jabartī. The Transformation of Mamluk Society in Egypt under the Ottomans," *JESHO*, III (1960, and "The Historian al-Jabartī," in *Historians of the Middle East*, cited p. 22; Stanford J. Shaw, *The Financial and Administrative Organization of Ottoman Egypt, 1517–1798* (1962); A. Raymond is preparing a work on the society of Ottoman Egypt. See also N. Tomiche, "La situation des artisans ... en Egypte (fin XVIIIe–milieu XIXe siēcle)," *SI*, XII (1960).

On the Fertile Crescent in general during the period of the Empire's decline, there is an important study by A. Hourani, "The Changing Face of the Fertile Crescent in the XVIIIth Century," *SI*, VIII (1957), which illustrates clearly not only the demilitarization of the government, but also the emancipation of non-Muslims, the Muslim opposition to orthodoxy, and the intrusion of foreigners. See also the introductory chapters in his *Arabic Thought in the Liberal Age* (1962).

On Mesopotamia in particular, in addition to C. Huart, *Histoire de Baghdad dans les temps modernes* (1901), S. Longrigg, *Four Centuries of Modern Iraq* (1925), and H. Gollancz, *Chronicle of Events between 1629 and and 1733* (1927), we now have the more recent *Ta'rīkh al-'Irāq bain al-iḥtilālain*, Vols. IV–VIII, by 'A. al-'Azzāwī (1935–1956), mentioned above, p. 173, which is a chronicle of events in the traditional manner, but very well informed.

Within the geographical area of Syria and Palestine, the only comprehensive work, apart from the general works mentioned above, p. 65 f., is concerned with Lebanon: M. Chebli, *Histoire du Liban sous les émirs druzes* (1955), which was preceded by his *Fakhreddin* (*1572–1635*) (1946); the article by F. Wüstenfeld in *AGG*, XXXIII (1886) still retains some value. A. Ismā'īl published the first and fourth volumes (1955 and 1959) of a wider *Histoire du Liban du XVIIe siècle à nos jours*, dealing with the periods 1590–1635 and 1840–1861 respectively; on foreign relations, P. Carali has produced a valuable edition of documents, *Fakhr al-Din II, principe del Libano e la corte di Toscana, 1605–1635*, two volumes (1936–1938). In addition, see A. Rustum and F. Boustani, *Le Liban à l'époque des émirs Chihab*, three volumes (1933); U. Heyd, *Ottoman Documents on Palestine, 1552–1615* (1960); I. Ben Zvi, *Eretz-Israel under Ottoman Rule* (1955), in Hebrew; a work which represents an encouraging study of archive material, by D. Chevallier, "Que possédait un cheikh maronite en 1859?" *Arabica*, VII (1960), and "Aspects sociaux de la Question d'Orient: aux origines des troubles agraires libanais en 1858," *AESC*, XIV (1959); and M. H. Kerr, *Lebanon in the Last Years of Feudalism, 1840–1868. A Contemporary Account by Antūn Dāhir al-Aqīqī and Documents*, no. 33 of the Oriental Series of the Faculty of Arts and Sciences of the American University of Beirut (1959).

F. Charles-Roux, *Les Echelles de Syrie et de Palestine au XVIIIe siècle* (1928), a study of the ports of the region, lacks sufficient research in Oriental sources; on Aleppo, see J. Sauvaget, above p. 92; on Damascus, see Bernard Lewis, "A Jewish Source on Damascus just after the Ottoman Conquest," *BSOAS*, X (1940–1942). For the organization of the country immediately after the conquest, see R. Mantran and J. Sauvaget, cited p. 194.

Arabia was incorporated into the Ottoman Empire for varying periods and then only partially. The most important event in its history, the formation of the Wahhābite Kingdom in the eighteenth century, has never been adequately studied. On Yemen, see Z. Ehiloglu, *Yemende Türkler* (Istanbul, 1952). For the rest of Arabia, there is an up-to-date bibliography in the article "'Arab (djazīrat al-)" in *EI²*. On North Africa, see p. 226 f.

The European provinces of the Empire have more often been the subject of study, but we are here concerned only with those works dealing with their relations with the Ottoman state or the presence of Muslims in their midst. Some general remarks will be found in the interesting work by G. Stadtmüller, *Geschichte Südosteuropas* (1950), and in the various national histories, by K. J. Jireček on the Serbs, by V. N. Zlatarski on the Bulgars, by N. Iorga on the Rumanians, by K. Paparrigopoulos or G. Hertzberg on the Greeks, and by B. Homan on the Hungarians. On the Turkish populations, see above, p. 160 f. On Rumelia, see M. T. Gökbilgin, "La Roumélie au début du règne de Soliman, districts, villes, bourgs," *Belleten*, XX/78 (April, 1956), 247–285, in Turkish with a summary in French. On Albania, which was strongly influenced by Islam, see the article "Arnāwutluķ" (the Turkish name for the country) by H. Inalcik in *EI*², which shows the recent trends on the question.

On the territories forming present-day Jugoslavia, consult in general the *Prilozi* cited on p. 195; see also F. Babinger, *Das Archiv des Bosniaken Osman Pascha* (1931); H. Duda, "Üsküb im 17. Jahrhundert," in his *Balkantürkische Studien*, *SBAW*, Phil.-Hist. Kl., 226/1 (1949); on Bosnia, where Islam is particularly strong, see B. Spuler and L. Forrer, cited p. 70.

On Bulgaria and Thrace, see the *Études historiques* of the Bulgarian Academy (1960); J. Kabrda, "Les problèmes de l'étude de l'histoire de la Bulgarie à l'époque de la domination turque," *Byzantinoslavica*, XV (1934); F. Babinger, *Beiträge zur Frühgeschichte der Türkenherrschaft in Rumelien, XIV–XV Jhdt.* (1944); Duda, "Schafsteuer und Schaflieferungen Bulgariens zur Osmanischen Zeit," in his *Balkantürkische Studien*, cited in the paragraph above; R. Anhegger, "Neues zur balkantürkischen Forschung," *ZDMG*, CIII (1953); and H. J. Kissling, *Beitrage zur Kenntnis Thrakiens im 17. Jhdt.* (1956). See also Dobruja, above, p. 161.

On Greece, apart from the national histories and the voluminous work by N. Svoronos cited on p. 210, one may also consult W. Miller, "Recent Works on Medieval, Turkish and Modern Greece," *Cambridge Historical Journal*, II (1926–1928) and VI (1938–1940), and A. Andréadès, "L'administration financière de la Grèce sous la domination turque," *Revue des études grecques*, XXIII (1910), which is of use but no longer up to date. Among more recent studies, see T. Papadopoulos, *Studies and Documents Relating to the History of the Greek Church and People under Turkish Domination* (Brussels, 1952).

For Rumania, see the national histories and a few limited studies, such as N. Beldiceanu, "La crise monétaire ...," cited p. 209.

On Hungary, L. Fekete, "The Ottoman Turks and Hungary," translated from Hungarian into Turkish in *Belleten*, XIII/52 (1949), and the works of G. Jacob, "Urkunden aus Hungarns Türkenzeit," *Islam*, VII (1917), 171–185, and "Grosswardein, eine selbständige türkische Provinz," *Islam*, IX (1919), 253–254, which are useful for the student with no knowledge of Hungarian.

On Slovakia, see J. Kabrda, "Les sources turques relatives à l'histoire de la domination ottomane en Slovaquie," *ArO*, XXIV (1956).

For the provincial life of Asia Minor, there are but a few, generally inadequate monographs on particular towns. The more useful are *I. Koynalı, Akşehir, Nasreddin Hocanın Şehri* (Istanbul, 1945); C. Tarim, *Tarihte Kirşehri-Gülşehri ve Babailer, Ahiler, Bektaşiler* (3d ed., Istanbul, 1948); K. Otto-Dorn and R. Anhegger on Nicea (see below, p. 215); N. Çağatay

Uluçay, *Manisa'da ziraat, ticaret ve esnaf teşkilâti XVII yüzyilda* (Istanbul, 1942), in one volume and an appendix containing documents on economic life in Magnesia, and *XVII asırda Saruhan'da eşkiyalik ve halk hareketleri* (Istanbul, 1944), on banditry and popular movements in Saruhan; F. Dalsar, *Bursa'da ipekcilik* (Istanbul, 1960), on silk at Bursa. The older *Amasya Tarihi* by V. Hüsameddin, four volumes (1928–1935), which is often cited, is quite uncritical. See also A. Refik, cited p. 210, and the works cited on p. 161.

On Cyprus, see Vol. IV of G. Hill, *History of Cyprus* (1950).

On the Crimea and the territories of Southern Russia which came under Ottoman suzerainty, see V. Smirnov, *Krymskoe khanstvo pod verkhovenstvom Ottomanskoi Porty do nachala XVIII veka* (St. Petersburg, 1887), and the rather obsolete J. von Hammer-Purgstall, *Geschichte der Chane der Krim unter osmanischer Herrschaft* (1856).

RELIGIOUS LIFE, LITERATURE, AND ART

On religious life in the early period, the reader is referred to the works cited on pp. 161 f. and 209. To these should be added H. J. Kissling, "The sociological and educational role of the Dervish orders in the Ottoman Empire" in *Studies in Islamic Cultural History* cited on p. 112, translated from an article in *ZDMG*, CIII (1953), (see O. Barkan, page 208) and by the same author, "Aus der Geschichte des Chalvetijje-Ordens," *ZDMG*, CIII (1953); J. Birge, *The Bektashi Order of Dervishes* (1937); and H. Ritter, "Die Anfänge der Ḥurūfīsekte," *Oriens*, VIII (1954).

On interfaith relations see F. Hasluck, *Christianity and Islam under the Sultans*, two volumes (1929), the second volume dealing with popular beliefs; F. Giese, "Die geschichtlichen Grundlagen für die Stellung der christlichen Untertanen im Osmanischen Reich," *Islam*, XIX (1931), and in *Forschungen und Fortschritte*, VII (1931); A. Galanté, *Histoire des Juifs de Constantinople* (1941 and 1949), which does not entirely replace M. Franco, *Histoire des Israëlites de l'Empire Ottoman* (1897); especially U. Heyd, "The Jewish Communities of Istanbul in the XVIIth Century," *Oriens*, VI (1953); and I. Emmanuel, *Histoire des Israëlites de Salonique* (1936).

On the Armenians, see the histories of Armenia cited on pp. 108 and 125; E. Uras, *Tarihte Ermeniler ve Ermeni meselesi* (Ankara, 1950); and with the general study "Arminiyya" in *EI*[2] by M. Canard. A. Belin, *Histoire de la Latinité de Constantinople* (2d ed., 1894), is still useful on the question of the Catholic communities.

On intellectual and literary life, consult the histories of Turkish literature cited on pp. 103 and 161 f., which may be supplemented by E. J. W. Gibb, *A History of Ottoman Poetry*, six volumes (1900–1909), and A. Adivar,

Tarih boyunca ilim ve din, two volumes, Vol. I, to 1800 (1944), which goes considerably beyond his shorter work in French, *La science chez les Turcs ottomans* (Paris, 1939). The main research into documents has been done by A. Ünver in his *Fatih külliyesi ve zamanı ilim hayatı*, İstanbul Üniversitesi Yayınları, vol. 278 (1946), and his *Ilim ve Sanat bakımından Fâtih devri albumü*, in İstanbul Üniversitesi Tib Tarihi Enstitüsü. Yayınlar, XXIX (1945), the former dealing with the university and the latter with science and the arts under Mehmet II (the Conqueror). For the period immediately following, see especially O. Ergin, *Türkiye maarif Tarihi*, five volumes (1939–1943), of which only the first volume deals with the period prior to the reforms of the nineteenth century. See also P. Boratav, "Les travaux de folklore turc," *Anadolu*, I (1952), 71–95, and H. Ritter, *Karagös. Türkische Schattenspiele*, three volumes (1924–1953), on the shadow theatre.

On art, see above, p. 103 f.; C. Esad Arseven, *Türk Sanatı Tarihi* (1928); H. Glück, *Die Kunst der Osmanen* (Leipzig, 1923); B. Ünsal, *Turkish-Islamic Architecture in Seljuk and Ottoman Times* (London, 1959); C. Gurlitt, *Die Baukunst Constantinopels*, two volumes (1912); A. Gabriel, "Les mosquées de Constantinople," *Syria*, VII (1926); E. Egli, *Sinan, der Baumeister osmanischer Glanzzeit* (Zurich, 1954); A. Gabriel, *Une capitale turque, Brousse*, two volumes (1958); O. Aslanapa, *Edirne'de Osmanlı devri âbideleri*, in İstanbul Üniversitesi Edebiyat Fakültesi Yayınlarından. Sanat Tarihi Enstitüsü, 6 (1949); A. Saim Ülgen, "Iznik'te türk eserleri," *Vakıflar Dergisi*, I (1938), 53–69; on Nicea, K. Otto-Dorn and R. Anhegger, "Das islamische Iznik," *Istanbuler Forschungen*, XIII (1941); the regional monographs are cited on p. 211 f.; K. Yetkin, "The Evolution of Architectural Forms in Turkish Mosques, 1300–1700," *SI*, XI (1959); A. Refik, *Türk Mimarları 1453–1830* (1936), on architects; G. Migeon and A. Sarkisyan, "Les Faïences d'Asie Mineure du XIIIe au XVIe siècle," *Revue de l'art ancien et moderne*, XLIII-XLIV (1923); O. Aslanapa, *Osmanlı devrinde Kütahya çinileri* (Istanbul, 1949); on the miniaturists, A. Ünver, *Rassam Nakşi* (Istanbul, 1949), and *Levni* (Istanbul, 1951), E. Esin, *Turkish Miniature Painting* (Tokyo, 1960), and S. Tyulayev, *Miniatures of Babur Namak* (Moscow, 1960), in Russian and English; K. Otto-Dorn, "Osmanische Ornamentale Wandmalerei," in *Kunst des Orients*, I (1950); Tahsin Öz, *Türk kumaş ve kadifeleri* (Istanbul, 1946), on textiles; K. Erdmann, *Der orientalische Knüpfteppich* (1955), on carpets; A. Lane, cited p. 104, on pottery; J. von Karabaček, "Abendländische Künstler zu Konstantinopel im XV. und XVI. Jhdt.," in *Denkschriften der Akademie der Wissenschaften in Wien. Phil.-Hist. Kl.*, LXVI/1 (1918), on Renaissance artists in Turkey.

24

The Muslim West

SOURCES

Northwest Africa, Sicily for a time, and Muslim Spain until the end of the Middle Ages, as we have said, were countries in which the distinctive national characteristics merged with the common contribution of Eastern Islam. This in itself would perhaps not justify a separate chapter, except that the sources for their history, owing to their geographical remoteness from the Orient, are generally not those used for Oriental history; moreover, the modern works devoted to them tend to reinforce this distinction and have almost no relation to the bibliography on Oriental history. There are grounds for believing that the separateness of the Islamic West has been overstated and that the true autonomy of Western Islam would have been worked out more pertinently by authors less exclusively concerned with countries dominated by their own or from which they derived their heritage and on occasions better informed about non-Western Islam. With these reservations we still feel justified to devote a chapter to the Muslim West that parallels that which we devote to modern Iran, this time however going back to the very beginnings.

We are able to be fairly concise, thanks to the substantial and methodical bibliography compiled by R. Le Tourneau in the *Histoire de l'Afrique du Nord*, cited p. 67, which should be supplemented for the years 1951–1956 by the same author's contribution to the article "Vingt-cinq ans d'histoire algérienne," *RA*, XL/6 (1955–1956), and E. Lévi-Provençal's *Espagne musulmane*, cited p. 67, which replaces most of the earlier works to which it supplies all the necessary references.

The sources for the history of Western Islam are on the whole later and less abundant than those for the East. There are no archive sources for the Middle Ages, all we have being the *Vie de l'Ustadh Jaudhar*, edited by

K. Ḥusain (1954), translated by M. Canard (1958), a collection of Fāṭimid correspondence, and a series of Almohad letters, in particular *Un recueil de lettres officielles almohades*, published by E. Lévi-Provençal in the Collection de textes arabes publiées par l'Institut des Hautes Études Marocaines, X (1941). For the contribution of the Geniza see S. D. Goitein, "La Tunisie du XIe siècle à la lumière des documents de la Geniza," *Études d'Orientalisme dédiées à la Mémoire de Lévi-Provençal*, II (1962). A few Eastern historians have provided information on the West that is worthy of attention, such as Ibn 'Abd al-Ḥakam, for the beginning of the third/ninth century, cited p. 122, Ibn al-Athīr, for the twelfth and thirteenth centuries, of whom the sections concerned with our subject have been translated by E. Fagnan, *Annales du Maghreb et de l'Espagne* (1898), and Nuwairī, of whom De Slane has translated all that pertains to the early history of North Africa in the first volume of the *Histoire des Berbères*, cited below on this page.

Among the Western chroniclers the most important are Ibn 'Idhārī, *al-Bayān al-mughrib*, I and II, edited by R. Dozy (1848–1851), the first volume of which has been translated by E. Fagnan, *Histoire de l'Afrique du Nord et de l'Espagne* (1901–1904). A new edition of these volumes has been prepared by G. S. Colin and E. Lévi-Provençal (1948–1951), while the third volume was edited by Lévi-Provençal alone (1930); Ibn abī Zar', *Rawḍ al-qirṭās*, edited with a Latin translation by C. Tornberg, *Annales regum Mauritaniae* (1843–1846), especially concerned with the Berber dynasties from the time of the Idrīsids; Abū Zakariyā', *Kitāb al-sīra*, partially translated by E. Masqueray (1878), and a new edition and translation being prepared by J. M. Dallet and R. Le Tourneau, on the Ibāḍites; for the Fāṭimids, the sketchy *Histoire des rois Obaidites* by Ibn Ḥammād, edited and translated by M. Vonderheyden (1927), has lost much of its value since the discovery of the "Autobiography of a Mahdi's Chamberlain (Ja'far)," edited in the *Bulletin of the Faculty of Arts, Egyptian University*, IV (1936), and translated into French by M. Canard in *Hespéris*, XXXIX (1952). See also the manuscript works of Qāḍī al-Nu'mān, listed in the article by A. A. A. Fyzee (1934) cited p. 147.

The inadequacy of the sources often makes it necessary to rely on the *Histoire des Berbères* by Ibn Khaldūn, rich through its reliance on older sources, translated into French by De Slane (2d ed., 4 vols., 1925), the author being acquainted with other unknown histories. On Spain much of the important *Kitāb al-Muqtabis fī ta'rīkh rijāl al-Andalus*, by Ibn Ḥayyān, has been found. Three volumes have been edited: Vol. I, reigns of al-Ḥakam I and 'Abd al-Rahmān II, by E. Lévi-Provençal and 'Abd al-Ḥamīd al-'Abbādī (Alexandria, 1950), Vol. II, part 3 only, by M. M. Antuña under the title: *Chronique du règne du calife umaiyade 'Abd Allāh à Cordoue* (Paris, 1937), and Vol. III, by E. García Gómez, *Anales palatinos del califa de Córdoba al-Ḥakam II* (Madrid, 1950).

For the period of the Taifas, Lévi-Provençal has published fragments of the "Mémoires d''Abdallāh, dernier roi Ziride," *al-Andalus*, III (1935), IV (1936), and VI (1941). On Hispano-Maghribī history during the Almoravid and Almohad periods, much material has survived only in the late and voluminous work by the seventeenth-century historian, al-Maqqarī, *Nafḥ al-ṭīb* edited by R. Dozy, G. Dugat, L. Krehl, and W. Wright under the title *Analectes sur l'histoire et la littérature des Arabes d'Espagne* (Paris, 1855–1861); also edited by M. M. 'Abdalḥamīd, ten volumes (Cairo, 1949), translated in part by P. de Gayangos, under the title *The History of the Muhammadan Dynasties of Spain* (London, 1840–1843). We do, however, have valuable chronicles in al-Marrākushī, *al-Mújib*, edited by R. Dozy. *The History of the Almohades* (1847; 2d ed., 1881), translated by E. Fagnan in *RA*, XXXV–XXXVII (1891–1893) and reëdited by A. Huici Miranda in the *Colección de crónicas . . .* , LV (1952–1955); al-Zarkashī, *Histoire des Almohades et des Ḥafsides*, edited (Tunis, 1289/1872), and translated by E. Fagnan (1895), and the anonymous *al-Ḥulal al-Mawchiyya. Chronique anonyme des dynasties almoravide et almohade*, edited by I. S. Allouche in the Collection de textes arabes publiées par l'Institut des Hautes Études Marocaines, VI (Rabat, 1938), and translated by Huici Miranda (1951–1952). Above all E. Lévi-Provençal has discovered a chronicle written by a contemporary witness of the early Almohads, al-Baidaq, and which he has published in his *Documents inédits d'histoire almohade* (1928). For the end of the Middle Ages, we may also cite Yaḥyā b. Khaldūn, *L'histoire des Beni Abdel Wad*, edited and translated by A. Bel (1903–1913). On Spain, see also Ibn al-Khaṭīb's multifaceted work, which was unfortunately not continued for the last years of the kingdom of Granada.

Valuable supplementary information may be obtained from the encyclopedic or biographical collections such as the *Dhakhīra* by Ibn Bassām, the first, second, and seventh volumes of which were edited in Cairo (1939, 1940, and 1947); the *Classes des savants de l'Ifriqiya* by Abū 'l-'Arab, edited and translated by M. Ben Cheneb (1914–1920), or the *Riyāḍ al-nufūs* by Abū Bakr al-Mālikī, edited by Ḥ. Mu'nis (Cairo, 1951), with a translation of numerous extracts by H. Idris, "Contributions à l'histoire de l'Ifrikiya," *REI*, IX–X (1935–1936). Similarly, see the Mālikite and Fāṭimid juridical works, cited pp. 44 and 147, and especially the collections of *fatwās*.

Historians should particularly note the *Aḥkām al-sūq* by Yaḥyā b. 'Umar, writing at the end of the Aghlabid period, of which extracts have been edited by M. Makkī in the *Revista del Instituto Egipciano de Estúdios Islámicos*, V (Madrid, 1957), on which is based the translation by E. García Gómez in *al-Andalus*, XXII (1957); for the Almoravid-Almohad period, the *ḥisba* treatises, properly speaking, such as that by Ibn 'Abdūn, edited by E. Lévi-Provençal in *JA* (1934), reëdited in his *Documents inédits*, I, *Trois traités hispaniques de ḥisba* (Cairo, 1947), which was published by the Institut Français d'Archéologie Orientale, translated into French in his *Séville au début du XIIe siècle* (1947), into Spanish by himself and García Gómez (1948), and into Italian by F. Gabrieli in *RL*, VI/11 (1935). See also Saqaṭī, edited by Lévi-Provençal and G. S. Colin, *Un manuel hispanique de "hisba." Traité d'Abū Abd Allāh Muḥammad al Saḳatī de Malage sur la surveillance des corporations et la répression des fraudes* (Paris, 1931). The collections of notes are also important; see Lévi-Provençal, *Histoire de l'Espagne musulmane*, III, 242, n. 1, and 116, n. 4, and the collections of *nawāzil* such as the *Mi'yār* by Wansharīsī, translated by E. Amar (Paris, 1908–1909). See the excellent analysis of consultations on the trade agents by M. Talbi in "Les courtiers en vêtements en Ifriqiya au IXe et au Xe siècle," *JESHO*, V (1962). For currency see Abū 'l-Ḥasan b. Yūsuf al-Ḥakīm, *al-Dawḥa al-mushtabika fī ḍawābiṭ dār al-sikka*, edited by H. Monès (Mu'nis) (Madrid, 1960).

The geographers of the East generally should be consulted, such as Ya'qūbī, cited p. 122; Ibn Ḥawqal, whose *Descriptio al-Maghrebi* has been translated by De Slane in *JA* (1842), and others: Ibn Khurradādhbih, Ibn al-Faqīh, and Ibn Rusteh, edited and translated by M. Hadj-Sadok, *Description du Maghreb et de l'Europe au IXe siècle*, Bibliothèque arabe-française, VI (Algiers, 1949), and al-Muqaddasī, edited and translated by C. Pellat, *Description de l'Occident musulman au Xe siècle*, *ibid.*, IX (Algiers, 1950); devoted especially to the West, the valuable *Kitāb al-masālik* by al-Bakrī, edited and translated by De Slane, *Description de l'Afrique septentrionale* (2d ed., 1913); the complete works of Idrīsī, the Muslim geographer who wrote for Roger II of Sicily, are to be published in Italy; for the time being, see R. Dozy and M. J. de Goeje, *Description de l'Afrique et de l'Espagne* (1866); for the later periods, apart from Ibn Baṭṭūṭa, cited p. 170, mention should be made of al-'Umarī (cited, p. 179) and al-Tījānī, edited under the supervision of Ḥasan Ḥusnī 'Abdulwahhāb (Tunis, 1958). Reference may also be made to the extraordinary description of Africa on the eve of the Ottoman conquest by Leo Africanus, a Moroccan by birth. He wrote his work in poor Italian. A French translation (1556) was made only six years after the publication of the Italian. The first English translation dates back to 1600. More recently there was an annotated translation by A. Epaulard *et al.*, *Description de l'Afrique*, two volumes (Paris, 1956).

The definitive edition of the original is being prepared by Angela Codazzi. For the section on Morocco, L. Massignon, *Le Maroc au début du XVIe siècle d'après Léon l'Africain* (1906), should be consulted.

In other areas the religious work by Ibn Tūmart, edited by J. D. Luciani (1903) and by E. Lévi-Provençal (1928), and also the abundant Hispano-Maghribī agricultural works, on which see E. García Gómez, "Sobre agricultura arábigo-andaluza," *al-Andalus*, X (1945), beginning with the famous *Calendrier de Cordoue*, edited by R. Dozy (1873), and by C. Pellat (1961), deserve special attention. To the epigraphical documents mentioned by R. Le Tourneau, should be added the *Corpus des inscriptions arabes de Tunisie* begun by S. Zbiss, I (1955).

For European documents see for example L. de Mas-Latrie, *Traités de paix et de commerce des Chrétiens avec les Arabes de l'Afrique septentrionale au Moyen Âge* (1866), with a supplement (1872).

NORTH AFRICA, SICILY AND SPAIN (TO THE ELEVENTH CENTURY)

The general introductory works for the history of North Africa by C.-A. Julien and R. Le Tourneau, H. Terrasse, G. Marçais, *et al.*, and the works of geographers and anthropologists are listed on p. 67. Particular mention must be made of a work famous in its time and the subject of considerable controversy, E. Gautier, *L'Islamisation de l'Afrique du Nord. Les siècles obscurs du Maghreb* (Paris, 1927). The author issued a revised edition in 1937 under the title *Le passé de l'Afrique du Nord*, in which he attempted to explain the first four centuries of the history of Muslim North Africa on the basis of interesting geographical and sociological considerations, attractively and enthusiastically developed, but insufficiently supported by historical evidence, and on which see the review by W. Marçais in the *Revue critique d'histoire et de littérature*, XCVI (1929), reprinted in his *Articles et Conférences*, Publications de l'Institut d'Études Orientales de la Faculté des Lettres d'Alger, XXI (Paris, 1961). Consult also *L'Afrique du Nord française dans l'histoire* (1955), by E. Albertini, G. Marçais, and G. Yver, and the excellent short account by R. Brunschvig, *La Tunisie au haut Moyen Âge* (Cairo, 1948). See also a general history of Algeria, published by al-Jīlālī, *Ta'rīkh al-Jazā'ir*, four volumes (1954). On a great many questions the best statements are to be found in *EI*.

For the period of the conquest, see the preliminary reflections by R. Brunschvig on p. 26. On the long process of Arabization, see the two lectures by W. Marçais, "Comment l'Afrique du Nord a été arabisé," *AIEO*, IV (1938) and XV (1957), on the country and the towns, respectively, in which he demonstrates how the historian can utilize linguistic material; both are reproduced in *Articles et Conférences*, cited above. Along similar lines, see C. Courtois, "De Rome à l'Islam," *RA*, LXXXVI (1942).

On the history of the principal dynasties, the works at our disposal are of unequal value. Pending the publication of a study on the Aghlabids, we must still rely on M. Vonderheyden, *La Berbêrie orientale sous la dynastie des Benoû 'l-Arlab* (Paris, 1927), which may be supplemented by H. Idris, "La vie intellectuelle et administrative à Kairouan sous les Aghlabides et les Fatimides," *REI*, IX–X (1935–1936). On the Khārijites, there are some recent studies by T. Lewicki, among which may be mentioned "La répartition géographique des groupements Ibadites dans l'Afrique du Nord," *RO*, XXI (1957); A. de Motylinski, *Les livres de la secte abadhite* (1885); R. Strothmann, "Berber und Ibaditen," *Islam*, XVII (1928), and a meticulous study by C. Bekri, "Le Kharidjisme berbère: quelques aspects du royaume rustumide," *AIEO*, XV (1957). Concerning the Fāṭimids in the Maghrib, see especially M. Canard's studies, "L'impérialisme des Fatimides, cited p. 149 f., and "Une famille de partisans puis d'adversaires des Fatimides," *Mélanges ... G. Marçais*, II (1957); R. Le Tourneau, "La révolte d'Abû Yazîd au Xme siècle," *CT*, I (1953), whose study should be supplemented by the new sources mentioned in the article "Abū Yazīd" by S. M. Stern in *EI*². The same author's "Abū 'Abdallāh" in *EI*² is recommended for the same reason. See also Ḥasan Ibrāhīm Ḥasan and T. Sharaf, *'Ubaidullāh al-Mahdī* (Cairo, 1947). On the Zīrids, we now have considerable information thanks to H. Idris, *Les Zirides*, two volumes (1962); L. Golvin has published *Le Maghrib central à l'époque des Zirides* (1957), which actually deals with the Ḥammādids and is especially valuable on account of the author's archaeological knowledge. In general, see also J. Hopkins, *Muslim Government in Barbary until the Sixth Century A.H.* (1960). On the Hilālian invasion and its effects, the basic work is still G. Marçais, *Les Arabes en Berbêrie du XIe au XIVe siècle* (1913), summarized by the author in his *La Berbêrie*, cited p. 67, although J. Poncet, "L'évolution des 'genres de vie' en Tunisie," *CT*, II (1954), has attempted to provide a less extreme interpretation of the invasions; the question must perhaps remain undecided. Also see by G. Marçais "Les villes de la côte algérienne et la piraterie au Moyen Âge," *AIEO*, XIII (1955). The inadequacy of the sources makes the findings of archaeological excavations of even greater interest, such as M. van Berchem, "Sedrata, Un chapitre nouveau de l'histoire de l'art musulman," *Ars orientalis*, I (1954); S. Zbiss, "Mahdia et Sabra-Mansouriya," *JA* (1956); and M. Solignac, "Recherches sur les installations hydrauliques de Kairouan et des steppes tunisiennes du VIIe au XIe siècle," *AIEO*, X–XI (1952–1953), which shows clearly how the historian can profit from archaeological research conducted with a view to his requirements.

The Muslims dominated Sicily from the ninth to the eleventh century, leaving many traces behind them. At various times they also spread into Southern Italy, the islands of the Western Mediterranean and even into Southern France. Apart from the writings of a few poets, the history of the Muslims in Sicily is based entirely on the evidence of authors foreign to the country, collected by M. Amari in his *Biblioteca Arabo-Sicula*, two volumes (1880–1881), and used in his *Storia*, cited p. 67; a new text has been published by H. H. Abdulwahab and F. Dachraoui in *Études d'orientalisme dédiées à la mémoire de Lévi-Provençal*, II (1962), under the title "Le régime foncier en Sicile au Moyen Âge ... , un chapitre du Kitāb al-Amwāl d'al-Dāwudī," but generally speaking nothing new has come to light since the first edition. On the state of research on this subject, see the remarks by F. Gabrieli in his "Un secolo di studi arabo-siculi," *SI*, II (1954). The *Storia* also provides the necessary information on the Arab expansion in Italy and on the survival of the Muslim populations after the Christian reconquest. On the Muslims under the Norman regime, we have the archive sources cited p. 18. There is a good study on the influence of institutions by L. Ménager, *Amiratus, l'émirat et les origines de l'Amirauté* (1960).

The old but well-documented monograph by J. T. Reinaud, *Les invasions des Sarrazins en France, en Savoie-Piémont et dans la Suisse* (1836), has not been replaced and was translated into English at Lahore (1956). On the battle of Poitiers (732), see M. Mercier, *Charles Martel et la bataille de Poitiers* (1944).

For Muslim Spain, add to the general works by E. Lévi-Provençal and H. Terrasse, cited p. 67 and on art, p. 104, the regular bibliographies which appear in the review *al-Andalus* and, for the centuries not covered by Lévi-Provençal, A. González Palencia, *História de la España musulmana*, (4th ed., 1951), or M. 'Inān, *Dawlat al-islām fī 'l-Andalus* (1949). On the Arabized Christians, see A. González Palencia, *Moros y cristianos en la España musulmana* (1945), and I. de las Cágigas, *Los Mozárabes*, two volumes (1947–1948); on the Jews, E. Ashtor-Strauss, in Hebrew [*History of the Jews in Muslim Spain*], I (1960), and M. Perlmann, "Eleventh Century Andalusian Authors on the Jews of Granada," in *Proceedings of the American Academy for Jewish Research*, XVIII (1949); on the towns, the numerous articles by L. Torres Balbás, such as "Les villes musulmanes d'Espagne," *AIEO*, VI (1947), or "Extensión y demografia de las ciudades hispano-musulmanas," *SI*, III (1955), "Ciudades hispano-musulmanas de nueva fundación," *Études d'orientalisme dédiées a la mémoire de Lévi-Provençal*, II (1962), and *Resumen histórico del urbanismo en España* (Madrid, 1954). For science, see J. Millás Vallicrosa, *Estúdios sobre história de la ciencia española* (1949).

For the period of the kingdom of the Taifas, which is beyond the scope of E. Lévi-Provençal's *Histoire*, see R. Dozy, *Histoire des musulmans d'Espagne*, second edition by Lévi-Provençal (1932), of which only the third volume is still of real use, due to the lack of a corresponding volume by Lévi-Provençal; A. González Palencia, *História de la España musulmana* (4th ed., 1951); A. Prieto y Vives, *Los Reyes de Taifas, estúdio histórico-numismatico*, 1926); and above all R. Menéndez Pidal, *La España del Cid* (1947). See also the articles "'Abbādids," "Afṭasids," and "Andalus" in *EI*[2]. On cultural life up to the eleventh century, see González Palencia, *História de la literatura arâbigo-española* (2d ed., 1945); A. Nykl, *Hispano-Arabic Poetry* (1946); H. Pérès, *La poésie andalouse en arabe classique au XIe siècle* (2d ed., 1953); and A. J. Arberry, *Moorish Poetry* (1953). Also read the *Kitāb Ṭauq al-Ḥamāma* by Ibn Ḥazm, edited and translated into French by L. Bercher, *Le collier du pigeon, ou, de l'amour et des amants*, Bibliothèque arabe francaise, VIII (Algiers, 1949); into English by A. Nykl, *A Book Containing the Risāla Known as the Dove's Neckring, about Love and Lovers* (Paris, 1931), and by A. J. Arberry, *The Ring of the Dove: A Treatise on the Art and Practice of Arab Love* (London, 1953), and into German by M. Weisweiler, *Das Halsband der Taube über die Liebe und die Liebenden* (Leiden, 1944). E. García Gómez, in his "La poésie lyrique hispano-arabe et l'apparition de la lyrique romane," *al-Andalus*, XXI (1956), French translation, *Arabic*, VI (1958), deals in fact with the influence of ancient Spanish poetry on that of the Muslims. On ideas and thinkers, Asín Palácios, *Aben Masarra y su escuela*, reprinted in his *Obras escogidas*, I (1946–1948), and *Aben Hazm de Cordoba y su história crítica de las ideas religiosas*, five volumes (1927–1932), and R. Arnaldez, *Grammaire et théologie chez Ibn Hazm de Cordoue* (1956).

ALMORAVID AND ALMOHAD PERIODS, AND THE KINGDOM OF GRANADA

The history of North Africa during the period of the Almoravids and the Almohads cannot be dissociated from that of Muslim Spain. On the Almoravids, we now have the general study by J. Bosch Vilá, *Los Almorávides* (1956), which does not, however, replace the work by R. Menéndez Pidal on the Cid (see previous paragraph), on which see E. Lévi-Provençal, "Le Cid de l'histoire," *RH*, CLXXX (1937), or in *Islam d'Occident* (1948). Also F. Codera, *Decadência y disparición de los Almorávides en España* (1899). On the Almohads, who are also discussed in the latter study, the works available are more abundant though less complete, because of the complexity of the movement, which was at once political and religious in character. A. Huici Miranda has published a *História política del Imperio almohade* (1956), replacing the outdated work by R. Millet, *Les Almohades* (1923). The doctrine of Ibn Tūmart, the founder of the dynasty or rather of the movement, has been brilliantly studied by I. Goldziher in his introduction to the edition of the *Livre d'Ibn Toumert*, above, p. 220, many points of Almohad history are covered in the *Documents inédits*, cited p. 219, by Lévi-Provençal, who is also the author of an up-to-date biographical sketch of the second founder of the regime in his article "'Abd al-Mu'min" in *EI*². The latter has also been studied by Ali Merad, "'Abd al-Mu'min à la conquête de l'Afrique du Nord," *AIEO*, XV (1957). It is still useful to read A. Bel, *Les Banou Ghânya, derniers représentants de l'empire Almoravide et leur lutte contre l'empire Almohade*, Publications de l'École des Lettres d'Alger, XXVII (Paris, 1903), on the Mediterranean activities of the Almoravids who took refuge on the Balearic Isles.

On the economy of both the Christian and Muslim sections of Spain, see C. Dubler, "Über das Wirtschaftsleben auf der iberischen Halbinsel vom XI. zum XIII. Jhdt.," *Romanica Helvetica*, XXII (Geneva, 1943). On the economy of North Africa as seen by the Italians, see A. Sayous, *Le commerce des Européens à Tunis. XIIe–XVIe siècle* (1929).

On Almoravid and especially Almohad art, see the fourth volume of the *Ars Hispaniae* by L. Torres Balbás, and the synthesis by H. Terrasse, "L'art de l'empire almoravide," *SI*, III (1955). In conjunction with J. Meunié he has written a study of an interesting Almoravid monument, *Nouvelles recherches archéologiques à Marrakech* (1957), and J. Caillé has also described in great detail *La mosquée Ḥasan à Rabat* (1954), built by the Almohads. References to earlier works on the subject will be found in G. Marçais, *Architecture*, and in Torres Balbás, *Ars Hispaniae* mentioned above. See also G. Deverdun, *Inscriptions arabes de Marrakech*, Publications de l'Institut des Hautes Études Marocaines, IX (Rabat, 1956).

A knowledge of the intellectual life of the Almohad period is particularly important because of its direct contribution to Western thought at a time when the Christian West was beginning to show an interest in the science and philosophy transmitted and developed in Muslim countries. For its influence on Europe, see p. 229. We shall mention here only the works dealing with Ibn Rushd (Averroes), such as L. Gauthier, *Ibn Rochd* (1948), not forgetting E. Renan, *Averroès et l'averroisme* (1852), reprinted in his *Œuvres Complètes*, III (Paris, 1949), which played an important part in the history of our studies. See also M. Alonso, *Teología de Averroes* (1947) and R. Brunschvig, "Averroès juriste," *Études d'orientalisme dédiées à la mémoire de Lévi-Provençal*, I (1962). There are many editions of Averroes' works, such as *Kitāb faṣl al-maqāl*, edited by G. Hourani (Leiden, 1959), and translated by the same (Leiden, 1959).

The literature of the period is no less interesting, and essentially for the same reason. We should mention here Ibn Quzmān, on whom see *EI*, *s.v.*

On the relationship between Spanish Arabic poetry and that of the troubadours, see p. 230.

From the thirteenth century onward, the kingdom of Granada, the sole surviving part of Muslim Spain, almost lost contact with Africa and fell at the end of the fifteenth century. Pending the completion of the *História de España*, see the article "Naṣrids," by E. Lévi-Provençal in *EI*. Concerning the Muslims who were incorporated into the states recovered by the Christians, see I. de las Cágigas, *Los Mudéjares*, two volumes (1948–1949), which does not however replace A. González Palencia, *Los Mozárabes de Toledo en los siglos XII y XIII*, four volumes (1926–1930), containing archival documents. On the last of the Muslims and their expulsion, see J. Baroya, *Los moriscos del Reino de Granada* (1957), R. Ricard and R. Aubenas, *L'Église et la Renaissance (1449–1517)*, Volume XV of *Histoire de l'Église* edited by A. Fliche and V. Martin (Paris, 1951), and H. Lapeyre, *Géographie de l'Espagne morisque* (1959). The Muslim influence on Spain has received considerable attention from the historians of that country, and the question has been defined by M. Cruz Hernández, "Spanien und der Islam," *Saeculum*, III (1952). See also Amérigo Castro, *The Structure of Spanish History* (Princeton, 1954), and G. Sánchez Albórnoz, *España y el Islam* (Buenos Aires, 1943) and *La España musulmana según los autores islamitas y cristianos medievales*, two volumes (Buenos Aires, 1946).

NORTH AFRICA (FROM THE THIRTEENTH TO THE NINETEENTH CENTURY)

North Africa has remained a part of the Muslim world to the present day. For two and a half centuries the eastern region belonged to the Ḥafṣids, on whom we now have a work which deserves to become a model for future historians of Maghribī Islam, R. Brunschvig, LA BERBÉRIE ORIENTALE SOUS LES HAFSIDES, two volumes (1940 and 1947), reflecting as it does his wide range of interests, his searching method, and his attempt to circumvent the inadequacy of the records in order to deal with the fundamental problems involved. On the 'Abdalwadids, who occupied the western part of present-day Algeria, the most up-to-date references will be found in G. Marçais, *Tlemcen* (1950), with equally interesting text and illustrations, and the article by the same author in *EI*². On the Marīnids of Morocco, there is no satisfactory general study, but R. Le Tourneau, *Fez in the Age of the Marinids* (1960), provides useful information. On the Waṭṭāsids, their successors, we have a monograph by A. Cour, *La dynastie marocaine des Beni Waṭṭâs (1240–1554)* (Constantine, 1920), which has not been superseded. There are some observations of a general nature on institutions in the introduction by M. Gaudefroy-Demombynes to his partial translation of al-'Umarī, cited p. 179. For a general understanding of the circumstances of their history, much may be gained from R. Montagne, *Les Berbères et le Makhzen* (1930), even though he discusses mainly modern times. See also E. Pröbster, cited p. 91.

Politically undistinguished, this period of Maghribī history has nevertheless contributed most illustrious names to the realm of culture and civilization. The work of Ibn Khaldūn, today considered to have surpassed medieval thinking in many respects, was not held in the same esteem by his contemporaries. Among the studies devoted to him, one should mention especially Muhsin Mahdi, *Ibn Khaldun's Philosophy of History* (1957), in which a bibliography of earlier works will be found. See also above, p. 217. It would be unpardonable to neglect the comprehensive *Muqaddima*, either in Arabic or in translation, such as the rather free version by De Slane into French in *Notices et extraits de mss.*, XIX–XXI (1862–1868), or the more recent and more reliable English translation by F. Rosenthal in three volumes (1958).

The end of the Middle Ages witnessed a considerable movement of Islamic expansion toward the Sudan. In this connection see C. Monteil, "Les empires du Mali. Étude d'histoire et de sociologie soudanaises," *Bulletin du Comité d'études historiques et scientifiques de l'Afrique occidentale française*, XII (1929), 291–447; D. Westermann, *Geschichte Afrikas. Staatenbildungen südlich der Sahara* (1952); R. Cornevin, *Histoire de l'Afrique* (1956); and E. Bovill, *The Golden Trade of the Moors* (1958); R. Mauny, *Tableau géographique de l'Ouest Africain au Moyen Âge d'après les sources écrites, la tradition et l'archéologie* (Paris, 1959). See also the interesting works by J. Trimingham, *Islam in the Sudan* (1949), *Islam in Ethiopia* (1952), and *Islam in West Africa* (1959).

In dealing with the history of the Maghrib, we must distinguish—from the sixteenth century onward—between Morocco, which was an independent territory ruled by the Sharīfian dynasties (i.e., claiming descent from the Prophet), and the rest, which was more or less effectively incorporated into the Ottoman Empire. The historiographical sources for Moroccan history have been discussed in an important monograph by E. Lévi-Provençal, *Les historiens des Chorfa* (1922). After an immense amount of research in European archives, H. de Castries undertook the monumental publication of the *Sources inédites de l'histoire du Maroc* (1905——), continued by P. de Cenival and R. Ricard, in twenty-four volumes, devoted to the Sa'dian period and classified according to the countries in which the documents are to be found. The most up-to-date synthesis is the *Histoire du Maroc* by H. Terrasse, cited p. 67, although we would remind the reader of the work by A. Cour, *L'établissement des dynasties des chérifs au Maroc et leur rivalité avec les Turcs d'Alger* (1904), and, on the Sa'dians, the account by P. de Cenival in the first series of the *Sources inédites de l'histoire du Maroc* (1926). The work on Fez by R. Le Tourneau, cited p. 92, is also mainly concerned with this period.

On the intellectual and religious life, see the stimulating monograph by J. Berque, *Al-Yousi, Problèmes de la culture marocaine au XVIIe siècle* (1958). It is also useful to consult the juridical treatises or treatises on modern legal practice, such as L. Milliot, *Les démembrements du habous* (1918), and *Recueil de jurisprudence chérifienne*, four volumes (1920–1923 and 1952), or J. Berque, *Essai sur la méthode juridique maghrébine* (1944), which possibly overestimates the originality of this jurisprudence.

The history of Algeria and Tunisia under the Turks has been studied more from the point of view of their relations with Europe than for their own sake. In addition to Arabic and Turkish texts, the European sources are becoming increasingly important, and both these sources are dealt with in C.-A. Julien and R. Le Tourneau, *Histoire de l'Afrique du Nord*, cited p. 67. Note particularly the *Ghazawāt 'Arūj wa-Khairuddīn* (i.e., Barbarossa), edited by A. Noureddine (1934), and the *Riḥla* by al-'Ayyāshī, two volumes (Fez, 1306). Among the European authors, see G. Salvago, *Africa overo Barbaria, relazione al doge de Venezia* (1625), edited by A. Sacerdoti (1937), with notes by P. Grandchamp in *RT*, XXX–XXXII (1937) and in *RA*, LXXXI (1937). For the archives, see section on the Ottomans, above, pp. 193–201. For a general survey on modern literature, see the article "Algeria" in *EI*². Apart from H. de Grammont, *Histoire d'Alger sous la domination turque* (1887), and R. Lespès, *Alger* (1930), which is geographical, almost all the valid studies are works of external history written from the European point of view, such as F. Braudel, cited p. 209; P. Masson, *Histoire des établissements et du commerce français dans l'Afrique Barbaresque* (1903); Y. Debbasch, *La nation française en Tunisie, 1577–1835*, Bibliothèque juridique et économique, IV (Paris, 1957), published by the Institut des Hautes Études de Tunis; R. Merriman, *The Rise of the Spanish Empire*, four volumes (1918–1934), on Spanish settlements; the first and second volumes of F. de Almeida, *Historia de Portugal*, six volumes (1922–1929), on the Portuguese settlements; and A. Ilter, *Şimali Afrikada Türkler*, two volumes (1936–1937), which provides Turkish information chiefly for the nineteenth century. One-sided accounts of Barbary piracy should be viewed with caution, if isolated from the general picture of piracy during the same period. On this question, see for example, P. Hubac, *Les Barbaresques* (1949).

25

The Influence of Muslim Culture in Europe

We have noted, on several occasions in the preceding chapters, the expansion of Islam beyond the confines of the great Muslim empires. Its effect upon Europe is a case not perhaps of expansion in the true sense, but at least of an influence that is a fact of major historical interest. It is not in our province to deal at length with the material and spiritual aspects of Muslim influence in Europe, as this is a subject that lies within the scope of European rather than Islamic history and would inevitably lead us away from our subject. We must nevertheless include what is after all an essential aspect of Islam, especially during the Middle Ages.

We are not concerned with the dissemination of the Islamic faith in Europe, which lay outside the political frontiers of Islam, but rather with those elements of Muslim culture which were felt either to be superior or not restricted to a particular religion, and thus capable of being assimilated by Christian Europe. Islamic culture was known in Europe partly through the commercial contacts (see pp. 92 ff., 209 f., 224, and 227), sometimes through the travels of Christian missionaries in the East, but mainly through the countries in which Christian reconquest had brought Muslim populations under the rule of Christian states, namely Italy and above all Spain under the Norman regime. The partly Arabized indigenous Christians and Jews, rendered polyglot by their commercial activities, often served as translators. For in fact what occurred was first and foremost a work of translating comparable to that by which the Hellenic heritage had been transmitted to the countries of Arab tongue; and it is precisely this heritage that she had not directly preserved which Europe seeks out in its Arab garb.

The influence of Islamic culture in Europe is evident, but there is nothing more perilous than the accurate definition of its channels and its exact nature in any given period or region. Many hasty, exaggerated, or erroneous assertions have been made, particularly in connection with the Crusades. In this field of study the student cannot be too often advised to exercise the greatest possible caution and to be as objective as he can.

Concerning Frederick II, see F. Gabrieli, "Frederico II e la cultura musulmana," *Rivista Storica Italiana*, LXIV (1952), or in his *Dal mundo dell'Islam. Nuovi saggi di storia e civiltà musulmana* (Milan and Naples, 1953).

The nature of European borrowings from Islamic culture has been well defined by H. A. R. Gibb, "The Influence of Islamic Culture in Medieval Europe, "*Bulletin of the John Rylands Library*, XXXVIII (1955). For the earliest periods, see "Rapporti fra Oriente e Occidente durante l'alto Medioevo," by B. Spuler *et al.*, in *Relazioni del X Congresso Internazionale di scienze storiche, Roma 4–11 Settembre 1955*, seven volumes (Florence, 1955), Vol. III, *Storia del Medioevo*, pp. 189–209, with bibliography. From the European point of view, the basic general study is still C. Haskins, *Studies in the History of Medieval Science* (2d ed., 1928). See also Sir T. W. Arnold and A. Guillaume, cited p. 96.

The prevalent ignorance of Islam as a religion from the beginning to modern times is the subject of an interesting but uneven work by A. Malvezzi, *L'Islamismo a la cultura europea* (Florence, 1956); more detailed and wider in scope, but more restricted in time, is U. Monneret de Villard, "Lo studio del Islam in Europa nel XII e nel XIII secolo," *Studi e Testi*, 110 (1944); one should still consult A. d'Ancona, "La leggenda di Maometto in Occidente," *Giornale storico della letteratura italiana*, XIII (1889); most especially, see the exhaustive examination of the formation of ideas concerning Islam by N. Daniel, *Islam and the West, The Making of an Image* (1960); also R. W. Southern, *Western Views of Islam in the Middle Ages* (1962). On Latin translations of the Koran, one of the best recent studies is by M. T. d'Alverny, "Deux traductions latines du Coran au Moyen Âge," *Archives d'histoire doctrinale et littéraire du Moyen Âge*, XXII–XXIII (1947–1948), to which can be added J. Kritzeck, *Peter the Venerable and Islam* (Princeton, 1964).

For the philosophical and scientific influence easier to define, there are a great many works of varying quality. General indications will be found in the general works on the history of Muslim science and thought cited on p. 100 ff. Translations are the basis and starting point on these questions. The only general guide, in this respect, is by M. Steinschneider, "Die europäischen Übersetzungen aus dem Arabischen bis Mitte des XVII. Jhdt.," *SBAW*, *Philos.-Hist. Kl.*, CXLIX (1905) and CLI (1906), reprinted separately in 1955; on astronomy, it may be replaced by the valuable study by F. Carmody, *Arabic Astronomical and Astrological Sciences in Latin Translation* (Berkeley, Calif., 1956). The general outlines on the influence of Muslim medicine will be found in D. Campbell, cited p. 101; on the part played by Spain, in the transmission of science, see J. Millás Vallicrosa, "La corriente de las traducciones cientificas de origen oriental hasta fines del siglo XIII," *JWH*, II/2 (1954–1955), and the *Estúdios* cited p. 223.

On the transmission of the philosophy of the ancients, see F. van Steenberghen, *Aristote en Occident, les origines de l'aristotélisme parisien* (1946–1948).

The influence of Arabic literature on the poetry of the troubadours and on the French *chansons de geste*, especially in Spain, has been the subject of much discussion. The question is increasingly complicated by the fact that the Spanish romances are known to have influenced the popular Hispano-Arabic literature. Concerning some of the influences on the *chansons de geste*, see A. González Palencia, "Precedentes islamicos de la leyenda de Garin," *al-Andalus*, I (1933), while on the wider and more diffuse influence upon the troubadours, a good statement will be found in A. Roncaglia, "La lirica hispano-araba e il sorgere della lirica romanza," *ALFAV*, XII (1957). Concerning the Islamic influence on Dante, which was suggested but not definitely proved by Asín Palácios, *La escatologia musulmana en la Divina Comedia* (1919), see also E. Cerulli, "Dante e l'Islam," *ALFAV*, XII (1957). The question is now practically proved thanks to the discovery, especially by Cerulli himself, of Latin translations of the Ascension of Muḥammad: E. Cerulli, "Il libro della Scala e la questione delle fonti arabo-spagnole della Divina Commedia," *Studi e Testi*, 150 (1949), on which compare G. Levi Della Vida, "Nuova luce sulle fonti islamiche della Divina Commedia," *al-Andalus*, XIV (1949), and M. Rodinson, "Dante et l'Islam d'après des travaux récents," *Revue de l'histoire des religions*, CXXXIX (1951). Cerulli has also established the interchange of legends, especially Christian, between East and West.

In the field of art, see É. Mâle, "Les influences arabes dans l'art roman," *Revue des deux mondes*, Sér. XVII, Vol. XVIII (1923), reproduced in his *Art et artistes du Moyen Âge* (1927), which ought to be read for its balanced judgments; the review of A. Fikry's *L'art roman du Puy et les influences islamiques* (Paris, 1934) by L. Bréhier, "Les influences musulmanes dans l'art roman du Puy," *Journal des savants*, n.v. (1936); the best points are made by E. Lambert in his *Études médiévales*, III (1958). This influence is particularly marked in Catalan art, as has been shown by G. Moreno, *Iglesias mozárabes, arte español de los siglos IX a XI* (1919), and by G. Gaillard, "La Catalogne entre l'art de Cordoue et l'art roman," *SI*, VI (1956).

One way of appreciating the general influence of Muslim culture in Europe is to list the words of Oriental derivation occurring in European languages and to attempt to determine the period and region in which they first appeared. The basic work on this question is by E. Lokotsch, *Etymologisches Wörterbuch der europaischen Worter orientalischen Ursprungs* (1927); also see A. Steiger, *Origin and Spread of Oriental Words in European Languages* (New York, 1963). Arabic loanwords are naturally most numerous in the Iberian Peninsula, concerning which, see R. Dozy and W. H. Engelmann, *Glossaire des mots espagnols et portugais dérivés de l'arabe* (1861; 2d ed., revised and enlarged, Leiden, 1869), which is still useful, and Steiger, *Contribución a la fonética del hispano-árabe y de los arabismos en el ibero-románico y el siciliano* (Madrid, 1932). For French, L. Devic, *Dictionnaire etymologique des mots français d'origine orientale* (1876), and H. Lammens, *Remarques sur les mots français dérivés de l'arabe* (Beirut, 1890), merely initiated the study of the subject, while G. S. Colin, "Origine arabe du mot français 'ogive'," in *Romania*, LXIII (1937), and M. Rodinson, "Sur l'etymologie de 'losange'," *Studi orientalistici ... Levi Della Vida*, II (1956), show the method to be followed in such studies. For German, see E. Littmann, *Morgenländische Wörter im Deutschen* (2d ed., revised and enlarged, Tübingen, 1924).

The Muslim influences we have discussed are mainly medieval. In modern times, when Europe has been the dominant cultural influence, the part played by the East in European culture is smaller. The modern period, however, has seen the rise of Orientalism, and the study of the Orient is at last pursued not for what can be gained from it but for the sake of the knowledge itself. Since the peoples of the East have fallen behind the West, this Orientalism may become in many respects the means of revealing to them their own past and of suggesting how it may be regarded and reassessed. For the history of Orientalism, see above, p. 6. A certain image of the East also plays a general cultural role in literature and thought, from the *Lettres persanes* by Montesquieu to the French and German Romantics. On this question, see for example, P. Martino, *L'Orient dans la littérature française au XVIIe au XVIIIe siècle* (1906), and C. Rouillard, *The Turk in French History, Thought and Literature, 1520–1660* (1941). For the special effect of Islam in Sicily and Spain, see above, p. 222 ff.

We cannot repeat too often that all the suggestions given in this book must be regarded as nothing more than a guide to the diversity and the richness of the research still to be done.

INDEX OF NAMES

The spelling of names of authors varies in accordance with the language in which the author wrote his book and we have followed the author's preference title by title. The spelling of the name of an author of a book written in a transliterated language is in the correctly transliterated form. When the book is published in a Western language, the spelling the author himself used is given. In the index all forms of the name are alphabetically listed, each with cross references to the other(s). Recent authors are listed under the legal or customary surname, older authors according to the custom of the times and scholarly tradition.

'Abbās (uncle of Prophet Muḥammad), 26
'Abbās, Shāh (of Iran), 185
'Abbāsī, M., 170
Abbott, N., 15, 17(2), 29, 117, 130, 137, 138
'Abdalḥamīd, M. M., 218
'Abdallāh b. al-Zubair, 123
'Abdallaṭīf Ḥamza, 179
'Abd al-'Azīz Dūrī. *See* Dūrī, A. A.
'Abd al-Bāqī. *See* Abdelbaky, M. F.
'Abd al-Bāqī, Muḥammad, 117
Abdelbaky, M. F., 28
Abd-eljalil, E., 97
'Abd al-Ḥamīd al-'Abbādī, 217
'Abd el-Jalil, J.-M., 102, 119
'Abd al-Qādir al-Jīlānī, 157
'Abd al-Raḥīm, 188
'Abd al-Rahmān b. Naṣr al-Shaizarī, 165
Abdulaziz, 189
'Abdullāh al-Māzandarānī, 171
'Abdulwahhāb, H. H. (Abdulwahab, H. H.), 133, 219, 222
'Abdurrazzāq Samarqandī, 171
'Abd al-Wahhāb 'Azzām. *See* 'Azzām, 'Abd al-Wahhāb
Abel, A., 99, 167
Abū 'l-'Arab, 218
Abū Bakr al-Mālikī, 218
Abū Bakr Tihrānī, 174
Abū 'l Faḍl 'Allāmī, 188, 189
Abū 'l-Faraj al-Iṣfahānī, 123
Abū al-Fidā', 31, 38, 164, 180
Abū 'l-Ghāzī Bahādūr Khān, 187
Abū Ḥanīfa, 42
Abū Ḥanīfa al-Dīnawarī, 122
Abū 'l-Ḥasan b. Yūsuf al-Ḥakīm, 219
Abū Ḥayyān al-Tawḥīdī, 134
Abū Isḥāq al-Ṣābī, 131
Abū 'l-Maḥāsin b. Taghrībirdī. *See* Ibn Taghrībirdī, Abū 'l-Maḥāsin
Abū Muslim, 24
Abū Ṣāliḥ, 165
Abū Shāma, 163
Abū Shujā' al-Rūdhrawārī, 131
Abū 'Ubayd b. Sallām, 134
Abū Ya'qūb al-Sijistānī, 147
Abū Yūsuf, 42, 43, 134
Abū Zaid Ḥasan al-Sīrāfī, 135
Abū Zakariyā', 217
Adıvar, A., 214
Afḍal al-Dīn Kirmānī, 155
Affifi, A., 167
Afnan, S., 144
Africanus, Leo. *See* Leo Africanus
Afshar, I., 70, 185
Āghā Buzurg al-Ṭihrānī, 50
Aghnidès, N., 207
Ahlwardt, W., 51, 123
Aḥmad b. Ḥanbal, 142
Ahrens, K., 116
Aigrain, R., 108, 112, 113(2)

Akdağ, M., 161, 208(2)
al-Akhṭal, 124
Akın, Himmet, 192
Alarcón y Santón, M. A., 18
Alazard J., 7, 67
Albertini, E., 7, 197, 220
Albright, W. F., 110, 112
Alderson, A., 206
'Alī (b. abī Ṭālib, caliph), 126(2)
'Alī (Turkish historian, sixteenth century), 198
'Ali (Turkish scholar, twentieth century), 207
'Alī, A. A., 188
'Alī, H., 187
'Alī, Jawād, 111
al-'Ālī, Ṣāliḥ, 77, 128
'Alī al-Harawī, 156
'Alī Ibrāhīm Ḥasan. *See* Hasan, 'Alī Ibrāhīm
'Alī b. Nāṣir, 155
'Alī Shīrāzī, 172
Ali-Zade, A., 172
Allen, W. E. D., 108
Allouche, I. S., 134, 218
'Almāwī, 179
Almeida, F. de, 227
Alonso, M., 224
Altheim, F., 111
Amar, E., 34, 219
Amari, M., 18, 67, 222
Amedroz, H., 131, 132, 133, 163
Amélineau, E., 125
Amīn, Aḥmad, 66
al-Āmir, 148
Ammar, H., 79
'Amar bar Ṣlībā, 132
Anasian, A., 198
Anastase Marie, 110, 157
Anawati, M., 97, 99
Anderson, J. N. D., 96
Andrae, Tor, 116, 119
Andréadès, A., 213
Anhegger, R., 194, 206, 208, 213(2), 215
Antuña, M. M., 217
Aqsarāyī. *See* Kerīm ül-dīn Maḥmūd
Arberry, A. J., 7, 15, 68, 96, 98, 99, 102, 118, 144, 223(2)
el-Aref, Aref, 79
Arendonk, C. van 142
Arends, K., 169
'Arīb, 131, 132
Arin, F., 91, 94, 97
al-'Arīnī, al-Sayyid al-Bāz, 165
Arnakis, G., 202
Arnaldez, R., 100, 223
Arnold, Sir T. W., 95, 96, 99, 104, 229
Arseven, C. Esad, 215
Arslan, S., 131
Asad, M., 28
Asal, M., 183
al-Ash'arī, 136
Ashton, J. F., 70
Ashtor, E. *See* Ashtor-Strauss, E.
Ashtor-Strauss, E., 92, 94, 166, 177, 182(3), 222
'Āshūr, Sa'īd 'Abdalfattāh, 181
Asín Palácios, M., 157, 167, 223, 230
Aslanapa, O., 193, 215(2)
'Aṭā-Malik Juwainī, 156
Ateş, A., 162
Atiya, A. S., 18, 124, 162, 163, 165, 181(2), 182, 203
Attaliates, Michael, 159
Aubenas, R., 225
Aubin, H., 173
Aubin, Jean, 157, 171(2), 173(2), 174, 186, 187, 190
Auboyer, J., 172
Averroes. *See* Ibn Rushd
Avicenna, 144
'Awad, G., 134
'Awnī, M., 185
Ayalon, D., 90, 181, 200, 211
al-'Aynī, 177
Ayrout, H., 79
al-'Ayyāshī, 227
'Azīz b. Ardashīr Astarābādī, 173
'Azīzī, M., 140
'Azzām, 'Abd al-Wahhāb, 131
al-'Azzāwī, 'Abbās, 173, 211

Babcock, F., 165
Babinger, F., 51, 161, 194, 197, 203(3), 204, 213(2)
Badā'ūnī (Badāōnī), 188
Badawi, A., 143
Badī' al-Zamān al-Hamadhānī, 133
Bagdatlı Ismail Paşa, 50
al-Baghdādī, 134
Bagley, F., 66
Bahā' al-Dīn al-Baghdādī, 156
Bahā' al-Dīn al-Janadī, 150
Bahār, Malik al-Shu'arā', 132
Bahmanyār, A., 156
Baibars, 176, 177
al-Baidaq, 218
Baihaqī, 132
Bailey, T., 189
al-Bakrī, 219

al-Baladhurī, 26, 122, 123
al-Balkhī, 135
al-Bāqillānī, 143
Barakāt, M., 117
al-Barawī, R., 150
Barbarossa, Khair al-Dīn, 198, 204
Barbier de Meynard A. C., 34, 78, 122, 164(2)
Bar Hebraeus, 165, 169
Barkan, O., 194, 205, 207, 208, 209, 210(2), 214
Baron, S. W., 89
Baroya, J., 225
Barozzi, N., 197
Barthélémy, A., 14
Barthold, V. (W.), 6, 67, 95, 141(2), 153, 154, 156, 170, 172, 188
Basset, A., 67
Bauer, H., 100
Baumstark, A., 50
Bausani, A., 103, 162
Bayani, K., 187
Bayānī, Khān-Bābā, 171
Bayānī, Mahdī, 155
Baykal, B., 174
Baynes, N., 108(2)
Becker, C. H., 16, 86, 90, 95, 98, 99, 116, 126, 127(2), 128, 140, 149
Behrnauer, W. F. A., 165, 199
Bekri, C., 221
Bel, A., 79, 80, 218, 224
Beldiceanu, N., 194, 209, 213
Belenitskii, A. M., 67
Belin, A., 207(2), 208, 214
Bell, H. I., 17, 108, 127
Bell, R., 113, 118(2), 119
Bellan, L., 186
Belot, J., 13
Ben Cheneb, M., 218
Ben-Horin, Uri, 101
Bennigsen, A., 188
Ben Shemesh, A., 134
Ben Zvi, I., 212
Berchem, Max van, 52(2), 53(2), 54(3), 90, 126, 166, 221
Bercher, L., 41, 43, 96, 223
Berchet, G., 197(2)
Berg, C. C., 190
Bergasse, L., 210
Bergsträsser, G., 118
Bernard, A., 76
Berque, J., 42, 79(2), 227(2)
Bertels, E., 102, 149, 173, 187
Berthelot, M., 101
Bertholet, A., 97, 98
Besançon, J., 79
Beveridge, A., 188(2)
Biberstein-Kazimirski, A. de, 13
Billoud, J., 210
Birge, J., 201, 214
Birkeland, H., 119
Birot, P., 76
al-Bīrūnī, 144(2)
Birzālī, 178
Bitlīsī, Idrīs, 198
Björkman, W., 21, 93, 179, 181
Blachère, R., 12, 15, 24, 38, 102, 110, 116, 117, 118(3), 124, 129, 133, 144
Blake, R., 169, 202
Blanchard, R., 76
Blau, J., 45
Blochet, E., 99, 164, 177
Blochmann, H., 189
Boer, T. de, 100
Boilot, D., 144
Boldyrev, A., 173
Bombaci, A., 103, 161, 198
Boor, C. de, 124
Boratav, Pertev, 80, 215
Boris, G., 79
Bosch Vilá, J., 223
Bosworth, C., 141, 156
Boucheman, A. de, 79
Bourrilly, J., 79
Bousquet, G.-H., 43, 67, 79, 80, 87, 88, 119, 157, 190
Boustani, F., 212
Bouthoul, B., 149
Boutruche, R., 90
Bouvat, L., 138, 172
Bovill, E., 226
Bowen, H., 138, 140, 156, 205
Bowen, R. le Baron, 110
Boyle, J., 156
Bräunlich, E., 79(2)
Braudel, F., 62, 204, 209, 227
Braun, H., 68, 96, 186
Braune, W., 157
Bravmann, M., 118
Bréhier, L., 108, 230
Briggs, G., 188
Brillant, M., 112, 113
Brinner, W. M., 178
Broadhurst, R., 164
Brockelmann, C., 12(2), 49, 50, 51, 66, 68, 102, 122, 154
Brooks, E., 125, 138
Brosset, M., 51, 169(2), 185
Brown, P., 189

Browne, E. G., 7, 101, 103, 169
Brünnow, R., 124, 133
Brunet, L., 79
Brunhes, J., 80
Bruns, E., 45
Brunschvig, R., 26, 42, 44, 88(2), 92, 93, 95, 97(2), 118, 122, 220(2), 224, 225
Bruyn, J. T. P., 28
Bryennios, Nikephoros, 159
Buckler, F., 139
Budge, E. A. Wallis, 165
Buhl, F., 116(2), 126
al-Bukhārī, 28
Bukhsh, S. Khuda. *See* Khuda Bukhsh, S.
al-Bundārī, 154
Bunz, H. 147
Burgess, J., 189
Burhān al-Dīn of Sıvas, 173
Bursalı Mehmet Tahir, 51
Burski, H., 204
Busbecq, Ogier de, 201
Busse, H., 21, 174, 185
Bussi, E., 87, 94
Butcher, E., 165
Butler, A., 125
Butorin, D. N., 170
Butzer, K., 78

Caetani, L., 115, 125, 131
Çağatay, N., 207 209(2)
Cágigas, I. de las, 222, 225
Cahen, C., 21, 66, 86(2), 90(3), 91(2), 92(2), 93, 95(2), 98, 128(2), 131, 134, 137, 139, 140(2), 147, 148, 150(2), 154, 156(3), 158(2), 160(2), 162(2), 163(2), 164, 165(4), 166(4), 171, 183, 193
Caillé, J., 224
Campbell, D., 101, 230
Canaan, T., 79
Canard, M., 7, 24, 38, 91, 96, 125, 132, 134, 135, 138(3), 140, 149, 182(2), 214, 217(2), 221
Cantor, M., 101
Carali, P., 212
Cardahi, C., 94
Carmichael, J., 66
Carmody, F., 230
Carra de Vaux, B., 96, 136
Carré, J., 201
Carrière d'Encausse, H., 188
Casanova, P., 119, 160
Caskel, W., 23, 79, 110, 112
Castagna, J., 96
Castries, H. de, 226
Castro, Amérigo, 225
Cattenoz, H., 81
Caussin de Perceval, A., 111
Cavaignac, E., 65, 172
Cenival, P. de, 226, 227
Cerulli, E., 182, 230(4)
Chabot, J., 109, 124, 165(2), 170
Chalandon, F., 160
Champdor, A., 166
Chardin, J., 185
Charles, H., 114, 124
Charles-Roux, F., 212
Charrière, E., 197, 201
Chauvin, V., 69
Chebli, M., 211
Chehade, A., 167
Chehata, C., 94
Cheikho, L., 178
Cheīra, M., 125
Chejne, A., 95
Chelebi, Eremya, 200
Chelebi, Evliyā, 199, 200(2)
Chelhod, J., 112
Chesneau, I., 201
Chevallier, D., 212
Choniates, Niketas, 159
Christensen, A., 107
Chubua, M., 185
Clavijo, 171
Clerget, M., 92
Clermont-Ganneau, C. S., 109
Codazzi, Angela, 220
Codera, F., 223
Codrington, O., 57
Cohen, M., 12
Colin, G. S., 80, 217, 219, 231
Collier, R., 210
Colombe, M., 195
Combe, E., 54
Conder, C. R., 164
Conti Rossini, C., 110, 114
Cooke, H. Lester, 77, 78
Corbin, H., 99, 144, 147(2), 149, 157, 186
Cornevin, R., 226
Coulbeaux, J., 114
Coulborn, R., 90
Coulson, N. J., 41, 42, 88
Cour, A., 225, 227
Courtois, C., 108, 221
Cowan, D., 12
Cowan, J., 12
Crawford, J., 190

Creswell, K. A. C., 60, 104(2), 129, 150, 167
Crouzet, M., 66, 172
Cruz Hernández, M., 100, 225
Cuinet, V., 202
Cusa, S., 18

Dachraoui, F., 222
Dağlioglu, H., 195
Dahhān, S., 135, 164, 165
Ḍaif, Shawqī, 131
Dallet, J. M., 217
Dalman, G., 79
Dalsar, F., 214
d'Alverny, M. T., 229
d'Ancona, A., 229
Daniel, N., 229
Danişmend, I., 202
Darke, H., 155
Darmaun, H., 38
Darrag, A., 180, 181
al-Dawādārī, 177
Dawes, E., 159
Dawson, M., 188
De, B., 188
Debbasch, Y., 227
Decourdemanche, J., 83
Dedering, S., 34
Defrémery, C., 170, 171
Déhérain, C., 7, 211
Della Valle, P., 185
Demeerseman, A., 79
Demirtaş, F., 202
Denizeau, C., 13, 14
Dennett, D., 95, 126, 127
Deny, J., 14, 153(2), 193, 194, 195(2), 207, 208, 211
Dérenbourg, H., 148, 150, 164(2)
d'Erlanger, R., 102
Dermenghem, E., 80, 99, 103, 116
Deschamps, P., 167
Desmaisons, J., 14, 187
Desparmet, J., 79
Despois, J., 76
Deverdun, G., 224
Devic, L., 231
Devonshire, R., 178
Devreesse, R., 114
al-Dhahabī, 34, 177(2)
Dib, E., 95
Dickson, H., 79
Dickson, M., 186
Diehl, C., 66, 108
Dietrich, A., 17, 137
Diez, E., 103, 157
Diez, F., 193
Diez, H. F. von, 199
Digenis Acritas, 24
Dimand, M., 103, 104
Dionysios of Tell-Maḥré, 124
Dochez, L., 201
Dodge, B., 97
Dölger, F., 182
d'Ohsson, A., 172
d'Ohsson, C. M., 205
Donaldson, D. M., 98, 100
Dopp, H., 180
Dorn, B., 171
Doughty, C., 77
Doutté, E., 79
Dozy, R., 13(2), 217, 218(2), 219, 220, 223, 231
Dresch, J., 76(2), 80
Drewes, G., 190
Dubler, C., 119, 224
Duda, H., 159, 161, 194, 213(2)
Dugat, G., 218
Dujcev, I., 203
Dulaurier, E., 169
Du Mans, Raphael, 185
Dunlop, D., 125
Duplessy, J., 93
Durdev, B., 195
Dūrī, A. A., 94, 95, 137, 139, 140
Dussaud, R., 78, 113

Eberhard, W., 80
Ebersolt, J., 180
Edhem, Halil, 54, 161
Edib, H., 97
Edwards, S., 189
Eflākī, 159
Eghbāl, A., 155, 156
Egli, E., 215
Ehiloglu, Z., 212
Ehrenkreutz, A. S., 56, 140, 166
Ehrhard, A., 51
Eichhoff, E., 126
Eichler, P., 118
El Ali, S. *See* al-'Ālī, Ṣāliḥ
Elejovič, G., 195
Elgood, C., 101
Elisséeff, N., 6, 166
Elker, S., 196
Elliot, H., 188
Emmanuel, I., 214
Engelmann, W. H., 231

Enveri, 192
Epaulard, A., 219
Erdmann, K., 104, 161, 215
Ergin, Osman, 210, 215
Ernst, J., 18
Ertaylan, I., 203, 204
Erzi, A., 158(2)
Esin, E., 215
Ettinghausen, R., 70, 104(2)
Evans, A., 84, 180
Evetts, B., 124, 165

Fagnan, E., 13, 134, 217(2)
Fahmy, A., 93
al-Fākhūrī, Ḥannā, 102
al-Fārābī, 144
Farès, B., 113
Faris, N. A., 96, 110(2), 111
Farmer, H., 102
Fattal, A., 89
Febvre, L., 62
Fekete, L., 21, 194, 195, 213
Fekhner, N., 210
Fergusson, J., 189
Feridun, 194
Ferrand, G., 101, 183, 190
Fevrier, J., 113
Fikry, A., 230
Filipovič, N., 208
Finkel, J., 133
Finkelstein, Louis, 50
Firdausī, 24
Firishta, 188
Fischel, W., 93, 140, 170, 180, 182
Fischer, A., 13
Fisher, G., 204
Fisher, S., 203
Fisher, W. B., 76
Fleisch, H., 12(2)
Fliche, A., 108, 225
Flügel, G., 50, 117(3)
Forrer, L., 70, 188, 213
Fränkel, S., 114
Franco, M., 214
Fraschéry, S., 202
Fraser, C., 199
Freeman-Grenville, G. S. P., 190
Frey, U., 76
Fries, N., 125
Fritsch, E., 99
Frye, R., 133, 141, 169
Fück, J. W., 6, 13, 68(2)
Furlani, G., 142
Fyzee, A. A. A., 87, 147, 148(2), 217

Gabain, A. von, 68
Gabriel, A., 161, 185, 204, 215(2)
Gabrieli, F., 66, 102, 104, 112, 127, 138, 141, 143, 163, 219, 222, 229
Gabrieli, G., 34, 83
Gändschäi, T., 68
Gätje, H., 13
Gafurov, B. G., 187
Gaillard, G., 231
Galanté, A., 214
Gantin, J., 169
Garbuzov, V., 160
García de Linares, R., 18
García Gómez, E., 218, 219(2), 220, 223
Gardet, L., 86, 91, 97(2), 99, 144
Gardīzī, 133
Gateau, A., 122
Gaudefroy-Demombynes, M., 12, 65, 85, 95, 98, 112, 117(2), 143, 164, 179, 181, 225
Gaulmier, J., 179, 201
Gauthier, L., 224
Gautier, E., 220
Gayangos, P. de, 218
Gegaj, A., 203
Geiger, A., 119
Gelzer, H., 51
Gevay, A., 197
al-Ghazālī, 100, 157(2)
Ghāzī, M. F., 140, 144
Ghedira, A., 12
Ghirshmann, R., 108
Gibb, E. J. W., 214
Gibb, H. A. R., 69, 86, 95, 97, 102, 125(2), 128, 143, 163(2), 166(3), 170, 205, 206, 229
Gibbons, H., 202
Giese, F., 197, 214
Giragos of Kantzag, 169
Gismondi, P. H., 132
Glotz, G., 65
Glück, H., 103, 215
Godard, A., 157, 187
Goeje, M. J. de, 12, 13, 93, 121, 122(2), 125, 131(2), 135, 136, 148(2), 164, 219
Gökbilgin, M. Tayyib, 195, 204, 210, 212
Gölpinarli, A., 158, 159, 160, 162(2)
Goichon, A., 79, 144
Goitein, S. D., 18, 86, 89, 92, 93, 98, 119, 123, 139, 140, 150, 217
Goldziher, I., 25, 41, 97, 118, 224
Gollais, L., 76
Gollancz, H., 211

Golvin, L., 80, 104, 221
Gómez-Moreno, M., 104
González Palencia, A., 67, 222(2), 223(2), 225, 230
Goossens, R., 24
Gorce, M., 111
Gordlevskii, V., 158
Gottschalk, H. L., 95, 140, 166, 167
Grabar, O., 56, 104, 157
Graf, G., 50
Grammont, H. de, 227
Grandchamp, P., 227
Grasshof, R., 94
Grégoire, H., 24(2), 138
Gregory Abū 'l Faraj. *See* Bar Hebraeus
Gregory of Akner (or Aknac'), 169
Grekov, B., 175
Grenard, F., 76, 189, 191, 205
Griaznevich, P., 122
Grierson, P., 128
Griffini, G., 43
Grigorian, S., 144
Grimme, H., 116
Grønbech, V., 153
Grohmann, A., 15(2), 17(4), 21, 68, 77, 89, 95, 104, 111, 112, 139
Grousset, R., 108, 125, 154, 162, 172(2), 189
Grumel, V., 80
Grunebaum, G. E. von, 7, 66, 86, 92, 96, 97, 98, 112, 144(2)
Guboglu, M., 195
Gücer, L., 209
Gücüyener, F., 203
Guest, R. 123
Guidi, I., 43, 111, 121, 124
Guidi, M., 111, 141, 142
Guillaume, A., 41, 96, 97, 116, 229
Guillou, A., 70
Guirgass, V., 122
Gurland, A., 208
Gurlitt, C., 215

Haas, W. de, 28
Hadj-Sadok, M., 219
Ḥāfiẓ Abrū, 171
Haig, T. W., 81, 188
Haïm, S., 14
al-Ḥajjāj, 47
Ḥājjī Khalīfa, 50, 199
al-Ḥākim, 149
al-Ḥākim al-Nīsābūrī, Muḥammad b. al-Bayyi'. *See* Muḥammad b. al-Bayyi' al-Ḥākim al-Nīsābūrī
al-Ḥalabī, 43
Halil Edhem, 82, 201
Halkin, A. S., 50
Halphen, L., 65(2)
Hambis, L., 153
al-Ḥamdānī, 110
Al-Hamdānī, H. F., 148, 150(2)
Ḥamdullāh Mustawfī Qazwīnī, 169
Hamidullah, M., 97, 112, 117, 123(2), 134, 138, 139, 147
Hammer-Purgstall, J. von, 169, 194, 200, 201, 205, 214
Hanotaux, G., 67
Hanoteau, A., 79
Hardy, E., 108
Hardy, P., 188
Hartel, H., 68
Hartmann, L., 108
Hartmann, M., 24
Hartmann, R., 158, 178, 179
Hartner, W., 101
Hārūn b. Yaḥyā, 135
Ḥasan, 'Alī Ibrāhīm, 94, 181
Ḥasan, Ḥasan Ibrāhīm, 66, 94, 149, 221
Ḥasan al-Baṣrī, 128
Ḥasan Ḥusnī 'Abdulwahhāb. *See* 'Abdulwahhāb, H. H.
Ḥasan b. Muḥammad Qummī, 132
Ḥasan Rūmlū, 185
Haskins, C., 229
Hasluck, F., 214
Hassan, Z. M., 140
Hassinger, H., 210
Hatschek, J., 96
Hautecoeur, L., 104, 183
Hava, J., 13
Havighurst, M., 93
Hayek, M., 119
Hayton. *See* Hétoum
Ḥayyim. *See* Haïm, S.
Hazard, H., 77
Heffening, W., 93, 94, 96, 181
Heidborn, A., 205
Heller, B., 24
Hellert, J., 201
Hellige, W., 138
Hennig, R., 101, 140
Henninger, J., 79, 112(2)
Hertzberg, G., 212
Herzfeld, E., 54(2), 138, 145
Hess (von Wyss), J. J., 79
Hétoum, 169
Heuser, F., 14

Heyd, U., 93, 177, 203, 212, 214
Heyworth-Dunne, J., 132
Hilāl, 132
Hilāl al-Ṣābī, 131(2), 133
Hilāl b. Yaḥyā, 43
al-Hilālī, 158
Hill, D., 104
Hill, G., 182, 214
Hillelson, S., 103
Hilmy, A., 164
Hindūshāh Nakhjavānī, 171
Hinz, W., 68, 83, 93, 170(2), 171, 172(2), 174, 185, 186(2)
Hirschberg, Z., 119
Hitti, P. K., 66, 67, 122, 150, 164
Hodgson, M. G. S., 128, 150, 166
Höfner, Maria, 68, 78, 110, 112
Hoenerbach, W., 45, 126, 139
Hönn, K., 70
Holmyard, E. J., 101
Holt, P., 6, 22
Homan, B., 212
Hommel, F., 111
Honigmann, E., 125, 138, 161
Hony, H. C., 14
Hopkins, J., 221
Horovitz, J., 118, 122
Horten, M., 98, 100
Houdas, O., 28, 156
Hourani, A., 208, 211
Hourani, G., 93, 224
Houtsma, M. Th., 122, 154, 155, 158
Howorth, H., 172
Hrbek, I., 150
Huart, C., 65, 157, 159, 211
Hubac, P., 227
Hüsameddin, V., 214
Hüsrev, I., 208
Huici Miranda, A., 218(2), 223
Ḥusain, K., 147(2), 148, 167, 217
Ḥusain, S., 124
Ḥusain, Ṭāhā, 110, 126
Huuri, K., 89
Huyghe, R., 103

Iakubovskii, A. I., 140, 154, 175, 187
Ibn 'Abbād, 131
Ibn 'Abd al-Ḥakam, 26, 122, 123, 217
Ibn 'Abd Rabbihi, 123
Ibn 'Abdūn, 219
Ibn 'Abd al-Ẓāhir, 176
Ibn abī Ṭāhir Ṭaifūr, 132
Ibn abī Zar', 217
Ibn al-'Adīm, Kamāl al-Dīn, 33, 164
Ibn 'Arabshāh, 170
Ibn 'Asākir, 33
Ibn 'Āṣim, 43
Ibn A'tham al-Kūfī, 122
Ibn al-Athīr, 83, 154(2), 164, 217
Ibn Bassām, 218
Ibn Baṭṭūṭa, 170, 180, 183, 192, 219
Ibn Bībī, 158, 159
Ibn Bukair, 116
Ibn Faḍlān, 135
Ibn Faḍlullāh al-Umarī, 179
Ibn al-Faqīh, 135, 219
Ibn al-Furāt, 177
Ibn al-Fuwaṭī, 158, 169
Ibn Ḥajar al-'Asqalānī, 177
Ibn al-Ḥājj, 180
Ibn Ḥammād, 217
Ibn Ḥanbal, 43
Ibn Hasan, 189
Ibn Ḥawqal, 135, 219
Ibn Ḥayyān, 217
Ibn Ḥazm, 123, 223
Ibn Hishām, 116
Ibn 'Idhārī, 217
Ibn Isḥāq, 116
Ibn Iyās, 178
Ibn Jai'ān, 180
Ibn al-Jawzī, 155
Ibn Jubair, 164
Ibn al-Kalbī, 110
Ibn Kathīr, 177
Ibn Khaldūn, 89, 150, 170, 217, 226
Ibn Khallikān, 34, 199
Ibn al-Khaṭīb, 218
Ibn Khurradādbih (Khurdādbeh), 135, 219
Ibn Mājid, 183, 200
Ibn al-Mammātī, 147, 165
Ibn al-Mi'mār al-Baghdādī, 158
Ibn al-Mujāwir, 167
Ibn al-Mukarram, 148
Ibn al-Muqaffa', 141, 143
Ibn Muyassar, 147
Ibn al-Nafīs, 167
Ibn Qāḍī Shuhba, 177
Ibn al-Qalānisī, 147, 163
Ibn al-Qifṭī, 34
Ibn Qudāma, 43
Ibn Qutaiba, 122
Ibn Quzmān, 225
Ibn Rushd, 224
Ibn Rusteh, 135, 219
Ibn Sa'd, 116

Ibn al-Sā'ī, 157
Ibn al-Ṣairafī, 147
Ibn Ṣaṣrā, 178
Ibn Shaddād, 'Izz al-Dīn, 164(2), 177
Ibn Sīda, 14
Ibn Sīnā. *See* Avicenna
Ibn Taghrībirdī, Abū 'l-Maḥāsin, 178(2)
Ibn Taimiyya, 43
Ibn al-Ṭayyib, 45
Ibn Ṭūlūn, 178
Ibn Tūmart, 220, 224
Ibn al-Ṭuwair, 147
Ibn al-Ukhuwwa, 165
Ibn abī Uṣaibi'a, 34
Ibn Waḥshīya, 136
Ibn Wāṣil, 164(2)
Ibn Ẓāfir, 147
Ibn al-Zubair, 147
Ibrāhīm b. Ya'qūb al-Ṭurṭūshī, 135
al-Ibyārī, I., 13, 116
Idrīs (dā'ī), 147
Idris, H., 218, 221(2)
Idrīsī, 135, 156, 219
Ilter, A., 227
'Imād al-Dīn al-Iṣfahānī, 154, 163
Inalcik, H., 194, 195(2), 207, 208, 213
'Inān, M., 149, 222
'Ināyat Allāh Khān Kashmīrī, 189
Ingrams, W., 77
Iorga, N., 201, 206, 212
Iqbāl, M., 155(2)
Irani, R., 15
Irvine, W., 189
Işiltan, F., 159
Iskandar, 171
Ismā'īl, A., 212
Ismā'īl Ḥakkı (Uzunçarşılı). *See* Uzunçarşılı, Ismā'īl Ḥakkı
al-Iṣṭakhrī, 135, 136
Iuldashov, M. I., 187
Iushmanov, N., 12(2)
Ivanow, W., 146(2), 147, 148(3), 149, 150
İz, F., 14
Izzeddin, M., 135
Izzeddin, N., 177

al-Jabartī, 200
Jābir, 143
Jacob, G., 213
al-Jāḥiẓ, 133
Jahn, K., 169(2)
al-Jahshiyārī, 123, 133
al-Jaiḥānī, 136
Jamme, A., 112
Jansky, H., 14, 204
Jarrett, H. S., 189
Jaussen, A. J., 79
Jawād, M., 158(2)
Jawād 'Alī. *See* 'Alī, Jawād
Jazarī, 177
Jeffery, A., 98, 118(2)
Jensen, H., 14
Jewett, J. R., 154
al-Jīlālī, 220
Jireček, K. J., 212
Jockel, R., 96
Johannes of Nikiou, 124
Johnson, A. C., 108
Jomier, J., 119, 182
Jones, J. B. M., 116
Julien, C.-A., 67, 108, 220, 227
Justi, F., 83
Juwaida, Wadī'. *See* Jwaideh, Wadie
Juwainī, 169
Juynboll, T., 28, 43, 87, 134
Jūzjānī, 155
Jwaideh, Wadie, 39

Kabrda, J., 195, 213(2)
Kaempfer, E., 185
Kafesoglu, I., 156, 157
Kahane, H., 210
Kaḥḥāla, U. R., 70
Kahle, P., 18, 158, 178, 200
Kamāl, Yūsuf, 102
Kamāl al-Dīn b. al-'Adīm. *See* Ibn al-'Adīm, Kamāl al-Dīn
al-Kāmil, 164
Kāmil, Murād, 13, 176
Kammerer, A., 113, 114
Kapliwatzky, J., 12
Karabaček, J. von, 16, 215
Karal, Enver Ziya, 202, 205
Kary-Niyazov, T., 173
al-Kāshānī, 43
Kasravi, A., 141
Kātib Chelebi. *See* Ḥājjī Khalīfa
Katsh, A. J., 119
Kauffmann, A., 76
Kawar, I., 114
Kay, H., 150
al-Kāzarūnī, 142
Kedourie, E., 95
Kedrenos, Georgios, 159
Kees, H., 67
Keilani, I., 144

Keller, H., 132
Kemālpashazāde, 198
Kennedy, R., 12
Kerīm ül-dīn Maḥmūd (Aqsarāyī), 159
Kerr, M. H., 212
Khadduri, M., 43, 96
Khalīl, 176(2)
Khalīl b. Isḥāq, 43
Khalīl al-Ẓāhirī, 179(2)
al-Khaṣṣāf, 43
al-Khaṭīb al-Baghdādī, 33
Khāwar, G., 155
al-Khazrajī, 183
Khowaitir, A. A., 176
Khs-Burmester, O. H. E., 124
Khuda Bukhsh, S., 85
Khwānsārī, S., 185
al-Khwārizmī, 134
Khwondamīr, 171
Kiernan, R., 76
al-Kindī, 123, 144
Kinnamos, Johannes, 159
Kirfel, W., 181
al-Kirmānī, 147
Kissling, H. J., 14, 68, 202, 213, 214
Klibansky, R., 143
Klincke-Rosenberger, R., 110
Klingmüller, E., 68
Klute, F., 76(2)
Kocabeg. *See* Quci Beg
Köprülü, M. F. (Köprülü-zāde, Mehmed Fu'ād), 91, 150, 157, 161(2), 162, 173, 193, 202(2), 206
Köymen, M., 156, 198
Komnena, Anna, 159(2)
Kononov, A. N., 187
Koray, Enver, 70
Kovalevsky, I., 135
Krachkovskaia (Krachkovskaya), V. A., 55(2)
Krachkovskii, I. I., 6, 38, 122, 132
Kraelitz, F. von, 194, 196
Kraemer, C. J., 17
Kraemer, J., 13
Kramers, J. H., 38, 69, 86, 100, 135
Kratchkovsky, I. I. *See* Krachkovskii, I. I.
Kraus, P., 143, 144
Krehl, L., 28, 218
Kremer, A. von, 85, 86, 96, 139
Kreutel, R. F., 199
Krey, A., 165
Kriss, H., 79
Kriss, R., 79
Kritobulos (Kritovoulos), 198
Kritzeck, J., 229
Krumbacher, K., 51
Kühnel, E., 103, 104(2), 145
al-Kumait, 124
Kurat, A., 123, 194, 207
Kurd, 'Alī, M., 67
Kuthaiyir 'Azza, 124

Labib, S. Y., 182
Labriolle, P. de, 108
La Broquière, Bertrandon de, 180
Lacour-Gayet, J., 209
La Jonquière, A. de, 202
Lamb, H., 204
Lambert, E., 103, 230
Lambton, Ann K. S., 6, 14, 80, 90, 91, 94, 132, 155, 156, 172, 186
Lammens, H., 67, 97, 112, 116, 117, 124, 126(2), 182, 231
Lamouche, L., 202
Lane, Arthur, 104, 215
Lane, E. W., 13, 79
Lane-Poole, S., 13, 56(2), 67, 82, 84, 166, 201
Lang, D. M., 187
Langer, W., 202
Langmantel, V., 180
Laoust, H., 43, 142(2), 144, 167, 177, 178, 181
Lapeyre, H., 225
La Roncière, C. de, 196
Launois, A., 128
Laurent, J., 125, 160
Lavoix, H., 56
Lavrov, V., 173
Lazard, G., 14
Lecerf, J., 88, 112
Leclerc, L., 101
Lecomte, G., 12
Lees, W. N., 155
Lehmann, E., 97
Leib, B., 159
Lemerle, P., 80, 192
Leo Africanus, 219
Lespès, R., 227
Le Strange, G., 78, 169, 171
Le Tourneau, R., 67, 70, 80, 92, 163, 216, 217, 220(2), 221, 225, 227(2)
Letourneux, A., 79
Leunclavius, Johannes. *See* Löwenklau, Johann
Levi Della Vida, G., 96, 111, 116, 123, 139, 230
Lévi-Provençal, E., 67, 69, 83, 123(2), 216,

217(4), 218(2), 219(3), 220, 222(2), 223(4), 224, 226
Levy, R., 86, 137, 165
Lewicki, T., 128, 142, 221
Lewis, Archibald, 93, 126
Lewis, Bernard, 6, 7, 22, 66, 69, 92, 95, 98, 137, 148, 150(2), 166, 193, 195, 200, 203, 205(2), 209, 212
Leyerer, C., 95, 139
Linant de Bellefonds, Y., 91
Lippert, J., 34
Littmann, E., 109, 231
Lockhart, L., 185(2), 186
Loeb, I., 81
Löfgren, O., 110, 167(2), 183
Løkkegaard, F., 90, 95
Löwenklau, Johann, 198
Lokotsch, E., 231
Lombard, M., 93(2)
Longrigg, S., 211
López, F., 171
López de Meneses, A., 182
Lowe, W. H., 188
Lozach, J., 80
Lucas, Paul, 201
Luccioni, J., 90
Luciani, J. D., 220
Lugal, N., 158, 174
Lundin, A., 110
Luṭfīpasha, 198
Lybyer, A., 205

McCarthy, R., 143
MacDonald, D., 98
MacGregor, J., 85
Macler, F., 124
Macro, E., 70
Madelung, W., 149(2)
Madkour, I., 144
Magued. *See* Mājid, A.
Mahdi, Muhsin, 226
Mahler, E., 81
Maḥmūd of Ghazna, 132
Maḥmūd Kashgharī, 154
Maḥmūd b. 'Uthmān, 142
Maimonides, 45
Mājid, A., 147, 149
Major, R. H., 170
Makdisi, G., 143, 155
al-Makhzūmī, 148, 165
al-Makīn b. al-'Amīd, 31, 164, 177
Makki, A., 134
Makkī, M., 219
Malachy the Monk, 169
Mâle, Émile, 57, 230
Mālik, 43
al-Malik al-Nāṣir Nāṣir al-Dīn Muḥammad b. Qalā'ūn. *See* Muḥammad b. Qalā'ūn, al-Malik al-Nāṣir Nāṣir al-Dīn
Malik al-Shu'arā Bahār. *See* Bahār, Malik al-Shu'arā'
Malkiel-Jirmounskii, M., 183
Malvezzi, A., 229
al-Ma'mūn, 132
Manīnī, 132
Mann, J., 150
Mansuroğlu, M., 161
Mantran, R., 194(2), 196, 201, 202, 209, 210(2), 212
al-Maqqarī, 218
al-Maqrīzī, 147, 177, 179
Marçais, G., 66, 67, 92, 103(3), 104(2), 220(2), 221(2), 224, 225
Marçais, W., 12, 14, 28, 88, 128, 220(2)
al-Marghīnānī, 43
Margoliouth, D. S., 34, 83, 131, 133
Mari, 132
Maricq, A., 157
Marin, E., 121
Markov, A., 56
al-Marrākushī, 218
Martin, V., 108, 225
Martino, P., 231
Marvazī, 136
Mashkūr, M. J., 137
Mas-Latrie, L. de, 220
Masnou, P., 133
Maspero, J., 78
Masqueray, E., 217
Massé, H., 80, 97, 103, 122, 144, 147(2), 173
Massignon, L., 92, 99, 100, 104, 128, 140 142(2), 146, 220
Masson, D., 119
Masson, P., 207, 210(2), 227
Mas'ūd, 132
Mas'ūdī, 122, 136
Matthew of Edessa, 165
Maunier, R., 79
Mauny, R., 226
Maurette, F., 76
al-Māwardī, 44, 134
Mayer, H., 163
Mayer, L. A., 57, 60, 104, 179, 180, 183
Mayr, J., 81
Mazahéri, A., 92
Mehlitz, O., 59

Mehmet Pasha Qaramānī, 198
Meier, F., 99(2), 142(2), 157
Mélikoff, Irène, 160, 192
Ménager, L., 222
Menasce, J. de, 100
Menéndez Pidal, R., 67, 108, 223(2)
Mensing, J., 28
Menzel, T., 206
Merad, Ali, 224
Mercanligil, M., 203
Mercier, E., 90
Mercier, M., 222
Meriçli, E., 195
Merriman, R., 204, 227
Meunié, J., 224
Meyerhof, M., 144, 167
Mez, A., 86, 133, 137
Miall, B., 93
Michael the Syrian, 165
Mieli, A., 100
Migeon, G., 103(2), 215
Mignanelli, Beltram de, 180
Miklukho-Maklai, N. D., 186
Miles, G., 56, 57, 84, 95, 138
Millás Vallicrosa, J., 222, 230
Miller, B., 14, 206
Miller, K., 101
Miller, W., 213
Millet, R., 223
Milliot, L., 87, 227
Minorsky, T., 6, 172, 173
Minorsky, V., 67, 70, 136, 140, 141, 154, 170, 172(2), 173, 174(4), 186(2)
Miquel, P., 136
Mīrkhwond, 171
Mirza, M., 147
Mis'ab al-Zubayrī, 123
Miskawaih, 33, 131, 132
Mitchell, J., 199
Moberg, A., 176
Mones (Monès), H. *See* Mu'nis, Ḥ.
Monneret de Villard, U., 89, 170, 229
Montagne, R., 79, 226
Monteil, C., 226
Monteil, V., 12
Montgomery, J., 170
Mor, C., 139
Morand, M., 88
Moravcsik, G., 51, 83, 153
Moreland, W. H., 189(2)
Moreno, G., 230
Moritz, B., 15(2)
Mortier, R., 111
Moscati, S., 111, 128, 137(2)
Moss, H., 108
Mostafa, M. *See* Muṣṭafā, M.
Mostras, K., 202
Motylinski, A. de, 221
Moubarac, Y., 111, 119(2)
Mu'āwiya, 23
Mu'āwiya II, 123
al-Mu'ayyad al-Shīrāzī, 147
Müller, A., 34, 65
Müller-Wodarg, D., 91
Mufaḍḍal b. Abī 'l-Faḍā'il, 177
Muḥammad b. 'Alī al-Ṣūrī, 148
Muḥammad b. al-Bayyi' al-Ḥākim al-Nīsābūrī, 28
Muḥammad b. Qalā'ūn, al-Malik al-Nāṣir Nāṣir al-Dīn, 177, 181
al-Muḥāsibī, 142
Muḥibb al-Dīn al Khaṭīb, 110
Muhyī al-Dīn, M., 116
Mu'īn, M., 147
Mu'īn al-Dīn Naṭanzī, 171
Muir, W., 65, 116, 181
Mukhlis, A., 147
Mukrimin Halil. *See* Yınanç, Mükrimin Halil
al-Munajjid, Ṣ., 15(2), 33
Munajjim Bāshi, 199
Mu'nis, H., 77, 95, 218, 219
Munshī, Iskander, 185
Muntakhab al-Dīn Badī', 155
al-Muqaddasī, 136(2), 219
Murgotten, F., 122
Musca, G., 139
Musil, A., 77, 79
Muṣṭafā, K., 133
Muṣṭafā, M., 178
al-Musta'īn, 132
al-Mustanṣir, 148
Mutafciev, P., 161
Mžik, H. von, 123

Nader, A., 141
Nafid, R., 161
Nafīsī, S., 132, 133, 141(2)
Na'īmā, 199
Naja, S., 124
Nājī al-Qaisī, A., 158
al-Najjār, A., 158
Najm al-dīn Kubrā, 157
Nallino, C. A., 67, 88, 101, 111, 124, 129
Nallino, M., 138
Narshakhī, 133
Nasawī, 156

Naṣīr al-Dīn Ṭūsī, 173
Nāṣir-i Khusrav, 135, 147
Nāṣir Muḥammad. *See* Muḥammad b. Qalā'ūn, al-Malik al-Nāṣir Nāṣir al-Dīn
Nau, F., 114
al-Nawawī, 43
al-Nawbakhtī, 136
Nāẓim (Nazim), M., 133, 141
Nedgoff, B., 207
Nemtinov, B. M., 170
Neşrī, 198
Nève, F., 170
Nicholson, R., 99, 102, 103, 144, 159, 169
Niedermeyer, O. von, 76
Nielsen, D., 111
Nieuwenhuijze, C. A. O. van, 99
Nikitine, B., 6, 67, 171
Nikitine of Tver, 170
Niẓām al-Dīn Aḥmad, 188
Niẓām al-Dīn Sāmī, 170
Niẓām al-Mulk, 155, 156
Nöldeke, Th., 13, 113(2), 118, 137, 140(2)
Noradounguian, G., 197
Norberg, M., 199
Noureddine, A., 227
al-Nu'mān, Qāḍī, 147, 217
Nūr al-Dīn (Zangī), 166
al-Nuwairī, 177, 217
Nyberg, H., 141
Nykl, A., 223(2)

Ocaña Jiménez, M., 81
Öz, Tahsin, 193
Özerdim, S., 203
O'Leary, De Lacy E., 96, 111, 149
Omant, H., 201
Oppenheim, M. von, 79
Orbelian, Stephen, 169
Ortiz, López, 87
O'Shaughnessy, T., 118
Ostrogorsky, G., 108, 198, 202
Otto, W., 111
Otto-Dorn, K, 213, 215(2)
Ouechek, E., 179

Pagliaro, A., 102
Pallis, A., 206
Palmer, E., 117
Papadopoulos, I., 138
Papadopoulos, T., 213
Paparrigopoulos, K., 212
Papazyan, A. D., 185
Parain, C., 80
Pareja, F. 66, 70, 190
Paret, Roger, 24, 25, 114, 116, 118
Paris, R., 210
Parry, V., 204
Partington, J. R., 90
Patton, W., 142
Pavet de Courteille, A. J.-B., 122, 188, 198, 204
Pearson, J. D., 60, 70, 102, 145
Pedersen, J., 98, 104, 156
Pegolotti, Balducci, 84, 180
Pellat, C., 69, 102, 122, 136, 142, 143, 219, 220
Pelliot, P., 153
Penzer, N., 206
Pérès, H., 79, 124, 144, 223
Périer, J., 127
Perlmann, M., 12, 66, 182, 222
Perron, M., 43
Perroy, E., 66, 93, 172
Pesle, O., 88, 91
Peters, L., 14
Petersen, E., 126
Petrushevskii (Petrushevsky), I., 172(3), 185 186
Pevzner, S. B., 182
Pfannmüller, G., 69
Pfeffermann, Hans, 204
Philby, H., 77(2)
Phillipe le Bel, 170
Phillips, C., 188
Phillott, D. C., 14, 189
Pigulevskaia (Pigulevskaya), N. V., 108, 111, 112, 170
Pihan, A., 15
Pijoan, J., 103
Piloti, Emmanuel, 180
Pinder-Wilson, R., 173
Pines (Pinès), S., 143, 144
Pinto, O., 123, 138
Pirenne, H., 93
Pirenne, Jacqueline, 76, 111
Pīrī Re'īs, 200
Planhol, X. de, 80, 208
Platonov, S. F., 65
Platts, J. T., 14
Plessner, M., 96, 100, 136, 143
Poliak, A., 90(2), 128, 182
Polonus, Martinus, 169
Poncet, J., 221
Pontecorvo, V., 187
Pope, A. U., 103, 173, 186
Popper, W., 178(2)
Predelli, R., 18

Pribitkova, A. M., 157
Prieto y Vives, A., 223
Pritsak, O., 154(2)
Pröbster, E., 91, 226

Qāḍī al-Nu'mān. *See* al-Nu'mān, Qāḍī
al-Qairawānī, 43
al-Qalānisī, 32
Qalā'ūn, 176(2), 181
al-Qalqashandī, 19, 150, 179(2)
al-Qāsim b. Ibrāhīm, 141
Qazwīnī, M., 155, 156
Quadri, G., 100
Quatremère, E., 13, 169, 177, 179
Quci Beg, 199
Qudāma b. Ja'far, 134
al-Qudsī Ḥusām al-Dīn, 83
al-Qudūrī, 42
Querry, A., 87

Rabin, Chaim, 13, 78
Rabino di Borgomale, 141
Rackow, E., 79
Rahman, F., 98
Rambert, G., 210
Ramsay, W., 161
Ranking, G. S. A., 14, 188
Rashīd, 199
Rashīd al-Dīn, 169, 172
Rathjens, C., 77
Ravaisse, P., 179
Raverty, H., 155
Rāwandī, 155
Raymond, A., 211
Raynaud, F., 93
Raynaud, G., 165
al-Rāzī, 144
Redhouse, J., 14, 183
Refik, A., 195, 207(2), 209(2), 210, 214, 215
Reichmann, J., 195
Reinaud, H. P. J., 101
Reinaud, J. T., 180, 222
Reinaud, M., 38
Remondon, R., 17
Renan, E., 224
Renaudot, E., 124
Rescher, O., 28, 39, 122, 199
Resmī, 199
Reynolds, J., 132
Rhodokanakis, N., 111
Ricard, R., 225, 226
Rice, D. S., 60, 167
Richter, G., 46
Ricoldo da Montecroce, 170
Reifstahl, R., 193
Rifat, K., 154
Riggs, C., 198
Rikabi, J., 167
Ringgren, H., 113, 118
Rippe, K., 156
Ritter, H., 15, 34, 89, 128, 136(2), 148, 162, 214, 215
Ritter, K., 201, 202
Rizzitano, U., 127
Roberts, R., 119
Robson, J., 28
Rodinson, M., 90, 92(2), 111, 117, 120, 230, 231
Rodwell, J., 117
Röhricht, R., 166, 180
Roemer, H. R., 16, 171, 173, 177, 184, 186, 187
Rohrbach, P., 76
Roncaglia, A., 230
Roolvink, R., 77
Rosenthal, E., 100
Rosenthal, F., 22, 50, 96, 144, 226
Rouillard, C., 231
Roux, J., 202
Rūmī, Jalāl al-Dīn, 159(2)
Runciman, S., 139, 162, 203
Ruska, J., 144
Rustum, A., 212
Ruyter, H. C., 28
Ryckmans, G., 111
Ryckmans, J., 110(2)
Rypka, J., 102
Sabā, M., 70
Šabanovič, H., 195
Sacerdoti, A., 227
Sachau, E., 45, 87, 116, 126
Sacy, Sylvestre de, 12, 90, 150
Sa'd al-Dīn, 198
Sadeque, M., 176
Sa'dī, 198
Sadighi, G., 141
Sa'dullāh Enverī, 199
al-Ṣafadī, 34, 50, 177
Safvet, 204
Ṣafwat, A. Z., 130
Sagnac, P., 65
Saif b. Muḥammad b. Ya'qūb al-Harawī, 171
Sakhāwī, 50, 178
Saladin, 163, 165, 166(3)
Saladin, H., 103
Sale, M., 164

Salem, E., 128
Salemann, C., 14
Sāliḥ al-ʿĀlī. *See* al-ʿĀlī, Ṣāliḥ
Ṣāliḥ b. Yaḥyā, 178
Salim, M., 77
Salīm, Maḥmūd Rizq, 183
Salinger, A., 158
Salvago, G., 227
al-Samʿānī, 83
al-Sāmir, Faiṣal, 140
Sanāullāh, F., 156
Sánchez Albórnoz, G., 225
Sanders, H., 170
Sanger, R. H., 77
Sanguinetti, B., 170
Sanson, N., 185
Santillana, D., 43, 87
Sanuto, Marino, 180, 200
Saqaṭī, 219
Saqqā, M., 116
al-Sarakhsī, 43
Saran, P., 189
Sarkar, Sir Jadu-Nath, 189(2)
Sarkis, J., 70
Sarkisyan, A., 215
Sarkisyanz, E., 188
Sarre, F., 145, 161
Sarton, G., 100
Sarwar, G., 186
Sauvaget, J., 15, 35, 54, 59, 83, 92(2), 128, 129, 135, 157, 161, 166, 167(2), 177, 178, 179, 180, 181, 194, 212(2)
Sauvaire, H., 83, 179
Savary, J., 200
Savory, R., 186
Sawīrūs b. al-Muqaffaʿ, 124
Sayili, A., 173
Sayous, A., 224
Sayyid Baṭṭāl Ghāzī, 24
Scanlon, G., 90, 180
Schabinger von Schowingen, K. E., 155, 156
Schacht, J., 25, 41, 42, 44, 87, 88, 91, 94, 97, 98, 128, 143, 167
Schaube, A., 93
Scheel, H., 68, 153, 158, 202
Schefer, C., 133, 135, 155(3), 180, 185, 201
Schiaparelli, C., 164
Schiltberger, J., 180
Schimmel, A., 178, 181
Schlössinger, M., 123
Schlumberger, D., 113, 129, 145
Schmidt, F., 91
Schneider, A., 210
Schroeder, E., 103
Schumann, G., 164
Schwally, F., 118
Schwarz, P., 78
Schwarzlose, F. W., 113
Scott, H., 77
Sebeos, 124
Seddon, C., 185
Seignobos, C., 16
Serjeant, R., 89, 119, 134, 183(2), 190
Seston, W., 113
Setton, K., 156
Severus. *See* Sawīrūs b. al-Muqaffaʿ
Şevket, İ., 14
Seybold, C. F., 124(3)
Seyrig, H., 113
al-Shābushtī, 134
Shafi, M., 123, 171, 172
al-Shāfiʿī, 43(2)
al-Shaibānī, 42
Sharaf, T., 221
Sharaf al-Dīn ʿAlī Yazdī, 170
Sharaf al-Dīn Bidlīsī, 185
Sharbatov, G., 12
Shaw, Stanford J., 194, 211
Shay, M., 205
Shayyāl G., 147(2), 164
al-Shīrāzī, 43
Shukovski, V., 14
Shumovskii, T. A., 183
Sibṭ b. al-ʿAjamī, 179
Sibṭ b. al-Jawzī, 154(2), 164, 177
Siddiqi, A., 95, 156
al-Ṣiddīqī, Muḥammad Zubair, 171
Sidersky, D., 119
Silberschmidt, M., 204
Singer, C., 89
Sinor, D., 7
Skylitzes, Johannes, 159
Slane, Wm. MacGuckin de, 34, 217(2), 219(2), 226
Slaughter, L., 166
Smirnov, N., 6, 204
Smirnov, V., 214
Smith, M., 142
Smith, S., 111
Smith, V. A., 189
Smith, W. Robertson, 12, 88, 112
Snouck Hurgronje, C., 88, 89, 95, 97, 190
Sobernheim, M., 54, 178
Socin, A., 12
Solignac, M., 221
Solmi, A., 108

Sourdel, D., 56, 95, 123, 134, 139, 142, 143, 165, 167
Sourdel-Thomine, J., 15, 54, 103, 145, 156, 157, 167(2)
Southern, R. W., 229
Soysal, I., 207
Speiser, M., 198
Speyer, H., 119
Spiers, R. P., 189
Spies, O., 45, 68, 92, 94
Spitaler, A., 13
Sprenger, A., 78(2), 116
Sprengling, M., 128
Spuler, B., 66, 67(3), 68(4), 70, 81, 140, 172(2), 175, 188(2), 213, 229
Stadtmüller, G., 212
Stapel, F., 190
Starcky, J., 113
Stavrianos, L., 205
Stchoukine, I., 173, 187
Steenberghen, F. van, 230
Steiger, A., 231(2)
Steingass, F., 14
Steinschneider, M., 50, 99, 143, 229
Stern, G., 88
Stern, S. M., 18, 21, 147, 148, 149, 221
Stevenson, W., 162
Stiehl, R., 111
Storey, C., xxi, 51
Strauss, E. *See* Ashtor-Strauss, E.
Streck, M., 78
Stripling, G., 211
Stroieva, L. A., 67
Strothmann, R., 68, 142, 173, 221
Struve, V., 187
Stuart-Poole, R., 56
Sümer, Faruk, 154, 174
Süreyya, Mehmet, 197
al-Suhrawardī, 157
Sulaimān Mahrī, 200
Sulaiman Qānūnī, 204
al-Ṣūlī, 32, 132
Sultan Veled, 159
Surāqa b. Mirdās, 124
Surūr, Jamāl al-Dīn, 181
Susa, A., 145
Suter, H., 101
al-Suwaidī, Amīn, 83
al-Suyūṭī, 83, 180
Svoronos, N., 210, 213
Sweetman, W., 97
Sykes, Sir Percy, 184, 187
al-Ṭabarī, 26, 35, 118, 121, 122, 126, 131(3), 132
Tabrīzī, S. A. Kasravī, 186
Taeschner, F., 68, 92, 158, 159, 160, 179, 198(2), 200, 202(2), 203, 209
Tafel, G., 18
Tāj al-Salmānī, 171
Talas, A., 156
Talbi, M., 94, 100, 219
Tāmir, ʿA., 148
al-Ṭanjī, M. b. Tāwīt, 170
al-Tanūkhī, 131, 133
Taqizadeh, H., 81
Tarim, C., 213
Tarkhān, Ibrāhīm ʿAlī, 181
Ṭashköprüzāde, 199
Taton, R., 100
Tauer, F., 170, 204
Tavernier, J.-B., 185
Tchalenko, G., 59
Tekindağ, Şehabeddin, 181
Telfer, J. B., 180
Terrasse, H., 67(2), 104, 220, 222, 224, 226
Testa, A. de, 197
Tevhid, Ahmed, 56
Texeira, Pedro, 190
al-Thaʿālibī, 134
Thābit b. Sinān, 131
Theophanes Confessor, 124
Thesiger, W., 77
Thiriet, F., 200
Thomas, B., 77
Thomas, G., 18(2)
Thomas of Metsop, 170
Thomin, R., 80
Thomsen, P., 70
Thomson, W., 128
Thorning, H., 92, 158
Thuasne, L., 204
Tibawi, A., 145, 148
Tiesenhausen, W., 174
Tietze, A., 210
Tihrānī, Jalāl al-Dīn, 132
al-Tījānī, 219
Timur, 170
Tischendorf, P. A. von, 208
Togan, A. Zeki Velidi, 68, 90, 134, 153(2), 161
Tolstov, S., 59, 144, 145
Tomiche, N., 211
Tornau, N. E., 205
Tornberg, C. J., 154, 217
Torres Balbás, L., 104, 222, 224(2)

Torrey, C., 122
Traboulsi, A., 144
Trask, W. R., 144
Trever, K. B., 187
Trimingham, J., 226
Tripathi, P., 189
Tritton, A., 89, 97(3), 145, 165
Tschudi, R., 198
Tucci, U., 200
al-Tūnkī, 50
Turan, O., 159(2), 160, 162
Turan Ş., 198
Tveritinova, A., 199
Tyan, E., 94, 95
Tyulayev, S., 215

Ubach, E., 79
Ülgen, A. Saim, 215
Ülgener, S., 209
Ünsal, B., 215
Ünver, A., 215
Uluçay N. Çağatay, 213
Ulugh Beg, 172, 173
'Umar (b. al-Khaṭṭāb), 47
'Umar b. 'Abdal'azīz, 127
'Umāra al-Ḥakamī, 150
al-'Umarī, 192, 219, 226
Unat, F., 198
Uras, E., 214
Usāma b. Munqidh, 164
al-'Utbī, 132
'Uthmān (caliph), 123, 126
'Uthmān b. Ibrāhīm al-Nābulsī, 165
Uzluk, F., 159(2)
Uzunçarşılı, Ismā'īl Ḥakkı, 160, 161, 192, 194, 202, 203, 205, 206(3), 210

Vajda, G., 15, 50, 100, 141
Van den Berg, L., 43, 87
Van den Branden, A., 110
Van Loon, J. B., 28, 171
Vasdravellis, I., 195
Vasiliev, A., 128, 132, 138
Vatikiotis, P., 150
Vattier, P., 170
Vaughan, D., 207
Veccia Vaglieri, L., 126, 142(2)
Veljaminov-Zervov, V., 185
Venture de Paradis, 179
Verlinden, C., 88
Veselovskii, N., 185
Vesely, R., 126
Vesey-Fitzgerald, S., 87
Veth, P., 83
Vidal de la Blache, P., 76
Vloten, G. van, 127, 133, 134
Volney, C.-Fr., 201
Vonderheyden, M., 217, 221
Vryonis, S., 203

Waardenburg, J., 229
Wächter, A., 192
Wätjen, H., 210
Wahb b. Munabbih, 26
Waisī, 199
Waldschmidt, E., 172
Walker, J., 56
Walzer, R., 96, 100(3), 143
Wangelin, H., 183
Wansharīsī, 219
al-Wāqidī, 116
Washshā', 133
Wāṣif Efendī, 199
Wathīma, 122
Watt, W. Montgomery, 98, 99, 112, 117, 128, 141, 143, 157
Watzinger, C., 92
Wehr, H., 12
Weil, G., 65
Weir, T., 65, 116
Weisweiler, M., 97, 223
Wellhausen, J., 112, 116, 125, 126, 127
Wensinck, A. J., 28(3), 97, 119, 157
West, L., 108
Westermann, D., 226
Westermarck, E., 80
Weulersse, J., 80(2)
Wickens, G., 144
Widengren, G., 24, 119
Wiedemann, E., 101
Wiet, G., 54(3), 66, 67, 78, 89, 103, 104, 122, 135(2), 136, 140, 145, 149, 157, 178(2), 179, 180(2), 181, 182, 183(2), 200
Wilber, D., 173
Wilhorsky, Count, 170
William of Tyre, 165
Williams, Alden, 98
Wilson, A. T., 70
Winckler, H., 79
Winnett, F., 109
Wissmann, H. von, 77, 78, 112(2)
Wittek, P., 95, 160(2), 161, 192, 193, 197, 202(2), 203(3), 206
Witteschell, L., 76

Wolfson, H. A., 100
Wood, A., 210
Worms, M., 208
Wright, W., 12, 164, 206, 218
Wüstenfeld, F., 34, 39, 81, 82, 116, 133, 149, 179, 181, 212
Wulzinger, K., 92

Yaḥyā b. Ādam, 26, 134
Yaḥyā al-Anṭākī, 132
Yaḥyā b. Khaldūn, 218
Yaḥyā b. 'Umar, 218
Yakubovsky, A. *See* Iakubovskii, A. I.
Yaltkaya, M., 177
Yaman, T., 161
al-Ya'qūbī (Ibn Wāḍiḥ), 122, 135, 219
Yāqūt, 34, 39, 50, 156
al-Yāsīn, 144
Yassā 'Abd al-Masīh, 124
Yaziji-Oghlu, 159
Yetkin, K., 161, 215
Yinanç, Mükrimin Halil, 160, 173, 198
al-Yūnīnī, 177
Yver, G., 220

Zāhid 'Alī, 149
al-Ẓāhir, 149
Ẓahīr al-Dīn Mar'ashī, 171
Ẓahīr al-Dīn Nīshāpūrī, 155
Zaid b. 'Alī, 43, 134
Zaidān, Jurjī, 85
Zajączkowski, A., 195
Zakhoder, B., 155
Zakī, A., Pasha, 110
Zambaur, E. von, 82
al-Zarkashī, 218
Zbiss, S., 220, 221
Zeki Pakalın, M., 197
Zeki Velidi. *See* Togan, A. Zeki Velidi
Zettersteen, K., 177, 194
Ziadeh, N., 182
Zinkeisen, J. W., 201
Ziyāda, M. M., 177, 178
Zlatarski, V. N., 212
Zotenberg, H., 121, 124
Zurayk, C., 177

www.ingramcontent.com/pod-product-compliance
Lightning Source LLC
Chambersburg PA
CBHW021659230426
43668CB00008B/666
9780520376281